Country Music Culture

Studies in Popular Culture
M. Thomas Inge, General Editor

Country Music Culture

From Hard Times to Heaven

CURTIS W. ELLISON

UNIVERSITY PRESS OF MISSISSIPPI
Jackson

98 97 96 95   4 3 2 1

The paper in this book meets the guidelines for permanence and
durability of the Committee on Production Guidelines for Book
Longevity of the Council on Library Resources.

Library of Congress Cataloging-in-Publication Data

Ellison, Curtis W.
    Country music culture : from hard times to heaven / Curtis W.
Ellison.
        p.   cm. — (Studies in popular culture)
    Includes bibliographical references and index.
    ISBN 0-87805-721-8. — ISBN 0-87805-722-6 (pbk.)
    1. Country music—History and criticism. I. Title. II. Series:
Studies in popular culture (Jackson, Miss.)
ML3524.E4 1995
781.642\09—dc20   94-36518
                                                          CIP
                                                          MN

British Library Cataloging-in-Publication data available

remembering
James I. Ellison
1910–1994

CONTENTS

PREFACE

This book seeks perspective on contemporary behavior by looking into the past for its roots. It relies upon histories and scholarly sources, fan and music business publications, studies of musical genres, performer biographies and autobiographies. Recordings, radio programs, documentary and Hollywood films, and video and television are important to the story. The perspective has been significantly shaped by first-hand observation of more than seventy-five major country music artists in live concerts and other public events between November 1991 and August 1993. Interactions of artists and fans, and of fans with one another, were observed where they occurred and were translated into written descriptions yielding suggestive patterns of behavior. More than 5,000 miles of travel involved with this activity also allowed for visits to country music historic sites, shrines, festival events, museums, theme parks, and tourist destinations.

In 1991, at the invitation of Peter Williams, Elliott Gorn, and Mary Cayton, I wrote an essay surveying the history of country music for the *Encyclopedia of American Social History*. A review of sources then suggested the possibility of writing an interpretive history of country music as a cultural phenomenon, one that might build on impressive institutional studies and writings for fans that already existed and pursue more deliberately the music's relationship to gender, class, and political values. Richard Abel, of the University Press of Mississippi, encouraged me, and Miami University allowed me a semester of leave from other duties to begin active work.

My plan was to do an exhaustive review of scholarly writing about country music, of biographies and autobiographies revealing the lives of key figures, and of studies exploring the music's genres and expression in particular states and regions. I also meant to listen to a lot of music on albums and radio. Jack Temple Kirby advised me to investigate the workings of the country music business, and that seemed right. From these beginnings I thought I could assemble written materials, build up my collection of recordings, sit at my desk with a CD player, and make a satisfactory synthetic account relying on much that was already known, yet inspecting it from new angles.

Then, almost on a whim, I went out.

Because I was working in Dayton, Ohio, in 1991, I was unknowingly located in a community rich with expressions of country music culture. In November, I decided to see a live country performance at Dayton's Hara Arena. I had grown up in a coal-mining town in north Alabama, and had performed in pop groups, dance bands, early rock bands, symphonic bands, marching bands, and church choirs. When the Byrds hit rock music with *Sweetheart of the Rodeo* during my graduate school days in Minnesota during the late 1960s, I discovered an affection for country stylings that possibly expressed my own regional nostalgia; since then, I had been listening to country music recordings and radio. I taught undergraduate courses on country music at Miami University in southwestern Ohio and took students to country music sites and shrines in Tennessee. None of this, however, prepared me for what I found in Hara Arena. After one evening of observing George Jones and Conway Twitty with their fans, I realized that I had much to learn about the social and cultural functions of country music performance.

In February 1992, I saw Alan Jackson with his younger fans at the University of Dayton Arena and met there another face of country music. That same month I went to Canal Street Tavern to hear fiddler Mark O'Connor. His instrumental virtuosity—which demonstrated intricate ties of commercial country music to folk, pop, and even symphonic traditions—raised more questions. Then, at the end of March, I attended Norm's Gospel Sing, at Dayton's Memorial Hall, where the Singing Cookes, Spencers and McKameys— and their followers—suggested an important link between the performance functions of secular country music and the ritual expression of evangelical religion. By now I was rethinking my approach to the entire project and seeking ways to interpret live performance situations, the nature of fan behavior, the interaction of fans and artists, and the social significance of public events in what I was increasingly sure was a complex, yet distinctive popular entertainment culture.

For the next two years, at every available moment, I was on the road, taking in country music concerts, festivals, theme parks, museums, and public events (see Appendix A). To my gradually increasing astonishment, this journey occurred just as the music seemed to explode in popularity, marketing zeal, media attention, and artist creativity. I was taking copious notes along the way and translating them into a computer database. In late 1993, I slowed down and began trying to make written sense of a cultural phenomenon I had entered as an observer but now had to respond to as a participant.

My desire to interpret both live performance situations and the nature of artist-fan behavior led to consideration of the assumptions inherent in ritualistic events. The work of Randall Balmer on the culture of evangelical religion was suggestive for organizing my thoughts about the performance expressions I wished to interpret. The writings of Jack Temple Kirby and Ronald D. Eller on regional modernization provided a backdrop for thinking about broader contexts of social change affecting country music. Writings by Mary A. Bufwack and Robert K. Oermann, Robert Cantwell, Douglas B. Green, Bill C. Malone, Richard A. Peterson, Neil V. Rosenberg and Charles K. Wolfe were indispensable for constructing a sense of the music's past. I relied on biographers for the lives of figures central to this story—Wilber Cross and Michael Kosser for Conway Twitty, Don Cusic for Reba McEntire, George William Koon and Roger M. Williams for Hank Williams, Edward Morris for Garth Brooks, Ellis Nassour for Patsy Cline, Nolan Porterfield for Jimmie Rodgers, Ronnie Pugh for Ernest Tubb, and Charles K. Wolfe for George D. Hay. Don Cusic published the songs of Hank Williams at a timely moment. Books by Peter Guralnick, Neal and Janice Gregory, and Cindy Hazen and Mike Freeman helped me find a perspective on Elvis Presley.

I benefited greatly from personal discussions along the way. Phil Campbell and Jerry Clower gave generously of their private time to help me consider the significance of country humor. Ellen A. Long shared information about Dollywood and activities of the Dollywood Foundation, and Chris Praetor described the evolution of

Twitty City. At the Country Music Foundation, Ronnie Pugh encouraged the work as a whole and assisted me several times as I pursued scarce resources. The International Country Music Conference and its co-chairs, Jim Akenson and Bill McNeil, offered a model of supportive scholarly conversation and follow-up aid. Contributions there by Thomas Poole, Jimmie N. Rogers, Wayne W. Daniel, and Cecelia Tichi were particularly helpful. Eddie Bishop and Jean Dollar Bishop, at the Jimmie Rodgers Museum, shared materials documenting a history of the Jimmie Rodgers Memorial Festival, in Meridian, Mississippi. Sam Marshall provided access to festival events, and Elliott Street, of the Grand Opera House, sent detailed information about the history of Meridian as a regional entertainment center. Lynne Gaines, at The Nashville Network, made it possible for me to see a live production of the TNN/*Music City News* Awards show. Donnie Beauchamp, of Opryland USA, provided important photographs. I thank Bill Malone for valuable assistance, and Richard Abel and Anne Stascavage for sound editorial advice and admirable patience.

I had extraordinary personal support in Ohio. Jan McLaughlin, of Miami University's Amos Music Library, aided me often, and Barbara Wheeler, of Miami Applied Technologies, helped with illustrations. Marjorie McLellan gave me timely information. Faculty and students of the School of Interdisciplinary Studies were always sympathetic to my enthusiasm and kept an amazing flow of music, articles, clippings and cultural artifacts drifting my way. Virginia Moore and Cheryl Ellis helped me think about what I was doing from a fan's perspective, and Cheryl Ellis typed and corrected drafts in an impressive display of competence and zeal. Celia Knight literally made it possible for me to do this work, ensuring her fame with me as an indispensable colleague. She also shared in preparation of the final manuscript. Peter Williams commented on the project regularly and offered references, personal contacts, ideas, insights, and inspiration. The book might be seen as an attempt to answer some questions that Peter and Elliott Gorn raised, though only I can be responsible for what I have said.

Barbara C. Ellison supported my commitment to this project from beginning to end. She joined Karin and Evelyn Ellison, as well as our entire extended families, by enduring my immersion in it with fine charity and grace.

INTRODUCTION

From Hard Times to Heaven

It's Saturday night at the Grand Ole Opry in Nashville, Tennessee. The date is January 22, 1994, and fans, artists, family, friends, and well-wishers are gathered to welcome the Opry's newest member, Hal Ketchum. Opry star Bill Anderson tells a national television audience that Opry backstage has so many floral arrangements honoring Ketchum it smells like a flower shop. Ketchum has told the same audience that he's "scared to death," but that he is having fun visiting with friends and family who have flown in from around the country. His father, Frank Ketchum, who introduced Hal to country music, has come from a hospital bed to be present. Frank Ketchum will soon die of cancer, but tonight he will see his forty-one-year-old son, who has been playing music since the age of fifteen, inducted as the seventy-first living act of the Grand Ole Opry. The artist seems awed by his father's determination to be present. He tells Bill Anderson in a pre-Opry interview, "My dad is pretty sick right now, and it's such—just a real—he's quite a role model. He decided to get himself out of the hospital Tuesday. He said, 'Get my pants. I'm going to Nashville.' And he's here tonight. He's out there watching the show right now—in heaven."

At 7:30 P.M. Central Standard Time, the Opry goes live on The Nashville Network. Hillbilly rocker Marty Stuart, decked out in a glittery black and white jacket and blue jeans with riding chaps, is tonight's Opry host. He begins the induction with a story meant to illustrate the special character of the moment just ahead.

> Not too long ago—I guess it was November last year—one of the most wonderful things happened to me that could happen to any country

performer. When you grow up singing country music the ultimate milestone is to become a member of the Grand Ole Opry. And if you're just gonna have to get inducted, there's one man that can do it probably better'n anybody in this world. And it's kinda like gettin' married by the right preacher—you know it took. And you know it took when this guy does it. Would you give a hand to Mr. Jimmy Dickens, and he has a special event he's gonna talk about. (TNN 1994)

As Stuart leaves the visible stage, another performer comes forward, dressed in his signature fire-engine-red rhinestone suit and large cowboy hat. Only two Opry acts performing in 1994 have been here longer than Little Jimmy Dickens, who has been a member of the Opry for forty-six years. Jimmy Dickens, who will preside at the formal induction of the Opry's newest initiate, begins by politely thanking assembled fans and artists. Then, with a serious expression, he turns to his subject:

Well, many times I've had the added pleasure of standing on this stage and bringing in new members and inducting 'em to our Grand Ole Opry family. And tonight certainly is a special night for all of us, because one of the most talented young men to come along in a long time—not only as a singer and performer, ladies and gentlemen, but a guy that's paid his dues in the small clubs all over the nation—this young man—all of you out there tonight have a program like I have here in my hand—and I read his little note to all of you, and to all of us. And I thought that I would just take a little part of it and let you know how this man feels: "My father brought these people home." By record, of course. "One by one/And they all stayed/They told me even then/That I was welcome/They knew I understood/A thousand souls and singers/Have beckoned me to this/Hallowed place/And tho' some would say/I've come a long way/I would say simply/That tonight, I arrive." Ladies and gentlemen, the newest member of the Grand Ole Opry family is Mr. Hal Ketchum!

As Ketchum comes vigorously on stage with his acoustic guitar, shaking a mane of full steel-gray hair and dressed in black jeans, black shirt, and a black fitted jacket sporting a relatively subdued glittering sheen, the packed house comes to standing ovation and Ketchum's younger fans, particularly the women, scream. Ketchum walks deliberately to center stage and formally shakes hands, first with Jimmy Dickens and then with Marty Stuart, who has returned briefly. He then moves to the stage extension projecting into the audience and bows from the waist. Turning to the microphone, Ketchum's first words are "God bless you, one and all. Thank you." Then he tilts his head far backward, yells a sharp "Owoo!," and leans into the microphone to begin Ferlin Husky's sixties-era hit, "On the Wings of a Dove."

Written in 1959 by Bob Ferguson, this is a song Husky originally had difficulty recording for the secular market because of its overt religious content. By 1994, Husky claimed there were more than 400 cover recordings of his original. Hal Ketchum has a special feeling for the song; it was the first one he performed on the Opry stage in his 1991 debut here, and he closes all his live performances with it.

Ferguson based "On the Wings of a Dove" on the scriptural account of the aftermath of the baptism of Jesus, when a dove was sent to earth as a sign of God's love. Here, the image of a dove is a reminder that God does not forget ordinary people during hard times. The opening words are "When troubles surround us, when evils come/The body grows weak, the spirit grows numb" (Horstmann 1975, 69). After delivering this beginning, Ketchum gestures to stage right and gently says, "Mr. Ferlin Husky." Husky himself then strides to Ketchum's side at an eager clip, and together, the 68-year-old star and the Opry's newest member sing the chorus: "He sends His pure, sweet love/A sign from above on the wings of a dove." For the second verse, Ketchum respectfully stands back for Husky to perform alone. He continues to play a guitar accompaniment and, near the end, adds harmony vocal. When Ketchum again takes the lead, Husky raises his hands toward the fans in a gesture of evangelical praise, and the television camera cuts to a young woman in the audience singing ardently with the second chorus. By the third verse the camera is panning the audience, where female fans are crying while Ketchum solos and Husky waves to the crowd, urging them to sing along. During the final chorus, fans are gazing in awe at the stage, swaying back and forth, singing in unison with Hal Ketchum as Ferlin Husky signals the crowd-rousing finale by taking the song's last line up an octave. Then the two country singers—the old and the young—embrace as Marty Stuart reclaims center stage and a long ovation rolls.

Later in this same televised Opry segment, reigning Country Music Association Entertainer of the Year Vince Gill complimented Hal Ketchum's behavior at the moment of his induction: "What meant more to me than anything is, he had enough respect for where he learned how to do what he does, and that showed me an awful lot about Hal Ketchum." Fans greeted this remark with immediate applause. When Ketchum returned to sing his own hit song, "Small Town Saturday Night," Marty Stuart greeted him with a comment about having become a member of one of the most exclusive fraternities in the world. At that, an unidentified fan called out, "He's worth it." Stuart turned to the fan and replied, "He *is* worth it." Ketchum acknowledged these informal confirmations with a gentle smile and a soft "Thank you."

Hal Ketchum was the twelfth star to become a member of the Grand Ole Opry after Garth Brooks joined in 1990. His induction ceremony was a vivid example of a confirmation tradition reserved for stars who have demonstrated sincerity, worthiness, and fidelity to the conventions of country music culture, as well as popularity. Foremost among these conventions is active homage to a living past. Ketchum's confirmation featured a touching of hands, embracing of younger by older stars, presentation of the inductee to fans who shower applause, compliments, and flowers, and a symbolic performance that in the Ketchum-Husky duet was a literal representation of the presence of the past. The song Ketchum chose amplified basic themes of country music culture by suggesting the transcendent power of heavenly love over earthly hard times. And this authentic moment of country music culture went out to fans across the nation in prime time from a multimillion-dollar entertainment and telecommunications complex that is a prime example of popular music marketing in the 1990s.

Commercial country music was invented during a period of intense modernization in the twentieth-century American South. It evolved rapidly from rustic radio programs of the mid-1920s through the marketing of recording artists to an extensive national network of performers and fans unparalleled in other forms of popular music. That network supports a distinctive, self-conscious entertainment community within American society that I call "country music culture." Borrowing *culture* from its anthropological use, here I mean to focus on the accumulation and reinforcement through time of shared attitudes, values, traditions, gestures, rituals and ceremonial events. The culture of country music includes many vernacular or "amateur" expressions in private jam sessions, traditional local sites like VFW halls, neighborhood barn dances, and small-town semi-professional gospel singings. In this study, however, I focus on "professional" country music—the commercial phenomenon promoted aggressively by business interests through print and electronic media, recordings, radio, network and cable television, movies, public occasions, festivals, theme parks, and tourist destinations. Yet, for nearly seventy years, even with its complexity, this entertainment has maintained a distinctly personal tone and a sustained focus on domestic social life. This persistence has achieved an impressive irony in American society: while the marketing of commercial country music and its trappings fully embrace modernity, the resulting popular culture community functions as an imaginative means for transcending the negative effects of modernity.

In everyday life, participants in country music culture behave something like a vast extended family at an endless church supper in a rural American small town. This behavior suggests a sustained affection for social convention, perhaps as an antidote to the dislocations that pervade the lives of twentieth-century white Southerners and working-class Americans. Indeed, country music culture is probably best known to nonparticipants as a popular expression of heartbreak, hard times, and personal failure. The image of a lonesome cowboy, homesick Appalachian migrant, or displaced farmer who can't cope with city life, big business, the boss, the wife, or the girlfriend—that is, the traditional rural American male suffering from negative effects of social change—is probably the most pervasive stereotype the uninitiated see in country music, along with the stereotypical antidotes for emotional pain, whiskey, and beer. Yet country music culture has itself been a substantial agent of social change as it has built a lucrative entertainment, media, and tourist business. Because the music business has made impressive fame and wealth for many informally-trained performers who were fans before becoming an inspiration for the success dreams of others, it, too, has become an object of romance. That romance, in turn, feeds an awareness of its own past linking country music artists, professionals, fans, and interpreters of the music in an evolving sense of community.

While it maintains distinct conventions that look to the past, country music is also actively innovative in capturing diverse elements of other musical traditions for use both in vocal and in instrumental styles. It blends these elements into musical formulas expressing personal emotion about romantic love, spiritual love, and loving relationships in family life. Country songs feature a dominating commitment to stories of broken hearts and hard times—an emphasis that masks the culture's assumption that such traumas can be overcome. The public and private lives of major stars are regularly made into object lessons that illustrate this assumption. Their lives provide fans with exemplary images of personal tragedy and spiritual salvation, demonstrations of individual grit, lessons in handling the financial rewards of a popular success ethic, or living commentaries about gender relationships.

True fans of country music tend either to ignore or sometimes to revel in the implicit irony of an entrepreneurial and increasingly complex entertainment business focused mainly on evocations of hard times, painful personal relationships, romantic love, salvation, or its own traditions. By their public adulation of stars, their affection for country music events, sites, and shrines, and their active identification with one another in organized groups, fans are essential agents of the culture who forgive its sinners, adore its saints, and pass on its conventions. An underlying question of this book is: Why do fans of country music show it such persistent devotion? Responding to this question requires that we think about the nature of the music culture as a whole, as well as about its social functions. An important motif at the heart of this entertainment is a sense of living in hard times. Hard times are usually expressed as financial distress, marital discord, family problems, personal loneliness, or the disorderly behavior that results from some of these features of modern life, such as drinking and domestic violence. Here, the stereotype of the lonely troubadour singing to rowdy hillbillies in an urban bar drenched with beer and cigarette smoke resonates as a theater of good times often wedded to desperation. Whatever their exact description, hard times in country music typically are presented as an intimately *personal* condition—one that can best be confronted romantically or spiritually. Hard times are usually not the result of economic conditions or tensions between social classes that might be remedied by collective political action (Peterson 1992). This emphasis on one's personal experience in country music parallels the emphasis on individual salvation in Protestant evangelical religious traditions. And, just as salvation can follow sin, if hard times are the principal topic of country music culture, its consistent hope is to escape them.

Through endless elaborations on formulaic singing and instrumental stylings, country music affirms the possibility of finding better times in the rewards of romantic, familial, or heavenly love. The prospect of love is a given—always offered as an ultimate goal and frequently in contrast to deceptive desires for wealth or social status. In that respect, country music is a distant cousin to domestic fiction such as gothic novels, where intense lovers regularly triumph over the vividly depicted hardships of broken hearts and social maladies. Yet fans of country music have opportunities not available to the readers of novels. At concerts, festivals, theme parks, historic sites, shrines, and tourist towns, they are invited to participate in the ceremonies and rituals of country music. Although few fans do all these things, most are aware that country music culture offers opportunities both to acknowledge a sense of living in hard times and to renew their faith in earthly love, religious salvation, or both. So country music culture has a working dynamic: It deliberately means to move our attention *from* hard times *to* heaven.

Singing stars are the culture's central agents. Their efforts to illustrate, draw out, examine, and affect feelings about hard times mean they must repeatedly demonstrate personal sincerity in order to have authentic standing with fans, and their pervasive sincerity lends a somber tone to much country singing. However, the culture has never valued *unrelieved* seriousness. It has so deliberately tried to blunt seriousness that, upon first encountering country music, one is struck by its exuberant character—whether descended from barn dance shows or rowdy bars. This exuberance is particularly expressed by the unrestrained instrumental virtuosity cherished among string bands and legendary pickers. Almost all country playing features something of that virtuosity, which, since the 1930s, has supported rhythms of interest in various forms of country dancing.

Another deviation from the press of sincerity is country comedy and humor. Comedy has been a staple of country stage performance since the mid-1920s, when it was adapted from vaudeville, medicine shows, and minstrel acts. Its earliest versions were hayseed performers who wore rustic costumes of self-parody. Laughter was crucial to the radio barn dance era that spawned the Grand Ole Opry, and its specialists have lingered on television's *Hee Haw* and on live stage shows. Although remnants of the minstrel tradition have never been entirely rejected in country music culture, by the 1950s some leading comics had replaced being laughed at with telling humorous stories that honor the daily lives of rural and working-class Americans by describing them affectionately in amusing ordinary moments. Through this strategy, country humorists offer fans and artists relief from the various hard-times predicaments that are the main concern of country music. Humorists also provide witty relief from the music's sincere prescriptions for dealing with those predicaments, while maintaining a poise that laughs with, but not at, their subjects. In live performance, such humor amplifies the underlying message of country music, that hard times can be transcended.

The growth of country music as a business parallels that of modern electronic media and has accompanied significant economic and social change. In the Depression era of the 1920s and 30s, a musical and comic motif of rusticity, coupled with nostalgia for an imagined rural past and the surety of gospel salvation, was advanced by radio and recording entrepreneurs, among whom George D. Hay was exemplary. Ralph Peer, agent of the Victor Recording Company, was instrumental in promoting the stylized playing and singing of the Carter Family and Jimmie Rodgers after 1927. While the Opry provided a keen sense of location through its imagery of common values and extended family descending from a warm and rustic past, the public images of the Carter Family and of Jimmie Rodgers provided imagery of wandering from home and of untimely death. They also demonstrated a novel devotion to country singing as a profession with attractive financial rewards. The examples of the Opry, the Carters, and Jimmie Rodgers encouraged scores of imitations and elaborations by vernacular musicians who entered the emerging country music business. Devoted radio listeners and record buyers in these years became an early community of country music fans.

During the 1940s, 50s, and 60s, country entertainers and promoters capitalized on the growth of record sales, on local and network radio programs, and on television exposure. Artists and their commercial sponsors welcomed improved highways and transportation that provided access to concert venues where performers could personally meet their fans. Through media promotion and live appearances they built a regional and national audience for country music and brought Nashville, Tennessee, to prominence among urban contenders for the geographic and business center of country entertainment. In these decades, Hank Williams, Patsy Cline, and Elvis Presley became influential models of vocal performance and artist behavior. After their untimely deaths, mass media, popular culture accounts, commercial films, and their own fans magnified the legendary dimensions of these artists in examples of sustained fan devotion seasoned with references to spiritual salvation. During this period, public death-memorials became a fixture of country music culture, and artist affiliations with both evangelical theology and personal philanthropy evolved to a ritualized norm.

Building on the styles of female predecessors, Loretta Lynn in the 1970s offered the nation an important image of personal success through country music. Her aura of attractive ambition—overcoming Appalachian poverty while maintaining domesticity, family loyalty, and personal warmth—was promoted in popular literature and in an award-winning Hollywood movie. During this same decade three sisters who headed Lynn's fan club—Loretta, Loudilla, and Kay Johnson—became country music's most entrepreneurial fans. They formalized a national network of fan clubs, advanced expectations about appropriate relationships among artists and fans, and influenced the creation of country music culture's most famous annual public event—Fan Fair.

By the 1980s, Dolly Parton was able to both stay close to and elaborate on established conventions of country music culture—a sense of the living past, rusticity and nostalgia, evangelical salvation, media images of legendary performance behavior, and a personal commitment to fans and to their organization. To these, Parton added a sophisticated national tourist destination associated with her life story at Dollywood in the Smoky Mountains, the social appeal of organized philanthropic activity for Appalachia, and media recognition in the mainstream popular culture that celebrated her successes in Las Vegas shows, Hollywood movies, and network television. As she became a favored icon of American life, Parton's diverse activities and financial success became indicators of how elaborately country music might be promoted as a phenomenon of popular culture.

The 1990s are exhibiting an expansion of country music well beyond the base of its traditional fans. Recognized in 1992 for having earned $44 million, Garth Brooks is the lead entertainer among a host of emerging country artists. In this same decade, the postwar generation of American music consumers is moving into and past midlife just as the rock music so much a part of their youth has fragmented into diverse subgenres of varied political and ethnic affiliation. Promoting images of sincere masculinity and devotion to wives and children as well as popular middle-class social concerns, Brooks and his male cohorts join such forceful female singers as Reba McEntire in advocating a new awareness of women's needs. In this same decade, aging but lively country artists have become successful tourism entrepreneurs in country music towns like Branson, Missouri—where traditional migratory patterns of country music culture are being reversed.

Through almost seventy years of dramatic growth, country music has elaborated on consistent styles of performance and on social values that yield sustained fan support and a distinct market niche in popular culture. In the focus years of this study, 1992 and 1993, that market niche was expanding rapidly. In March 1992, *Forbes* claimed that country music had become the leading American popular musical genre. Yet its culture remained most alive in local performance events. In June of that year, the International Country Music Fan Fair attracted 25,000 faithful fans to the Tennessee State Fairgrounds to hear and mingle with their stars for a week in the largest gathering of its kind since the parent event in 1967. Near the end of April, the Dollywood Ambassadors gathered at their theme park to meet Dolly Parton; and the Singing Cookes, of Kingsport, Tennessee, an active gospel family who have toured since the 1960s, held their thirtieth anniversary concert for close family, friends, and fans at Lincoln Memorial University in Harrogate, Tennessee. In May 1993, the Jimmie Rodgers Memorial Festival—held in Meridian, Mississippi, the hometown of Jimmie Rodgers and the site where he is buried—marked the fortieth year since an event was inaugurated there to commemorate Rodgers on the anniversary of his death. Meridian's week of concerts and special events for artists, fans, Rodgers's family, and the local business community has become a major municipal festival of country music culture. In Dayton, Ohio, in 1992, the Ervin J. Nutter Center became one of the world's ten top-grossing concert venues seating ten to fifteen thousand fans. This achievement was aided by booking concerts of country artists increasingly attractive to a growing suburban audience. That same year, in Branson, Missouri, thirty-five theaters for live country-music performance welcomed more than 5 million visitors.

The effects of active participation in country music culture have exceeded most expectations for musical entertainment. For artists, it's their lives; for fans, though not their lives, it isn't just music, either. Fans can hear it, sing with it, dance to it, go to shrines evoking a sense of its past, and participate in concerts, festivals, and public events with others who embrace the emotions and understandings of this culture. Fans can imagine what big success must be like by following the life stories of stars they adore—in print, on television, and in the movies—then they can meet and talk informally with those stars after concerts, at Fan Fair, at their county fair, in Branson, or even on a Caribbean cruise. The places and ceremonies of country music culture work up feelings that are nostalgic, sad, romantic, amused, happy, even spiritual. They stimulate fans and artists to imagine their own hard times and to imagine better ones. In an era of relentless social change, country music culture offers one path to a sense of identity.

Country Music Culture

*I was standing on this stage here at the
Grand Ole Opry, and I said this was like
stepping into a picture I've been looking at
all my life.*

—Clint Black, 1989

CHAPTER 1   **Mother Church**

If you have a good radio in your car or truck, when you drive into the southern Ohio countryside any Friday or Saturday evening you can tune to AM 650 and listen to the Grand Ole Opry from Nashville on clear channel WSM. Or you can find a thirty-minute segment of this world's longest-running radio program each Saturday night on The Nashville Network cable channel. If you try this, you'll be tuning in to the spiritual center of country music culture.

Country Music Hall of Fame member Little Jimmy Dickens recalled his first appearance on the stage of the Grand Ole Opry in 1948. Already a veteran of country radio performance, Dickens nevertheless was awed by the Opry stage: "I realized how many greats had stood there, and wondered whether or not I was worthy to follow them, and my knees started knocking, and I felt like I was doing my first talent contest even though I had ten years' experience" (Eiland 1992, 58). Garth Brooks, country music's most vivid example of hit-making stardom and extravagant stage performance in the 1990s, is not immune to the mystique of the Opry. In November 1992, he told Jane Pauley, of NBC television, how it felt to play the specially designed center circle of the Grand Ole Opry stage at Opryland USA:

> This is the floor of the old Ryman. So they took the old Grand Ole Opry and brought it here. So you get to stand on here. And when you think of *Elvis*, and Hank Williams, Sr., and of course Minnie and Roy, it's like—*there it is*. And it's, it's the most wonderful feeling in the world. That's it. You're *there*. It's great. I wish I could explain to you what it feels like to play here. (NBC 1992)

For rising stars, the Opry readily generates awe. At a 1992 showcase program for Fan Fair, Collin Raye told the audience, "This is my second time at the Opry. The first time I didn't stand in the circle from the Mother Church of Country Music downtown. I didn't feel worthy. But I feel a little more comfortable tonight."

 The self-consciousness at the Opry shared by living legends, superstars, and newcomers alike derives partly from a strong sense of tradition shared by country music performers. Every artist knows how their music modifies and yet builds on the music of the legendary performers who preceded them. In addition, the Opry exemplifies a distinctive link between artists and fans that characterizes country music culture. Brooks describes the link this way: "You're playing to millions of people for the past sixty-five years and you try and uphold what you feel the Opry has worked their butts off to establish" (NBC 1992). Alton Delmore—who wrote more than a thousand songs and, as part of the Delmore Brothers, influenced a long tradition of country harmonic singing after the 1930s—called the Grand Ole Opry "the Bible of radio achievement," where artists worked hard to please fans. "We were practicing for the *people* who listened to WSM, not the bosses," he said. "I don't care how much money you have, or have made, your supreme happiness is in moments when you have your audience captivated" (Delmore 1977, 50–51).

I had been to the Grand Ole Opry perhaps a half dozen times before. This time—June 13, 1992—was the traditional Saturday night performance marking the end of Fan Fair, a week in Nashville when 25,000 fans gather with country artists for performance, club events, autographing, small talk, friendship, and music-industry promotion.

This had been the strongest year in decades for country music; Fan Fair had had its largest turnout ever, and anticipation at the Opry was high. The curtain rose promptly at 6:30 P.M., with the hall sold out for two shows that ran consecutively.

As a radio program, the Opry proceeds in segments, each with its own commercial sponsor. The first segment was hosted by Porter Wagoner, a thirty-five-year Opry veteran known for flamboyant stage costumes and a memorable television program that introduced Dolly Parton to the nation. Wagoner features a comedic style that combines rustic jokes with exaggerated hamming for the fans. His first performers evoked the rural barn dance tradition of the Opry. The Melvin Sloan Dancers, a group in its fortieth year, led off the evening with a clogging act. Wilma Lee Cooper, another thirty-five-year veteran whom Wagoner introduced as "a great girl," performed a Hank Williams song, "The Evening Train." During commercial announcements and between songs, Wagoner frequently came to the edge of the stage to talk with fans, sign autographs, mug for snapshots, or model his purple-rhinestone suit to a cordial reception.

Grandpa Jones hosted the second Opry segment, sponsored by the Country Music Hall of Fame. Jones, an Opry member since 1947, was elected to the Hall of Fame in 1978. His stage persona is reminiscent of the early Opry performer Uncle Dave Macon, featuring rustic banjo-playing in the character of an old man Jones created when he was a young entertainer in Ohio during the 1930s. One of Jones's guests, "Jumpin' Bill" Carlisle, has promoted the rustic motif on the Opry since 1953. Carlisle told the audience that if we cross a hog with an octopus, ham would come down because we'll have hog in the middle and ham all around. The third Opry segment was hosted by crooner Jack Greene, an artist initially popular in the late 1960s, who, in recent years, has promoted gospel singing and Christian testimony. Three of Greene's four guests—Skeeter Davis, George Hamilton IV, and Jean Shepard—are also active in the Opry's Sunday Morning Gospel movement. During the show, Hamilton performed a gospel song, "Cabin in the Corner of Gloryland."

Through all this, the Opry audience demonstrated fan behavior characteristic of country music culture: they were polite; for lively numbers, they clapped and cheered; for quiet numbers about heartbreak and pain, they sat silently in close attention; for the famous signature songs of stars, they sang along. Many songs were greeted by applause at their beginning as fans recognized the importance of hit-making for stars as well as the music itself. For true fans, coming to the Opry is a memorable event, and the entire evening was marked by an orderly but steady stream of movement toward the stage to photograph performers. The mood of the audience is informal, as is their dress. Concessions flanking the stage on either side sell soft drinks, sandwiches, and candy; these are freely brought into the audience during the show. The Opryhouse at Opryland USA is a multimillion dollar concert hall with excellent acoustics and impressive technological sophistication, yet the Opry audience is in constant movement; it never sits contemplatively. For Jean Shepard's "Slipping Away," the entire hall was clapping. When Jack Greene ended his segment with "Statue of a Fool" (a hit song recently remade successfully by Ricky Van Shelton), people seated around me in every direction were singing, and they all knew *all* the words.

Fans present for the Grand Ole Opry are watching the production of a radio program, thus there are moments of "stage wait" when taped advertising is played, backup musicians are changed on stage, or people close to particular stars are allowed to be seated on stage. This atmosphere itself contributes to the air of informality. Most fans sit in an array of benches that sweep in a gentle arc in front of the stage for 180 degrees on the main floor or in a corresponding balcony above. This organization was adapted from the Ryman Auditorium, a gospel tabernacle in downtown Nashville completed in the 1890s and home to the Opry from 1943 to 1974 (Eiland 1992, 51, 85). The original Ryman, designed to seat 3,755 people, became legendary as an intimate venue (Eiland 1992, 18). The 1974 Opry House at Opryland, which seats 4,400, is described by its owners as "the world's largest broadcast studio," yet the auditorium design and informal behavior by fans and artists contribute to maintaining the feeling of intimacy for which the Ryman was known (Adkinson 1992, 3).

The evening's fourth segment was hosted by Jim Ed Brown, a pop country stylist who joined the Opry in 1963. Brown wears a businesslike dark suit and gray tie. This segment was presented live on national television via The Nashville Network. Compared with other segments, it was tightly structured. Two guests who were not yet members of the Grand Ole Opry were presented—the singing group Shenandoah and Hal Ketchum, who had recently been voted by a fan poll the best-looking man in Nashville. These guests each performed songs of theirs currently on the hit charts, and Brown closed the segment with a nostalgic number-one song from thirty years ago, "The Old Lamplighter." For that, the audience sang along, swaying back and forth in collective appreciation.

The fifth segment was hosted by Mr. Roy Acuff, "The King of Country Music." By 1992, Acuff, a member for fifty-five years and a member of the Country Music Hall of Fame, had become an Opry legend. His segment was sponsored by Martha White Flour, the longest-running sponsor for the current Opry. He opened with the "Wabash Cannonball," a train song performed by Acuff's band at their first recording session in 1936 (Schlappi 1980, 28). Acuff brought out the Whites, a family trio consisting of a father and two daughters who feature rustic vocal performance and acoustic instrumentation, and a young man who won the Fan Fair fiddling contest, Dale Morris, Jr., to fiddle a Bill Monroe bluegrass tune, "Uncle Pen." The Acuff segment concluded with Connie Smith, a member of the Opry for twenty-one years, leading a fast rendition of "Louisiana Man" that had a jam-session quality. As the curtain come down, Buck White returned to sing, Acuff and Connie Smith danced, and the Melvin Sloan Dancers clogged to "Golden Slippers" while fans clapped vigorously.

The last segment of the show was hosted by Hank Snow, a Canadian who became a member of the Opry in 1950 and was elected to the Hall of Fame in 1979. His four guests—Charlie Walker, Jan Howard, Roy Drusky, and comic Mike Snider—closed the first show. Snider is a young banjo player who combines rustic country humor with virtuoso picking and an extremely exaggerated rural manner of speech; yet, for this appearance, he was dressed in a suit and tie. The Opry ended with Hank Snow's benediction to the fans: "Good night, God bless you, and may the Good Lord always be proud of you."

The second Opry show was essentially a reprise of the first. Porter Wagoner again hosted the first segment, but this time he brought out twenty-six-year veteran Ray Pillow, and the newest member of the Grand Ole Opry, Alan Jackson. Jackson thanked the fans for a warm reception and told them he had just gotten off his bus from a trip to Ft. Payne, Alabama, where he played the Alabama June Jam. "I can't think of a better way to top off Fan Fair week than to do the Grand Ole Opry," he said. Then he sang three of his hits, all number-one songs, and thanked fans for voting him three awards presented by *Music City News* and TNN just prior to Fan Fair. The last two years "have been really great," Jackson said, because "the music business has been so blessed."

The second Opry show introduced Justin Tubb, son of Ernest Tubb and a member of the Opry since 1955. Jeannie Pruitt sang her signature number "Satin Sheets," and invited fans to her restaurant in the Opryland Park. Ricky Skaggs, a ten-year Opry member who has been an important figure in the revival of traditional musical motifs in the 1980s and 90s, introduced as his guests a family band from Grant Pass, Oregon, which had played at his Fan Fair party and won awards in the fiddling contest. They received a standing ovation and a compliment from Skaggs: "I'm thankful to God for their music." The evening at the Opry closed with Skaggs joining the Whites in a sing-along performance of "Honey Won't You Open That Door." He, too, left the fans with a benediction: "Good night and God love you. Come back and see us every chance you get."

The Grand Ole Opry of the 1990s is directly descended from its original forms of the 1920s. For nearly seventy years it has consistently entertained with rusticity, nostalgia, humor, dancing, and informal invitations to fans to participate actively in the creation of a musical event. From its earliest years the Opry has evoked images of older times and after more than a half century rightly cherishes a self-consciousness about its own traditions.

In 1992, the Opry was weighted toward aging performers. At the June 13 show, twenty-five members of the Grand Ole Opry performed. They represented a total of 708 years of Opry performing and an average tenure of 28.3 years. The youngest performer had been a member for only one year, the oldest for fifty-five. Four artists had been on the Opry stage for forty years or more, thirteen for thirty years or more, and eighteen for twenty-five years or more. Only four had been Opry members for ten years or less. The 1992 cast was heavily weighted toward male singing stars—sixteen of these appeared this June 13, compared with six female soloists and three groups, one of those groups dancers.

On this night the audience appeared to be a cross-section of American working- and middle-class fans, with a slight weighting toward females and a notable weighting toward fans middle-aged and older. Families, children, and all age groups were present, however. Midway through the evening, a young couple, probably in their twenties, held their infant son high in the air for a memorial snapshot with Hank Snow on stage in the background. Perhaps this was the first visit of a future Opry star.

Today's Opry is notable for fan participation. Fans can talk with the stars on stage between numbers, receive autographs, take memento snapshots up close to performers, sing and clap along, even shout if the mood is right. It's clear that a visit to the Opry is a memorable moment for country music fans, just as performing there is for country music artists. The tone of an evening at the Opry—its intimate feel and sense of a living tradition—can be known best at first hand, in the scene. For both artists and fans, at its best the spirit of the Grand Ole Opry yields an active sense of continuity with an imagined past.

Yet the Grand Ole Opry is a business enterprise invented at a specific time and carefully designed to create a sense of the past. When George D. Hay left Chicago's National Barn Dance on WLS radio in 1925, he brought with him to Nashville a broadcasting strategy and marketing concept that left indelible marks on the forms of commercial country music.

In 1924, the National Life and Accident Insurance Company moved to its new building in downtown Nashville, Tennessee. Responding to the popular novelty of radio broadcasting, National Life the following year opened a radio station in its new building with call letters WSM adopted from its advertising slogan, "We Shield Millions." The new station promptly hired as program director a former Memphis newspaperman then broadcasting the National Barn Dance program from the Sears, Roebuck and Co. Chicago radio station WLS, for the "World's Largest Store."

The new program director, George Hay, had in his early years as a court reporter with the *Memphis Commercial Appeal* written a minstrel-style newspaper column in black dialect that derived its humor from court proceedings. For Hay, it was a short step from black racial rusticity to white racial rusticity in the mid-1920s. First in Memphis, then Chicago, and then Nashville, he promoted the appeal of old-time music and hillbilly characters for a growing radio audience. He even rusticated his own image in Nashville, adopting the stage persona "The Solemn Old Judge," although he was just thirty years old. Hay first programmed old-time fiddle-playing by

Uncle Jimmy Thompson, achieving a considerable audience response of telephone calls and telegrams. Then a rival radio station paid his strategy a compliment by broadcasting a fiddling contest which they claimed stimulated 360 telephone responses in two hours. Within two months Hay was producing press releases suggesting that commercial hillbilly entertainment was a folk culture evocative of rural life. "Much has been said for and against the old time tunes but the fact remains they are taking the country by storm," he said. "There is some delightful little folk strain that brings us all back to the soil, which runs through each of the numbers" (Wolfe 1973, 16).

The predecessor program to the Opry began Saturday, December 26, 1925, as an "old time music" show. Hay marketed this program carefully. In 1927, he renamed it the "Grand Ole Opry" in what Charles K. Wolfe calls "a deliberate rustic burlesque of formal and classical music" (Wolfe 1973, 17). Hay's performers were asked to shed their business suits and dress in overalls while assuming hillbilly stage names such as the "Gully Jumpers" and "Dixie Clodhoppers." From its beginnings the demeanor of the Grand Ole Opry thrived on apparent informality. Hay called this "a distinctly human affair which may be termed a big get-together party of those who listen in" (Wolfe 1973, 18). Rustic informality worked. By 1927, *The Tennessean* could report that a typical show "received over 200 messages from thirty-two states" (Wolfe 1973, 22). In the spring of 1927, WSM joined the NBC Radio Network and became a clear-channel broadcaster at 650 kilocycles, assuring it a national frequency without interference. By then, WSM had an 878-foot broadcasting tower outside Nashville, said to be the tallest in the world.

In the late 1920s, the Grand Ole Opry was strategically positioned to reach a growing mass market of sympathetic listeners, and it had a sponsor interested in broadening that market. In 1928, the National Life Company began selling life insurance on a monthly premium basis and using field collection agents. According to Wolfe, "this new installment system opened up a new market for insurance: the working class and the rural middle and lower middle class" (Wolfe 1973, 23).

Building musician popularity and insurance sales went hand in hand. By 1933, WSM had formed the Artist Service Bureau to assist its performers in booking concert venues, as live performance became a means for supplementing artists' incomes so they could afford full-time commitments to the music business. Artists wanted to perform full time, and for their sponsors the interest was mutual. Thus, the original institutional bonds of country music culture formed. Media images of rustic musical performance generated elaborate fan desires to associate with the artists depicted by that imagery. Personal appearance concerts and informal relationships among fans and artists built a sense of trust and shared values. In this setting, sponsors of products designed for personal security, health, and consumption—such as insurance, food, laxatives, tobacco, candy, cooking ingredients and soft drinks—found country music a lucrative advertising medium. New profits for music business entrepreneurs could, in turn, support investment in new artists and further elaboration of the musical genre. By the time America's Great Depression was well under way, country music as a popular entertainment culture had found a workable economic niche.

Historian Bill Malone has said that "roughly from 1880 to 1910, cowboys, mountaineers and their music were 'discovered' and 'memorialized' in the context of a national hunger and nostalgia for simpler times and a simpler society" (Malone 1993, 73). In the southern United States after 1920, where an insurance company catering especially to working-class and lower-middle-class customers set up a powerful radio voice for nostalgic entertainment, longings for simpler times grew in fertile ground.

In just forty years after 1920, the southern United States underwent significant social changes as it was transformed from a primarily rural and agricultural society to an urbanized, industrialized one. During this period the region endured severe economic depression, participated in a world war, and encountered new government programs meant to modernize both agriculture and home life. Migration across the region and out of it increased dramatically, and personal economic traumas, as well as family disruptions, were widespread. Ronald Eller has described the sequence of industrializing patterns in Appalachia that displaced nineteenth-century family farming. The lumber industry was followed by coal mining and textile mills, which generated commercial manufacturing towns tied together by railroads and highways. Land acquisitions were used to create national parks and tourist attractions, to control flooding, and build hydroelectric projects. The social displacement that followed these changes yielded a new market for government welfare. By

1930, three-fifths of employed Appalachians were in nonfarm jobs, and in 1936, almost half the mountain population was on federal relief (Eller 1982, 229, 240). Describing the broader transformation of Southern agricultural regions between 1920 and 1960, Jack Kirby reports that the region lost 1,532,793 farms in this forty years of modernization and estimates that if each 1920 Southern farm household consisted of five persons, by 1960 nearly 8 million people had left farming and 9 million had left the region entirely (Kirby 1987, xv, 276). This unprecedented displacement of rural people was important to the creation of a market for commercial country music.

An early reflection of that market was proliferating radio barn dances styled in the manner of the Grand Ole Opry. Indeed, the WLS National Barn Dance in Chicago preceded the Opry as a highly successful venture. Charles Wolfe has documented radio barn dance programs during the 1930s at Wheeling, Charlotte, St. Louis, Cincinnati, Louisville, Tulsa, Richmond, Atlanta, Shreveport, Des Moines, and New York City. It is probably no coincidence that rustic barn dance programming, beginning as early as January 1923 in Fort Worth, Texas, and still alive today in the Grand Ole Opry, achieved its broadest market in the Depression era of the 1930s in cities that may be said conceptually to encircle the southeastern United States (*Country* 1988, 77). Consistent with Judge Hay's commitment to make rustic radio "down to earth" (Wolfe 1973, 17), barn dance programs during the Depression and thereafter set about creating an active sense of a more attractive rural past. Created in 1937, the Renfro Valley Barn Dance is an enduring example. In 1992, it still attracts tourist groups to its replica of an imagined nineteenth-century Kentucky town now located just off Interstate 75 between Lexington and Nashville. The story of its inventor, John Lair, is a suggestive vignette in the history of commercial country music. Wolfe describes Lair as the grandson of an old Southern judge from Livingston, Kentucky, located "near the junctions of the Big and Little Renfro creeks" (Wolfe 1982, 52). Operating a family farm there after military service in World War I, Lair became "discouraged at the way his valley was being modernized." He migrated north to Battle Creek, Michigan, where he worked in an art institute, then moved to Chicago, where, in 1927, he became program director and music librarian for WLS radio. There he encouraged mountain string band players, whom he described as "folk" musicians.

In 1937, Lair, singer Red Foley, and comedian Whitey Ford ("The

Duke of Paducah") bought land in Rock Castle County, Kentucky, where they intended to build a campground and music barn. Just at that time, the Crosley radio station WLW, in Cincinnati, moved dramatically into the radio market with 500,000 watts of broadcasting power and considerable country music programming. Persuaded to join WLW, Lair brought several acts from the WLS Barn Dance and in October 1937 initiated the Renfro Valley program from Cincinnati Music Hall with "a wildly enthusiastic crowd and a huge listening audience" (Wolfe 1982, 77–78). In 1938, he broadcast from Memorial Hall in Dayton, Ohio, moving the next year to a newly constructed site in Kentucky. Lair's initial radio christening for the Kentucky version of the Renfro Valley Barn Dance proclaimed it "the first and only barn dance on the air presented by the actual residents of an actual community" and offered to mail listeners photographs of the barn. According to Wolfe, fan response to this offer was dramatic: Lair received 253,000 requests for the barn photograph; initially, the 1,000-seat barn was selling out for every show. Like Judge Hay, John Lair dressed his performers in rustic costumes and favored old-fashioned string band musical stylings. The "Little Red Schoolhouse" museum of Kentucky mountain music and stylized rustic performing can still be visited in Renfro Valley, Kentucky, on any Friday or Saturday evening (Wolfe 1982, 78–79).

Neil Rosenberg, a historian of bluegrass music, has provided a generic description of the "show form" associated with early barn dance programs and their relatives in the country music business:

> The show is best thought of as the dramatic equivalent of an idealized family "get-together." The total ensemble was symbolic of a small community or an extended family; to this day shows like "Hee-Haw," the WWVA "World's Jamboree," and the Opry allow and even encourage performers to appear casually onstage; most shows of the thirties featured everyone onstage whether they were actively performing or not. They constituted an audience within an audience, a kind of framing device which suggested that the audience was viewing an old-time corn-shucking or evening of parlor entertainment. This emphasized the communal aspects of the show, projecting a feeling of onstage group solidarity. (Rosenberg 1985, 57)

Rosenberg emphasizes other elements of family relationship within "this communal or extended-family aggregation," such as the duet of brothers (Rosenberg 1985, 58). Singing family groups were numerous, and such appellations as "cousin" and "brother" were frequent, as in "Cousin Minnie Pearl," "Brother Oswald" in Roy Acuff's band, "Uncle Dave Macon," or "Grandpa Jones."

When I visited the WWVA Jamboree USA at Capital Music Hall in Wheeling, West Virginia, and the Renfro Valley Jamboree in Renfro Valley, Kentucky, during the spring of 1992, these contemporary descendants of radio barn dance shows were still presenting themselves as communal get-togethers of friends, family, and extended family. For each program, a major portion of the audience was senior citizens who had traveled to the site in tourist coaches. As a warm-up for the WWVA Jamboree USA, an announcer polled the audience on their points of origin. For the Saturday night show on March 28, 1992, the audience included travel tours from Pennsylvania, Ohio, Virginia, New York, Michigan, New Jersey, and Canada. About half the crowd reported that they were first-timers, and half were returnees.

Promptly at 6 P.M., Jamboree USA went on the air. The program featured three performers. Anita Stapleton and Brad Paisley offered highly competent professional singing performances that covered better-known artists. Stapleton performed songs by Buck Owens, Tanya Tucker, and George Jones. Paisley, a clean-cut young man who showed instrumental virtuosity on mandolin and guitar, covered numbers by contemporary artists Rodney Crowell, Steve Wariner, and Hal Ketchum. Stapleton did five songs and Paisley six, but neither had elaborate strategies for significant audience involvement with their acts.

After an intermission and advertisements for program sponsors, the announcer welcomed more travel groups, then the main act for the evening—Tom T. Hall and the Storytellers. Hall was introduced as an artist who has written and recorded more than 300 songs. A Grand Ole Opry star who has written seven books, served as a television show host, and won a Grammy award, Hall appeared wearing a well-tailored black business suit with an off-white shirt and black string tie. His costume of country respectability was combined with a folksy, humorous manner that included extensive banter onstage as well as the performance of thirteen songs, at least ten of them Hall's own compositions. After a nostalgic opening with "Country Is," Hall spoke to the audience about how wonderful it was to be in Wheeling, West Virginia, with country music on a Saturday night. He asked the audience to tell all the people listening on radio how good he looked because he had lost weight, then welcomed and introduced some of his closest fans and family who were present. The linkage of immediate family and the extended fan family was clear when he introduced a fan couple he said had seen 148 of his shows, introduced four more fans in the audience, and then four members of his family—two sisters and their husbands. Hall concluded his introductions with another nostalgic touch by introducing an "old childhood sweetheart" named Barbara. After Hall's second song, during which picture-takers filed forward to record memorial snapshots, he introduced a couple in the audience who, he said, "brought me a picture of their baby."

Hall had strategies to involve fans with his stage act. Song five was an exaggerated kidding cover of the Johnny Cash hit "Folsom Prison Blues," in which Hall, to the delight of the crowd, parodied Cash's inflections. In Hall's own "Fox on the Run," he played a banjo break that demonstrated his ability to mimic the facial expressions of *Hee Haw* star Roy Clark. The seventh performance was a two-song medley honoring Hank Williams; Hall played keyboard on "You Win Again," which he presented as a cover of the piano styling of Jerry Lee Lewis. One effect of these stage strategies was to invoke the heritage of country music performing traditions. Hall concluded with a song for children, "Sneaky Snake," and a sing-along where he encouraged the audience to boisterously join in the refrain, "I like beer." After Hall signed off with his signature nostalgic ballad "Old Dogs, Children and Watermelon Wine," the announcer closed the program with the benedictory statement, "Good night and God bless."

In April 1992, Renfro Valley, Kentucky, appeared to be a recently constructed old town featuring a town hall, general store, church, post office, firehouse, mill, schoolhouse, cafeteria, and gift shop organized around a "Main Street" pedestrian mall. A large paved parking lot was nearby. There was a new Renfro Valley barn, as well as an old one converted into a museum celebrating Renfro Valley's founding entrepreneur, John Lair. The atmosphere in Renfro Valley is a cultivated rusticity consistent with the spirit of its originator.

The Friday Night Jamboree that I saw on April 24 is staged in the new barn, a technologically sophisticated auditorium in the style of the Grand Ole Opryhouse. The 7:00 P.M. show filled two-thirds or more of the hall with a tourist audience, most of whom had arrived on tour buses. The audience appeared to be heavily oriented toward senior citizens. They saw a program of nearly two hours, produced on a stage that simulated the interior of a barn and featured a rustic pump organ, a quilt, an old radio, a rocking chair, old musical instruments, and an early radio microphone in addition to hay bales, rustic farm tools, straw hats, a mule harness, and large thermometers advertising Royal Crown Cola.

The cast of the Renfro Valley Jamboree consisted of about a dozen people ranging in age from a preteen female who did a clogging act to an aging white-haired male crooner wearing a blue sport coat and slacks. There was a hayseed comic who appeared several times in the show wearing red pants, a checked shirt and flop hat, and told rustic country jokes. And there was a gospel quartet whose work was said to be popular with tourists who buy cassettes in the Renfro store. There were also covers of contemporary hits by Vince Gill, Lorrie Morgan, Collin Raye, and Mary Chapin Carpenter.

The performing troupe appears in glossy group photographs in Renfro Valley's promotional literature, and all performers but one on this show appeared to be regulars. The exception was a singer introduced by a young woman performer as her "real good friend from Berea, Kentucky." This guest thanked his grandmother, his mother, and his aunt for their support and said, "My grandmother has waited a long time to see me on this stage." He performed a cover of Martha Carson's gospel number "Satisfied Mind" while accompanying himself on a dulcimer. For the finale of the Renfro Valley Barn Dance, the entire cast took a common bow while the clogger danced to a well-fiddled hoedown. The communal design of the Renfro Valley Barn Dance show was a direct representation of an idealized family event. When the show ended at 8:45 P.M., the audience was invited to meet that idealized family in the "General Store," where autographs were available and recordings could be purchased.

The pervasive emphasis on images of extended family since early barn dance days finds some of its most vivid expression in bluegrass music. Robert Cantwell has described the musical subculture descended from Bill Monroe and the Blue Grass Boys as a quasi-religious sense of extended family expressed through the music's performance choreography, its formulaic musical structure, and the situations in which it is played. Since the 1970s, enthusiasm for bluegrass music among both working- and middle-class Americans has generated an array of festival events as well as localized bluegrass scenes. The lead example is Bill Monroe's Bean Blossom Festival in southern Indiana, which Cantwell calls a "camp meeting, an evangelical retreat" structured in an "absolute, liturgical sense." A legendary figure in his eightieth decade in the 1990s, and a member of the Country Music Hall of Fame, Monroe has gathered informally with other string instrument players at Bean Blossom for a communal jam session. When Cantwell saw that event in the early 1970s, Monroe said to the assembly: "I call you all my children" (Cantwell 1972, 54). In response, Cantwell described Monroe as "the first modern man" of mountain music and a "religious teacher" who restores "a private and inward dimension to people whose lives have become dominated by outward forms" (Cantwell 1972, 58). Bill Monroe formed the Blue Grass Boys in 1938. More than any other figure in popular culture, he is responsible for standardizing vernacular string band music of the Appalachian heritage into a marketable style and an endlessly repeatable format that allows for improvisation while retaining a basic structure. Monroe's band features five instruments: mandolin, fiddle, banjo, guitar, and bass. In 1939, he joined the Grand Ole Opry with an inaugural performance that updated Jimmie Rodgers's "Blue Yodel No. 8 (Muleskinner Blues)." The standardized instrumentation, formulaic "high lonesome sound" vocal harmonies of charismatic rusticity, and up-tempo rhythmic motifs of bluegrass music are innovations that extend the novelty of radio barn dance programming initiated in the 1920s and 30s.

A variety of other innovations adapted to new media have come from this heritage. An important one was the *Hee Haw* television program. Beginning as a summer replacement for the Smothers Brothers' show on CBS television in June 1969, by its third week of national broadcasting it had achieved television's number-one audience rating—a distinction it held for two years before going into syndication. *Hee Haw*, which lasted until 1993 on The Nashville Network and still appears as reruns in prime-time weekend slots, was a variety show featuring extreme rustic comedy heavily indebted to vaudeville and minstrel traditions. It offered actors in skits where they wore exaggerated rural garb and presented comedic stereotypes of Southern and small-town characters. This basic formula was interspersed with country music solo singers, as well as gospel acts, singing groups and virtuoso bluegrass and string instrument players (Campbell 1981, 125–28). Like the Opry stage show, the

Renfro Valley Jamboree or Bill Monroe's Bean Blossom, *Hee Haw* represented an idealized rural community setting, and this time it was a funny one.

A more recent variant is the Riders in the Sky program, *Riders' Radio Theater*, originating from public radio station WVXU in Cincinnati and syndicated to National Public Radio outlets. Members of the Grand Ole Opry since 1982, Riders in the Sky is a trio. Douglas B. Green ("Ranger Doug") is a scholar who has written histories of country music and sings lead vocals featuring impressive yodeling; Fred LaBour ("Too Slim") is a comedian and bass player; and Woody Chrisman ("Woody Paul") is a fiddling champion with a Ph.D. from M.I.T. Chrisman also satirizes mainstream honky-tonk singing in the persona of "High Sheriff Drywall." The Riders' stage act features comedy skits, serious covers of western harmonic vocals descended from The Sons of the Pioneers and movie westerns, trick roping, vaudeville joke routines, and a variety of skits. The tone is tongue-in-cheek and literate, pitched to an educated upper-middle-class audience as well as to traditional country music fans. Riders host a Saturday morning children's program on CBS television for their "saddle pals." Their amalgam of 1950s television cowboys and singing cowboys combined with moralizing about American heroes and "the cowboy way" is meant humorously, but for its overall effect their act depends on an honorific, not cynical, attitude. While satirizing elements of country music culture, ultimately Riders in the Sky magnify it (Riders 1992).

Bill Malone has described Riders in the Sky as "a modern fantasy of a musical world that was never anything more than a fantasy itself" (Malone 1993, 110). An even more striking example of an invented world directly in debt to the barn dance tradition is Garrison Keillor's *A Prairie Home Companion*. This creation on Minnesota Public Radio between 1974 and 1987 (it returned to the air in the early 1990s), was a Saturday night variety hour that Keillor said was inspired by watching the final program of the Grand Ole Opry in Ryman Auditorium (Lee 1991, 1, 11). Keillor's biographer describes *Prairie Home Companion*, a verbal evocation of incidents in the fictitious rural community of Lake Wobegon, Minnesota, as "an imaginary place based on his experience of many small Minnesota towns—including Freeport, Marine on St. Croix, and Anoka— without representing any of them." Keillor called the program "a throw back" to older radio programs (Lee, 1991, 11). Like the Opry and other programs in the barn dance tradition, *Prairie Home Companion* emphasized casualness, rusticity, family dramas in daily life, humor, and a spirit that would have been readily recognizable to George Hay and John Lair. "I set out deliberately to be warm and folksy and Middle America and down to earth," Keillor has said (Lee 1991, 31–32).

In a piece originally published in *The New Yorker* in 1974, Keillor reported his feelings at the Ryman Auditorium on the Opry's last night there. At first seated in the balcony, he thought that the Opry on stage, even with its mass assembled performers, seemed "small compared with what you'd imagined at home as you listened to the radio." Keillor left the balcony and went to the control booth backstage. "The best place to see the Opry that night," he said,

> was in the booth with my eyes shut, leaning against the back wall, the music coming out of the speaker just like radio, that good old AM mono sound. The room smelled of hot radio tubes, and, closing my eyes, I could see the stage as clearly as when I was a kid lying in front of our giant Zenith console. I'd seen a photograph of the Opry stage in a magazine back then, and, believe me, one is all you need. (*Country* 1988, 367–71)

A Prairie Home Companion features country and folk musicians—usually those who play gospel music and acoustic instruments and display vocal consistency with rustic mountain stylings. It's also a venue for Keillor's humorous monologues, which have a counterpart in country humor. Moreover, the dramatic structure is analogous to that of radio barn dance programming and particularly the Opry, because the performers, especially Keillor, speak intimately to listeners about concerns in their daily lives through stories about incidents of family life, home, love, heartbreak, and hard times. It may be an exaggeration to say that in the popular success of *A Prairie Home Companion*, Garrison Keillor invented a rustic upper Midwest regionalism that parallels the formulaic Southern regionalism represented by George Hay's Grand Ole Opry. Yet there is a consistency.

In the film version of Loretta Lynn's autobiography, at the moment when the young Loretta first arrives outside the Ryman Auditorium the building is pictured at an angle emphasizing its imposing stability. This image magnifies both the grandeur of Lynn's musical aspirations and the solidity of the Opry's position as a central institution of country music culture. After the Grand Ole Opry left the Ryman Auditorium, Garrison Keillor admitted his reluctance to go to the new Opryhouse at Opryland USA. He feared that its modernity might diminish the Opry's emotional power. Indeed, the Opry has never entirely "left" the Ryman, because continuing fan and artist affection has elevated that building to the status of a major shrine of popular culture.

The Ryman Auditorium is well suited to be a shrine. In fact, it is a church, a nineteenth-century gospel tabernacle that memorializes a Cumberland River steamboat captain who was converted to prohibition and saving souls by the flamboyant Southern evangelist, Samuel P. Jones. After his conversion, Captain Thomas Greene Ryman led a life of personal sacrifice, urging the citizens of Nashville to build a community center for evangelistic church services (Eiland 1992, 4–23). When Dwight L. Moody preached here in 1896, so dramatic was his effect that the *Nashville Daily American* enthusiastically christened Nashville the center of the nation (Eiland 1992, 16). In the early years of this century, the Ryman became the site of operatic performances and legitimate theater. It was well known to touring companies in the eastern United States and played an important role in building Nashville's middle- and upper-middle-class artistic community. Before the arrival of the Grand Ole Opry, the Ryman Auditorium had hosted such luminaries as the opera star Enrico Caruso, popular singers Nelson Eddy and Jeanette Mac-Donald, evangelist Billy Sunday, race spokesman Booker T. Washington, and actress Sarah Bernhardt (Eiland 1992, 25–45).

The Ryman became the Grand Ole Opry's fifth home. Originating in the National Life Building, it moved to the Hillsboro Theater, then to the Dixie Tabernacle in east Nashville and to Nashville's War Memorial Auditorium. Each move was prompted by growth in fan desire to see the Opry in live performances. In 1943, the Opry moved to the Ryman, where it remained until March 1974.

The Opry's thirty-one years at the Ryman are still regarded by many fans and artists as its best years. As a performing site, the Ryman is acoustically effective and intimately arranged. A celebrated inefficiency of backstage accommodations probably contributed to the familiarity and camaraderie among artists. Fans were also extremely close to artists here, and the larger-than-life imagery of country music stars (illustrated by Keillor's favorable memory of listening to the Opry in comparison to actually seeing it) mixed readily with opportunities for personal encounter. If you talk with older country music fans and ask if they have been to the Opry, almost invariably you will be told whether they saw it at the Ryman and that, if they did, when that was, who they saw, and how it felt to be there.

In the early 1990s, many artists committed to traditionalism in country music performing choose to play the Ryman. In 1992, for example, Emmylou Harris did a live album concert there with her acoustic band, the Nash Ramblers (Eiland 1992, 47–72, 87). The June 1992 official Grand Ole Opry Fan Club newsletter, *The Opry Observer*, carried a front-page picture from that concert, along with a picture of Connie Smith singing "Amazing Grace" on stage at the Ryman.

In 1989 and 1990, the Ryman had a million-dollar exterior restoration to prepare for celebrating its hundredth birthday in 1992. Listed on the National Register of Historic Places since 1971, and owned outright by the Grand Ole Opry since 1963, today the Ryman is a venue for special events and a site visited by more than 200,000 fans annually (Eiland 1992, 85). An $8.5-million interior renovation was done for another official reopening in June 1994, as a museum and 2,000-seat performance hall. On Saturday night, June 4, Garrison Keillor broadcast *A Praire Home Companion* from the stage of the renovated Ryman to 2 million listeners on the American Public Radio network.

If you go to the Ryman, you can stand in the center of its stage and the tour guide will invite you to sing. And, if you have a fan's appreciation for the history of country music culture, even with your own distance from the experience of Garth Brooks, you, too, may feel something like "you're *there*."

If the Ryman Auditorium is the mother church of country music and its most important shrine, the Opry's latest home on an outer freeway loop adjacent to the Cumberland River in Nashville is country music culture's most elaborate theme park and museum site. Roy Acuff presided at Opryland USA's groundbreaking in 1970 by blowing the steamboat whistle that Judge Hay blew regularly on the Opry. The longtime Dobro player in Acuff's band, Brother Oswald, broke the ground by plowing it with mules. Acuff also got his wish to be the first performer on the new Opry stage and the first to walk across the six-foot circle of oak flooring brought to the center of the new stage from the Ryman Auditorium (Schlappi 1978, 60). This deliberate symbolic continuity, a public self-consciousness of the Opry's history, pervades Opryland.

Opryland is a musical theme park featuring live productions depicting the full range of popular music in American history. The total site is 757 acres located nine miles from downtown Nashville. In 1992 the Opryland Hotel featured 1,891 rooms, a spectacular two-acre conservatory, and numerous conference and tourist amenities, including "more meeting, exhibit and public space than any other hotel in the country." The Nashville Network (TNN), a cable television channel since 1983, produces shows here, including 1992's number-one rated cable television program, "The Statler Brothers." Opryland Music Group, one of country music's premier music publishing operations and a descendant of Acuff-Rose Publishing, is headquartered here. In 1985, Opryland christened *The General Jackson*, a showboat named for President Andrew Jackson (who lived near Nashville). This is a 300-foot, four-deck riverboat that includes a theater of 1,000 seats. WSM radio, in both AM and FM versions, is located here. Television productions, sightseeing tours, travel agencies, and operating offices for hotels and theme parks the company owns elsewhere in the nation are here, as well as Country Music Television cable video network (CMT) and TNN Radio.

The initial construction cost of Opryland USA was $182.5 million. Between 1972 and 1992, 41.7 million people visited Opryland, 1,924,801 in 1991 alone. The Opryland Hotel had a phenomenal 86 percent occupancy rate in 1991. In its first eight years The Nashville Network grew from 7 million to more than 53 million subscribers, and Country Music Television in 1991 had more than 15 million subscribers. *The General Jackson* hosted 439,500 passengers that year, and 795,000 people attended the Grand Ole Opry. In October 1991, Gaylord Entertainment Company, the parent company of Opryland USA, was listed on the New York Stock Exchange (Adkinson 1992).

For several years before his death in 1992, Roy Acuff lived in a home built for him in the park near the Opryhouse. Stars such as Porter Wagoner, Mike Snider, and Jeannie Pruitt are commonly seen in the park. Several theaters feature contemporary hit-making performers, as well as established ones, along with performers not yet well known, who depict figures from country music history. The theme park also features important museums. The Roy Acuff Museum and musical instrument collection is here, as is the Minnie Pearl Museum. The Grand Ole Opry Museum features separate sections for such important stars as Patsy Cline, Hank Snow, Little Jimmie Dickens, and Marty Robbins. Star automobiles, memorabilia, musical instruments, clothing, and restorations of actual rooms—Marty Robbins's office or Patsy Cline's kitchen—are on view here. Admission to the Opry requires separate tickets, but most performances and all museums are open to the fans with park admission.

Roy Acuff favored the move to Opryland USA from the Ryman Auditorium because he felt that the accommodations for fans would be much better. During the last Opry show at the Ryman, Acuff told the fans, "You just don't know how much we do appreciate you people. It's *you* who have made the Grand Ole Opry so successful." Before leaving the fans with a benediction for their spiritual comfort—"God bless you all"—Acuff talked about their physical comfort:

> Certainly there are certain memories of this old house that will go with us forever. Not all of them are good. Not all of them. Many of them are. But some of them are *punishment*. Punishment in a way that we ask you to come visit with us and then we sit you out in this audience here and in the hot summer we sell you a fan for a dollar. You do your own air conditioning. And some of you, we sell you a cushion to sit on because the seats are not just the most comfortable as they can be. But out in Opryland, when you come to see us, we'll furnish the air-conditioner. We'll furnish the cushion seats. (Schlappi 1978, 67)

The spirit of the Grand Ole Opry is one of commercial enterprise and, simultaneously, extended family. For Roy Acuff, it was both his business and his home. In June 1992, Chris Praetor, manager of Conway Twitty's Twitty City theme park, told me that major stars who can fill concert halls in the 1990s don't perform on the Opry even though they may be members of it. As a strictly business proposition, the Opry pays them comparatively little. Praetor said, "When Garth Brooks plays the Opry, he's donated $100,000. It used to be that you had to be part of the Grand Ole Opry to get airplay on the radio. Not any more." Yet Brooks does play the Opry. In 1992 and 1993, his appearances usually coincided with a Saturday night television broadcast, with the release of a new record album, or with the beginning of a concert tour. While his timing probably had commercial implications, there may also have been emotional ones. "I have always been treated like family when I was at the Opry," Brooks has said; "but now to be recognized as a member is among the class of honors that will never be topped no matter how long or how far my career goes" (Strobel 1992, 10). The matter of low financial return for playing the Opry is widely noted among entertainers. After Hal Ketchum sang his hit song "Small Town Saturday Night" on the June 13, 1992 Grand Ole Opry, host Jim Ed Brown asked him if he would be willing to sing another song but added, "We don't pay you nothin.'" Ketchum's response was immediate: "You pay in history and beauty."

Direct financial return appears never to have been the Opry's entire attraction for entertainers. In his autobiography, *Every Highway Out of Nashville*, steel guitarist Howard White included a reproduction of a 1965 check stub for September 11—his gross earnings were $10 and his net was $8.44 (White 1990, 24–25). Alton Delmore looked back on his early days at the Opry with mixed emotions. Citing an instance of manipulation by Opry management to keep him on the Opry when he might have had a chance to go elsewhere for higher pay, Delmore says: "But if I could recall my decision, knowing what I do today, I would have never gone up there to play" (Delmore 1977, 56). Yet that conclusion is overmatched by competing memories.

> So you see we had a dedicated attitude toward the Grand Ole Opry. It was like something like Cinderella felt when she made her big splash. It was ambition with an amazing intensity—just longing for something that is seemingly impossible to attain. I still remember very clearly how I felt and I'm sure Rabon felt the same way. Two country boys longing for the chance to perform in what was to us, like heaven. (Delmore 1977, 44)

While the Opry is definitely a business, as country music's mother church it is also much more. The rustic informality of stage production—combined with professional dedication of the stars, the immediate sense of extended family rooted in a historic place, and the sense of collective personal bonding among fans and artists—has been a source of identity for this music culture since the 1920s. In a society experiencing intensive modernization, the Opry has been simultaneously an effect of modernization and a means for imaginatively transcending its disruptions. The Opry's warm sense of the past is a congenial invention of tradition that provides an image of common values and a location in time and place. While the Opry is about fame, fortune and making money, it is also about supporting people, about being at home and being with family.

In 1992, Iris DeMent recorded a song that suggests the spiritual attraction of the Opry in country music culture. In "Mama's Opry" DeMent tells a story about her mother, who grew up in a farm community where neighbors would come to her home for hoe-downs. Her mother's family also listened to the Carter Family, Jimmie Rodgers, and the Grand Ole Opry on radio—and her mother dreamed of singing on the Opry stage. As a child, Iris sang along with gospel records played on her mother's phonograph. In 1992, she remembered those songs: "Sweet Rose of Sharon," "Abide with Me," "The Gospel Ship to Heaven's Jubilee," "I Don't Want to Get Adjusted to This World" and others. From her adulthood, DeMent now sees "that I was singin' in the grandest opry" (DeMent 1992).

There are eleven songs on Iris DeMent's album, *Infamous Angel*; "Mama's Opry" is the tenth. It's an image of her memory of her own past, of her family's past, of a link to a larger spiritual tradition that the Opry provided its fans. In "Higher Ground," the last song on *Infamous Angel*, Iris DeMent sings this traditional gospel number and features her mother, Flora Mae DeMent, as lead vocalist. By moving from an artist's remembered image of family to active realization of actual family through a shared gospel heritage, *Infamous Angel* enacts the spirit of the mother church.

I'm a thousand miles away from home
Just waiting for a train.
                    —Jimmie Rodgers, 1928

I wouldn't mind dyin', gotta stay dead so
long . . .
And I wouldn't mind dyin' if dyin' was all.
                    —Carter Family, 1932

CHAPTER 2   **Tragic Troubadours**

In "Mama's Opry," Iris DeMent invokes her mother's childhood in a farming town where her grandfather played fiddle at hoedowns and where she could sing along with the Carter Family, Jimmie Rodgers, and the Grand Ole Opry on the family radio. If she did, DeMent's mother participated in more than one country music tradition as a child. The barn dance tradition of the Opry represents a lively spirit of the living past in country music culture. The Carter Family and Jimmie Rodgers, however, present another face of the past—a pervasive evocation of transience, of present things fading away, of personal tragedy and death. As early as 1927, and especially after the Depression years of the 1930s, the war years of the 1940s, and the intensive urbanization of the 1950s, this note of pain emerged to dominate country music culture. By the 1990s, newcomer Doug Stone could sing, "they ought to put warning labels on those sad country songs." Robert Cantwell finds this painful note in bluegrass music. "In its subject matter," Cantwell discovered, "in its performers and their performances, even in its most antic moods, it is pervaded by death. Often it is actually about death, in pious, morbid or sentimental ways." Because Cantwell regards bluegrass as principally celebratory and communal, he sees its focus on death as mystical, "a kind of rude cosmology" that underscores the bluegrass attempt to transcend worldly forms (Cantwell 1972, 58–59). Yet the tone Cantwell identified in bluegrass exists throughout country music culture, where it lends the poignancy of pathos to many traditions. In the spirit of the barn dance, the living past serves the present; the spirit of tragic troubadours, however, is one of present time becoming "old," a sense of approaching change that may not be for the better, a sense of impending loss, of sadness. Perhaps a variant of Victorian nostalgia and perhaps a mood that resonates with the historical experience of Southerners, this spirit in popular music echoes the more complex renditions of Southern novelists who perceive history as a grand trauma acting on the daily lives of ordinary people.

In country music culture, sadness takes on a magnified preciousness that is nevertheless meant quite seriously. In the 1970s, entertainer Johnny Cash presented himself as the "Man in Black," dressed to mourn for the poor, the beaten down, the hungry, the prisoners, the sick, the lonely, the old, reckless drug users, and Vietnam war dead (Cash 1971). Twenty-one years later, newcomer Billy Ray Cyrus scored with another memorial song to Vietnam veterans, "Some Gave All." At his appearance in Dayton's Hara Arena, September 12, 1992, Cyrus spoke seriously to his fans when introducing the title song from his first album: "If you remember anything from tonight remember this. Someday it will be chiseled in stone when they bury me in Kentucky. My tombstone will read *Some Gave All*."

Charles Reagan Wilson has studied the theme of death in country song lyrics and found an indicator of regional distinctiveness:

> Rather than establishing institutions of death avoidance, as scholars now believe that the Northeast did, Southerners from the last nineteenth century to the mid-twentieth had what can best be characterized as a culture of death. An examination of country music shows six categories of death—the pervasiveness of death, violent and tragic death, songs of love and death, death and the family, celebrity death, and religious influences on death. (Wilson 1992, 114–15)

Wilson attributes this theme to the historical experience of the South: "White Southerners, both individually and collectively, have known much suffering in their long history, and especially since the Civil War. The evidence from country music is that this reality has sensitized them to the tragedy of human mortality in a distinctively regional way" (Wilson 1992, 126–27). It's possible to elaborate on Wilson's insight. Four country acts—the Carter Family, Jimmie Rodgers, Hank Williams, and Patsy Cline—have been particularly important to the use of mortality in country music culture. Each had a difficult life; three died prematurely, and the fourth dissolved prematurely as a family act. The sense of transience associated with the legendary performing lives of these entertainers has been an important influence in country music culture, one that nurtures the popular image of professional country musicians as tragic troubadours.

First recorded in Bristol, Tennessee, in 1927, by Ralph Peer, an agent of the Victor Recording Company who hoped to market hillbilly singers in response to the dramatic growth in popularity of radio barn dance programs, popular response to the Carter Family and Jimmie Rodgers may be regarded as the formative moment of commercial country music culture (*Country* 1988; Wolfe, 1987). A formal portrait of the Carter Family shows A. P. Carter—the group's founder, song collector, arranger, and manager—with his wife Sara and her signature autoharp, and with A. P.'s brother's wife Maybelle and her expensive L-5 Gibson guitar. The Carters, dressed in refined late-Victorian attire, are photographed against a plain background staring directly into the camera lens with entirely serious expressions. Nolan Porterfield aptly says that in this portrait the Carters are "grave as headstones" (*Country* 1988, 14). This demeanor is an apt visual representation of the impression on country music culture left by Carter Family songs.

Individual songs recorded and performed by the Carter Family had their origins in a variety of sources. A. P. Carter, sometimes working with the black guitar player and songwriter Leslie Riddles, is reported to have said he "worked up" songs collected from diverse informants and other resources. According to Archie Green, Carter "did not distinguish between direct borrowing, recomposition, and original creation" (Green 1972, 392). Green describes Carter music as a jumble of traditions.

When the Carters began to record, they sang old hymns, new gospel songs, timeless secular ballads, sagas of bad men, current journalistic pieces, songs of unrequited love, recomposed sentimentalities of the popular stage, and occupational songs of cowboys, railroaders, and hobos. (Green 1972, 397)

Even so, Carter Family singing was distinctive for several innovations that were to be widely imitated throughout subsequent country music culture.

Fundamental to Carter innovations was Maybelle Carter's guitar playing—a strong melody played on bass strings with her thumb, with driving rhythmic chords played on treble strings. If not unique, this fingering pattern was certainly distinctive. "Of course, such runs were not new," Johnny Cash explains:

but they were used differently by Maybelle, they were being used not only as a part of the lead instrument, but as fills and also for the "bottom" of the song. Throughout it all the strong emphasis on the bass was a must and this was gained in part by the use of a thumb pick and two steel finger picks. Later, this style was to be imitated to the note by literally thousands of guitar players. (Cash 1980, 4–5)

Maybelle Carter's use of this picking style created a steady rhythm wedded to a key innovation in vocal performance. Earlier hillbilly vocalizing—as well as the vernacular mountain and rural ballad, gospel, and pop singing that preceded it—had not been intimately controlled by its instrumental accompaniment. The Carters blended their vocal harmonies so carefully with their instrumental rhythms and riffs that, in effect, they standardized the country song. A. P. Carter arranged the songs he created or found so that complicated traditional melodies were reduced to repeating melodic lines fitted to a regular rhythmic pattern of basic instrumental chords. Earlier singers, says Johnny Cash, "were barely singing over the instruments. The Carter style was built around the vocals and incorporated them into the instrumental background, usually made up of the basic three-chord structure." In effect, the Carters "violated the main traditions of vocal and instrumental music" to create a new style and sound (Cash 1980, 5; JEMF 1977, 2).

Another singular feature of Carter Family music was its consistency. Between 1927 and 1941, they released some 300 recordings featuring their signature rhythm, instrumental motifs, and vocal harmonies. Their musical consistency put songs from diverse sources into a recognizable format that was precise in execution, one that could be imitated or elaborated on by other musicians. And aspiring country musicians had many opportunities to hear it.

In the late 1930s, the Carters lived for three years in San Antonio and Del Rio, Texas, where they made transcriptions for "border radio" stations licensed in Mexico as XEG, XENT, and XERA. These stations were built just over the Mexican border to avoid legal regulation of power limits by American authorities. Their colorful entrepreneurs (such as "John R. Brinkley, M.D., Ph.D., M.C., L.L.D., D.P.H, S.C.D.; Lieutenant U.S. Naval Reserves; member National Geographic Society") promoted patent medicines and such questionable health cures as goat gland transplants as a treatment for infertility. Seeking radio entertainment that would attract a broad audience of working-class listeners, these radio innovators employed Mexican balladeers, astrologers, numerologists, fortune-tellers, and hillbilly and western musicians. The test of success for an act on border radio was the ability to attract fan mail from listeners. By 1932, some stations reportedly were receiving nearly 28,000 pieces of mail per week. "A good mail puller was someone who generated numerous inquiries for products and services offered on the air, sometimes as many as several thousand per day. As long as a performer pulled mail, he or she was assured border stardom and job security" (Fowler and Crawford 1990, 13, 17, 29, 39). Along with the Grand Ole Opry and other radio barn dance programs, the impact of border radio programming in an era when radio listening was the country's most novel form of popular entertainment expanded the appeal of commercial country music.

As a standardized form of rustic popular music that could readily be recognized on radio and in recordings, Carter Family songs were crucial musical models for the formation of country music culture. They also served as a source for its characteristic pathos. Whatever their particular subject matter, whether sacred or secular, the bulk of Carter Family topics were sad ones. In their first recording session with Ralph Peer, at Bristol, Tennessee in 1927, they recorded six songs, now available on the Country Music Foundation release *The Bristol Sessions* (1987). In these songs, a daughter remembers her mother's Bible readings with sentiment and nostalgia ("Little Log Cabin by the Sea"), a young woman laments her unrequited love ("Bury Me Under the Weeping Willow"), a mother pines for her wandering boy ("The Wandering Boy"), lovers pledge their loyalty in trepidation over pending separation ("The Storms Are on the Ocean"), blessings are sought for poor orphaned children ("The Poor Orphan Child"), and a young bride complains of constraints in married life ("Single Girl, Married Girl"). At least five of these songs depict emotional hardship, and all connote a sense of the inexorable passage of time and of change that acts on individuals, not necessarily for their benefit.

A similar tone was apparently at hand when the Carter Family was introduced to America on border radio. In 1972 (and, in revised form, in 1977), the John Edwards Memorial Foundation issued a collection of twenty-three songs taken from electrical transcriptions played on border radio stations XERA at Villa Acuna, Choahilla, between 1938 and 1942. The songs in this collection include three brief instrumentals, seven gospel songs, nine songs depicting the circumstances of a broken heart, and four renditions of hard times (JEMF 1977). Gospel music seemingly was a prominent feature of Carter Family singing, yet Carter gospel theology did not yield unrelieved happiness. "Diamonds in the Rough" tells the story of a musician who gave up his profession after a conversion experience—an ironic incident apparently meant to encourage persistence by the converted in the work of saving souls. Other gospel numbers in the collection depict sorrow, pain, and praying as well as rapture ("When Our Lord Shall Come Again"), anxiety about meeting Jesus after death ("I Wouldn't Mind Dying"), an image of an afterlife where there are no drunkards ("There'll Be Joy, Joy, Joy"), a pledge of fidelity to Jesus so the singer can join his dead mother in heaven ("In Just a Few More Days"), and a warning to a brother who risks his soul by the way he lives ("What Would You Give in Exchange for Your Soul?"). The album is introduced and concluded by a trademark Carter song, "Keep on the Sunny Side," a gospel number in which the chorus encourages us to keep on the sunny side of life because that will help us every day. Apparently the words for this song were written by a woman who got the idea from an invalid cousin who wanted his wheelchair pushed on the sunny side of a street (JEMF 1977).

The evangelical religious tradition to which the Carter Family belonged is itself an elaborate commentary on the transience of worldly things and the passing away of worldly sorrows in sacred redemption. Three of the four secular songs of hard times in this collection implore children to write to their lonesome mothers when the latter are confined to the "old ladies' home"; they give an account of the homesickness of a wandering man in "Goin' Back to Texas"; and, in "Broken Down Tramp," tell of an alcoholic hobo whose story of another hobo's death is a warning against the hobo life. The fourth hard-times song, the "Cyclone of Rye Cove," is a disaster song about a storm that killed all the children in Rye Cove when the schoolhouse blew away.

Nine Carter songs of broken hearts from the border radio collection warn a lover to go away because a girl's father may kill him ("Who's that Knocking"), lament a lost childhood sweetheart whose parents arranged a marriage for wealth ("One Little Word"), reveal a suicide note addressed to an indifferent or turncoat lover ("The Last Letter"), depict the rejection of a late declaration of love by one already betrothed ("I Cannot Be Your Sweetheart"), give a balladeer's account of a broken engagement where a woman dies before the man realizes he actually loved her ("Broken Engagement"), reveal the anxiety of a man about forgiveness in Heaven because a quarrel with his lover resulted in her death ("Why There's a Tear in My Eye"), pray for the end of armed conflict when a woman's lover has been taken to war ("Soldier's Sweetheart"), and depict the lament of a wronged lover ("Bonnie Blue Eyes"). A blues cover in this collection, "I'm Sitting on Top of the World," is a past-broken-heart song in which a rejected lover claims to have recovered from his emotional trauma.

The Carter Family was influential in the creation of country music culture because of their styling innovations and their popularity as personalities of 500,000-watt border radio stations that could reach most homes in America. They also influenced the character of country music culture by their choice of songs dealing with hard times, broken hearts, and gospel salvation from the troubles of a worrisome world. The actual life experience of A. P. and Sara Carter may have affected that choice. Never able to make their living solely from musical performance, family members at times worked in locales distant from their Scott County, Virginia, homes, and A. P. maintained a variety of local occupations such as farming, blacksmithing, carpentry, and selling fruit trees (JEMF 1977). For an act that become famous as a singing family, there were ironies. Four years before the Consolidated Royal Chemical Corporation sponsored the Carters' move to Del Rio, A. P. and Sara Carter separated. They continued to perform as the Carter Family, however, and frequently brought their children into the act for live performances. While in Texas, they divorced; then in 1939, Sara married A. P.'s first cousin, Coy Bayes, and moved to California. In 1942, the Texas arrangement ended. After a short engagement in Charlotte, North Carolina, the original Carter Family broke up (JEMF 1977).

Through the influence of the Grand Ole Opry and the "folk" revival movement of the 1960s and 70s, Maybelle Carter maintained a strong personal influence on the evolution of country music (she died in 1978). A. P. attempted unsuccessfully to record on more than one occasion after the demise of the family act. Nolan Porterfield quotes Jeanette Carter on this period in her father's life: "He seemed lonelier, he walked more, and his laughing blue eyes seemed sad." A. P. Carter died in 1960, never to know that the folk movement would lionize his family's memory (*Country* 1988, 26, 38).

If there was a mismatch between the actual lives of the Carters and the family image of their act, they represented a larger historical irony as well. The Carter Family canonized a rustic music that steeped songs of hard times, broken hearts, and gospel salvation in nostalgia for a rural past. Yet their work appeared, and achieved its greatest popularity, just at a moment when regional modernization, economic dislocation, and world war were profoundly transforming rural life. In his introduction to *The Carter Family on Border Radio*, Archie Green makes this point by describing the anthology as a "time capsule."

> [It] helps us relive one brief span of the past—the period when America began to emerge from the Depression into the era of world superpower. Nothing that the Carter Family recorded at Del Rio foreshadowed the pace of life in the United States after Pearl Harbor. Much that was cut onto aluminum discs at Del Rio actually revealed the erosion of the Carter Family's cosmos—in part by the very radio transmitter that broadcast the Family's music. (JEMF 1977)

The lives of country music artists sometimes exemplify in popular culture the ways social and historical forces act on ordinary people. By 1941, the popularity of the Carter Family was a national phenomenon. Then times changed quickly. June Carter Cash remembered the coming of World War II: "That war had knocked the Carter Family right off the front cover of *Life* magazine. We were scheduled to be on the cover the week of December 7, 1941, but Pearl Harbor took our place" (Cash, June [1979], 1981, 41). The original family act ended the following year, but by 1950, "Mother May-belle" Carter and daughters Helen, June, and Anita had joined the Grand Ole Opry. Johnny Cash, who married June, described the next seventeen Opry years as "The Carter Family home—at least for the second generation of the family" (Cash 1980, 9–11).

With the charismatic stylist Chet Atkins as a guitar player for the group, the new Carter Family on the Opry impressed many profes-sional entertainers as well as such radio fans as Iris DeMent's moth-er. Singer Dottie West recalled the special combination of Carter Family singing and the Ryman Auditorium: "We all know it was built as a tabernacle, and I would cry sometimes when I heard An-ita's pure sweet voice in that old building. It was just like hearing an angel sing" (Eiland 1992, 59). So, Mother Maybelle Carter and the Carter Sisters replaced the tragic troubadour experience of the origi-nal Carter Family with the living spirit of the Grand Ole Opry—but not before A. P., Sara, and Maybelle Carter made an indelible print of pathos from the rural Southern past on country music culture.

In his introduction to a song collection showcasing *The Original Carter Family Songbook* in 1980, music publishing executive Roy Horton, a member of the Country Music Hall of Fame who helped establish that institution in the late 1960s, described Jimmie Rodgers in the vivid way that many country music artists, business people and fans remember him.

> In the 1920s, Ralph Peer was recording manager for RCA Victor Re-cords. He decided to tour the country with portable equipment and record regional groups. After moderate success, he discovered a Sing-ing Brakeman named Jimmie Rodgers and a group of folk singers in Virginia called the Carter Family. He recorded both in Bristol, VA. in August, 1927. Jimmie Rodgers became a phenomenal success and out-sold every artist in America. Although he lived only six more years, his songs (110) published by Peer became the nucleus of a giant pub-lishing empire with branches all over the world. Rodgers' songs have earned millions in royalties and have been vehicles for dozens of super-stars through the years. (Cash 1980)

Rodgers was "phenomenal"; his songs "earned millions" and built a "giant publishing empire." Instantaneous recognition, big money, songwriting, wide and lasting influence—these are important criteria by which the success of singing stars has been measured in commercial country music since the late 1920s. Jimmie Rodgers gave country music an innovative vocal performance and stage presence; but, even more important, he gave it a lasting image of artist success. Ironically, this was an image of a tragic troubadour, dedicated to his art, in frail health and dying, and singing of hard times and broken hearts during the nation's Great Depression of the 1930s.

As a formative act of commercial country music, the original Carter Family had played to fan interest in America's fading rural past and "folk" traditions. In a sense, A. P. and Sara Carter never became "professional" country singers in a contemporary style. Off stage, they kept to their private lives; their renditions of old mountain ballads, spiritual appeals for gospel salvation, and adaptations of Victorian parlor and disaster songs faded with them into the changing Southern past. As the original Carters went back to makeshift farming in Virginia or off to California, the extended Southern family seemed to be dissolving. Before they went, however, they left country music a consistent rhythm, a standardized song, and a great guitar.

Jimmie Rodgers left a quite different impression. In him, we have the type for a lonesome individual, a tragic troubadour beset by human frailty and ill health, dedicated passionately and publicly to becoming a "professional" artist. During the Great Depression, as Rodgers sang songs of hard times, broken hearts, domestic violence and personal pain, he brought to country music a charismatic stage presence, an innovative vocal signature in the "blue yodel," and a public flair, presence, and highly visible image that would stimulate generations of country music performers. Jimmie Rodgers could turn fans into aspiring professionals, and he could generate the sincerest flattery—imitation.

Jimmie Rodgers became country music's model of the professional commercial entertainer. Many patterns of star behavior evident in country music culture today originated with him. In 1961, he was the first entertainer elected to the newly formed Country Music Hall of Fame in Nashville. Rodgers was also elected to the Alabama Music Hall of Fame in 1993 (when its officials came to believe that he was born on their side of the Alabama—Mississippi state line at Geiger, Alabama).

Yet, throughout his life, Rodgers regarded Meridian, Mississippi, as his home. A central Mississippi railroad town nine miles from the Alabama state line destroyed by General Sherman in the Civil War, Meridian came back in the early twentieth century as a regional center of economic and entertainment activity. Rodgers's youthful experiences in Meridian were definitely urban ones; by the time he was thirteen, in 1910, Meridian was Mississippi's largest city, with a population of 23,285. Its 1915 population was nearly 30,000. Nolan Porterfield describes the tone of Meridian at this time:

> The diverse and sprightly Southern metropolis boasted multi-storied office buildings and hotels, an electric streetcar line, two telephone companies, brick streets, a professional baseball team, and, according to publicity, a "splendid" police force. In addition to lumber mills and cotton gins, a cannery, and a harness-and-saddle works, there were factories which produced steam boilers, eight-wheel lumber wagons, brooms, mattresses, and a variety of farm and household goods. Products were distributed from the complex of warehouses and shipping facilities of the seven rail lines which served the city and operated "shops" (roundhouse and repair stalls) there. (Porterfield 1979, 15)

Not only was Meridian urban, it was relatively urbane as well. It featured colleges for men, for women, and an institute for girls, as well as a medical college, a normal school for blacks, and a music conservatory. By the time Jimmie Rodgers had reached professional stardom, Meridian was an even more impressive Deep South city. Its Threefoot Building, a fifteen-story downtown structure built in 1929–30, was designed by Frank Fort for the *Chicago Tribune* Tower competition in Chicago, where it won third place (Meridian Historic Preservation Commission 1992, 9). It's likely that Rodgers's perspectives were considerably influenced by the urban milieu of Meridian and the industrial culture of the railroad. In those respects his musical sensibilities were born in modernity.

Located between Jackson, Hattiesburg, and Tuscaloosa—and, beyond them, Memphis, New Orleans, and Birmingham—the Meridian of Rodgers's youth was a place where trains came and went daily. Positioned on the Southern Crescent Route from New York City to New Orleans (with Atlanta and Washington also on the line), Meridian became a stopover for theatrical and musical touring groups. The city featured seventeen different theaters, where Rodgers may have encountered professional entertainers (*Country* 1988, 39). A 1991 study for Meridian's Grand Opera House elaborates: "In fact, the crucial factor in the growth and success of theater in Meridian was its location as a junction point for five major rail lines: the Mobile and Ohio; N.E. and N.O.; Illinois Central; Great Southern; and the Vicksburg and Meridian. Any show traveling to New Orleans (a major theatrical center) from New York would have to pass through Meridian" (Castagno 1991, 4).

Winner of a talent contest in Meridian at the age of twelve, in 1911, Rodgers ran away with a medicine show before he was fifteen. Later, he would link his early years with the life of a vagabond railroader; but his biographers suggest that his railroad work was principally a means to the end of a music career. Rodgers followed carnivals, tent shows, and other opportunities to perform. After being recorded by Ralph Peer in Asheville in 1927, he toured extensively with vaudeville and tent shows, alternated touring with recording sessions across the country, from New York City to Louisville to Hollywood, and actively promoted himself as a professional recording artist and entertainer in urban centers across the South (*Country* 1988, 39–44; Malone 1985, 81).

The image of Rodgers as a touring entertainer going to meet his fans lingers powerfully in country music culture and especially among its artists. In accepting the 1993 Country Music Association Entertainer of the Year Award on CBS Television, Vince Gill referred not to Rodgers but to that image of the touring country entertainer. Comparing himself with characteristic humility to Garth Brooks, Gill said, "I know Garth hasn't toured this year but he played in front of more people in one weekend than I think I did all year." One legacy of Jimmie Rodgers is the notion that touring is essential to country music stardom, and even though Garth Brooks performed at spectacular events in 1993, the Entertainer of the Year, it seems, ought to tour.

In addition to modeling professional behavior, Jimmie Rodgers gave country music a formative example of solo vocal performance. His most commonly cited vocal innovation is the "blue yodel." In 1992, humorist Jerry Clower told me that the first country music he ever heard was black people coming home from the cotton fields and hollering to one another in order to communicate over great distances. Bill C. Malone has cited such field hollers as a possible antecedent of Rodgers's blue yodel, along with the work of street criers in Southern cities, cowboy wailing, train whistles, and adaptations of Tyrolese yodeling in minstrel shows and vaudeville (Malone 1985, 87). Whatever its exact origin, and even though others had preceded Rodgers as yodelers in American pop and vernacular music, Rodgers created a yodel with a distinct tone of blues lament indebted to African-American musical traditions and redolent with pathos. Henry Pleasants, a professional musician trained at the Curtis Institute in Philadelphia and an expert on opera, said of Rodgers's yodel, "I had heard plenty of yodeling during tours of duty with the Army and the Foreign Service in Switzerland, Bavaria, and Austria, but never anything quite like this. It was sweeter than any yodeling I had ever heard, more melodious, wider in range—a true falsetto extending upward to the E flat above high C—more accurate in pitch, more imaginative in its figuration and somehow compellingly and uniquely plaintive" (Porterfield 1979, 364).

Despite the power of Rodgers's yodel, country music scholars emphasize the range of his interest in song stylings. Bill Malone, for example, cites his "multi-faceted repertoire" as railroad songs, "rounder" songs, risqué novelty songs, cowboy songs, hobo songs, sentimental, nostalgic, romantic, semireligious, and popular love songs (Malone 1985, 88). Rodgers also drew eclectics on popular sources—parlor music, tin pan alley stylings, jazz, blues, Hawaiian music and orchestral music—and he recorded with a jug band, a whistler, and a musical saw. Rodgers was one of the first white performers to record with black artists, including Louis Armstrong, Clifford Gibson, and the Louisville Jug Band (*Country* 1988, 45–46). Jimmie Rodgers's voracious borrowing from other musical traditions —which was consistent with A. P. Carter's song-collecting, though far more entrepreneurial and wide-ranging—was again influential for country music culture. Subsequent country songwriters, music publishers, and performing artists would range freely over popular, folk, blues, jazz, African-American, Mexican-American and other traditions to enrich their work.

Despite the diversity of Rodgers's sources, his music yet left a consistent, recognizable tone that would give resonance to the imagery of his life as a tragic troubadour. Porterfield reports an incident when, in rehearsal, Rodgers told his accompanists to play in a distinctive way: "It's gotta have pathos. Make folks feel it—like we do, but we gotta have the feelin' ourselves first. This is supposed to be pathetic" (Porterfield 1979, 75–76). One device for magnifying pathetic effect was the steel guitar. Introduced to pop music earlier as an Hawaiian instrument, the steel guitar was used by Rodgers as early as 1928, and often thereafter (Malone 1985, 86). This is one origin of the haunting musical motif that in contemporary country music routinely accompanies songs of pain and sadness.

In addition to the yodel, the steel guitar, and an emphasis on pathos, Rodgers pioneered another important feature of country music stage performance—the relaxed, informal but lively interaction with fans while in performance on stage. Lawrence Levine argues that a process of sacralization occurred in the early decades of the twentieth century, where several arenas of cultural expression—particularly theater, symphonic music, and museums, gained the status of "highbrow" art "free from the contamination of lesser works or lesser genres, free from the interference of audience or performer, free from the distractions of the mundane." This status was represented by formal expectations about artist-audience interaction: "Audiences were to approach the masters and their works with proper respect and proper seriousness, for aesthetic and spiritual elevation rather than mere entertainment was the goal" (Levine 1988, 46). In the area of musical performance, the creation of permanent professional orchestras in the late nineteenth century was partly, Levine believes, a "step in the direction of creating passive audiences." Conductors lectured audiences on their decorum at concerts, in order to "render audiences docile, willing to accept what the experts deemed appropriate rather than play a role themselves in determining either the repertory or the manner of presentation" (Levine 1988, 189). Decorum was regulated in the theater as well. In Ohio, by action of the state legislature, women were forbidden to wear large fashionable hats in the theater (Levine 1988, 191).

Such governing terms for community ritual probably originated in a desire to differentiate entertainment culture along class lines. As a form of "lowbrow" art, commercial country music—as pioneered by Jimmie Rodgers—deliberately violated "highbrow" canons of behavior. In his stage performances, Rodgers frequently appeared alone, accompanying himself only with his guitar, and often seated on a single stool in an extremely relaxed, unaffected manner. He wore relatively casual stage attire, usually a light suit and a bow tie, and he wore a hat—cocked at a jaunty angle. In his singing, Rodgers lengthened or shortened words for emotional expression in the manner of blues and jazz singers and during performances carried on a stream of commentary to enliven his audience or encourage an accompanist. The general effect was vivacity and a sense of bonding with fans. Rodgers did not lecture his fans. Malone says, "he kidded his audiences in a whimsical fashion and beguiled them with songs that seem to catalogue the varied memories, yearnings, and experiences of small town and rural Americans" (Malone 1985, 86).

It's likely that the full effect of a Jimmie Rodgers act was more than relaxation or relief from the stiffness of formal art. Rodgers's famous informality—when combined with his emphasis on pathos, hard times, broken hearts, and personal hardship—served as a kind of model testimony, a living analogy to the traumas of working-class people undergoing intense modernization and economic depression. There's a quasi-religious element to this, where fans respond to an emblematic voicing of their troubles. Rodgers's biographer puts it this way:

> Whatever Rodgers lacked as a polished musician he made up for in the simple authenticity and intense emotion he brought to every performance. Whether the song was humorous or bluesy, sentimental or bawdy, Rodgers sang it like testament, as if he'd lived every line and suffered every change. (Country 1988, 49)

Rodgers provided a different testimony in his public lifestyle, which was to become another convention associated with artists of country music culture. He was the first "overnight sensation" of country music as a media culture. Many aspiring performers quickly took note of his 12 million record sales in a recording career that lasted from 1927 to 1933. A free spender of a newly acquired fortune, Rodgers modeled lavish public consumption of automobiles as well as jewelry, expensive guitars, clothing and a fancy home in Kerrville, Texas. He was also reputed to enjoy good whiskey, and his star status no doubt led fans to believe he had easy access to it despite prohibition (Malone 1985, 85). Rodgers's conspicuous consumption probably was a way of living out a working-class notion of American success: He made it his way, and he was enjoying it. Importantly, his high living was connected to another trait that became indelibly associated with country music artists—personal generosity. Steel guitar player Cliff Carlisle, who recorded and performed with Rodgers after 1931, left a testimony to Rodgers's good nature. "He was a swell guy, yes sir. He was just real relaxed, an everyday guy and the same every time you saw him," Carlisle said. "When you was with Jimmie, he'd want to take care of everything—any way in the world he could keep you from spending your money" (*Country* 1988, 43). Here, a key image of country music stardom was being forged: A rising star makes big money and spends it lavishly in public, while both fans and other entertainers offer enduring support because the big star has an even bigger heart, and shows it.

If Jimmie Rodgers modeled embryonic conventions of country music culture—by borrowing freely from other musical fields, adapting popular music to his particular vocal signature, promoting pathos in tone and subject matter, cultivating familiarity with his fans by a charismatic stage manner that made his personality part of the act, parading his newfound wealth in conspicuous living and yet making his heart visible through personal generosity—he modeled yet another convention that subsequently would be repeated by important country music stars: he died a premature death and was elevated to country music legend.

In the winter of 1925, Rodgers worked as a railroad brakeman through states of the mountain west, then came back to Meridian "nursing a bad cold and hacking cough." The doctor in Geiger diagnosed Rodgers's condition as tuberculosis, then a dreaded disease that killed 90,000 people in the United States that year (Porterfield 1979, 52–53). Ordered to bed and hospitalization, after a short period of recovery Rodgers instead joined a traveling medicine show as a black-face entertainer, touring as far north as Ohio and Indiana (Malone 1985, 79). By 1927, he was in Asheville, North Carolina, perhaps in part for his health; there he learned of Ralph Peer's recording opportunity in Bristol. Rodgers's next, and last, six years were a dramatic display of professional commitment to musical entertainment. By the end of 1927, he had a million-selling record in the Victor release "Blue Yodel" ("T for Texas"). After that came a dramatic demonstration of touring shows, live performances, recording sessions, and a brief movie. Rodgers's audience increased throughout this period as measured by record sales, and he died in legendary fashion immediately upon completing his final recording sessions in New York City in 1933. Later generations remembered details of that event:

> The moving story of Rodgers's last sessions in New York has been recounted many times. Too sick to stand up for long, he rested between takes on a cot set up in a rehearsal hall. A couple of studio

musicians were called in to help with some sides, but on the last day, Jimmie finished up alone, as he'd begun. Among the numbers recorded in those last days were such tragically prophetic titles as "I'm Free from the Chain Gang Now," "Yodeling My Way Back Home," and "Women Make a Fool Out of Me," released as "Jimmie Rodgers' Last Blue Yodel." It took eight hard, grueling days, but he had completed the contract and done what he set out to do. Less than thirty-six hours later, on May 26, 1933, he was dead of a massive lung hemorrhage in his room at the Taft hotel. (*Country* 1988, 46–47)

Homage to Rodgers began immediately, even as he was brought home on the Southern Crescent Line from New York City to Meridian.

> When his death train pulled into Meridian, Mississippi, late at night, the engineer, Homer Jenkins, blew the whistle in a long moaning wail that grew in intensity as the train rolled toward the terminal station. This was the train crew's tribute to the "Singing Brakeman" who now lay in a coffin in one of the baggage cars. (Malone 1985, 83)

Fifty-four years later, that specific moment lived on in country music legend when The Nashville Bluegrass Band (the 1992 International Bluegrass Music Association Vocal Band of the Year) recorded a story song about it. In "The Train Carryin' Jimmie Rodgers Home," a young man who has lost his farm in the Depression calls his wife and young son to walk down to the railroad track as Rodgers's death train passes by. Holding up his son, the father tells him to remember the pride and sadness of his mother and dad as they look on in awe. For them, Rodgers's dedication was an inspiration. When we heard him sing, the speaker says, "we knew somehow we'd make it through" (Nashville Bluegrass Band 1987).

Between the time that Rodgers died in 1933 and the time he was remembered by the Nashville Bluegrass Band over half a century later, Rodgers influenced countless country music artists. When Roy Acuff joined the Grand Ole Opry in the 1930s, he was singing Jimmie Rodgers's songs, and he still sang them on the Opry until he died in 1993. Rodgers's home in Texas and his occasional cowboy clothing stimulated an emphasis in country music on western themes, beginning with Gene Autry, who recorded twenty-four of Rodgers's songs between 1929 and 1933 before becoming a singing star in cowboy movies. In 1932, Ernest Tubb began his half-century career with the endorsement of Rodgers's widow Carrie, who gave him Jimmie's guitar. Bill Monroe's first performance on the Grand Ole Opry in 1939 featured an adaptation of Jimmie Rodgers's "Blue Yodel Number 8" ("Muleskinner Blues"), played in a driving bluegrass style that has subsequently been copied by Dolly Parton for a signature rendition she still performs in the early 1990s. Hank Snow, from Nova Scotia, began recording in 1936 as the "Yodeling Ranger" and joined the Opry in 1950, where he featured such allusions to Rodgers as the train song "I'm Movin' On." Snow, elected to the Country Music Hall of Fame in 1979, still performs in the early 1990s. Merle Haggard, a California-based singer who has earned notice for his elaborations on western swing stylings, recorded a tribute album titled *Same Train, A Different Time* (Hemphill 1975, 332). Malone cites Ernest Tubb's estimate that "perhaps 75 percent of modern country-music performers were directly or indirectly influenced to become entertainers either through hearing Rodgers in person or through his recordings" (Malone 1985, 84). In addition to his memorable yodel, Rodgers produced train-whistle sounds in his throat that have a lonesome, distant quality. These have been widely imitated in performances by Acuff, Snow, and especially Boxcar Willie, a flight engineer from Sterrett, Texas, who in the 1970s began dressing as a hobo to become a professional country act. Initially popular in England and Scotland, Boxcar Willie became a member of the Grand Ole Opry in 1981, where he is billed as "America's Favorite Hobo" (Strobel 1992, 134).

Young artists of contemporary country music have kept allusions to Jimmie Rodgers in their music. Hal Ketchum and Joe Diffie, for example, have recorded songs that feature yodeling in the Rodgers manner, and Aaron Tippin's "Blue Angel" uses voicing techniques indebted to yodeling, which give a signature quality to a hit song. Perhaps 1992's most interesting (and perhaps most distant) derivation from the Jimmie Rodgers legacy was the monster hit by Billy Ray Cyrus, "Achy Breaky Heart." This initial release by a new artist for Mercury Records broke precedent in numerous ways. It rose to the top of both country and pop sales charts and was played as a single hit on both country and pop radio stations. The Cyrus album that included "Achy Breaky Heart," *Some Gave All*, sold more than 7 million copies in the United States and won three Grammy nominations (Rhodes 1993, 22). Part of the appeal of this song is its adaptability to country music dance clubs where a line dance named for it helped escalate the popularity of country dancing in 1992 and 1993. As a media personality, Billy Ray Cyrus—a frenetic, weightlifting, pony-tailed performer described by an agent who worked with him early in his career as "Elvis on steroids" (Faragher 1992, 245)—was promoted by a video of "Achy Breaky Heart" that depicted both the line dance and the charismatic Cyrus stage persona.

Reputed to have worked as a Chippendale dancer early in his career (Faragher 1992, 257), Cyrus achieved a success often attributed partly to his sex appeal. *Billboard* magazine quoted an Oklahoma City radio program director who described him as "a stud muffin"—"there was just a vibe on this guy out there, especially among women" (Stark 1992, 89). When I saw him in live concert at Dayton's Hara Arena on September 12, 1992, Cyrus attracted an audience of working girls, middle-aged women, mothers with young children ranging from ages two to six, young couples with small children, young married couples, and Vietnam veterans. His Dayton audience appeared to be mostly working-class and lower-middle-class fans; its diversity (especially the appeal to children) suggests that, in addition to his personal magnetism, the song itself, as Cyrus performs it, has considerable appeal to fans.

Even if Billy Ray Cyrus was unaware of them, his performance of "Achy Breaky Heart" included motifs pioneered in country music by Jimmie Rodgers. First of all, it's a song of broken hearts, a plea based on rejection by a lover. The speaker in the song addresses the coldhearted lover, saying you can tell the world, your friends, your Ma, your dog, brother and Aunt Louise, and you can tell my arms, feet, lips, fingertips, eyes and mind, that "you never was my girl." But while friends, family, and the worldly body can bear rejection, the "achy breaky heart" won't understand. More important, the rhythmic structure of "Achy Breaky Heart" alludes to train songs. Sung in a chanting manner tied directly to a steady and rough guitar beat reminiscent of a driving-wheels locomotive motif, this effect is magnified in instrumental breaks when a ringing percussion sound, probably tambourine, adds a metallic ting evoking the sound of a spike driver. The resulting effect is relentless inevitability, reinforcing the song's essential rhetoric, which is a warning: if the heart is told of this rejection, it "might blow up and kill this man" (Cyrus 1992). A warning of pending explosion, in the context of rushing locomotive rhythms and spike-driving motifs, suggests an image of a boiler accident on a steam locomotive. One of Billy Ray Cyrus's stage mannerisms reinforces such a suggestion, when he clenches his fists and pumps his forearms parallel to the floor in the rhythmic manner of driver arms on locomotive wheels.

Imagery of a looming wreck brings to mind the long tradition of train-disaster songs in American folk and country music (Cohen 1981; Lyle 1991). Rodgers recorded such train-disaster songs as "Ben Dewberry's Final Run" and a variety of other pathetic train-related scenarios such as "Hobo Bill's Last Ride" and "Waiting for a Train" (Smithsonian 1986). In "Waiting for a Train," Jimmie Rodgers imitated a lonesome train whistle, stimulating similar whistle techniques by later country singers. That train whistle imitation is the most direct connection to "Achy Breaky Heart," for, at the end of each refrain, Cyrus renders a lonesome wailing train whistle sound (Cyrus 1993).

If the biggest single hit of the country music boom for 1992 was perhaps obscurely indebted to Jimmie Rodgers, Rodgers was also remembered in that year by direct imitation. Fiddling virtuoso Mark O'Connor hosted an American Music Shop memorial program to Rodgers on The Nashville Network, featuring Van Williams, an elderly blind performer from Rayville, Louisiana, famous for reproduction of Rodgers's vocal performance, guitar work, yodeling, and train sounds. In Ft. Payne, Alabama, on July 20, 1991, a live reenactment of a performance by Jimmie Rodgers at the Ft. Payne Opera House on July 22 and 23, 1932, was produced by the Big Wills Arts Council with support of a grant from the Alabama Humanities Foundation. This program was directed and produced by Russell Gulley and starred Dean Mitchell as Jimmie Rodgers. Mitchell dressed in period costume and sang Rodgers's songs in close imitation with yodeling, train sounds, and guitar work imitative of Rodgers.

Mitchell, who first heard Rodgers on the radio during the 1930s, said he later talked to a man who walked fifteen miles to Ft. Payne in 1932 to see Rodgers perform. Mitchell has recorded tribute albums to Rodgers and his own compositions about Rodgers, in addition to gospel music and country novelty songs. The lineage of Rodgers's influence in Ft. Payne has been traced. In addition to Mitchell, Vince Clayton Stanley (who later played steel guitar for Hank Williams in Montgomery) heard Jimmie Rodgers at the Ft. Payne Opera House in 1932. Later in his life, Stanley gave music lessons in Ft. Payne to Jeff Cook of the band Alabama, a vocal group named Artist of the Decade for the 1980s by the Academy of Country Music and Entertainer of the Year for 1982, 1983, and 1984 by the Country Music Association. Grammy winners in 1982 and 1983, Alabama has been described as the "most popular band in the history of country music" (Richards and Shestack 1993, 19).

Creators of the Jimmie Rodgers reenactment in Alabama saw it as an opportunity for public education about social history in the Depression era. A newspaper interview with Rodgers in 1932 was reprinted in newspaper format, a flyer on the social history of the period was written, and the reenactment was videotaped for loan to public schools. On August 14, 1992, Dean Mitchell appeared at the Center for Cultural Arts, in Gadsden, Alabama, to again depict Jimmie Rodgers live at the Ft. Payne Opera House in 1932. To begin this performance, Russell Gulley introduced the character of Jimmie Rodgers as a worker on the Southern Railroad from Birmingham to Gadsden to Ft. Payne, and an artist whose records sold what would be the equivalent of 8 million records today. Rodgers, Gulley said, stayed at a hotel in Gadsden the night before he performed in Ft. Payne. Then Mitchell entered from the back of the room in the Rodgers persona, wearing a white suit and hat and a bow tie. Mitchell performed fourteen Rodgers songs accompanied by his own guitar, then stepped out of character to introduce himself as a farm boy from Sand Mountain, Alabama, who first heard Rodgers on WCKY radio from Cincinnati as a child. Mitchell said he worked for eleven years as a performer in Gatlinburg, Tennessee, that he grew up in the Methodist church and had written a gospel song he could yodel in, "From Jimmie to Jesus." He sang this to conclude his program.

Although the middle- and upper-middle-class audience for Dean Mitchell's performance was small, it was enthusiastic, lingering afterward to talk with him at length, to get autographs and buy his albums. Eventually the entire crowd gathered around Mitchell, who strapped on his guitar and did several impromptu and effective imitations of country singers. The tone of the event by this time was decidedly informal, with patrons of the arts, figures associated with the Big Wills Arts Council, local musicians, and Gadsden townspeople mingling over talk of Mitchell's performance, country music, and Jimmie Rodgers.

In January 1935, the Delmore Brothers and Uncle Dave Macon drove from Nashville to New Orleans for a recording session. Along the route they decided to spend the night in Meridian, Mississippi. There they paid an unscheduled visit to Jimmie Rodgers's brother, Tal Rodgers, and his wife. They took along their musical instruments and played a song Alton Delmore had meant for Rodgers to record, "Blue Railroad Train." Tal Rodgers welcomed the Opry stars and encouraged them to sing in Jimmie's memory: "If he was just here he would be the happiest guy you ever saw. He always liked to be with people, especially other musicians." By the time the singing session was over, the hosts were crying. "I nearly did myself," Delmore says, "and I barely made it through." Delmore explained this by testifying to Rodgers's legendary status:

> That is how people felt about Jimmie Rodgers, The Great Blue Yodeler! I can say one thing and tell you how I feel about Jimmie Rodgers. He was simply the greatest. There has never been one man in the whole history of entertainment that packed the wallop he did by himself. There have been good singers, good players and performers that have made great hits with the public and made millions of dollars. But there has never been one man with a single instrument that could sing and play like he did. I say there never has been, and I don't believe there ever will be another just like Jimmie Rodgers. And I'm not meaning just style, either. (Delmore 1977, 98)

The Delmore Brothers and Uncle Dave Macon visited with Jimmie Rodgers's relatives in Meridian less than two years after Rodgers died (Delmore 1977, 96). Their account of gathering in Meridian to remember him may be the earliest recorded instance of remembering Rodgers in this way, but it is certainly not the last. On May 16, 1953, a Meridian newspaper carried a story about a memorial celebration for Rodgers that later became the Jimmie Rodgers Memorial Festival. Four elaborate scrapbooks lovingly kept by Eddie Bishop, which I read at the Jimmie Rodgers Museum in Meridian in May 1993, detail the history of the Jimmie Rodgers Memorial Festival (JRMF). Intermittent for more than forty years, and continuous since 1972, this festival features a unique mingling of Rodgers's relatives, country music artists, entertainers who were heavily influenced by Rodgers, Rodgers's descendants who still perform, Meridian townspeople, civic entrepreneurs, and, in the last decade, scholars of country music and its history. No other event shows more clearly than the JRMF the atmosphere of extended family and spiritual cousinry that marks contemporary country music culture.

The celebration in 1953 featured Mrs. Jimmie Rodgers (Carrie), Mrs. Casey Jones (wife of the famous railroad engineer), Elsie Mc-Williams (co-writer of many Jimmie Rodgers songs), the governors of Mississippi and Tennessee, railroad and union officials, and Nashville figures Roy Acuff, members of the Carter Family, Lew Childre, Cowboy Copas, Jimmie Dickens, Jimmie Davis, Tommy Duncan, Red Foley, Lefty Frizzell, Bill Monroe, George Morgan, Moon Mullican, Minnie Pearl, Webb Pierce, Marty Robbins, Carl Smith, Hank Snow, Charlie Walker, Ernest Tubb, Bill Bruner, and Jimmie Skinner. The first memorial program appears to have been an initiative of highly visible stars Ernest Tubb and Hank Snow in combination with Meridian publishing and civic officials. A clipping from the *Meridian Star* for May 27, 1953, indicates that it was named National Hillbilly Music Day, organized to commemorate the twentieth anniversary of Jimmie Rodgers's death, and drew 30,000 people. A steam locomotive dedicated to deceased railroad men of Meridian and a granite monument memorializing Jimmie Rodgers were dedicated in Meridian's Highland Park. A representative from *Billboard* said of the memorial that there was "nothing like it in the nation before." Twenty-five Grand Ole Opry stars were present, along with Ralph Peer of RCA Victor Records; Peer dedicated the Rodgers monument. Hank Williams's mother from Montgomery, Alabama, Mrs. W. W. Stone, was present, as was Sim Webb, a "colored fireman for Casey Jones" (JRMF 1 1953). For country music insiders, part of the event's intent was apparently to enshrine Rodgers as tradition— during the first memorial Rodgers's first guitar was given to Jimmie Rodgers Snow, son of Hank Snow.

The early years of the festival attracted attention. In 1954, midway between his two presidential campaigns, Adlai Stevenson was present. In 1955, Elvis Presley, a Sun recording artist from Memphis who then had eight songs released on four records, entered the festival talent contest. The *Meridian Star* noted that "this young recording artist has been rained with tremendous enthusiasm . . . and is well on his way to becoming one of the top artists in the nation." Elvis, however, had the same fate here that he met when auditioning for the Grand Ole Opry: "he placed second, first place going to Linda Coker of Gulfport, Miss" (JRMF 1 1955). When Jimmie Rodgers was elected to Nashville's Country Music Hall of Fame in 1961, this honor was first announced in Meridian. Between 1959 and 1972, the festival was held in other Mississippi towns, and in Mobile, Alabama, in 1967. Jerry Clower was master of ceremonies for the return of the Festival to Meridian in 1972. In 1974, the Jimmie Rodgers Foundation was established with funds derived from previous festivals. It contributed $20,000 toward building a museum to honor Rodgers, and groundbreaking occurred that year.

By the mid-1970s, the Jimmie Rodgers Memorial Festival was taking shape as a major civic enterprise for Meridian, while Nashville-based country music figures apparently continued to regard their participation as something like homage, a contribution to the Rodgers legend. On May 26, 1976, Bill Monroe, Ernest Tubb, and Pee Wee King were present for the official opening of the Jimmie Rodgers Museum. And in that year, the *Meridian Star* printed thanks to Charlie McCoy, Tony Douglas, Ray Griff, Hank Locklin, O. B. McClinton, and Melba Montgomery for "repeated performances without pay." The Nashville Songwriters Association Hall of Fame Award was presented to Rodgers at the 1976 festival. In that year, the festival's public performances moved to the Temple Theater, an elaborate venue in downtown Meridian designed for movies as well as stage shows (Castagno 1991, 15). Erected in 1924 by the Hamasa Shriners, the Temple Theater was leased by the Sanger movie chain, who completed the building and opened it in 1928. In 1978, Elsie McWilliams, a sister-in-law of Jimmie Rodgers who wrote many of his songs, performed at the festival and the U.S. Post Office offered a stamp commemorating Rodgers, first issued May 24 in Meridian. Ken Ramey became a show producer that year. Subsequently, many well-known performers have appeared, including Merle Haggard, Conway Twitty, Tammy Wynette, Randy Travis, Mel Tillis, George Jones, George Strait, Charlie Pride, Patty Loveless, J. D. Sumner and the Stamps, Alan Jackson, Doug Stone, Tanya Tucker, and others.

I attended the Jimmie Rodgers Memorial Festival in both 1992 and 1993. My introduction to it occurred on Tuesday night of the festivities week in 1992, when I walked into a large room located at street level behind the main auditorium of the Temple Theater during an intermission between two shows by "The Songwriters" (Paul Overstreet, Paul Davis, Dean Dillon, Fred Knobloch and Mark Gray) and the evening's headliner, Travis Tritt. The scene reminded me distinctly of community festivals sponsored by the local Lions Club and held in the junior high school gymnasium of the coal-mining town in Walker County, Alabama, where I grew up in the 1950s. The crowded room was buzzing with animated conversations occurring in circles and clumps of Meridian's middle- and working-class people, who were dressed up for "going out." Around the perimeter of the room were booths set up with local exhibits—the tourist bureau, the community college, country radio stations. Local musicians were selling their tapes, an artist was sketching pictures, and most poignantly for my 1950s nostalgia, ladies were selling home-cooked food. At the opposite end of the room from the door was a small stage where participants in the JRMF beauty pageant and other local singers were vigorously performing country music. To the right was a table for Nashville-based performers to sit after their shows for signing autographs and posing with fans for pictures. People of all age groups were here; there were lots of families, and it seemed everyone knew everyone. Jim Akenson, professor of curriculum and instruction at Tennessee Technological University and co-founder of the International Country Music Conference, captured the tone of the intense socializing all around us which, it became apparent, lay at the heart of the festival. "This," Akenson said, spreading his arms in an embracing gesture, "is charming."

Public performances for 1992 began on Saturday, May 23, with Sawyer Brown and Aaron Tippin appearing at the Mississippi–Alabama Fairgrounds. On Monday night, Vern Gosden and Mark Gray appeared at the Temple Theater. On Tuesday it was Travis Tritt and the Songwriters; Wednesday, Tanya Tucker, Collin Raye, and Rick McWilliams; Thursday, Joe Diffie, the all-female group Wild Rose, and Jimmie Dale Court, grandson of Jimmie Rodgers. Friday featured T. G. Sheppard and Karon Blackwell, a California-based singer born in Mississippi, and Jason D. Williams, a Jerry Lee Lewis sing-a-like from Memphis whose hands, Dean Mitchell believed, had appeared in the Lewis biographical movie *Great Balls of Fire*. On Saturday, May 30, the JRMF concluded in an outdoor venue at Ray Stadium with the Budweiser Rock 'n Country tour starring Hank Williams, Jr., with Paulette Carlson and the Jimmie Rodgers Talent Contest winners as opening acts. Charlie McCoy, a harmonica player who, in 1992, was appearing at the JRMF for his twentieth year, and Justin Tubb, son of Ernest Tubb, hosted the Midnight Jamboree to be broadcast over the Ernest Tubb Record Show on WSM in Nashville, Saturday evening.

The 1992 JRMF was much more elaborate than headliner concerts and community socializing. It included a beauty pageant with queens in four age categories, a crawfish boil and street dance, a children's talent contest, and a runner's event at the fairgrounds. At Highland Park the Jimmie Rodgers Museum welcomed up to one hundred visitors a day. A celebrity fishing rodeo was held on nearby Lake Eddins, hosted by Bill Dance of TNN and featuring country stars. A celebrity golf tournament took place at the Briarwood Country Club, hosted by Paul Overstreet and Paul Davis. Barbecues, flea markets, crafts and "Old Timey Day" occurred in Highland Park. A major talent contest in the tradition of the one Jimmie himself won was held for two consecutive days.

At the Country Music Conference, academic papers by scholars from the Country Music Foundation in Nashville, the Ozark Folk Center in Mountainview, Arkansas, the Texas Music Museum in Austin, Traditional Concepts of New Milford, Connecticut, and faculty members from the University of Louisville, the University of North Carolina, Tennessee Technological University, the University of Arkansas, and Mississippi State University were featured. A high school teacher who offers a class in country music composition in Nashville, Tennessee, spoke, and creators of "Jimmie Rodgers at the Fort Payne Opera House, 1932" described and illustrated their project. The Peavey Electronic Corporation received visitors all week at its Visitor Center and Peavey Museum. There you can learn the story of Hartley Peavey, an entrepreneur who created his first high-powered guitar amplifier as a high school science fair project in the basement of his Meridian home in 1957, patented his amplifier in 1964 while a student at Mississippi State University, opened a manufacturing plant in 1967 and today has 2,000 employees, exports to 103 countries, and in 1991 experienced a 20 percent overall growth and a 40 percent growth in exports. Exhibits here show visitors how Peavey amps, mixers, guitars, recorders, microphonic speakers, keyboards, and digital audio transducer technology have transformed the character of country and rock concerts since the 1960s.

Eddie Bishop's JRMF scrapbooks include historical information about the changing financial condition of the festival as reported by the *Meridian Star*. In 1980, the JRMF balance sheet showed receipts of $48,544.48 from tickets, a dance, concessions, a staff barbecue, and donations. Entertainers expense in 1980 was $33,170.27, and other expenses for concert preparation, publicity, transportation, photography, and related operations brought total costs to $42,883.62. The balance sheet for 1980 shows a profit of $5,660.86 (JRMF 2). In 1987, the year Jimmie Rodgers's Martin guitar was brought to the museum, a bluegrass concert kicked off the festival and Tanya Tucker and Alabama closed it, yielding a reported profit of $30,000. In 1990, Tanya Tucker sold out the final concert, a celebrity cookbook was produced for the first time, TNN ran a ninety-minute salute to Jimmie Rodgers on Ralph Emery's *Nashville Now*, and Waylon Jennings appeared, yielding a profit of $21,759.51. That same year, Mississippi native Charlie Pride gave a $5,000 donation on behalf of himself and his family. The 1991 profit was reported at $28,000, with net income for that year $154,885, and artist costs $120,996.

These figures suggest that the Jimmie Rodgers Memorial Festival, when measured by its direct profits, has not operated as a major fund-raising event. That conclusion is consistent with the impression that the festival was founded and has grown out of a genuine desire to honor Jimmie Rodgers and his legendary status and to participate in community rituals. The total economic impact of the festival, however, is considerably greater than its direct proceeds might indicate. The chair of the Business and Industry Department at Mississippi State University, Meridian, is engaged in a long-term study of the character of festival participants and the festival's larger economic impact. Habib Bazyari told me that in 1990 the full effect of the JRMF was $1.8 million direct, without calculating multiplier effects, which he estimated at nearly $4 million. Economic activity in Meridian during 1992 was approximately $1 billion annually; thus, an impact of this magnitude for a single eight-day event was described by Bazyari as "very, very significant."

Those attending JRMF concerts and spending their money in Meridian are a diverse group, and the Bazyari study suggests a broadening audience—one that is becoming younger. In 1990, the initial festival concert was gospel music; it attracted an audience with an average age of fifty-eight. As the festival progressed, the average age dropped to thirty-five for the concluding concert with Alan Jackson. The Travis Tritt concert in 1992 attracted an audience with an average age close to thirty. The gender distribution of JRMF audiences is slightly more female than male, with the closest distribution 55 percent female to 45 percent male. The work orientation of 1990 JRMF participants was 20 to 25 percent professionals, 17 percent blue collar, 16 percent white collar, 17 percent retired. For the Aaron Tippin-Sawyer Brown opening concert of 1992, 17 percent of the audience identified themselves as "entertainers." The festival has a decidedly local orientation. Most people attending festival concerts live within fifty miles of Meridian. Only 5 to 6 percent come from a greater distance, although five foreign countries were represented in 1990—Germany, England, Japan, Australia, and Canada. Asked where they heard about the festival, most fans learned of it on radio.

The Bazyari study reinforces the impression that country music festival events draw heavily from working- and middle-class groups, that the typical age is thirty and up, while in the early 1990s, younger fans are joining, that women slightly outnumber men, and that there are few black participants. The visual impression, that this festival is an occasion for friends and acquaintances to both socialize and contribute to community ritual, is borne out by an inadvertent result of the Bazyari study. He and his coworkers take a systematic selection sample, strictly random, by counting the seats in the Temple Theater and assigning questionnaires to specific seats. They hand out a questionnaire and pencil, simply asking that it be filled out and returned. This gets amazing results. For the Travis Tritt concert, on Tuesday, May 26, 1992, 3,600 people appeared and 90 were sampled—45 in each of two shows—and only *one* person failed to return the form! This trait of friendly cooperativeness and participatory enthusiasm is a pervasive feature of the JRMF and of country music culture generally (Bazyari 1992).

When you observe fans at JRMF concerts, the mixture of appearances is striking. Here you can meet yuppie-styled younger couples, working people in blue jeans, overalls, and workshirts, retired people in leisure clothes, and community leaders in business suits. You can see T-shirts, fancy "western" clothing, party dresses, polyester pant suits, rhinestone cowgirl outfits, boots, suits, sport coats and teenage designer clothing. You can see infants, children, preteens, teenagers, high school people, young professionals, middle-aged people, retired people, and the elderly. There are handicapped people here, including some in wheelchairs. At the May 30, 1992, outdoor concluding concert, I saw other people of color attending, but the only blacks seen were stadium workers.

The JRMF is notable for attracting people associated with the music business. Numerous entertainers—from major stars to those whose jobs seem to be principally in bar bands—come here. People associated with broadcasting are prolific. Families and groups who follow particular artists are visible. I met a woman who claimed that her daughter first showcased Joe Diffie in Nashville. If you enter one of the crowds that regularly gathers during the festival, such as backstage at the Temple Theater or in a line waiting to enter a concert, the character of overheard conversation is people greeting old friends, inquiring about the health of acquaintances, congratulating one another on business deals, making vacation plans as groups or couples. Before concerts in the Temple Theater, individuals swapped seats so that couples might sit together, and snapshot picture-taking—not only of stars—was common.

The JRMF is an event where artists celebrate one another and very consciously remember Jimmie Rodgers. In the Temple Theater they perform on a stage where an image of Rodgers is projected behind them constantly. Tanya Tucker, C.M.A. Female Vocalist of the Year for 1992, has been a festival favorite in recent years. In 1992, she introduced Travis Tritt by walking on stage before his concert and talking with the audience—telling them she had a wonderful time in Meridian during the week, that everybody associated with the festival had been wonderful to her and her family, that the food had been good, and that she was here to present "a dear friend" and "a great performer." Travis Tritt then performed fourteen songs, at least eight of them his own hits, one a cover of Hank Williams, Jr., one an extraordinary impromptu duet with Tucker on a gospel rendition of "Amazing Grace," and two Jimmie Rodgers songs. In "No Hard Times Blues," Tritt played a massive virtuoso guitar and yodeled like a master, and for his finale, covered a Lynyrd Skynyrd version of Rodgers's "T for Texas." The Travis Tritt concert with Tanya Tucker lasted from 7:00 to 9:30 P.M. and included, in addition to Tritt's impressive performance and fan-pleasing numbers with Tanya Tucker, a great deal of intimate talk with the audience. At the end, Tritt took flowers from fans, spent time shaking hands at the edge of the stage, then stood at attention in center stage with his back to the audience and saluted the picture of Jimmie Rodgers before exiting.

The 1993 festival repeated motifs and events of the 1992 one, including its pervasive conviviality, informality, and sense of extended family. The gospel concert was revived for 1993 and featured J. D. Sumner and the Stamps. Hit-makers Tracy Lawrence, T. Graham

Brown, Billy Joe Royal, Marie Osmond, and Ricky Skaggs appeared. The final outdoor concert paired Tanya Tucker with Willie Nelson. They followed Patsy Montana, the first woman singer in country music to sell a million records (her yodeling version of "I Want to Be a Cowboy's Sweetheart"). The lieutenant governor of Mississippi, Eddie Briggs, proclaimed the week of May 22–29 Tanya Tucker week in Mississippi. The final multi-concert event lasted from 7:25 P.M. to 12:26 A.M. Headliner Tanya Tucker chose to open for Willie Nelson. Elected to the Country Music Hall of Fame the following September, Nelson played nonstop for over two hours, giving the audience twenty-seven songs and concluding with the "Milk Cow Blues."

The JRMF spun off numerous informal gatherings where Rodgers's descendants, people in the music business, and their friends could mingle. A suite at the Best Western Hotel served as a hospitality room for festival insiders. Homemade ice cream was available here between 5 and 9 P.M., the room was open from 10 to midnight, members of the International Singing Brakeman's Association gathered, and relative-artists Jimmie Dale Court and Rick McWilliams (Jimmie Rodgers's nephew) played here.

The central symbolic event that brings together surviving relatives and persons close to Rodgers is the wreath-laying ceremony at the Rodgers gravesite, which occurs annually on Rodgers's death date—May 26, the date that governs scheduling of the festival each year. In 1992, Sam Marshall, President and Executive Director of the Jimmie Rodgers Foundation, presided. He introduced and invited brief comments from people who had come to the gravesite, explained that single roses had been distributed as a gesture to remember Rodgers's wife Carrie, and conducted the wreath-laying. In 1993, the sixtieth anniversary of Rodgers's death and the fortieth anniversary of the first memorial festival in Meridian, the ceremony was considerably more elaborate.

By 9:45 A.M., May 26, 1993, sixty years to the day from the time of Jimmie Rodgers's burial, a collection of his descendants, descendants of his wife Carrie Williamson, Meridian civic leaders, festival officials, entertainers, Rodgers admirers, media, and the press gathered in Meridian's Oak Grove Cemetery to pay homage to "America's Blue Yodeler." The atmosphere prior to the beginning of the ceremonies was decidedly social, an extension of country music culture's family reunion motif which, in this case, is a fact as well as an image. Folding chairs were provided for some elderly participants, and Carl Fitzgerald, a Meridian Shriner instrumental in returning the festival to Meridian in 1972, presided. As Fitzgerald made a sound check of the portable amplification system situated beside a podium decorated with a festival poster, participants greeted one another like old friends with such phrases as "how you doin', darlin'," "I'm gonna hug your neck," "everybody who's here be sure you sign the program," "you remember me?" "oh, hi, look who's here," "he just lost his wife," "I'm glad you told me," and "go over there and see Charlie." Two flag bearers—one holding the American flag, the other, the flag of Mississippi—positioned themselves either side of the Rodgers family headstone and the service began.

The Reverend Jimmy John of a local Methodist church opened with prayer. "We come together in fellowship," the preacher said, "because our friends around us, from all around the world, from across the United States, right across the street, and everywhere they are, they're friends of ours." The Reverend John then thanked God "for these pioneers that start things out in life that turns into such great things," those "individuals in life who are willing to venture out, be that pioneer, be that grower, be the one to reach out and touch people, bring them something in their heart that is really needed, share with 'em the life of the world." Brother John asked God's blessings on the local fellowship, America, country music, the blues, and "the love we have for Jimmie Rodgers and their family." "Rodgers," he said, "may have passed on but his memories are so cherished, they're so exotic, they're so great, there's no way they'll ever die in our lives."

Following this invocation, Carl Fitzgerald introduced some of Rodgers's relatives who were present: Ann Shine Landrum, a second cousin of Jimmie Rodgers; and Mildred Williamson Pollard from Texas, sister of Elsie McWilliams (Rodgers's sister-in-law, who wrote many of his songs). Jimmie Dale Court, Rodgers's grandson, was present. Other relatives now living in nursing homes and unable to attend were mentioned. Fitzgerald then introduced state senator Terry C. Burton, who spoke briefly, asking God's blessings on those assembled and on Mississippi. James Skelton took the podium. Skelton was president of the festival for thirteen years after it was reorganized in 1972. Commending Fitzgerald's role in bringing the festival to Meridian, he said that action was stimulated by a sidewalk conversation between them downtown. Jim Akenson of the International Country Music Conference that celebrated its tenth anniversary in 1993 commended participants, Rodgers, and Rodgers's international reputation.

Fitzgerald gave an extended comment on Rodgers's life, constructed as a fan's view of country music history. When Rodgers died, Fitzgerald remembered, he was brought back by train and laid to rest here. Without Rodgers, we probably would never have had Jim Reeves, Hank Williams, Merle Haggard, Alan Jackson, "The Tennessee Waltz," "The Cattle Call," Peer International, guitar teachers like Fitzgerald himself, the Martin Guitar Company, and Peavey Electronics. Fitzgerald made an analogy between aspects of Rodgers's life and career and those of Hank Williams, describing the parallels as "ironic." "Both," he said, "had a six-year career that began and ended in similar numbers, 1927–33 for Rodgers and 1947–53 for Williams." Both wives had six-letter names with a similar sound—Carrie and Audrey. Rodgers was "discovered" by a music publisher whose name had four letters (Peer) and so was Williams (Rose). Rodgers, from Mississippi, wrote his own songs and played guitar; Williams, from Alabama, did the same. Rodgers bought a $50,000 home in Kerr*ville*, Texas, and Williams a home in Nash*ville*. Rodgers is buried in Oak Grove Cemetery, Williams in Oak Hill Cemetery. Rodgers's first record carried a song with the word "Sleep" in the title ("Sleep Baby Sleep") and Williams's first record had the song "Last Night I Heard You Crying in Your Sleep." The crowd listened with solemnity to this comparison and received Fitzgerald's conclusion thoughtfully: "We don't know why these things happen but I just want to pass them on to you." Fitzgerald ended with an observation on the historical significance of the festival, claiming that Meridian held it between 1953 and 1959 with the exception of the year 1958, that it "died in '59 because of politics and other things," and was revived in 1972. "I think," said Fitzgerald, "we should keep the legacy of Jimmie Rodgers and country music that's known as basic country." He ended with a story of Elsie McWilliams's last days and told the crowd, "We still miss the legend, James Charles Rodgers, America's Blue Yodeler."

The Reverend Jimmy John presided over the wreath-laying ceremony. The wreath was donated by a Swedish citizen not present—Peder Gustawson, who had served in the U.S. Marines and admired

American heroes like Davy Crockett and Jimmie Rodgers. The wreath itself was a large creation of blue carnations that John described as a symbol of the blue sky which, just like love, even on a cloudy day, is going to "open back up." Jimmie Dale Court carried the wreath to the grave. Single red roses were distributed to several close participants and Elsie McWilliams's granddaughter from Spokane, Washington, was recognized. John asked participants to bring their state flags and country flags to the ceremony next year, and referred to flag-bearers as symbols of love and sharing.

No major public event of country music culture fails to provide live performance meant to amplify the event's social meanings. Here, Van Williams was brought forward and introduced as someone who had recently been on television. Williams played his guitar and sang "The One Rose," a Rodgers number which includes the phrase "you're the one rose that's left in my heart" and features an elaborate yodel. When Williams finished, Mildred Williamson Pollard, seated in the audience, spoke up to tell another death memorial story about the "one rose." For the funeral of Carrie Rodgers, Johnny Cash sent a bouquet eight feet across with "1,000 single roses." Bruce and Nancy Langhum were introduced for Nancy to sing "Daddy and Home," which she described as "just one of my 110 favorites that belong to Jimmie Rodgers." Although at one emotional point she almost forgot the words, someone in the audience prompted her. Rick McWilliams, grandson of Elsie McWilliams, came to the microphone to conclude the musical tribute by leading assembled participants in the communal gesture to gospel salvation, "Amazing Grace." The ceremony closed with Carl Fitzgerald reciting the words to a tribute song that ended with "I can almost hear him yodel . . . ," and Reverend Jimmy John asking for God's blessing on each one here today. He concluded with "thank y'all for comin'." At this, Van Williams stepped to attention beside Rodgers's grave and saluted. It was now 10:43 A.M. As Williams continued to stand, the buzz and bustle of talking, socializing, handshaking, touching, and memory-sharing returned (Akenson 1993).

In his description of Billy Ray Cyrus as "truly one of the nicest and most genuine people I have ever met," one who "has paid his dues and is deserving of the renown he is rapidly acquiring," talent agent Scott Faragher seemed to be justifying Cyrus's authenticity as a country performer (Faragher 1992, 258). The authenticity question was raised for participants in country music culture shortly after the Rodgers graveside memorial in Meridian. At Nashville's Fan Fair in June 1992, Travis Tritt told a radio audience (and repeated to reporters) that, in his opinion, "Achy Breaky Heart" failed to make "a statement." Tritt implied that Cyrus's live performance scene in the song's video was staged, and charged that Cyrus's popularity was obscuring the writing of country songs "that really talk to the public" in favor of "an ass-wiggling contest" (Kingsbury 1993, 14). Debate about this charge erupted at Fan Fair, spilling into television talk shows and print and in position messages scrawled on car windows and printed on fan T-shirts. Tritt soon apologized for any harm that his remarks might have caused Billy Ray Cyrus "or his family," but did not recant. Cyrus was eventually to say, "I believe Travis Tritt has a personal problem" (Rhodes 1993, 23).

This media spat and fan debate may seem, on first encounter, to be a publicity stunt or an unmanaged moment of star frustration that went public; yet it points to a deeper issue, that of the formation of artist identity in country music culture. For Jimmie Rodgers, "the father of country music," paid ultimate dues—he died painfully during a schedule of prolonged touring and live performing, at the close of an exhaustive recording session. The legend of his life and performance, its amplification in the public memory of his death train, and the annual festival in his hometown that draws luminaries from all segments of country music culture to remember him on his anniversary are indicators of popular mythmaking signifying a high cultural standard for appropriate sincerity. Emerging artists are definitely expected to meet such a standard. Faragher puts it this way: "This business of music concerns a great deal more than singing. It is a metaphysical thing in many ways, like the search for the Holy Grail. This might sound strange and farfetched, but it's not. It is a calling that only the person who gets it hears or understands" (Faragher 1992, 246). Faragher's perhaps unintended analogy between country music artists and ministers in the evangelical faith is revealing. As we shall see, country music stars function for fans in some ministerial ways; to be effective in this culture, their musical sincerity must be unquestioned. The relentless gravity and pathos of Carter Family musical stylings and the exemplary behavior and legendary memory of Jimmie Rodgers come together on the authenticity issue to form perhaps the most esoteric and, possibly, the most important discrete convention of country music culture. For, despite the celebratory barn dance spirit of the Opry that echoes in festival behavior of the music's extended fan and artist families, the legacy of tragic troubadours is clear. Because their lives were "tragic," country music is deadly serious.

During the years of America's Great Depression, country music's leading singing stars furnished the nation with both an enduring tone of pathos that reflected the sadness of hard times and an indelible image of entertainers as tragic troubadours. When tragic troubadours are remembered, their tenacity in the face of personal hardship takes on heroic elements and they become illustrations in a legacy of collective endurance.

Without their being named directly, the country music heritage of the original Carter Family, of Mother Maybelle Carter and the Carter Sisters, and of their musical descendants in singing families featuring women was lovingly remembered by Lee Smith in her 1992 novel, *The Devil's Dream*. "This book is dedicated," she wrote, "to all the real country artists, living and dead, whose music I have loved for so long" (Smith 1992).

Based on seven years of research in country music history and resources, and influenced by Jean Ritchie's music and her account of "growing up in a real 'singing family'" (Ritchie 1988, 314–15), Smith's novel appears to draw freely on incidents in the lives of the original Carter Family and their descendants. R. C. Bailey—born in 1881 in a mountain valley not far from Bristol, Tennessee—is a quiet, mysterious man of dubious lineage who, with his wife, sister-in-law, and sister-in-law's daughter, records their "mournful" mountain music for Ralph Peer at the Bristol sessions. Wife Lucie plays a "little Gibson guitar," sister-in-law Tampa Rainette plays autoharp, and her daughter Virgie plays "the big arch top guitar." R. C. sings and occasionally plays fiddle. "Their harmony is perfect. It is a simple, direct, appealing sound" (Smith 1992, 123). Likely an allusion to A. P. Carter, R. C. Bailey become a patriarch of an elaborate extended family replete with musicians beset by hard times, domestic turmoil, and untimely death. The twenty-eight principal figures who populate this novel (six of them R. C.'s ancestors, five his close family as brothers, sisters and wife, and the rest his descendants directly or by marriage) experience a graphic array of accidental deaths, suicides, homicides, excessive alcohol and drug use, rampant pre- and extramarital romantic sexual entanglements, unwanted pregnancies, automobile accidents, and crippling diseases. Before he is married, R. C.'s stepfather, Ezekiel, experiences a direct visitation from God as he walks home from a night of dancing and drinking. God warns Ezekiel against singing worldly music and orders him to sing the gospel songs an aunt had called "true singing" in contrast to "pretty singing" (Smith 1992, 40). R. C. and Lucie's only daughter, Rose Annie, runs away from her husband and children to marry Black Jack Johnny Raines, and the two become known as the "King and Queen of Country Music" before their marriage deteriorates into drug-ridden domestic violence ending on "Blue Christmas, 1959," when Rose Annie kills a mean and drunken Johnny with her .32 pistol (Smith 1992, 206).

Despite this array of exotic hillbilly rusticity, many individual characters in R. C. Bailey's extended family are drawn sympathetically and with effective human detail. The central perspective of the novel is provided by Katie Cocker, granddaughter of Tampa Rainette, R. C.'s sister-in-law who "tells it like it is" (Smith 1992, 207). Katie's story is the story of a tragic troubadour who survives to become a successful country singer. As the story ends, she reunites her extended family at the Opryland Hotel to record an album memorializing their musical heritage.

Katie Cocker's singing career began in high school. A granddaughter of Tampa Rainette (of the original Grassy Branch Girls), Katie believes that she was born for stardom. Her first taste of it was winning the "Miss Holly Springs High" talent contest by singing Patsy Montana's "I Want to Be a Cowboy's Sweetheart." Katie's reward is feeling appreciated by the fans, a feeling that provided career-long motivation:

> The audience loved it. People from all over the auditorium jumped up and whistled and clapped and yelled when I finished. It went to my head, I guess. I felt hot and tingly all over, a feeling I *still* get, believe it or not, at the end of every show. And every time it's just as exciting as it was that first time, honestly. It gets in your blood, you know. Finally you can't live without it. I was probably *born* with it in my blood but I didn't know it until that night I was crowned Miss Holly Springs High. (Smith 1992, 212)

In 1947, Katie and her cousin Georgia ran away to Richmond with their Aunt Virgie to form a singing trio, The Raindrops. In Richmond, Katie, the daughter of an alcoholic father and a devoted fundamentalist Christian mother, quickly becomes enamored of both boys and the music business. A series of marriages follows. Her first husband leaves her with a young child who has polio; her second husband is killed in prison. The third—an older musician whom she loves—dies in the flaming wreckage of his touring bus on a foggy highway near Chattanooga. Katie sings on the Old Dominion Barn Dance in Richmond, then spends time in California during the 1970s folk revival living a sexually "liberated" life and suffering from homesickness.

There are two moments of salvation in Katie's life narrative. One is her personal religious conversion. After an automobile accident and DWI charges in Nashville, Katie checks into Vanderbilt Hospital for an alcoholic rehabilitation program. There she meets Brother Billy Jack Reems, who talks of God's love and invites her to an evangelistic meeting at the Y.M.C.A. Katie hears Reems tell his flock that "everything we ever do in our lives has got something to do with His search for love," and responds immediately. "This hit me like a bolt out of the blue. It is the story of my life." Her recognition give Katie a religious evaluation of her autobiography.

> Now I can understand that I was starving for God's love, that I had been denying that part of myself ever since I was a child, ever since I'd been cut off somehow from the love of God at the church on Chicken Rise. I'd cut myself off, to be exact—out of arrogance, out of pride, out of not wanting to be like my Mamma. (Smith 1992, 295–97)

During an altar call, Katie experiences salvation as a release from pain: "I could feel my pain rushing up from all over my body, feel the shock when it hit the air, feel it shatter and blow away, nothing but dust in the wind. Then I felt God come into me, right into me through the mouth, like a long cool drink of water." By the story's end, no longer "dazzled by the things of the earth," Katie finds God to be "an endless source of pure energy for me" (Smith 1992, 298).

God's love is not Katie's only salvation experience. Years earlier, she had an earthly one when she first sang on the Grand Ole Opry. Before her performance, as she stands backstage waiting her turn, she is uncommonly nervous. Katie wants a drink but knows she can't get one at the Opry because the atmosphere is definitely not right for being tipsy. She explains:

> There was something like a church about the Opry in those days when it was still at the Ryman Auditorium—why, shoot, the Ryman used to

be a church, come to think of it. It's got those pews, and the balcony, and stained glass in the windows. There's something solemn about the crowd, too—even now, over at the new Opry House—something worshipful, which has to do with how far the fans have driven to be there, and how long they've been listening to their favorites, which is *years* in most cases. For you know, the country music fan is like no other, they'll follow you for years, through good times and bad, and never tire of hearing your old tunes one more time. They are the biggest hearted, most devoted folks in the world and they are the ones that have made the business what it is today. It's not the stars. It's the fans. (Smith 1992, 273)

Here, Lee Smith has Katie Cocker understand a central convention of country music culture: Fan devotion to artists is a symbolic expression of collective love that sustains tragic troubadours through hard times. Katie's direct reference to the gospel heritage of the Ryman Auditorium and to the "worshipful" atmosphere of the Opry suggests a parallel between country music culture and the nurturing collective identity of evangelical religious life. Katie Cocker also perceives a similarity between worshipers and devoted fans:

Standing backstage at the Ryman was when I really realized this, watching them get up and slip forward as their favorites came on, walking one at a time right up to the footlights to take their own photos to carry back home. It's exactly like people going up for Communion in a big Catholic church, if you ask me, the fans moving forward in a steady stream to pause and snap, pause and snap, and then move on, back to their seats, back to Ohio and Maryland and West Virginia and all the places they came from, where they will get these pictures developed and put them in frames where they can point to them and say, "I was there. I was right there." (Smith 1992, 273)

The Devil's Dream is a series of family recollections, a living past. The occasion for all these recollections is an extended family reunion that begins in the lobby of the Opryland Hotel, where descendants of R. C. Bailey are gathering to make a memorial event album to be produced by Katie Cocker and titled after the gospel song, "Shall We Gather at the River." The novel is framed by commentaries in present time. At the end of the novel we learn the diverse fates of family members. Katie has a new two-month-old granddaughter whom she introduces to her own mother, who in turn overcomes a reluctance to hold the baby, in an image of healing family tradition. R. C.'s granddaughter, Sugar, daughter of Rose Annie (who is specially released from prison to sing on this album) has earned a Ph.D. in "deconstruction" at Duke University. There are plans to turn R. C.'s barn at Grassy Branch into a Bailey Family Museum that will be open to the general public as a country music shrine; but exactly at the moment when the family gathers in Nashville, R. C. Bailey, listening to his old record and thinking of his own dead mother and wife, commits suicide in that barn.

Tragic endings and the promise of new life mingle in Lee Smith's parting image of country singers, yet their significance to fans is consistent from the very beginning of the novel. There a fan watches the singing family gather. It's Christmastime, the Opryland Hotel is lavishly decorated, and nostalgic singing groups perform Christmas carols; yet the fan's real interest is the prospect of meeting country music stars:

> This place is full of real stars, you have to keep an eye out. You might see anybody. And if you do, it's a good bet they'll give you their autograph or maybe even the shirt off their own back. Country stars are real nice. They love their fans in a deep way. They will give of themselves till they drop. (Smith 1992, 11)

As the fan walks through the hotel lobby she spies Katie Cocker, "One of the real superstars of country music, looking just as natural—looking just like herself!" Katie, says this fan, "don't put on airs. She don't have to. She don't have to take off those twelve extra pounds if she don't want to, either. She looks okay. She looks fine! She's made it, and made it her own way." Here we have a fan's acknowledgment of the star's aura of success and special standing blended with appreciation for the star's everyday humanity. Katie's key attraction is her authenticity, measured by her long survival of hard times, and she gets the ultimate fan compliment. "God knows she's paid her dues, too. Some of the events of her life are just tragic, but she's weathered them. She's still here. She's still singing her heart out." Not only is Katie a troubadour who has triumphed, she represents all country music artists whose endurance of traumatic personal lives seems to inspire ordinary people. "It does seem like more things happen to country artists than to anybody else, have you ever noticed?" the fan asks. "It's like they have more events in their lives" (Smith 1992, 12).

In *The Devil's Dream*, Lee Smith has captured important features of country music culture. In their larger-than-life experiences, country artists represent for fans the tragic dimensions of hard times and broken hearts, and they provide images of personal salvation. In this novel, the evolving cousinry of country music culture is tangible, actively linking the spirit of a living past with the domestic turmoil of relentless present experience. Since the radio and recording stardom of the Carter Family and Jimmie Rodgers, tragic troubadours have been fundamental to country music culture, but ultimately they are never alone. They have God, family, and the fans.

I'll never get out of this world alive.
                    —Hank Williams, 1952

I'm crazy for loving you.
                    —Willie Nelson, Patsy Cline, 1961

CHAPTER 3   **Domestic Turmoil**

Bill Malone remembers the death of Hank Williams as a turning point for country music:

> Almost 40 years have passed since that morning when I heard of Hank Williams's death. I spent most of that day dialing around on the radio looking for tributes and recorded reminiscences of the Boy from Alabama. I'm sure, though, that I was playing some of his records, and looking properly solemn, when my mother walked in. I wanted her to be aware of the tragic significance of the moment. I was 18 years old, and I *did* feel a deep personal loss. Several years passed before I equated his death with that of old-time country music. After all, Elvis Presley's emergence was still a year and a half away. (Malone, 1992, 9)

Carl Fitzgerald's sentimental comparison of Hank Williams and Jimmie Rodgers at the Rodgers graveside ceremony was the kind of moment in country music culture that consciously links legendary lives, giving them a parallel shape in the imaginations of country fans. The life, stardom, and untimely death of Hank Williams added significantly to country music's tragic troubadour tradition, and his music—especially his songwriting—magnified the emphasis on turbulent romance, broken hearts, and failing marriages in the postwar America of the late 1940s and early 50s. Patsy Cline, whose brief career in the late 1950s and early 60s helped transform country music styling for broader market appeal, also met an untimely death at an early age and was, like Williams, elevated posthumously to legendary status. In an era when nuclear families were virtually a mystique in popular culture despite the rising divorce rate, Cline's songs of compliant femininity gave added impetus to country music's commentary on domestic turmoil.

That commentary would last. A detailed study of the 400 most popular country songs from 1960 to 1987 found that 75 percent were love songs, and most of those were about unhappy or lost love. Next most frequent were songs about cheating situations; far less frequent were songs about happy love (Rogers 1989). Dorothy Horstman's review of country songs and their writers, *Sing Your Heart Out, Country Boy,* led her to observe that country songs are "full of death, sadness, and self-pity" (Horstman 1986). The persistent emphasis on wasted love in country music supplements themes of fading rural life and gospel salvation with the domestic nightmares of the urban honky-tonk.

Jimmie N. Rogers's documentation—that, between 1960 and 1987 country songs focused principally on broken hearts—indicates that by 1960, country music culture had found a consistent voice. That voice was linked to the effects of modernization. Jack Kirby's study of agricultural change suggests that the bulk of Southern migration to cities took place between the origins of commercial country music in the 1920s and the coalescence of the country music business in the 1960s. John Lomax III has written about the emergence of Nashville as an urban music center. He chose the year 1960 to illustrate the maturation of music business institutions. In that year, Nashville recording studios made number one singles on the *Billboard* charts for twenty-eight of fifty-two weeks. Just two years earlier, the Country Music Association was formed to promote traditional country music in response to the growing popularity of rock and roll. In another response, such innovative producers as Chet Atkins, at R.C.A. Victor Studio B, and Owen Bradley, producer of Patsy Cline, pioneered country pop musical stylings intended to broaden the market for country music. According to Lomax, in the decade after 1956, "118 songs written or recorded in Nashville made the pop Top 10" and twenty-seven of them went to number one (Lomax 1985, 150–52).

When Horstman reviewed sixty years of "best loved songs" in 1986, she was able to sort them into fifteen categories: home, religion, death and sorrow, comedy and novelty, winning love, lost and unrequited love, cheating, honky-tonk, social comment, war and patriotism, prison, working, cowboy, traveling, and stories. That topical diversity, which undeniably exists, masks the evolution of country music culture's underlying cultural imagery. By 1960, the tragic troubadour singing songs of domestic turmoil and broken hearts had become the characteristic figure of a country singer. Bill Malone's feeling that "old-time country music" died with Hank Williams, expressed in 1992, suggests the sustained appeal of the tragic troubadour dying an untimely death and ascending into legend. There's reason for this. Country singers have repeatedly suffered Jimmie Rodgers's fate of an untimely death at the height of their career. Fans can easily remember Jim Reeves, Hawkshaw Hawkins, or Buddy Holly dying in a plane crash, the murder of Opry star David "Stringbean" Akeman, Marty Robbins dying from a heart condition, or Dottie West dying from injuries sustained in an automobile wreck. The deaths of two country stars in particular— and the way they were memorialized in popular movies and in artist memory—have amplified country music's postwar concern with domestic turmoil. These two stars are Hank Williams and Patsy Cline.

Charles K. Wolfe is another country music historian who has considered the parallel between Hank Williams and Jimmie Rodgers: "Williams' influence on country music of the 1950s was as great as that of Jimmie Rodgers in the 1930s, and like Rodgers, Williams had a brief meteoric career filled with personal tragedy" (Wolfe 1977, 77). That career affected the contemporary tone of country music significantly, for the life, death, and memory of Hank Williams magnified the tragic-troubadour tradition by focusing attention on domestic traumas of marriage and troubled nuclear families.

Hank Williams's life has been examined with considerable attention (Malone 1968, 1985; Williams 1973; Flippo 1981; Koon 1983;

Cusic 1993). Born in 1923 to Lon and Lillie Williams of Mount Olive, Alabama, Williams was the offspring of a working-class couple who lived a modest but independent life in rural southern Alabama during the Depression years. The Williams family operated a store out of their home at one time, sold strawberries, and Lon drove a locomotive for the W. T. Smith Lumber Company. Lillie ran boarding houses (Williams 1973, 6–8). From his earliest years, Hank Williams was entrepreneurial. His father claimed that he sold peanuts in a logging camp by the time he was three years old, and later he "shined shoes, delivered groceries, and did whatever odd jobs he could to make a few cents" (Williams 1973, 11). Hank's entrepreneurship also focused on music from a very early age. Lillie was organist for the Mount Olive Baptist Church, where Hank learned gospel singing. He also followed an old-time fiddler in a local shoe shop and formed a friendship with Rufus "Tee-Tot" Payne, a black street singer who introduced him to the blues in the mid-1930s. By age thirteen, Hank had become serious about a musical career; that year, he won an amateur talent show in Montgomery by singing his own song, "The W.P.A. Blues." He put together his "Drifting Cowboys" band, got a radio spot on Montgomery's WSFA, and was traveling with a medicine show when he met Audrey Sheppard, "Miss Audrey," who was to become his wife and in their turbulent marriage provide Hank Williams his life-long musical inspiration. When it started, he was eighteen years old. Before his marriage, Hank's mother had assisted him in his musical ambition; after it, Audrey became his informal manager—taking care of money, booking shows, and serving as a "stabilizing force" of "responsibility and of ambition" (Cusic 1993, ix–x).

In 1946, Hank and Audrey went to Nashville. They met Fred Rose, a respected New York songwriter and staff pianist at WSM radio who had formed a music publishing partnership with Roy Acuff that year (Country 1988, 418). Hank Williams was a hit with Fred Rose, who soon had him in a recording studio for the New York label Sterling, then in 1947 for M-G-M. Williams joined the radio barn dance Louisiana Hayride at Shreveport's KWKH in 1948 (Cusic 1993, xiii). In the last year of the decade, he repeated the phenomenon that Jimmie Rodgers had inaugurated in country music by making a single record that became a national sensation. Williams's recording of "Lovesick Blues," a pop tune written in the 1920s in New York City that Hank sang in a style distinctly reminiscent of Jimmie Rodgers's blue yodel, became *Billboard's* top country record for 1949 after spending more than two months at the top of the country charts (Cusic 1993, xiv; Malone 1985, 242). In June 1949, Williams went to the Grand Ole Opry, where his first guest appearance earned an unprecedented six standing ovations (Williams 1973, 83). For three years at the turn of the decade, Hank Williams was one of the most visible figures in American popular culture, touring military bases in Europe with Opry Groups, appearing on network television with Kate Smith and Perry Como, and traveling with Milton Berle and Bob Hope in the Hadacol Caravan, "America's Last Great Medicine Show" (*Country* 1988, 263; Williams 1973, 146, 154). Like Jimmie Rodgers, Hank Williams at the peak of his career had record sales that were sustained and dramatic.

> In 1950 alone, according to one source, M-G-M sold over a million Hank Williams records, with Hank getting his cut from every one. Throughout his best years, his releases sold an average of a half-million records each. The big hits—"Cold, Cold Heart," "Lovesick Blues," "Why Don't You Love Me," "Jambalaya"—sold well above that. "Your Cheatin' Heart," the biggest of all, sold way over a million. (Williams 1973, 157)

Hank Williams imitated Rodgers's flair for the visible public image of overnight sensation. He bought big Cadillac automobiles, a fancy house in Nashville and a farm outside it, and opened a clothing store ("Hank and Audrey's Corral") in 1951 (Williams 1973, 158; *Country* 1988, 244). Also like Rodgers, Williams was said to be extremely generous with those around him—giving hundred-dollar tips to hotel clerks, privately supporting an orphanage, chartering an airplane so as not to miss a show date in Mississippi for someone who had befriended him (Williams 1973, 137–39). Williams apparently loved the flair of doing it "his way," often seen in country artists who emerge from working-class origins into sudden wealth. Roger M. Williams reports that a Nashville songwriter once saw Hank scattering thousands of dollar bills around his den. "I was so poor most of my life," Hank reportedly told him, "I've always dreamed about being able to do this" (Williams 1973, 138).

Hank Williams's stage persona was carefully constructed but not elaborate. His band featured a lead guitar, bass, fiddle, and steel guitar derivative from western swing-band playing in the 1930s and 40s. Song arrangements were "rather regimented," but the steel guitar played by Don Helms was given prominence and Helms was encouraged to improvise. Bass player Hillous Butrum described the rationale for this emphasis: "The lonesome sound of Don's steel guitar fit right in with the lonesome sound of Hank's singing" (Williams 1973, 100). With the exception of a pop music cover such as "Lovesick Blues," Hank Williams's songs were standardized in musical form and relatively uncomplicated.

> The songs Hank sang, his own and those written by others, were almost invariably simple, musically unsophisticated pieces that followed the classic country music patterns: a verse followed by the chorus; a melodic line that is often the same for both verse and chorus; a chord progression that seldom ventures beyond the stock 1-4-5 (e.g., G-C-D), with a "passing chord" (e.g., A) occasionally thrown in; a rhythm that does not vary from one part of the song to the next. (Williams 1973, 80)

This musical form is an evolution from Carter Family songs, bringing together their standardized rhythm structures with a vocal emphasis adapted from Jimmie Rodgers's pathos in the "blue yodel." Like Rodgers, too, Hank Williams encouraged his musicians with vocal commentary during performance and at breaks, and he talked with his audience in an extremely folksy manner featuring an unrelieved country boy's drawl. Bill Malone remembers Williams as "a quintessential *rural* singer" with a "distinctive sound and phrasing" that "reflected the milieu of the country fundamentalist church and the styles of people like Roy Acuff as much as it did the noisy, sin-saturated honky-tonk world of Mobile and the Alabama Gulf Coast" (Malone 1992, 9).

A vivid example of Hank Williams's mature style as he neared the height of his popularity in October 1949 is available on the *Hank Williams Health & Happiness Shows*, eight 12-minute radio shows produced originally for radio broadcasts sponsored by the patent medicine Hadacol and transcribed from acetate discs in the Country Music Foundation for a collection produced by Colin Escott in 1993 (Escott 1993). These radio programs were done in two settings by Hank Williams and the Drifting Cowboys. They offer forty-nine song selections that include a mix of Hank Williams's songs, covers of other pop and traditional tunes, gospel songs, and barn dance fiddle and guitar instrumentals. Each show begins with the theme song "Happy Rovin' Cowboy," a Bob Nolan western tune that presents the cowboy as penniless ("I ain't gotta dime") but happily herding dark clouds from the sky and singing until he is called "to the land beyond the blue." Each show concludes with the hot fiddling barn dance number "Sally Goodin," fiddled by Jerry Rivers. Excluding the standard opening and closing numbers, the eight shows offer thirty-three live performances. Each show presents one gospel number, one instrumental, and two songs either written by Hank or adapted by him from pop or other sources.

In his annotation, Escott describes these transcriptions as "beautifully preserved," "vital," and "the way it really, really was." For Escott, the authenticity of Hank's production in this format is particularly important because "this was how he won over his first fans" (Escott 1993, 7). That claim deserves attention. The *Health & Happiness Shows* were recorded just four months after Williams joined the Opry and exactly at the time he was making a move to broaden his appeal. Their syndicated radio format elaborates on the radio success of the Grand Ole Opry and the Carter Family, and Williams's mannerisms and speech patterns amply embrace Judge Hay's prescription for rustic nostalgia: Keep it "down to earth."

Hank's number-one hit for sixteen weeks, "Lovesick Blues," appears here just six months after it reached the top of the charts. Perhaps more important for building a lasting fan following, Williams was able to showcase on syndicated radio a generous selection of his own compositions. Excluding theme songs, ten of the thirty-three songs included in this collection were written by Williams. Those ten songs provide a clear indicator of the central theme in Williams's songwriting: domestic turmoil. Of the ten, four deal with domestic situations of romantic love where partners complain about, defy, or warn one another, or express their loneliness, and three are songs of broken hearts. Seventy percent of the total depict romantic trauma; the other 30 percent include two songs of gospel salvation and one train song. The overall effect of Williams's songwriting for this syndicated radio program was quite pointed: a protracted lament about the hard times of unhappy love punctuated by hope for salvation in heaven, with a passing nod to the image of worldly escape embodied in the celebration of a speeding train. One of the two gospel songs, "I Saw the Light," is personal testimony that became important to the way Hank's fans remembered him in legend.

One of the most celebrated contributions of Hank Williams to country music culture was his song-writing partnership with Fred Rose. Jimmie Rodgers partnered successfully with his sister-in-law Elsie McWilliams, but Hank Williams and Fred Rose took that precedent considerably further. Williams's biographer, Roger M. Williams, describes their relationship as one of blending Hank Williams's genius with Fred Rose's craftsmanship. Rose, he said, "polished" Williams's originals, which sometimes included changing their tone (as in the shift of "Kaw-Liga" from an unrequited love song featuring Indians to a novelty wooden Indian with a broken heart). Rose was official cowriter on six of Hank Williams's songs but his influence was likely greater (Williams 1973, 129–31). Wesley Rose, Fred Rose's son, credited Hank Williams with two firsts, making country music national and gaining the acceptance of pop artists and record managers. In 1951, Fred Rose took "Cold, Cold Heart" to Mitch Miller who, in turn, gave the song to Tony Bennett, who made it into a pop hit that reached number one and sold a million records. Polly Bergen, Frankie Lane, Jo Stafford, and other pop stars of the 1950s recorded Williams's songs as well (Williams 1973, 117–18).

Despite their wide adaptability, Williams's songs maintained consistent grounding in the tragic-troubadour tradition and pointedly elaborated the theme of domestic turmoil. Williams himself described the goal of a "hillbilly" singer, thus:

> He sings more sincere than most entertainers because the hillbilly was raised rougher than most entertainers. You got to know a lot about hard work. You got to have smelt a lot of mule manure before you can sing like a hillbilly. The people who has been raised something like the way the hillbilly has knows what he is singing about and appreciates it. . . . what he is singing is the hopes and prayers and dreams of what some call the common people. (Williams 1973, 107)

No account of Fred Rose describes him as a "hillbilly," yet he understood the appeal of sincerity in the country music tradition. When Rose observed Roy Acuff crying while singing a country song, the incident exemplified for Rose the role of the artist in bonding with country music fans: "And that's when I got it—the reason people like hillbilly tunes. 'Hell,' I said to myself, 'the guy *means* it'" (Williams 1973, 122).

In his study of popular country songs, Jimmie N. Rogers observed that, to be effective, artists are expected to establish a "sincerity contract" with their fans (Rogers 1989, 17). Hank Williams's songwriting played an important role in defining the nature of sincerity within country music culture. His achievement can be scrutinized in *Hank Williams: The Complete Lyrics*, a 1993 compilation edited by Don Cusic. Cusic describes Williams's style as featuring three prominent elements: "his sense of self-mocking humor, of faith and devotion, and of deep, sad loneliness" (Cusic 1993, xviii). All these elements are present in the 138 songs Cusic included; scrutiny of their content yields additional complementary patterns.

The distribution of themes in the songs Hank Williams wrote makes clear his preoccupation with domestic turmoil in romantic love and marriage (see Appendix B). Love is itself the most consistent theme in Williams's songwriting; 39 percent of his songs deal with domestic situations, 27 percent with broken hearts, and 9 percent with happy love—a total of 75 percent of all his songs. Another 15 percent deal with the love of God expressed through images of gospel salvation. Together, earthly love and heavenly love are the focus of 90 percent of Williams's work.

The leading concern with domestic situations further illustrates Williams's preoccupation with romantic trauma. Of these fifty-four songs, 91 percent focus on romantic relationships, and all are negative: 57 percent are songs of complaint, 19 percent songs of loneli-

Total Themes in Hank Williams's Songwriting

THEMES	NUMBER OF SONGS	PERCENT
Domestic Situations	54	39
Broken Hearts	37	27
Gospel Salvation	21	15
Happy Love	13	9
Hard Times	5	4
Death Lament	3	2
Trains	2	2
Other *warning about fighting men, prison lament, against war*	3	2
TOTAL	138	100

Domestic Situations Themes

THEMES	NUMBER OF SONGS	PERCENT
Complaint	31	57
Loneliness	10	19
Defiance *warning, satisfaction, kissoff*	8	15
Family *mother, dad, son*	5	9
TOTAL	54	100

Domestic Complaints

THEMES	NUMBER OF SONGS	PERCENT
Women's Changing Mood	5	16
Loveless Marriage	4	13
Remorse	4	13
Shame	4	13
Infidelity	3	10
Warning About Women	2	6
Other *ambitious wife, unresponsive wife, doubt of love, waiting for love, unreturned love, fear of marriage constraints, divorce trauma, sympathy for broken hearts, rambling man*	9	29
TOTAL	31	100

Wit in Hank Williams's Songwriting

THEMES	NUMBER OF SONGS	PERCENT
Laughing at Treatment by Woman	21	75
Laughing at Hard Times	5	18
Other *putdown of city folks, laughing at shy man*	2	7
TOTAL	28	100
PERCENT OF TOTAL SONGS (138)		20

ness, and 15 percent songs of defiance. The range of concerns within the theme of domestic complaint has suggestive features as well, especially complaints about a woman's changing mood, a loveless marriage, infidelity, and such associated feelings as remorse and shame.

It's important to add that many songs written by Hank Williams are done in a tone of sardonic, wry wit and ironic worldly observation. One implication of this tone is that since events are beyond our ability to influence them by conscious action, humor can be a defense against the pain of romantic trauma and hard times. In Hank Williams's 138 songs, a total of twenty-eight—20 percent—can be regarded as songs embodying this form of wit or humor. Yet even here, the overwhelming preoccupation is with romantic relationships; 75 percent of these songs evoke laughter at a man's treatment by a woman. Another 18 percent suggest laughing at the effects of hard times. In the *Health & Happiness Shows*, 30 percent of Hank's own songs were selected from his witty repertory.

The overwhelming emphasis on unhappy love and broken hearts in Hank Williams's songwriting might be regarded as a by-product of changing gender roles in postwar America. In her critique of family nostalgia in *The Way We Never Were*, Stephanie Coontz describes a new focus on nuclear family life in prosperous suburbs of this period, where romantic sexuality and children were both focal points of marriage and became defining points of personal satisfaction for a generation. Quoting historian Clifford Clark, Coontz defines the changing character of romantic satisfaction:

> There was an unprecedented "glorification of self-indulgence" in family life. Formality was discarded in favor of "livability," "comfort," and "convenience." A contradiction in terms in earlier periods, "the sexually charged, child-centered family took its place at the center of the postwar American dream." (Coontz 1992, 28)

Coontz suggests that the unreality of this image of family life generated a market for domestic romance. "By 1989, the United States had the highest divorce rate in the world; since then, the divorce rate and the sales of romance novels have risen side by side" (Coontz 1992, 66). Even for those who chose not to divorce, Coontz concludes that one consequence of the nuclear family ideal was pervasive unhappiness:

Between one-quarter and one-third of the marriages contracted in the 1950s eventually ended in divorce; during that decade two million legally married people lived apart from each other. Many more couples simply toughed it out. Sociologist Mirra Komarovsky concluded that of the working-class couples she interviewed in the 1950s, "slightly less than one-third were happily or very happily married" (Coontz 1992, 35–36).

If these suggestions about the character of American domestic life provide some perspective on Hank Williams's dramatic popularity, it's also important to consider his stage manner in live performance as a production meant to stimulate significant fan response from women. Minnie Pearl, who seemed to be fascinated by Hank Williams, provided this description of his act:

> He had a real animal magnetism. He destroyed the women in the audience. They just had to have his autograph and get close enough to touch him. It wasn't sex per say, like with some artists. He appealed to their maternal instincts a lot. (Williams 1973, 145)

Hank's biographer goes further: "Hank had plenty of sex appeal," he suggests, "and there was nothing maternal about it." In a body-movement motif that was probably a forerunner of Elvis Presley, Hank "hunched forward toward the microphone, buckling his knees and swaying with the music." Hank's steel guitarist, Don Helms, described another stage effect: "He'd close his eyes and swing one of those big long legs, and the place would go wild" (Williams 1973, 145).

At the height of his popularity, Hank Williams combined a charismatic, sexually aggressive stage manner with a sardonic wit and a poetry of broken hearts to update the Grand Ole Opry's longstanding rusticity and flair for the common touch. This made him the most attractive star that country music culture had produced. Opry announcer Grant Turner described Williams on stage at the Ryman Auditorium in 1944.

> The fans just didn't want to let him go. When Hank would work that stage, he would appear to be suspended in a blue haze, very much as if you had a coat hanger in his suit holding him up over the microphone. He just had that way of being totally relaxed, and, he being a Southerner and knowing his audiences so well, had that easy-going drawl in his voice and manner that made people love him so much. (Eiland 1992, 58)

With million-selling records, a highly professional songwriting partnership, pop music artists making careers from his work, a storybook marriage that amply met postwar expectations of a fine house in the suburbs, wealth, and fancy automobiles, Hank Williams's rise to stardom perhaps left a stronger impression on American popular culture than had his closest ancestor in country music, Jimmie Rogers. Rodgers died quickly of a debilitating physical illness and Williams was to meet a tragic troubadour's fate as well—the rapid destruction of his career, his marriage, and his body by alcoholism.

Williams was probably introduced to hard liquor while he was a teenager in Montgomery. As a young entertainer he had a reputation for excessive drinking, and although he apparently reformed at his first major venue, the Louisiana Hayride, there may have been concern about his drinking habits at the time he joined the Grand Ole Opry in 1949. By August 1952, there was definitely concern about his habitual drunkenness, failure to appear for performances, and showing up on stage inebriated. Members of Hank's band took extreme steps to separate him from the bottle, and the Opry's Artist Service Bureau hired a detective to travel with Hank and the Drifting Cowboys, to "keep Hank Williams sober enough to fulfill his, and the Opry's, obligations." Many stories were told about Williams's drunken sprees. He was fascinated by guns, often carried pistols with him, and once shot up his room at Nashville's Hermitage Hotel. At the Tulane Hotel he set his bed on fire, and on another occasion, police were called to find "Hank and a lady wrestler chasing each other, nude, up and down the hallway" (Williams 1973, 178–79).

Exotic behavior influenced by alcohol was not rare in postwar America and certainly not foreign to country music stars. If performing obligations were met, such displays probably would not ruin a career, especially not the career of Hank Williams. But Williams did not meet his responsibilities; and, as his professional performance deteriorated, so did his relations with fans. After Williams fell off a stage, drunk, in Ontario, Canada, the fans were "furious." His promoter said, "They really wanted to get to him. We called the Mounties, and they escorted us all out of town" (Williams 1973, 180–81).

Grand Ole Opry management fired Hank Williams in August 1952. In January of that year, he separated from his wife Audrey, and they divorced in May. Hank returned to the Louisiana Hayride, and made a spectacular public marriage there to Billie Jean Jones Eshlimar, the nineteen-year-old daughter of a Shreveport policeman. Hank and Billie Jean were married three times—once by a justice of the peace and twice in the New Orleans Municipal Auditorium with 14,000 people in attendance for each public ceremony (Williams 1973, 203; Flippo 1981, 254). A honeymoon in Cuba was planned, but Hank passed out from drinking the wedding champagne. "That left Billie Jean to face the press alone, and she says she responded to that challenge by appearing, in wide-eyed innocence, in a translucent negligee and no shoes. Hank, she announced, was 'resting'" (Williams 1973, 204). Soon reports of alcoholism were augmented by reports that Williams was taking pills. His biographers say that by this time he suffered from hepatitis, a heart condition, malnutrition, agonizing back pain from the uncorrected birth defect spina bifida, and from chronic loneliness and insecurity, as well as the negative effects of drugs (Williams 1973, 174–76; Koon 1983, 8; Flippo 1981, 269). In Louisiana, Hank formed a relationship with a phony doctor, Horace "Toby" Marshall, who provided him with amphetamines, seconal, and chloral hydrate to use as a sedative. Hank's new wife, Billie Jean, and other friends placed him in institutions for recovery, but their efforts failed. More characteristic of his last days was an incident in which he refused to sing his signature song, "Lovesick Blues," on stage in southern Louisiana, with the result that "angry fans mobbed his car after the performance and rocked it until police arrived" (Williams 1973, 206). Minnie Pearl worked a show with him during this period, and again Hank called out her maternal instincts, but with a different tone: "He'd forget the words so often he could hardly get through a song. His voice was like the cry of a child or a wounded animal" (Williams 1973, 208). In this last year of his life, she described Williams as a "pathetic, emaciated, haunted-looking, tragic figure" (Koon 1983, 45).

Hank Williams was booked in Canton, Ohio, for the evening of New Year's Day, 1953. He was in Montgomery on December 31, following a short holiday with his family, and there hired a teen-age taxi driver, Charles Carr, to drive him to Ohio in his blue Cadillac convertible (Williams 1973, 213). George William Koon has written a detailed account of Williams's last hours (Koon, 1983, 51–52). When Hank and Carr left Montgomery, "Hank was in rough shape." A fight at one of his "old haunts" in Montgomery had done damage, leaving his left arm bandaged. Carr drove Highway 31 to Birmingham, then Highway 11 to Chattanooga and Knoxville, while Hank drank beer and took chloral hydrate. In Knoxville, they attempted to fly to Ohio, but bad weather prevented this and they checked into the Andrew Johnson Hotel. Unable to eat, Hank was carried to his room. A doctor was called who gave him B-12 shots with morphine. Koon believes they were probably for pulmonary edema—fluid in the lungs caused from either the fight or a drug overdose. At 10:45 P.M., Carr had hotel personnel help him dress Williams and carry him to the back seat of the Cadillac. They checked out and drove north in bad weather. About an hour later, stopped for reckless driving in northeast Tennessee, Carr told police that Williams—who was "lifeless-looking" in the back seat—had been sedated and drinking. Apparently their next stop was "about dawn on New Year's Day" in Oakhill, West Virginia, at a service station, where Hank was found to be immobile. Taken to a nearby hospital, he was pronounced dead, then removed to a funeral home and embalmed.

That evening in Ohio, Hank Williams's last booking went on as scheduled. When the announcer stepped into a single spotlight to tell fans that Hank Williams was dead, at first they laughed at "the ultimate in bad excuses." But when Hawkshaw Hawkins and other performers gathered to sing Hank's signature of gospel salvation, "I Saw the Light," believing fans joined them in a public mourning ritual that was to be repeated in coming years for other tragic troubadours of country music culture, including Hawkshaw Hawkins.

The elevation of Hank Williams to the status of an enduring American icon began the instant his waiting fans in Ohio sang his signature song of gospel salvation. The funeral that soon followed in Montgomery was a moment of collective grief for country music culture. The Nashville promoter who booked Williams in Canton, Ohio, booked his funeral for Montgomery's Municipal Auditorium the afternoon of January 4. Williams lay in state there in an open silver casket and held a Bible. An estimated 25,000 people attended the funeral—filing by the casket or listening to the service on outdoor loudspeakers. Others tuned in to live broadcasts on local radio stations. Two tons of flowers were sent to the funeral (Williams 1973, 54, 223).

Chet Flippo's biography gives a detailed account of the funeral service, including the main sermon delivered by Dr. Henry Lyon of Highland Avenue Baptist Church. Lyon supposedly told the assembly that he could not preach Hank's funeral because it had already been preached. "The preacher of the message on the radio—*Hank Williams*. The Congregation—the *American People*. His life is a real personification of what can happen in this country to one little insignificant speck of humanity" (Flippo 1983, 280). Yet, by 1953, Hank Williams was certainly not insignificant—he was a star of country music culture. His untimely death was an opportunity for other stars to publicly recognize their sense of community with one another and with their fans, and apparently they felt it was a good thing to do. Virtually the same entourage of Nashville artists who gathered as a memorial assembly for Hank Williams in January 1952 would gather again just sixteen months later, in Meridian, Mississippi, to initiate the annual memorial event for Jimmie Rodgers. They included Ernest Tubb, Jimmy Dickens, Carl Smith, Hank Snow, Webb Pierce, Red Foley, Bill Monroe, Lew Childre, and the star who by 1953 was already a father figure of the Grand Ole Opry, Roy Acuff.

Despite Hank Williams's erratic personal history and recent dismissal by Opry management, Acuff told the funeral assembly that Williams was a member in good standing with the community of country music stars: "Friends and neighbors, several years ago I came here to visit with you in this city and stood on this stage with this fine young gentleman that we're here to pay our respects to. No finer boy has ever come or gone as far as we're concerned" (Flippo 1981, 277). Musical performances at the funeral were vivid. Ernest Tubb sang "Beyond the Sunset"; a black gospel quartet, the South-wind Singers, performed to a filled auditorium that segregated blacks in the balcony. Red Foley—who had an agreement with Williams that if one died first, the other would sing at his funeral—sang "Peace in the Valley," and Roy Acuff led the entire assembly in a memorial rendition of "I Saw the Light" (Flippo 1981, 276–80).

Hank Williams's funeral was an important event for the self-consciousness of country music culture. Country radio stations magnified the moment by playing his records "for two hours at a time." In Troy, New York, WPTR radio "offered copies of 'Kaw-Liga' and its flip side 'Your Cheatin' Heart' in exchange for March of Dimes contributions of $25.00 or more," and listeners "flooded the station with letters and money" (Flippo 1981, 271). The demand for Hank Williams's records—all of them—increased dramatically, and within a month "one of M-G-M's plants was devoting itself exclusively to pressing them." In fact, the year 1953 was Hank Williams's biggest-selling year, earning him posthumous country music awards and designation by a *Downbeat* fan poll as "the most popular country and western performer of all time" (Williams 1973, 220–21).

In the years immediately after Williams's death, the fascination with remembering him increased. A memorial celebration sponsored by Shriners in September 1954, at his burial site in the Oakwood Cemetery Annex, near downtown Montgomery, drew 60,000 people and began with a parade that "included among the marchers three governors, Alabama Governor-elect Jim Folsom, Alabama Senator Lister Hill, and more than fifty country artists" (Williams 1973, 251). Roy Acuff led a memorial show for charity where "everyone paid to get in and no one was paid to perform" (Williams 1973, 257). The ill-fated star Jim Reeves and others played celebratory dances. There was a parade, with Hank's mother riding in his car, and an air show by the Alabama National Guard. The marble monument that has since become a shrine of country music culture, designed by Hank's mother and Willie Gayle of Henley Memorial Company and bearing a sentimental love poem from Audrey Williams, was unveiled at this event. It's an "upright slab" inscribed "Hank Williams" and "I Saw the Light" (Koon 1983, 56).

The number of visitors annually to Hank Williams's grave is not regularly reported, but in 1991, the image of such a visit proved important to emerging country star Alan Jackson. Jackson collaborated with song-writing partner Don Sampson that year to compose a tribute to the spirit of Hank Williams: "Midnight in Montgomery." This is a ballad telling an incident where Jackson, supposedly riding his Silver Eagle touring bus through Montgomery at midnight en route to Mobile for a New Year's Eve performance, stops at Hank Williams's grave. On this unnamed anniversary of Hank's death, his presence at the grave is strong—Jackson is surprised by "a drunk man in a cowboy hat" who wears "shiny boots, a nudie suit and haunting haunted eyes." The figure is quickly gone; but first he tells Jackson, "It's nice to know you care." The singer wonders if Williams was "ever really there," yet the song's refrain echoes "that lonesome chill" when there is "whiskey in the air" because "Hank's always singing there" (Jackson 1991). In 1993, a compelling music video of this song was released. Here, Jackson is depicted as standing before Hank's gravestone to sing his tribute, and Williams makes a ghostly appearance (Jackson 1993). This video created a sensation among fans. The annual TNN/*Music City News* Country Awards— the only major awards voted entirely by fans—elected Alan Jackson 1993 Entertainer of the Year and Male Artist of the Year and celebrated "Midnight in Montgomery" as Video of the Year. Whether Hank Williams actually appeared to Alan Jackson in Montgomery, the memory of Hank Williams as a tragic poet of domestic turmoil was still vivid in country music culture forty years after his death.

It's interesting to consider the attention Alan Jackson and his choreographers may have given to the image of Hank Williams in positioning his own act. In 1992 and 1993, I saw Jackson perform four times. The first event was a sold-out concert at the University of Dayton Arena on the evening of February 15, 1992. Jackson presented himself on stage in a manner visually reminiscent of Hank Williams. He was positioned as the solo center of attention in an essentially empty stage front, standing with a single guitar behind a single microphone stand. A bank of lights on three sides crossed the stage from one end to the other, separating members of Jackson's band, the Stray Horns, behind him on a riser. The visual effect of this arrangement was to make the band part of the backdrop to the star.

While the production was technically sophisticated—using strobe lights, spotlights, colored lights, and choreographed lighting to position a mood for each song—Jackson's stage demeanor was understated. Like Hank Williams, he is a tall, slender performer whose clothing, tight white jeans and soft blue shirt, boots, and white cowboy hat for this concert, accented his height. He stood directly behind the microphone stand for the entire performance, often with the slightly cocked leg and stoop reminiscent of descriptions of Hank Williams on stage. Jackson also swings his legs in a manner suggesting the movements of Hank Williams and the effect is similar: screams of delight from fans who, in this instance, probably were at least 60 percent women.

Jackson's female fans include conservatively dressed middle-aged women sitting in couples; young women with short tight dresses or denim skirts, high heels, loose hair and pronounced make-up; casually dressed teen-age women in jeans and sweatshirts, often in couples; overdressed preteen women in couples; and working-class women dressed out in tight jeans, flashy tops, country music T-shirts, pronounced make-up, home perms, hairspray, and costume jewelry. Women at this concert were frequently accompanied by men dressed in attire analogous to Jackson's dress on stage—blue jeans and casual shirts, tight jeans and fancy western shirts, cowboy hats, and now and then, the splurge of long western riding coats. This youngish audience was entirely polite. Most fans remained seated during most of the performance and, except at the end, listened attentively to the words of Jackson's songs. Women fans filed to the edge of the stage throughout the concert offering flowers to Jackson, who collected them carefully. For the finale, the entire audience came to its feet, and encores were demanded. During slow songs this audience lit cigarette lighters in emotional communion and stage lighting was dimmed to enhance audience participation in the theatrical effect.

Alan Jackson has often mentioned his admiration for Hank Williams. Clearly, he seeks some of Williams's charismatic effects in the design of his show. While on stage, he talks with the audience between songs, sometimes mentioning Hank Williams. But the most essential similarity is his "traditional" and "straight" vocal delivery, one that commands attention by its solidity, by Jackson's pronounced regional accent (from Noonan, Georgia), and by a soft-spoken, small-town, Deep South, good-ole-boy manner of talking. Jackson writes or coauthors the majority of his songs, which focus on making it in the music business, domestic situations at home, people he left behind, his music idols, and the ability (or inability) to relate well to women. One of his biggest hits, "Don't Rock the Jukebox," is a homage number to George Jones—another Hank Williams admirer—and to honky-tonk music, a statement against rock and roll in favor of country music. When this song was performed, the stage backdrop showed a giant neon jukebox, which excited Jackson's fans considerably. A man sitting next to me, who introduced himself as a former concert promoter, estimated the crowd at between 8,000 and 9,000 people and thought its median age was 16. While that estimate seemed youngish, the crowd was very heavy with middle and late teenagers. The arena served beer from the opening of the concert at 8:00 until 9:20 P.M. The vocal band Diamond Rio provided an opening act, and the concert lasted until well past ten.

Jackson sang seventeen songs. He opened with one of his number-one hits, "Chasin' That Neon Rainbow," an autobiographical account of his own break into the music business. After five more songs from his first two albums, Jackson introduced "Midnight in Montgomery" by saying, "I think a lot of Hank Williams. I wrote this song about a visit to his grave." The rendition was highly produced—played very slowly in a tone of exaggerated and dramatic lament with a sophisticated colored light show playing across the darkened auditorium. The effect was to create a momentous quality intended as an emotional highlight of the concert. In other venues on this same tour, Jackson used a machine that spread smoke on stage from behind the backlights to increase the "ghostly" effect as he stood alone, spotlighted at stage center within a darkened hall; but this effect was not used in Dayton. Jackson stood still to render "Midnight in Montgomery." His white guitar, held steady before him at a cocked angle, glittered like an icon of the tragic troubadour it was surely meant to suggest. At the end of "Midnight in Montgomery," and for the first and only time this evening prior to the concert's conclusion, Jackson walked to the edge of the stage to shake hands with fans. He did this quietly, without talking. Variations on this bonding ritual between artists and fans occur often in country music performances at moments of heavy sincerity. This moment honored the memory and spirit of Hank Williams.

By the time Alan Jackson played the Arista Records Show four months later at Fan Fair in Nashville on June 11, his strong talent, songwriting, attractive rustic personality, professional achievement, and stylistic allusions to Hank Williams had made him a major star. Three days earlier, at the 1992 TNN/*Music City News* Country Awards, fan votes had made him their Male Artist of the Year, his "Don't Rock the Jukebox" their Single of the Year, and Jackson's album of the same name, which includes "Midnight in Montgomery," their album of the year. At his Fan Fair performance, a cameo event where stars thank their fans for continuing support, Jackson sang nine songs. Probably because he was appearing outdoors before 25,000 people at 4:20 in the afternoon, the special stage effects for "Midnight in Montgomery" were not attempted. Performed again at the center of the program, however, the song elicited the same somber audience response that had been achieved in Dayton. Two days later, Alan Jackson played the Saturday night Grand Ole Opry. Here, he did three songs and led off with "Midnight in Montgomery," introduced as a song he wrote "over on Music Row about a man who used to sing here." When hitmaking stars perform on the Opry, they follow the Opry stage format rather than their touring choreography, which again precludes special stage effects. Still, the Opry audience sat in respectful silence throughout the homage to Hank Williams.

On April 15, 1993, Alan Jackson returned to the University of Dayton Arena for a major show opened by John Michael Montgomery and Billy Dean. Montgomery played for forty-five minutes and Dean for an hour. At 9:39, Jackson's concert began with a sophisticated music video playing on large screens behind stage, depicting Jackson and his band on the road and talking to his fans in concert crowds. These images were intercut with logos of the tour sponsor, Miller Lite beer. As the video played, smoke rose from the stage and fans came to their feet across the sold-out concert hall. At 9:42, with the band already playing, Jackson walked casually on stage and, again in front of backlighting, opened with his autobiographical "Chasin' That Neon Rainbow."

A year after his first headline appearance in the same arena, Jackson's stage production was more technologically sophisticated, yet its fundamental structure was unchanged. Jackson remained separated from the band, which was arranged behind him on risers in a pyramid format that individualized the keyboard, drums, fiddle, bass, lead, and steel guitars. He continued to stand front and center on stage, carrying his acoustic guitar at a cocky angle; and his attire was consistent—light blue jeans, pink shirt, white cowboy hat. An addition to this concert was live video cameras showing close-ups of Jackson and other band members throughout the concert projected on screens behind stage. While this maneuver increased the visual sense of action, still Jackson did not move around significantly. By 1993, he had added a number of bonding mannerisms to his act— tipping his hat to fans, saying "whooo" at the end of songs, introducing a Hank Williams/Bob Wills "Ah Hah" to accent instrumental runs (especially of steel guitar), and when the band took a long instrumental bridge in a song, sometimes moving to the edge of the stage, shaking hands, and carefully taking flowers that he piled into a neat clump. In this concert, Jackson did nineteen songs and the positioning of "Midnight in Montgomery" changed significantly—

possibly to indicate its signature importance for the impression Jackson wished to leave. Now it was the penultimate, sixteenth song, preceding the finale, "Don't Rock the Jukebox." And now the song's video was shown on screen during the performance, smoke rose all across the stage, blue and green spotlights waved over the audience, and Jackson stood under a single spotlight as the hall was darkened. Fans brought out thousands of lighters to bring the candlepower significantly up again, creating an eerie flickering effect that magnified the plaintive musical moan of this song. During this performance the remarkable silence that had occurred in previous stagings of "Midnight in Montgomery" was punctuated by occasional screams and by people moving toward the stage. Overhead handwaving began, amplifying the visual effect of a darkened hall illuminated by weaving spotlights and flickering fan lighters. Without question, this production drew out fan involvement theatrically to become the emotional high point of the concert. The show lasted until 11 P.M. and ended on an upbeat, rocking note that offset the mood of "Midnight in Montgomery." This was the concert tour that helped earn Alan Jackson's Hank Williams video country music culture's official endorsement of voted fan approval.

Like Hank Williams, Alan Jackson has also focused his songwriting on themes of domestic turmoil. Nominated in 1993 for seven awards by the professional Country Music Association (Entertainer, Male Vocalist, Video, Song, Single, Album, and Vocal Event), Jackson shared the Vocal Event award with nine other singers who collaborated with George Jones, and Jackson's "Chattahoochee," co-authored with Jim McBride, won Single of the Year and Video of the Year.

"Chattahoochee" is an upbeat song with a danceable rhythm that focuses on nostalgia for the summer pleasures of home in his early years. It relies on themes which, in a different mood, could yield domestic turmoil even though here they are meant to convey innocence. The second stanza, for example, is an image of teenagers parking by the river on a Friday night and talking about cars and women, meanwhile drinking so much beer that the cans form a pyramid in the moonlight. We "never had a plan," Jackson says, "just a livin' for the minute" (Jackson 1992a).

By the time fans voted Alan Jackson Entertainer of the Year, he had released three albums featuring thirty songs, twenty-five of

Total Themes in Alan Jackson's Songwriting

THEMES	NUMBER OF SONGS	PERCENT
Domestic Situations	10	38.5
Broken Hearts	10	38.5
Happy Love	3	11.5
Home Nostalgia	1	3.8
Becoming a Star	1	3.8
Honoring Country Music Legend	1	3.8
TOTAL	26	100

them attributed to his own songwriting or to collaboration with others. Those twenty-five songs, plus one he wrote for a 1993 Christmas album, may be assigned to categories similar to those found in Hank Williams's songwriting. Although Hank Williams wrote many more songs in his lifetime than Alan Jackson had released by 1993, the distribution of themes is related. For Williams, the main focus of songwriting was domestic situations—39 percent of all songs. For Jackson, domestic situations account for 34.6 percent. Love songs of some type comprised 75 percent of Williams's output, while for Jackson, the comparable figure for love songs is 88.5 percent. A second frequent topic for each writer is broken hearts—27 percent for Williams, and a significantly higher 42.3 percent for Jackson. Williams's songs about happy love were 9 percent of his total compared to 11.5 percent of Jackson's. A significant divergence between the two is Hank Williams's concern with gospel salvation; 15% of his songs treated that theme while none of Jackson's do. In less frequent categories, Williams was concerned with hard times, death laments, and trains; Jackson has focused on nostalgia for home, songs about becoming a singing star, and in his "Midnight in Montgomery," honoring a country music legend. There are additional parallels. Within the category of domestic situations 76 per-

Domestic Situation Themes

THEMES	NUMBER OF SONGS	PERCENT
Complaint	7	70
Family	2	20
Loneliness	1	10
TOTAL	10	100

Domestic Complaint Themes

THEMES	NUMBER OF SONGS	PERCENT
Remorse	3	42.8
Abandoned	2	28.6
Women's Changing Moods	1	14.3
Waiting for Love	1	14.3
TOTAL	7	100

cent of Hank Williams's songs focused on complaint or loneliness; 77.8 percent of Alan Jackson's songs fit these two categories—in roughly equal distributions that similarly emphasize complaint. And, when songs of domestic complaint are scrutinized, remorse about a romantic relationship appears prominently in the work of each writer (see Appendix C).

Thematic parallels in the songwriting of Hank Williams and Alan Jackson are suggestive. Williams's focus on domestic life has been a lasting preoccupation of successor artists, and domestic turmoil still appeals powerfully to country music fans. New artists seeking to position themselves prominently in country music culture find that Williams's stage demeanor and manner of speech, as well as his songwriting themes, still resonate effectively. Beyond these considerations, there is a continuing preoccupation with Williams himself that, in Jackson's case, includes a degree of imitation. It appears that, for some artists and fans, the notion of a male tragic troubadour experiencing the hard times of domestic turmoil is virtually synonymous with country music authenticity.

Another young star of the 1990s, Marty Stuart, released a concept album in 1992 that brought him favorable attention. An aggressive celebration of authenticity in country music, the opening piece on Stuart's album is a "dream monologue" in which he imagines himself in "Hillbilly Heaven." There, Stuart talks with many dead stars. The first to appear is Hank Williams, whose voice can be heard opening the album with his familiar fatalistic banter to the country faithful, "If the Good Lord's willin' and the creek don't rise, we'll see you in the mornin'." Williams gives Marty Stuart some advice. "Just sing what's in your heart and God's gonna do the rest," Hank tells him. "Just be what you are at all times" (Stuart 1992).

The "Hillbilly Heaven" image appropriated by Marty Stuart in the lead song for his concept album has been recurrent in country music since at least 1954. Originally written the year after Hank Williams's death and public funeral as "I Dream of a Hillbilly Heaven," cowriter Hal Southern based the song on an actual dream he had, and it was first recorded by cowriter Eddie Dean. Southern told Dorothy Horstman that the song was inspired by a town in California with so many country music fans that a friend called it "Hillbilly Heaven" (Horstman 1986, 81–82); yet clearly the song was a memorial to Hank Williams. Other than Williams, the only inhabitants of the heavenly "Hall of Fame" in 1954 are Jimmie Rodgers and humorist Will Rogers (Southern and Dean 1954).

In 1961, Tex Ritter—who, as president of the Country Music Association, led fundraising for the Country Music Hall of Fame, was later elected to it, and may be memorialized there in Thomas Hart Benton's mural, *The Sounds of Country Music* (Fryd 1993, 89)—had a hit with a revised version of "I Dreamed of a Hillbilly Heaven." Will Rogers again greets the dreaming singer upon arrival in "Hillbilly Heaven" (which is again described as a "stars' hall of fame") and introduces him to an early figure of country music, Carson Robison—a Kansas City radio singer who performed in New York City in 1924 and remained active until his death in 1957 (Stambler and Landon 1984, 619). An actual stars' hall of fame was not created until 1967, when the Country Music Hall of Fame opened in Nashville. The heavenly hall of fame in the 1961 song, though, has gold guitars and fiddles on the wall, and standing in smiling statuesque array are Jimmie Rodgers, Hank Williams, Johnny Horton, and Will Rogers's pilot, Wiley Post. A "big tally" of ten future inhabitants is read, and when it comes to Ritter's name he awakens (Ritter 1961). Another remake of the song by Ritter some time between 1964 and 1974 (the rewrite is credited to Southern and Dean's wife, Dearest) brings Cowboy Copas, Hawkshaw Hawkins, Hank Martin, and the first female admitted to "Hillbilly Heaven": Patsy Cline (Ritter 1981). In Marty Stuart's 1992 derivation of "Hillbilly Heaven," in addition to Saint Peter and Hank Williams, upon his dream arrival, Stuart meets Elvis Presley, Keith Whitley, seven members of Reba McEntire's band (one of them a woman)—and Patsy Cline (Stuart 1992).

In 1993, Grand Ole Opry star Bill Anderson again remade the "Hillbilly Heaven" vision, this time as "Country Music Heaven." Now we meet no hillbillies, but many country music stars. Here,

Jimmie Rodgers plays the heavenly host. Rodgers introduces Anderson to Ernest Tubb, Marty Robbins, Red Foley, Lefty Frizzell, Tennessee Ernie Ford, Hank Williams, and Elvis Presley. They visit the Hall of Fame with its gold guitars and fiddles and there meet Tex Ritter, Johnny Horton, George Morgan, Dottie West, and Keith Whitley. When the "big tally book" of the future is again read, nine names concluding with Bill Anderson's own are given; and, true to form, Anderson wakes up. Just before awakening, Anderson saw a Grand Ole Opry-style stage show in "Country Music Heaven," which has "an all-star lineup like none I'd ever seen." That lineup showcased Roger Miller, Bob Wills and the Texas Playboys, Webb Pierce, Hawkshaw Hawkins, Red Sovine, Carl and Pearl Butler, Cowboy Copas, Lester Flatt, "String Bean," Jimmy Gateley, Mel Street, Jim Reeves—and Patsy Cline (Anderson 1993).

Hank Williams is given an honored position in five versions of "Hillbilly Heaven" between 1954 and early 1993. In 1954, all three heavenly inhabitants were male. In 1961, there were six male inhabitants and no women. The Ritter version, released between 1964 and 1974, has nine males in "Hillbilly Heaven" and one woman. In 1992, there were ten male inhabitants and two women. In early 1993, there were twenty-four male inhabitants, another all-male band, and three women. The only woman to appear consistently during four decades in this evolving vision of the spiritual fate awaiting country music culture's tragic troubadours is Patsy Cline.

In his biography of Patsy Cline, Ellis Nassour tells a story about Cline's interest in country music immortality. On the evening of December 26, 1963, sixty-eight days before she would die in a plane crash, Cline sat backstage in Las Vegas, talking with the cowriter of her first number-one record, "Walkin' After Midnight." Reflecting on her illnesses, accidents, hospital bills, and exploitive music publishers, she held out her hand to Donn Hecht. "Every time I've had what I wanted here," she said, "something pulls the rug out from under me." Hecht took this conversation as pensive reflection and tried to reassure her. "Patsy, you've got a lot of songs to sing before you join 'Hillbilly Heaven'." Cline responded with characteristic wit: "If there're a bunch of hillbillies up there, you can be damn sure I'll get in" (Nassour 1993, 209–10).

Six years after it opened in 1967, Patsy Cline became the first female solo artist elected to the Country Music Hall of Fame. Her marker reads, "Patsy will live in country music annals as one of its outstanding vocalists. Tragically, her career was cut short in its prime when she was killed in a plane crash" (Nassour 1993, 178). At a special tribute in Kansas City twelve days after her death, Tex Ritter sang a version of "Hillbilly Heaven," inserting the names of four new arrivals, crash victims Cowboy Copas, Hawkshaw Hawkins, Randy Hughes—and Patsy Cline (Nassour 1993, 246).

Jimmie Rodgers, the original Carter Family, Hank Williams, and Patsy Cline are the formative tragic troubadour acts for the social history of country music culture. The Carters and Jimmie Rodgers set the "tragic" image in popular culture and inaugurated its focus on hard times and broken hearts. Hank Williams and Patsy Cline refined that focus into a direct examination of romantic love traumas and domestic turmoil. Within this arena of popular romance, Hank Williams became the archetypal lonely, addicted, wasted, tragic man, a figure inspiring generations of male artists and their fans on into the early 1990s. Patsy Cline was the first female artist to have sustained popularity as both a country and pop performer in postwar America. Her legendary vocal styling helped Nashville entrepreneurs develop an antidote to the commercial challenge of rock and roll in the early 1960s. And her slow-tempo "torch" songs about the painfulness of compliant femininity, produced by Owen Bradley in renditions richly backed by harmonic vocals and string instrumentation, inspired many younger female artists who entered the country field after Cline's example had opened doors for them.

An audacious personality whose own domestic turmoil later became the basis for a Hollywood movie, Patsy Cline and her story have grown in significance since her premature death more than three decades ago. In *Finding Her Voice*, an elaborate study of women in country music, published in 1993, Mary A. Bufwack and Robert K. Oermann describe her distinction:

> To this day Patsy sells more records than any other country artist on MCA records. Her life and music have provided the raw material for a Hollywood film, a video documentary, two books, two stage productions, and several tribute albums. She was still making the country charts in 1981. Actress Jessica Lange garnered a 1985 Oscar nomination for bringing Patsy's personality to life on screen. In 1988 and 1989 two new Patsy Cline albums of live performances were successfully marketed. A seven-hour radio documentary on Patsy's life aired in Canada in 1990. In 1991 she sold millions via a TV record offer and

was saluted with a lavish CD boxed set reprising four hours of her music. In 1992 her *Greatest Hits* album passed the four-million mark in sales and was the only album from the 1960s still on the charts. Other country stars have come and gone. Patsy Cline endures. (Bufwack and Oermann 1993a, 243)

Virginia Patterson Hensley, who would become Patsy Cline (or, as she referred to herself, "The Cline"), was born near Winchester, Virginia, in 1932. Her mother Hilda was sixteen years old then. Ellis Nassour tells the story of Cline's long desire to become a country music star. Naturally gifted on the piano from the age of seven, at ten, Virginia became a devoted fan of the Grand Ole Opry and declared her intention to become a country singer. At twelve, she lied about her age to get a job in a chicken-processing plant. At thirteen, she had rheumatic fever, which she later said gave her a "booming voice like Kate Smith's." At fourteen, she approached Joltin' Jim McCoy who, with his Melody Playboys, had a live radio show Saturday mornings on WINC in Winchester. After an aggressive audition, she became a regular with McCoy's group. The next year, her father, who had problems with alcohol, left his family and moved to Ohio. Thereafter, Virginia saw him rarely. When Cline was sixteen, she quit school, took a day job in a drugstore, and began playing local clubs at night. Her mother sewed cowgirl costumes for her by hand and often drove her to club dates.

In 1948, Virginia approached gospel singer Wally Fowler, who was appearing in Winchester, and sang for him. He arranged an audition at the Grand Ole Opry, where Roy Acuff told her she had "one of the sweetest voices I've ever heard." She failed to get a contract, however, and her mother took her back to Winchester, where she played "church socials, benefits, fraternal parties, carnivals, and minstrels," fronted for a pop music band, sang in a restaurant, and continued to find nightclub engagements (Nassour 1993, 15, 17). By 1951, nineteen-year-old Virginia was playing regularly with the house band at Winchester's Rainbow Inn. Then she joined regional favorites Bill Peer and his Melody Boys. Peer paid $10 a show and gave Virginia the stage name "Patsy Hensley" (Nassour 1993, 20). Nassour provides numerous suggestions that Patsy Hensley and Bill Peer developed a romantic relationship, and that it lasted beyond Patsy's marriage, in March 1953, to a local playboy, Gerald Cline. Marriage and love affairs never diminished Patsy's ambition. A month after her marriage, she sang at Ernest Tubb's Record Shop on the new-talent showcase, "Midnight Jamboree." In this same year, in addition to her husband and Bill Peer, Patsy was reportedly involved with a 22-year-old sailor based at Norfolk. In June 1954, she had a miscarriage and, apparently, kept the knowledge from all her men. In the summer, she won Best Female Vocalist in a national country music contest sponsored by Washington D.C. broadcaster Connie B. Gay. This provided her a job doing commercials and an afternoon show with singer Jimmy Dean. Soon Patsy was making radio transcriptions for U.S. Army recruiting, and appearing in a variety of Washington area venues. Finally, just after her twenty-second birthday, she signed a two-year recording contract (Nassour 1993, 29–30).

Bill McCall, of Four-Star Records, was based in California; he sent Cline to New York City to record and bound her contractually to his song selections. Then he made a deal with Decca Records whereby he kept artist and publishing rights, but she recorded in Nashville. There, Patsy was introduced to producer Owen Bradley, an innovator important to Nashville's pioneering effort to broaden the appeal of country music by softening its modulation, muting its rusticity, and adding harmonized vocal and instrumental backings. Bradley and Decca executives saw great potential for Patsy Cline as a pop country stylist, even though she brought to the recording studio a number of distinctive country vocal maneuvers she had developed for stage shows and to which she was deeply attached—the yodel, a growl, and a song-ending style that speeded up and sometimes jumped an octave (Jensen 1982, 41–42). In 1956, Donn Hecht gave Bill McCall a song targeted for Cline's new style, "Walkin' After Midnight." Cline said she hated this number ("It ain't country."); but, as his contract permitted, McCall required Cline to record the song over her vigorous objection. Hecht reported later that Cline said, "Doing something I don't believe in makes me feel like a whore" (Nassour 1993, 64–65).

In 1957, the tempo of Cline's career increased rapidly. In January, she performed "Walkin' After Midnight" on Arthur Godfrey's televised talent scout show in New York City—wearing a cocktail dress selected by the show's female staff instead of the cowgirl costume she preferred. When audience applause "froze" response meters, Godfrey invited her to sing an encore. Patsy Cline chose to look backward: she sang Hank Williams's "Your Cheatin' Heart." Afterward, Godfrey offered her a regular position on his CBS television program "Arthur Godfrey Time," said to have an audience of 10 million people (Nassour 1993, 75). In the 1950s, network television was the leading novelty of American popular culture, and Patsy Cline was a decided hit there. Decca released "Walkin' After Midnight" on February 11, and on February 16, Cline was invited to appear on the Grand Ole Opry—an aspiration of hers for the previous nine years. "Walkin' After Midnight" stayed on *Billboard's* country chart for nineteen weeks, rising to number 2, and on the *Billboard* pop chart for sixteen weeks, where it went to number 12 (Nassour 1993, 81).

In late March, Gerald Cline divorced Patsy, leaving her free to develop a romantic relationship initiated the previous year with Charlie Dick. Charlie, another ladies' man from Winchester, "cocky, oozing with personality and sex appeal, with a distinct nose, wavy brown hair, and chiseled good looks," was said to be the focus of complete romance for Patsy, who described him as "a hurricane in pants" (Nassour 1993, 55). Charlie was drafted and sent to Ft. Bragg, North Carolina, in 1957. On August 5, Cline's first album was released, and on September 15, she married Dick (Nassour 1993, 91–92). By December, Patsy was pregnant, and in August, daughter Julie was born. Soon, however, Cline was complaining of "changing diapers and powdering the baby's behind." "Sitting around the house playing the wife and mother is starting to drive me crazy," she said. "I've got to get out. I've got to sing" (Nassour 1993, 101).

There's little doubt that Patsy Cline was restless for big success. As a struggling artist, she had developed a brash persona. Gordon Stoker of the Jordanaires, who backed Cline's late recordings, described her forceful personality:

> She was the sweetest person in the world if you played your side of the cards right. But, brother, she'd fix you fast if you didn't. She'd love you to death if you did something for her, but God forbid if you turned on her. I liked her because she was brutally frank. If you messed with her she'd strike like a snake. She'd look you right in the eye and say, "Don't you ever cross my path again, you sonofabitch!" (Nassour 1993, 102)

Apparently, this attitude was fully displayed in her marriage as well. Pregnant again before her first child was nine months old, Cline continued to appear regularly in performance and worked hard at her recording career, refining her new pop style. While appearing in

California at three months of pregnancy, she had another miscarriage. Still, she played dances, drive-ins, bars, carnivals, and county fairs. In 1960, Patsy and Charlie relocated to Nashville with the hope of securing a permanent position on the Opry from which her career could be developed. In Nashville, she was soon pregnant again, and buying new furniture and clothes with an advance from a new record contract (Nassour 1993, 105).

Charlie Dick, said to have a fondness for alcohol, apparently indulged it during their early Nashville years. Friends claimed he had difficulty with his wife's stardom. Faron Young (an Opry star with whom Cline may have had yet another brief relationship) described the couple's domestic turmoil:

> Charlie treated Patsy like a dog. He'd get her up in front of a bunch of people and call her a no-good whore, and everything else. He was drunk, just a drunk. And jealous. Once he'd see Patsy was getting attention from somebody, he'd be right on top of her and sometimes even say something to that person. (Nassour 1993, 125)

Charlie supposedly had other destructive strategies. "She'd come in from the road with money. He'd take it and blow it, gambling at pool, shooting dice. Stuff like that. Anything. He couldn't win. But he could drink" (Nassour 1993, 125).

On January 21, Patsy Cline played the Grand Ole Opry. Later that night, she gave birth to a boy. The next day her country pop styling of "I Fall to Pieces" was released. There was a lag in its popularity, but by April the song was receiving good play on radio. Then, on June 14, Patsy and her brother had a head-on automobile collision in Nashville while returning from shopping. Cline suffered severe facial lacerations, a dislocated hip, wrist fracture, and other traumas. Her brother's injuries were more modest, as were those of the woman at fault in the car that hit them; but two of that woman's passengers died. While Patsy Cline endured a major operation, members of the Grand Ole Opry kept a seven-hour vigil outside the hospital. Patsy's fans responded as well—she received two thousand cards and letters from them. During her stay in the hospital, Patsy Cline had, she said, a vision where Jesus appeared to her, saying it was not yet time for her to die (Nassour 1993, 149, 179). On July 22, Patsy Cline was wheelchaired onto the stage of the Grand Ole Opry, where she thanked fans for their support, and they gave her a standing ovation. Early the next month, "I Fall to Pieces" rose to number one on the

Billboard country chart and stayed there for thirty-nine weeks. By early September, it was also number 12 on the *Billboard* pop chart (Nassour 1993, 161, 169).

In 1961 and 1962, Patsy Cline released a series of "torch" songs written by men, produced by Owen Bradley, and rendered by Cline in a slow tempo, anguished vocal style. Many of these were major hits—"Crazy" by Willie Nelson, "I Love You So Much It Hurts Me" by Floyd Tillman, "Strange" by Mel Tillis and Fred Burch, and "She's Got You" by Hank Cochran. By now, Patsy Cline was leading a major wave of popularity for the new country music, as Nashville-based pop stylings entered the national market. Yet her personal life did not improve. In late December 1961, she was reported near a nervous breakdown, with blackouts and headaches, and there were more reports of marital violence (Nassour 1993, 185). Cline had a suburban dream house in Nashville, where she was personally waxing floors and having friends in for cooking sprees in a fancy kitchen (now on public view at the Grand Ole Opry Museum). She was said to be devoted to her children during this period, and repeatedly told manager Randy Hughes that she wished to spend more time with them. Caught between professional commitment and domestic mystique, she described her life to Dottie West and Loretta Lynn as a quest for values she felt might be behind her: "Y'all, I thought I wanted the future, when all along it was the past I was aching for." Yet soon, Cline was playing Hollywood and Las Vegas, while her nerves deteriorated and she smoked constantly (Nassour 1993, 196, 207).

On Sunday, March 3, 1963, Patsy Cline headlined at a benefit show for the family of Jack Wesley "Cactus Jack" Call, a Kansas City disc jockey killed in an automobile accident. This death-memorial event, booked into Kansas City's Memorial Auditorium, featured Roy Acuff, Cowboy Copas, Wilma Lee and Stoney Cooper, George Jones, Dottie West, Hawkshaw Hawkins, Billy Walker, and Ralph Emery (Nassour 1993, 218). The Nashville stars did three shows, and Cline earned a standing ovation; but her effort to return to Nashville was to precipitate an even more dramatic death observance in country music culture. On March 5, flying late and in stormy weather in a single-engine airplane, Randy Hughes, Cowboy Copas, Hawkshaw Hawkins, and Patsy Cline crashed and died in a wooded area eighty-five miles west of Nashville. Conditions were said to be "extremely turbulent" (Nassour 1993, 226–27).

One of Patsy Cline's last recordings was a melodramatic performance of a broken-heart testimony written by Don Gibson, "Sweet Dreams (of You)." This song provided the title for a 1985 movie biography of Patsy Cline starring Jessica Lange as Patsy and Ed Harris as Charlie Dick. The movie account keeps reasonably close to Cline's story as told by Nassour, though many details are modified. The Patsy Cline portrayed on screen by Jessica Lange is indeed brash and aggressive; she exhibits many of the ambiguities Cline showed during an era when American popular culture honored both a conventional success ethic and femininity, domesticity and motherhood above forceful female professional aspiration. In *Sweet Dreams*, conventional domestic values are assigned to Patsy Cline, and her defiance of sexual monogamy is downplayed. This tailoring of perhaps a more conventional Patsy Cline than actually existed heightens the "tragic" effect in her image, perhaps making it more palatable to the middle-class audience of HBO Video, memorable to female fans, and appealing to younger female singers who emerged in the late 1980s and early 1990s.

The smoothing of Patsy Cline's personality begins as the movie opens. We first see Patsy singing in the Rainbow Inn in 1956, where she belts out favorite songs by Bob Wills and Bill Monroe. Her alleged lover, Bill Peer, is nowhere to be seen, but her husband Gerald Cline is—in the movie, he's a quiet, conservative, nondrinking, gentle homebody who speaks politely to Patsy while building model ships—hardly the playboy Patsy's first husband was said to be. In fact, Gerald is boring, and the movie makes boredom Patsy's motivation for responding to the advances of Charlie Dick. They do have sex in his car on their first date (which Patsy explains by saying "I was starvin' and I didn't even know"), yet in that same encounter Patsy tells Charlie that her deepest personal goal as a country singer is to become a happy mother:

> I want it all and I want to make it right. . . . Since I've been about eleven or twelve years old I've had my life mapped out. . . . I'm gonna be a singer. I'm gonna make some money, have some kids, then I'm gonna stop singin' and raise them kids right. Have a big house with yellow roses all around it. (HBO Pictures 1985)

This encounter with Charlie occurs on Saturday night. The following morning—in another adjustment of Cline's actual experience—she packs and leaves Gerald, telling him she wants a divorce. This tidy sequence enhances the romantic effect of the infatuation Charlie and Patsy feel. When Patsy agrees to marry, Charlie describes their union as "good times all the time Sunday to Sunday," and Patsy responds, "I just want it to work out, Charlie. I want everything to be right."

Cline's image as a young singer is adjusted in the movie version of her life. When she appears on the Godfrey show in New York City, she does wear the cowgirl suit made by her mother that Godfrey's managers disallowed. This submerges early signs that Patsy's voice invited the pop stylings engineered by Owen Bradley, as well as her initial resistance to them. Those stylings were, in fact, to make her famous; in the movie they are suggested to Cline by her manager, Randy Hughes. When Cline tells Hughes that she wants to "be Hank Williams," he tells her how to go about it: "You've got a voice that was made to sing love songs. And if you work with me we're gonna take advantage of that fact." In the movie, Patsy readily agrees. She is soon recording her famous "torch" hits and appearing on the Grand Ole Opry.

But life is not easy. *Sweet Dreams* emphasizes domestic turmoil over professional conflicts, so that, privately, Cline's ready success as a pop sensation is foiled by Charlie's drinking and negative thinking. The movie has Charlie first hit Patsy while he's in the army, in a transference of his frustration and anger at the regimen of army life. He immediately apologizes, but Patsy, cast as innocent victim, moves home to mother. Patsy's mother warns her about Charlie: "They say if a man hits you once there's always another time." Yet Patsy stays with Charlie, rationalizing naively that she knew he drank when she married him. The image of Patsy Cline as victim is heightened by the treatment of random violence. The automobile accident that Cline survived, which killed two people and severely injured three, is depicted in the movie as Patsy and her brother being hit broadside by a large truck. She's the only person badly injured.

Cline's domestic victimization builds to a scene of severe wife-beating, in which Charlie attacks Patsy in their dream home under the frightened eyes of their young daughter. This occurs following an evening at an automobile demolition derby, where Patsy and Charlie argue and each takes up with a member of the opposite sex. Patsy's encounter is shown to be innocent defiance to "get even," but when she returns home Charlie calls her "a whore." At that point Patsy utters the movie's explanation for their domestic turmoil: "I looked at you tonight and I thought, 'God help you, Patsy. No matter how hard you try to make things right, 'ole Good Time Charlie just keeps draggin' you back down'." Charlie resists this characterization. "Where are you," he says, "when the kids want their oatmeal in the morning? Where are you when Julie pukes in bed at night? You sure as hell ain't here." Such a direct challenge to Patsy's domesticity angers her more than any other encounter in the movie. She accuses Charlie of lying, of dereliction in his own domestic duties; she taunts him with the possibility that she had sex with her man of the evening. This challenge, in turn, angers Charlie more than any other encounter in the movie. True to mother's warning, Charlie attacks Patsy again, this time with repeated physical blows. This scene is based on an incident reported by Patsy's friends to her biographer— and, just as allegedly happened in life—Patsy calls the police and Charlie is put in jail (Nassour 1993, 200).

Charlie's incarceration allows the movie to dramatize his story as well. Sitting overnight in a cell beside an older prisoner (played by the singing descendant of Jimmie Rodgers, Boxcar Willie), Charlie reveals that as a child he saw his father commit suicide by shooting himself between the eyes while sitting at the kitchen table. After that, Charlie adopted a tragic-troubadour philosophy of his own: He left home and thereafter has lived by the rule "just keep on movin'."

When he is released from prison, Charlie tries to apologize and begs to be taken back. Yet now Patsy has learned the lesson of mean drunks that her mother already knew:

> I just can't seem to find anything in my life to hold on to anymore. I keep saying to myself, "I don't have to lead that trashy dog's life that my Daddy led my Mama. I can make things different. I can make it right." And look at me. Here I am, my face all busted up, calling the cops in the middle of the night, and my kid saw it all.

So Patsy gives Charlie the message of failed romance after domestic turmoil: "I just don't know if I can live with you anymore."

The domestic turmoil of Patsy and Charlie is the central "tragedy" of *Sweet Dreams*. The movie's final scene of random violence—instant death in a plane crash—reinforces the image of innocence and good intentions betrayed. In the movie, part of the motive for flying a small single-engine aircraft in turbulent weather is that Patsy is eager to return home to be with her children. At every stop along the way, she calls home to talk with her mother about them. It may be more likely that Randy Hughes actually took this flying risk because he learned in a telephone call to his wife that his father-in-law and passenger Cowboy Copas was requested in Nashville immediately to serve as pallbearer at the funeral of a well-liked musician in Hank Snow's band (Nassour 1993, 226, 240). The circumstances of the crash are modified for effect, as well. Flying without instruments in cloudy weather, Randy Hughes may have thought his aircraft was climbing when it hit the ground, rather than flying upside down. In the movie, however, the plane runs out of gas; Hughes switches tanks, drops the nose to restart the engine, then fails to clear the side of a mountain. The result is spectacular, head-on, unavoidable flaming destruction.

Sweet Dreams concludes with a dignified funeral showing close family and a modest crowd of friends and mourners, followed by Patsy's mother taking her children so that Charlie can continue to work. The last scene emphasizes the tragic effects of domestic turmoil for the survivors. A grief-stricken Charlie stands in the living room of Patsy's dream house, remembering their romantic ecstasy when he first danced with Patsy in the parking lot at the Rainbow Inn. "I'm crazy," Patsy sings on the lush sound track, "crazy for loving you."

I dreamed I was there in Hillbilly Heaven.
> —Hal Southern, Eddie Dean, 1954
> —Tex Ritter, 1961
> —Loretta Lynn, Dolly Parton,
> Tammy Wynette, 1993

Last night I dreamed I went to Hillbilly Heaven.
> —Marty Stuart, 1992

I dreamed I was there in Country Music Heaven.
> —Bill Anderson, 1993

CHAPTER 4   Salvation

Patsy Cline crashed ten years and two months after the death of Hank Williams. Williams's death in 1953, the occasion for an important assembly of country music artists and fans, may have influenced another artist assembly later that same year to honor the memory of Jimmie Rodgers. The deaths of Patsy Cline, Cowboy Copas, Hawkshaw Hawkins and Randy Hughes in 1963 extended and amplified the tradition of memorial assembly by fans and artists in country music culture.

The Tennessee highway patrol escorted the bodies back to Nashville from the crash site. Charlie Dick held Patsy Cline's wake in her dream house, where her gold casket was arranged before the draped picture window in her living room (Nassour 1993, 238). The extended spiritual family of country artists appeared and, Nassour reports, "everyone took on chores."

> Minnie Pearl and Pearl Butler stood watch at the door. Anita Carter
> and Jan Howard went into Madison and bought a Barbie doll for Julie

and toys for Randy. Dottie and Loretta carved ham while Skeeter Davis served potato salad. Del Wood and Mooney Lynn scrambled eggs and bacon. Hank and Shirley Cochran kept the trays full of sandwiches, ham, and chicken. Roger Miller and Ann Tant kept hot biscuits coming. Teddy Wilburn and Wilma Burgess made iced tea. Billy Walker and Owen Bradley filled glasses with ice. Faron Young spiked drinks when asked. (Nassour 1993, 240)

While artists came together in private, fans came together in public. Prayer services were held in a Nashville funeral home on Thursday and Friday. Fan response was reminiscent of that for Hank Williams, with closed streets, loudspeakers, and an avalanche of flowers—615 arrangements (Nassour 1993, 240).

Emotion at Patsy Cline's memorial service deepened when the crowd learned that Opry star Jack Anglin had been killed in an automobile accident on his way to the event. The shock of six country music deaths within a few days was especially dramatic. Ralph Emery recalled rumors about "a jinx on the Opry," yet at the Opry's Saturday night radio performance, the power of tradition prevailed. The first hour was "music, laughs, and pure Opry entertainment." Then "Opry manager Ott Devine began a simple spoken tribute" while "all Opry members on hand gathered onstage." "What do you say when you lose such friends?" Devine asked. "We can reflect on their contributions to us through entertainment, their acts of charity and love. We can think of the pleasure they brought to millions and take some comfort in knowing that they found fulfillment in the time allotted to them. They will never be forgotten" (Nassour 1993, 241). The Opry ended with a standing silent prayer and the Jordanaires—who had backed Cline's most successful recordings—singing "How Great Thou Art," Roy Acuff playing "a rousing fiddle tune of celebration," and Minnie Pearl repressing her grief to transform fan and artist sadness into "a sea of howling laughter" (Nassour 1993, 241–42).

On Sunday afternoon, March 10, 1963, Patsy Cline's funeral and burial were held in Winchester, Virginia. Cline's biographer says the scene was "unmanagable" because so many fans appeared. Estimated to number in the thousands, they blocked streets, stopped traffic, and in general made it impossible for some of Cline's friends to reach the services. Traffic congestion lasted more than two hours and roads to the Shenandoah Memorial Park were blocked for up to a mile from the burial site. At the graveside service souvenirs were taken—flowers, decorations, cards, and the remains of wreaths and decorations. A reporter for the *Winchester Star* grasped the relic significance of these items for fans by quoting an unidentified honorary pallbearer: "It's like a religion with them" (Nassour 1993, 243–44).

The notion of country music stars entering into a heaven that is a perpetual replica of their earthly lives and family relationships, minus the pain of hard times and domestic trauma, has its antecedent in a popular American religion. Traditions of Southern gospel singing among white evangelicals suggest particular ways that images of salvation from personal and domestic tragedy have entered secular country music culture.

In a discussion of Victorian evangelicals, the American church historian Peter W. Williams describes an important refocusing of piety that occurred in the mid-nineteenth century. In addition to the fear of a masculine, wrathful God that had characterized American popular religion descending from Puritan antecedents, in nineteenth-century domestic literature such as *Uncle Tom's Cabin* a new strategy for redeeming sinners can be found. Here, says Williams, "Redemption came about not through the active mastery of the external environment and the aggressive conquest of sin, but through a passive, exemplary role exerted by the saintly." Preaching by the popular evangelist Dwight Moody exemplified this shift. Moody's theology, says Williams, "could be reduced to the proposition that salvation was available for the asking. All the sinner had to do was make a simple decision, symbolized in 'hitting the sawdust trail'" to public demonstration of conviction. The theatrical form of a Dwight Moody revival to which Williams alludes emphasizes the direct personal response of individuals to evangelistic preaching, culminating in the act of walking forward to an area near the evangelist where an emotional demonstration of redemptive love occurs. Moody was especially effective because he spoke to the everyday experiences of converts.

> Instead of theological reflections, Moody's sermons were anecdotal—usually pathetic stories invoking premature death, longing for mother, and a gentle Jesus whose message of redemption was open to all. Judgment was largely gone, and mercy was everything. Sentimentality —the appeal to the heart, even in contradiction to the dictates of the head—had been raised to an ultimate principle.

To emphasize the shift in gender orientation that accompanied this change, Williams adds: "And sentimentality was the province of woman" (Williams 1990, 233).

On March 27, 1992, Brother Norman Livingston sponsored his annual "Norm's Gospel Sing" at Memorial Hall in Dayton, Ohio. Advertised throughout the metropolitan area by posters, radio, television, and newspaper promotion, this event filled about two-thirds of a large auditorium with families, couples, and many women from the evangelical culture of the Miami River Valley—Baptist, Church of God, Church of the Nazarene, Assembly of God, and other groups. Promptly at 7:30 P.M. Brother Norm introduced the event with a long commentary on its religious intention: saving souls. For the next several hours, those present heard both personal-salvation testimony and fervent gospel singing from the Hoskins Family, the Spencers, Tim Livingston, the Singing McKameys, the Singing Cookes, and the Cooke Brothers.

The first song offered by the Hoskins Family, of nearby Franklin, Ohio, was a commentary on life in Heaven from the point of view of the afterlife. "We Wish You Were Here" is a testimonial hook on sending a vacation postcard from Heaven, where there is no more pain, to earth, where there's lots of it. The speaker for this group was Opal Hoskins. She introduced her husband Rick, her daughter Angie, and three other local singers who are part of the group. The display of the Hoskins Family on stage was characteristic of performance strategy by family singing groups in Southern gospel, which features and "frames" the lead female singer. Opal Hoskins stood at center stage, with Rick Hoskins to her right and behind her. Angie Hoskins stood to her left, and the lead guitar, drums and two other guitars were arrayed behind the singers. The stage costume was dresses for women, suits or sport coats with dress shirts and ties for men. The effect is a somewhat formal "dressy" image that centers visually on the woman singer, who is brought slightly forward to carry the message of personal testimony. In the tradition of Moody's sentimental appeal to the heart, here the lead female plays the exemplary role of the saintly figure who relates accounts of worldly experience meant to speak directly to individual members of the audience.

The second group—the Spencers, of Shiloh, Ohio—also presented themselves formally on stage, with one woman singer moved slightly forward and flanked by three men. This group, which has produced number-one songs on Southern gospel hit charts, led gospel-singing tours of the Virgin Islands, and documented their experience in music videos, brought the audience to its feet with "Let's Meet by the River." This song imagines a literal Heaven derived from a reading of the Book of John. It depicts Heaven as a city with walls of jasper, gates of pearl, streets of gold, and a "pure river of life" flowing from God's throne. This is a place "where loved ones live who've gone on before." The dramatic interest in the song is anticipation of a heavenly family reunion. The lead female singer asks her audience to wait for her by the river if they leave earth before she does, and she promises to do the same in return. With plans for a rendezvous intact, later verses make plans to visit Jesus, then Dad and Mother (Spencers 1990). During an extended performance of this song, Barbara Spencer cried profusely, introduced her own mother sitting in the audience, and extended dramatic gratitude to her mother and dad that stimulated many responses of "Amen" from the audience, as well as verbal encouragements to the singers. "We're on the road a lot," she said, "and I feel like I neglect my mother, but the Lord reminds me that if we stay true we'll be together then." In response to this expectation of redemption from the gospel troubadours' life, the audience stood to sing vigorously the chorus of "Let's Meet by the River" three times with the Spencers and one another. This motif of "leading the congregation in testimony" was often repeated throughout the evening by other groups.

The Singing McKameys were introduced by Brother Norm as singers from Clinton, Tennessee, for thirty-five years, who have had four number-one hits. McKameys feature one man and three women. Perhaps to illustrate a higher profile among Southern gospel performers, the women were dressed in long purple crepe dresses with an elaborate bead effect on the left shoulder—clearly tailored for a professional stage show. Again, the accompanying band was discreetly positioned as a backdrop to the quartet. The three women singers stood forward in a line, with the man slightly behind them at all times. Women stepped forward modestly to sing individual solos. Peg McKamey Bean (who in 1993 was chosen Favorite Female Singer for the fifth time by fans in *Singing News* magazine) performed a well-received number, describing a detailed tour of Heaven after the singer's arrival there, naming all the people she meets and highlighting family and friends. The McKameys performed thirteen songs during this appearance. By the midpoint of their show, Peg

McKamey Bean had become extremely animated. She removed her shoes, shook a white handkerchief over her head, and repeatedly generated standing ovations. In the middle of McKameys' finale, "The Rising of the Son," she testified at length about illnesses such as cancer and strokes within her family and the hardship of her mother giving birth to twelve children—ten without assistance of a doctor. "When Jesus comes," she said, "there will be no more cancer and no more heartbreak."

The concluding act prior to intermission at Norm's Gospel Sing was the Singing Cookes. Livingston introduced the Cookes as a lesson in family values: "If you bring up your children right, they'll not depart from you. This family is special." The Singing Cookes consist of a mother and father, three sons, and a granddaughter. The father, Hubert, was a coal miner until he became a full-time singer in 1963. Mother Jeanette, the daughter of a minister, has been a Southern gospel singer since she was eleven. Their sons, known on stage as the Cooke Brothers, are instrumentalists as well as singers, and granddaughter Tami plays keyboard. All the men dress in suits and ties, but the three brothers enliven their decor with snakeskin boots and guitar straps. In this appearance, Hubert wore a purple suit and Jeanette a print dress with red shoes. The Singing Cookes are displayed across stage in the formal manner associated with family gospel singing: Hubert stands slightly behind Jeanette; Jeanette is the central focal point on stage; and instrumentalists and harmony singers are spread across the background. Jeanette's high-pitched soprano voice exudes the charismatic energy of a gospel rouser, and Hubert frequently "talks" behind her in repetition or commentary on lyrics, to stimulate both the singers and the audience.

One of the Cookes' initial songs in this set is a literalistic depiction of the afterlife titled "First Day in Heaven." Again, we see gates of pearl and streets of gold where "all the saints will be singing." Loved ones, their faces "shining with a radiant glow," will be standing as they wait for our arrival. We'll meet Mom and Dad there, Jeanette says; "but best of all, I'll see my Jesus." In a long testimony centered in a video version of this song from 1991, Jeanette Cooke describes Heaven as a place where we will "never have to shed no more tears." She summarizes the strategy of Southern gospel singing—a present communal experience of happiness that anticipates salvation from worldly hardship—in animated conclusion to her testimony as she tells those assembled: "We're not home yet, but we can have a good time here while we're traveling on our way! Praise God, let's be happy tonight! Get your mind up on Jesus! Praise God!" (Singing Cookes 1991).

The Singing Cookes were the finale act for Norm's Gospel Sing. They performed only eleven songs but took extended time with each one, interspersing singing with testimony, crowd encouragement, and an altar call in which members of the audience came forward to demonstrate their faith in Christ's salvation. For Brother Norm and other local ministers attending to those who responded, this was the purpose of the singing. "If we miss this chance," said Livingston to the auditorium, "we'll miss what we're all about." At 11:15 P.M., after extended praying, counseling, and more singing, the Cookes left the stage for intermission. The groups that had appeared moved to the lobby to talk with fans, sign autographs, sell CDs, tapes, pamphlets, and books and to encourage interest in Caribbean cruises and other gospel singing events.

On April 25, 1992, the Singing Cookes held their thirtieth-anniversary concert at Lincoln Memorial University, in Harrogate, Tennessee. Norm Livingston came from Dayton, Ohio, for this event, and his son, Tim Livingston, produced a commercial video of it (Singing Cookes 1992). The Tex Turner Arena, at Lincoln Memorial University, was about a third filled for the event, which featured the Cookes, the Cooke Brothers, and the Redeemed quartet. Brother Norm opened with a prayer in which he took special note of the sound and camera crews. "You may be a Nazarene, Pentecostal or Baptist, but we are Interdenominational," he told the audience. "Let's have church tonight!"

The Singing Cookes came on stage in a display highly similar to their Dayton appearance, with Jeanette front and center, Hubert beside and slightly behind and the Cooke brothers and Tami farther back, playing keyboard, guitar, and drums; an additional guitarist from Nashville sat in. For this anniversary, Jeanette wore a frilly off-white dress and Hubert a purple suit. The Cooke Brothers, the guest guitarist, and Tami all wore conservative dark suits. Green plants and flowers were arrayed on the stage. The audience featured many extended family members who were introduced at various points during the concert. Other audience members appeared to be work-ing- and middle-class people dressed as though for church, with men in sport shirts and ties, dress shirts and suits, or dressy sport shirts and most women in dresses or better-quality sports clothes.

The Cookes played eleven songs, including their current hit, "Just on Time." The song allowed Hubert to testify at length. Two autobiographical songs were the centerpiece of the concert. Hubert's "Mama's Roses" is a nostalgic bluegrass recollection of returning home for his mother's funeral and seeing her roses still growing on a hillside, where, he says, they grow today. Hubert cried throughout this song, and many people in the audience did so as well. Jeanette interrupted Hubert's introduction to introduce her eighty-nine-year-old mother, seated in the front row beside two brothers, a sister, and various nieces and other relatives. "Singing for Jesus" is an autobiographical song that begins with Hubert's coal-mining years. It describes his decision to leave mining and form a singing family that would support itself by going on the road, testifying for Jesus. With the exception of these two autobiographical songs and three that featured the Cooke Brothers and Tami, the remaining six songs all featured Jeanette's crowd-arousing soprano testimonials to the redemptive power of Jesus and Heaven's reward for enduring worldly pain.

This thirtieth-anniversary concert featured an additional event suggestive of links between gospel music and its larger host, country music culture. The Cookes' first set lasted from 7:30 to 9:00 P.M. The Redeemed—three men and one woman—sang for an hour; and at 10:20, after a twenty-minute intermission to reset the stage, Jeanette and Hubert got married again. For this, Hubert wore tails and Jeanette a full wedding dress. A complement of attendants, as well as a lengthy marriage ceremony, concluded with an emotional rendition of Vince Gill's "I Still Believe in You," with Hubert and Jeanette Cooke singing to each other.

In 1989, and in an expanded version in 1993, Randall Balmer published a detailed first-hand account of the workings of evangelical institutions in America—"churches, missions, camp meetings, publishing houses, colleges, seminaries, Christian schools, Bible camps"—that he titled *Mine Eyes Have Seen the Glory* (Balmer 1993). Balmer describes the interior life of an evangelical subculture that, he says, withdrew from the mainstream popular culture following the Scopes trial of 1925 and remained relatively secluded until the middle 1970s. That subculture "promises intimacy with

God, a support community, an unambiguous morality, and answers to the riddles of eternity" (Balmer 1993, 283). Although Balmer takes pains to distinguish among the meanings of *evangelical, fundamentalist, charismatic,* and *pentecostal,* he looks for common ground. "Evangelicals generally believe," he says, "that a spiritual rebirth, a 'born-again' experience (which they derive from John 3) during which one acknowledges personal sinfulness and Christ's atonement, is necessary for salvation." Evangelicals also share an attitude or posture about their beliefs: "In greater or lesser degrees, evangelicals place a great deal of emphasis on spiritual piety." Many American evangelicals have been influenced by John Wesley's experience in London in 1783, when "Wesley felt his heart 'strangely warmed' and saw this as assurance that Christ 'had taken away *my* sins, even *mine,* and saved *me* from the law of sin and death'" (Balmer 1993, xiii–xiv).

The exemplary piety at the heart of evangelical practice in America pervades gospel singing. Demonstrating piety is an important role of gospel singers as they move the faithful to emotional demonstration that accompanies the personal assurance of salvation. In this way, contemporary gospel singing carries out the domestic commitments of Victorian evangelicals by showcasing the role of the saintly person. The sentimentality involved in gospel music's storytelling about life in a literal Heaven that is a victory over worldly hard times links it to the sentimental woman's sphere of nineteenth-century popular culture. So it is that Opal Hoskins, Peg McKamey Bean, and Jeanette Cooke are the focus of their family acts.

On July 26, 1992, the Sumiton (Alabama) Church of God choir conducted services at the Princeton Pike Church of God, in Hamilton, Ohio. On that day, this traveling choir featured sixty-four female singers, twenty-seven male singers, fifteen male musicians, and one male musical director. Among singers, the ratio was more than 2 to 1 female. In addition to male accompanists and director, six male ministers were present. This event had the singular purpose of saving souls and heightening evangelical piety. The congregation appeared to be entirely churchgoers, and the religious content of the service went well beyond public gospel singings in secular venues by including manifestations of spiritual gifts such as glossolalia ("speaking in tongues") spasmodic body movements (as individuals were "struck by the Holy Spirit"), and charismatic praying aloud in groups that formed and re-formed near the front of the church to touch, hug, hold hands and witness to the presence of "holiness." Female members of the choir took the lead in demonstrating piety. While the choir sang lengthy songs, women soloists came forward to testify about salvation and deliverance from such diseases as cancer, ovarian cysts, and heart conditions. The message was clear and unequivocal: Jesus will take you from hard times to Heaven, and you can know it right now.

This is a message within country music culture not confined to evangelical church services and gospel music: direct references to the saving power of Jesus are prolific across all forms of country music. The Grand Ole Opry has featured gospel singing prominently since its earliest days, bluegrass music is heavily devoted to an evangelical vision, one of Hank Williams's signature songs was the testimony to salvation "I Saw the Light," and Williams wrote twenty other gospel songs, for a total of 15 percent of his entire list. Although he had not yet released a recorded gospel number, the Hank Williams devotee Alan Jackson performed one, "Tell Me What Kind of Man Jesus Is," when he appeared in Dayton, April 15, 1993.

In June 1993, The Nashville Network showcased thirty-seven-year-old country singer Mark Collie on its autobiographical feature *Path to Stardom*. A native of Waynesboro, Tennessee, who lists Hank Williams, Jimmie Rodgers, John Lennon, Paul McCartney, Jerry Lee Lewis, Ray Charles, and Elvis Presley as figures he admires, Collie chose to base his life story for TNN fans around his spiritual values. A recognized songwriter responsible for such phrases as "My baby did but now she don't, and if I don't say 'I do,' it's a safe bet that she won't," on TNN Collie said: "I had a difficult time as a young man trying to understand, to resolve what I was doing, because my relationship to God is important to me. It's the most important thing, I think, in the lives of all of us."

Path to Stardom showed Collie as a hometown boy who has made good in an entertainment field that requires a difficult lifestyle for the diabetic that he is. A vivid stage performer who brought the 1993 Fan Fair audience to its feet with rockabilly renditions where he dressed in tight gold pants and wriggled energetically, on TNN, Collie spoke softly of his inner strength: "I believe in a higher power. I believe we all need to be connected spiritually . . . music is a very supernatural thing." At the end of *Path to Stardom*, Collie is shown listening respectfully to Parker White, eighty-eight years young, playing "We Shall See the King Someday" on his dulcimer. They are seated in Russell's Chapel Church, of Waynesboro, where Collie played piano and White had worked since 1932 (Richards and Shestack 1993, 59–60; TNN, 1993).

The spiritual values of country singers who devote most of their efforts to the secular side of the music have been expressed by the country music business in characteristic ways. One of these ways is recording a gospel music album while maintaining a secular career. Johnny Cash is a good example. One of seven children of a sharecropper family in Dyess, Arkansas, Cash was born in 1932. In *The Sound of Light*, Don Cusic tells Cash's life story as a secular and gospel singer (Cusic 1990, 178–79). As a young man, Cash worked in an automobile plant in Detroit, then joined the Air Force. Stationed in Germany, he learned to play guitar and sing country and gospel songs. An appliance salesman in Memphis in 1955, Cash formed "Johnny Cash and the Tennessee Two," a gospel group, and pitched the act to Sam Phillips at Sun Records. Phillips signed Cash as a country artist; and, with the rise of Elvis Presley, Carl Perkins, Jerry Lee Lewis, and Charlie Rich, Cash hit the charts as a rockabilly. Then, in a pattern reminiscent of Hank Williams, Cash spent ten years on pills and personal destruction. Of this time in his life, he said: "There is something important in worshipping together with other believers. And missing it left me vulnerable and easy prey for all the temptations and destructive vices that the backstage of the entertainment world has to offer" (Cusic 1990, 179).

Johnny Cash was saved by the Carter Family. June Carter, daughter of Mother Maybelle and E. J. Carter, took Cash on as a rehabilitation project. "June was never afraid of me," Cash said of her efforts; "and she was serious about the battle she was waging against the pills. 'I'm just trying to help,' she'd say. 'God has His hand on you, and I'm going to try to help you become what you are whether you want me to or not'" (Cusic 1990, 179). June Carter and her parents moved in with Cash and employed a doctor for assistance. In 1968, Cash and June Carter were married, and the following year he was able to perform without drugs. A network television show followed—then Grammy Awards, five CMA awards in 1969, and a public commitment of his life to Christ. Cash's autobiography was titled *Man in Black* and his novel about Jesus' disciple Paul, *Man in White*. Cash's albums include live recordings in prisons, social commentaries about Native Americans, and observations on war. In 1980, he was elected to the Country Music Hall of Fame.

Don Cusic compares Cash's story with a parallel account of Barbara Mandrell's spiritual values. A star of popular culture who has fronted a secular cable television series and has recovered from an automobile accident graphically depicted at her museum in Nashville, Mandrell speaks frankly about her religious faith. She told Don Cusic she was "saved" at the age of ten and grew up a pentecostal, but lacks denominational affiliation, and that her secular appeal is, in fact, related strategically to her spiritual commitment:

> I really feel like if He meant for me to be totally in gospel music, that is where I would be. Because He doesn't pull any punches with me. Besides, I reach so many, many people, and I don't say this in any ugly way—I am just stating fact—that I would never reach if I were not a secular singer. Introducing a gospel song into a secular show has a larger strategy. . . . And then, when I sing the gospel songs, they see something in my eyes that lets them know I mean what I'm singing about. I think that is why they turn to me. I've had kids who have gone back to church, that have gotten over family problems. Do you think they would have tuned into me had I been on a "gospel" music show?

Mandrell states clearly a broad commitment to evangelism that Cusic believes is typical among country entertainers: "You see, I don't record for me. I am a public servant and I record" (in Cusic 1990, 181–82).

Marie Osmond is another popular singer who chooses to emphasize her religious faith to her country music audience. When she performed at the 1993 Jimmie Rodgers Memorial Festival she opened with her secular hit "Meet Me in Montana" (recorded with Dan Seals) but centered her show on a rendition that achieved absolute silence from the fans, followed by a standing ovation: "From God's Arms to My Arms to Yours." This ultimate "family song" expresses gratitude to the biological mother of her adopted children. Osmond concluded with the gospel hymn, "How Great Thou Art," and a sung statement of spiritual conviction: "Let there be peace on earth, and let it begin with me." This show, surely religious, was delivered in a glitzy, Las Vegas pop motif that included an elaborate video celebrating Marie Osmond's twenty years in the music business at the age of thirty-three.

The Grand Ole Opry and the Renfro Valley Barn Dance have established separate gospel music events where secular performers can appear in an entirely religious setting. John Lair's Renfro Valley on Saturday nights featured the "Renfro Valley Sunday Morning Gathering" as its complement. Renfro Valley still sells John Lair's hymnbook, which includes thirty-five gospel favorites, a collection of sentimental poems about religious experiences, and a brief history of hymn-singing in America. In the 1990s, the tradition of a separate gospel program is still alive at the Grand Ole Opry. In 1986, Music City Christian Fellowship, Inc. celebrated the fifth anniversary of its *Sunday Mornin' Country*, a program in the Opryhouse featuring secular country music stars who testify and sing gospel music twice a year—once at the end of Fan Fair in June and once at the end of CMA week and the Grand Ole Opry birthday in October (MCCF 1986, 1990).

A performer featured in 1986 was Lulu Roman, a veteran comic from *Hee Haw*, who testified about overcoming her problems with drugs and sex: "I like to shine for Jesus because I tell you what, He did the greatest thing in my life when he shined his light on me." Tammy Wynette appeared in a medley of updated Carter Family and Hank Williams songs, including "Will the Circle Be Unbroken" and "I Saw the Light." She concluded her set with a solo (accompanied by her husband, George Richey, on piano), a rendition of a song written by her brother-in-law about miracles of Jesus that save people from personal hard times, "The Wonders You Perform." Most *Sunday Mornin' Country* programs conclude with Connie Smith testifying about her personal devotion to Jesus and singing "How Great Thou Art." In 1990, *Sunday Mornin' Country* celebrated its tenth year with a lineup that included Roy Clark, Roy Acuff, Hoyt Axton, Billy Walker, George Hamilton IV, Skeeter Davis, Lulu Roman, Connie Smith, Jack Greene, Paul Richey, Johnny Russell, the Fox Brothers, the *Hee Haw* Gospel Quartet, and Country Corral. For this program, Roy Clark, an entrepreneur of country television comedy, testified that, "behind all the foolishness that I do there is nothing but Jesus." He sang the Red Foley/Elvis Presley favorite, "Peace in the Valley." At the end of Fan Fair 1992, *Sunday Mornin' Country* concluded with an altar call led by the president of Music City Christian Fellowship, the reverend Stu Phillips, who introduced himself as an Episcopalian and a member of the Grand Ole Opry. "The world is a jungle," Phillips told the Opry audience, and

"Jesus said you must be born again." With the thirty-eight-member choir and six-piece band playing "Just as I Am" (a favorite Billy Graham altar call number), Phillips invited everyone to "raise your hands if you want to come to the Lord today." Counselors fanned out to meet individuals who were making a decision for Christ for the first time, and a pledge was read. Phillips concluded by saying, "We hope that you enjoyed what we've offered you and that when you leave this place you will take God's spirit with you."

Then, in a ritual common to spiritual and secular country concerts, performers adjourned to the lobby to mingle with the audience, sign autographs, and sell tapes, CDs, videos, and hats. Forms were available to order Christian-related items or join associated organizations. One of the fan favorites here was Jack Greene. Greene, a former member of Ernest Tubb's Texas Troubadours, became a solo artist in 1966 with a number-one hit written by Dallas Frazier, "There Goes My Everything." In 1967, Greene joined the Grand Ole Opry and in that year was named CMA Male Vocalist of the Year. His hit song—named Song of the Year and Single of the Year and its album, Album of the Year—earned two Grammy nominations (Stambler and Landon 1984, 277–78; Millard 1993, 139).

"There Goes My Everything" is a broken-heart lament of a rejected male whose domestic complaint is, "There goes my reason for living . . . my everything." "This song," Dallas Frazier said, "was inspired by a broken marriage between two friends of mine" (Horstmann 1975, 189). Since first writing this song, Frazier, a recovering alcoholic, has left the music business to become a minister. Before leaving, he rewrote the words to "There Goes My Everything" for a new rendition by Jack Greene, now titled "He Is My Everything." Greene, who often hosts a Saturday night segment of the Grand Ole Opry and sometimes wears a rhinestone lapel pin that spells "Jesus," sings the new gospel version out of his personal conviction as a member of the Music City Christian Fellowship. The words now say, "He is my reason for living . . . my everything" (Greene 1991).

In 1993, Andrew "Ace" Collins published a volume with the Christian book publisher, Vision Press, of Cheyenne, Wyoming, entitled *I Saw Him in Your Eyes*. This coffee-table volume, which comes in a leatherette case and features numerous color pictures, showcases personal testimony of twenty-nine country music figures, including secular hitmakers Reba McEntire, Ricky Van Shelton, Charlie Daniels, Marty Stuart, and Travis Tritt. The book's purpose is unabashedly to convert its readers to evangelical Christianity. Dexter Yeager says in the book's foreword: "Ricky Van Shelton cried out to God from the bottom of his drinking problem. Penny DeHaven whispered, 'God, I don't want to die,' following a childhood of violence and abuse. In story after story the message is clear. God can and will change your life, if you'll let Him!" (Collins 1993, ix–x).

Marty Stuart's testimony in *I Saw Him in Your Eyes* typifies evangelical conviction among country singers. Stuart, who also idolizes the tragic troubadour Hank Williams, shows us another face of this same figure—the tragic troubadour who is meant to be saved. As told here, Stuart's own story began in Philadelphia, Mississippi, where he was raised in singing schools and learned to play the mandolin at age eight. In 1970, he heard the Sullivan Family in concert with Bill Monroe and the Blue Grass Boys at the National Guard Armory in Jackson, Alabama. There, Jerry Sullivan played a number entitled "Born Again Experience," that hooked young Marty on music. "He had a way with it, and he just rocked the crowd. I felt the audience's excitement, and I felt the song's power. He encored the number and I was really blown away!" When he was twelve, Stuart got a job with the Sullivans playing in churches across the South. In less than a year he was invited to play with the bluegrass legend Lester Flatt on the Grand Ole Opry; thereafter, he toured with Johnny Cash, Bob Dylan, Billy Joel, Roger Miller, Willie Nelson, Emmylou Harris, and Randy Travis (Collins 1993, 137–39).

In the late 1980s, Stuart attempted a solo career; but his rockabilly act failed, and he went into a spiral of divorce, alcohol and drugs. At the bottom of this spiral he turned to his mother:

> "When things were at their worst," Marty remembered, "I went to my mama and said, 'Mama, what do I do?' And she said, 'When there is nothing to do on the outside, then there is always plenty of work to do on the inside. Be still, be patient, be quiet, and wait on the Lord. When you get confused where you are, always go back to the beginning and wait on the Lord.'" (Collins 1993, 139)

What Stuart did next was return to his musical roots. He began listening to Sullivan Family records, and miraculously the Sullivan Family invited him to tour with them again. That experience was a restorative spiritual revelation: "I was so full of darkness and misery and hurt and depression and anger and defeat and fear, and yet on the weekend I had so much fun. These people were still wide open, filled with happiness, joy, and peace, and all the other things that the fruit of the Spirit gives you" (Collins 1993, 140). Since that weekend, Stuart has restored his "born-again experience," assisted the Sullivans in gaining a recording contract, made major hit recordings, and achieved top billing as a star among Nashville's "neo-traditionalists" of the 1990s. Like Jack Greene, Barbara Mandrell, Johnny Cash, Mark Collie, and the Music City Christian Fellowship, Marty Stuart is a living link between the gospel and the tragic faces of country music.

The tragic and gospel traditions of country music culture reinforce one another. This perspective is helpful for absorbing the emotional force of one of Dolly Parton's most powerful songs, "Appalachian Memories." Here, Parton, another secular country artist with deep roots in the evangelical tradition, provides an autobiographical account of her family's attempt to move out of Appalachian poverty into a more economically secure life in the North.

When Dolly Parton played the Fraze Pavilion, in Kettering, Ohio, August 1, 1993, she used "Appalachian Memories" as the penultimate number within a four-song set of autobiographical ballads telling her life story. This cluster of songs, occupying approximately 20 percent of her concert of twenty songs, was positioned at the end of its first third. In that location, "Appalachian Memories" was a major production that set a lingering dramatic effect for the remainder of the performance.

Parton introduced the song by telling a story about her father. He was a hardworking farmer who never went to school and couldn't read or write. Told that he could "do better" in Detroit, he was able to stay there only two weeks. Returning home, he said to his family: "Whatever happens, I'm gonna live and die in these mountains." Parton wrote this song out of her own loneliness after first leaving home. "Appalachian Memories" evokes not only God and family but an active sense of the regional past. A ballad about a family leaving Appalachia told from the perspective of their Northern destination, the song is framed at beginning and end with a melancholy flute line supported by long violin strokes that evoke a wistful, nostalgic tone. The tempo of the song builds gradually from slow to moderately slow through two verses, a chorus, then another verse and chorus—all rising gradually to a climactic finale. The beginning features Parton's voice accompanied solely by piano-playing derived from evangelical church services. As the song builds intensity, violins enter to provide fills, then a more insistent sense of tension. The singer says the family was told to go north because there, "fortune falls like snowflakes in your hands." The family "hitched our station wagon to a star," but instead of finding a land of promise, they found life in the North to be "a struggle keepin' sight of who you are." The refrain evokes an image of old folks back home and promises to "keep leaning on sweet Jesus" because, "He'll love and guide and lead us." The family's religious faith and the regional past become one as the last line of the refrain (and of the song) pointedly affirms: "Appalachian memories keep us strong" (Parton 1987).

If Marty Stuart exemplifies a link between gospel and tragic traditions in country music culture, in "Appalachian Memories," Dolly Parton confronts migratory loneliness with gospel salvation, links secular and sacred traditions, and builds the culture's sense of the past. This may be regarded as another response to social traumas of modernization, one that has a parallel in regional religious expression. In a study of Baptist traditions, *Giving Glory to God in Appalachia*, Howard Dorgan concludes that the worship practices of Appalachian evangelicals are, in part, intended to create a usable sense of the past:

> The past is terribly important to these fellowships. Their particular understanding of it has fostered their sense of certainty, of place, of belonging, of heritage, of an ongoing covenant. And the value of this past to them does not diminish with the encroachments of modernity—just the opposite, in fact. (Dorgan 1987, 216)

Perhaps it is logical that gospel music emphasizes singing families as its lead performers, that it frequently emphasizes the saintly testimony of mothers, envisions Heaven as a literal destination where extended families will be reunited, and evokes nostalgic images of the Southern past alongside personal anecdotes of being rescued from illness, drugs, alcohol, and worldly pain. It may be that in addition to its spiritual qualities, salvation in country music culture is partly an antidote to the negative effects of modernity.

Being saved by the evangelist's Jesus is the persistent subject of sacred country music. There is a parallel tradition in secular country music culture that relies on the motif of salvation but replaces the love of Jesus with the love of women. This salvation strategy—good women working tirelessly to save men from the debilitations of domestic turmoil and the tragic troubadour's life—is central to many depictions of country music culture by Hollywood filmmakers and novelists. It's likely, too, that the salvation motif, borrowed from gospel traditions to enhance the power of women's domestic and romantic love, has fueled the growth of the distinctive fan culture associated with country music.

The figure of Hank Williams again looms large in the tradition of salvation by secular love; but this time, it derives less from his actual life than from a popular image of him promulgated in the movies. After Williams died in 1952, an effort was made to refashion his image. "We've made a superhuman effort to build Hank up since his death, and his earnings have been probably ten times what he got in his lifetime," Wesley Rose told Hank's biographer. Seventeen years after his death, Williams was estimated to have 15 million devoted fans (R. Williams 1973, 244). In 1961, the three charter members elected to the Country Music Hall of Fame were Jimmie Rodgers, Hank Williams, and his songwriting partner and agent, Fred Rose. By this time, country music insiders were steeped in the legend of Hank Williams; soon the American public would be reminded of it.

On November 4, 1964, *Your Cheatin' Heart*, a Hollywood movie biography of Hank Williams, premiered at the Paramount Theatre in Montgomery, Alabama (M-G-M 1964). Alabama's Governor George Wallace declared "Hank Williams Week" in Alabama, and Opry stars Roy Acuff, Johnny Cash, and Tex Ritter appeared for a special show at the opening (Koon 1983, 113). Roger M. Williams reported that in just over a decade, *Your Cheatin Heart*, which cost M-G-M $1.2 million to make, had grossed $10 million to become "the most successful country film ever made" (R. Williams 1973, 242). Williams's biographers almost universally condemned the movie version of Hank's life, some citing the casting of George Hamilton IV as Hank and Susan Oliver as Audrey because they regarded these figures as unrealistically pleasant for their roles. Biographers objected to the profound sentimentality in such concocted scenes as Rufus "Tee-Tot" Payne dying in young Hank's arms to open the movie. There were omissions of fact that bear significantly on Hank's life and artistic creativity (Koon 1983,113). Yet, for its viewing audience, this film had undeniable charm; it can still appeal powerfully to college students interested in the vagaries of country music, which, they believe, are important but do not fully understand. The Hank Williams movie appeals to some scholars as well. In a note at the conclusion of his collection of Williams song lyrics, Don Cusic makes a fan's confession:

> Finally, the movie *Your Cheatin' Heart*, starring George Hamilton, should be essential viewing. It is terribly inaccurate and plays loose with the facts, but somehow [it] captures the true spirit and essence of Hank Williams. For me and a number of others, this movie was our introduction into Hank's life, and it holds a dear spot in my heart. Without that movie, I don't believe I would have had such an early, compelling interest in Hank, and perhaps this book would never have emerged as its result. (Cusic 1993, 148)

How does *Your Cheatin' Heart* create a tragic troubadour who manages to transcend his worldly traumas? First, it underplays and sentimentalizes Hank's ambition by portraying him consistently as a down-home good ole boy who is vague and lost in the high-pressure world of commercial success. Much of that pressure is applied by Audrey, who is always talking business, organizing Hank, and thinking of the future. In *Your Cheatin' Heart*, Audrey Williams is well-intentioned, clear-minded, highly organized and "pushy." She proposes marriage to Hank and sends his songs to Fred Rose. She tells Rose that Hank is "natural," not "sophisticated"; Rose responds in appropriate awe during a memorable scene where Hank immediately produces "I Can't Help It (If I'm Still in Love With You)" in response to Rose's challenge to write an original country song.

After Hank and Audrey go to the Louisiana Hayride in Shreveport, they acquire a new child, a new home, and new stage clothing for Hank. Hank's success and the emergence of his family into middle-class consumption make him "edgy." "This ain't a house," he tells Audrey, "it's a warehouse." The night Hank is called to the Grand Ole Opry, he ends up in a bar playing to "my friends, my kind of people." Audrey accuses him of being scared, then proves it—her threat to leave him scares him into making his first Opry appearance even though he's drunk. Drunk or sober, Hank is a hit with the fans; as crowds, travel, and stardom increase, he drinks more. Hank's closest friend in the film, a band member named Shorty, defends Audrey's behavior. "You think she's pushing you? Well, buddy, all I can tell you is all she's doing is pull—pull you outta the gutter!"

The domestic tension between Hank and his wife builds to a climactic scene where they disagree about the rewards of country music stardom. Audrey begins by arguing innocently that "everything I've done, I'm only doing it to better ourselves." In turn, innocent country-boy Hank charges: "That's exactly what's wrong, Miss Biggety of 1952!" One of Audrey's answers to this charge is, "Whoever gave you the idea that it's a sin to be rich?" to which Hank has a prompt rejoinder: "I don't reckon it's a sin. Women shovin' babies at me to touch, cripple people, who do they think I am? A walkin' shrine? I gotta hard enough time tryin' to save myself." With this recognition of his personal agony under the pressures of fan adulation, Hank leaves home. Yet, after a period of drinking and rambling he returns home to find that Audrey has left him, his children are gone, and he's been fired from the Grand Ole Opry.

At this point the movie diverges even more significantly from Williams's actual life, to emphasize his personal salvation. The movie Hank sobers up, spends months off the bottle, and allows Fred Rose to arrange a top billing for him in Lebanon, Ohio, on January 1, 1953. Audrey—who, in the movie, never divorces Hank—reappears to tell him the good news of his return to show business, saying "everything will be so different, everything." This scene concludes with Hank looking out the window of his room and dreaming of stardom again. Yet, in the movie, tragedy inexplicably strikes down Hank Williams. Driving to Ohio in his Cadillac, he stops at a country store where a group of good ole boys invite him to have a social drink. Hank resists firmly but does agree to sing an impromptu "I'm So Lonesome I Could Cry." While singing, he sees through the window an image of his boyhood friend and musical mentor Rufus "Tee-Tot" Payne. The movie then cuts to its final scene in the auditorium of Hank's last no-show in Ohio. While fans wait and fidget, police go into the hall, and with Audrey and Hank's children standing in the wings, Shorty announces to the shocked audience that "some time between six and seven o'clock this morning" Hanks Williams died. "His heart," Shorty says, "just stopped." Then Shorty offers the lesson of Hank Williams's life as a country music star: "He was my friend. He was your friend. He was one of you, a poor boy who never forgot you. He was on this earth twenty-nine years. Now he's gone home." Spontaneously, the audience stands to sing Williams's signature gospel song, "I Saw the Light."

Your Cheatin' Heart is a salvation story. It suggests that country music stars can struggle mightily against worldly temptation and the stress of modernizing lifestyles with a combination of personal grit, the support of a determined spouse and loving friends, and the affection of working class fans from whom the star derives strength and who know they are not forgotten. Even if the struggle fails in this world despite the commitment of a faithful woman, spiritual salvation can still take the star "home" from hard times to heaven. Numerous subsequent movie and literary accounts of male entertainers offer variations on this image of salvation for male country singers. Willie Nelson, in *Honeysuckle Rose* (1980), and George Strait, in *Pure Country* (1993), play country stars saved from personal destruction by strong women.

Honeysuckle Rose, a.k.a. On the Road Again (Warner Bros. 1980) presents Willie Nelson as Buck Bonham, an aging honky-tonk singer whose Texas road life consists of one-nighters in beer joints, alcohol, drugs, adoring fans and casual sex. In the movie, road life is contrasted with farm life. Farm life means a vast network of extended family and friends in a rural setting. Early in the movie, we see the fifty-second Bonham Family Reunion, sponsored by the Future Farmers of America, attracting an entire community to a festive picnic and western swing dance that ends with a group singing of "Amazing Grace."

The movie's broadest dramatic tension centers on the contrast of road life with this domestic scene. Buck's wife, Viv Bonham (played by Dyan Cannon), challenges him about his devotion to family as he prepares to tour again: "You make all your efforts for strangers—people who don't even know you—none for us. You treat Jamie and me like we were an audience." Buck's response is characteristic of the road musician: "Well, you know I can't quit."

On the road again with Lily, a replacement guitar player who is the twenty-two-year-old daughter of Buck's best musician friend, Buck discovers that Lily is a fan who wants him to love her. "I've gone to bed with a song of yours every night since I was nine years old," she tells him. "I've always been scared that you'd get old before I grew up." Late at night, after a 1:00 A.M. closing and while smoking marijuana together, Buck and his friend's daughter begin a love affair that soon has them singing romantic duets on stage. Toward the end of the tour, Buck's wife appears during a live performance in Amarillo and, observing the lovers' sexual performance of "You Show Me Your Tongue and I'll Show You Mine," takes the stage unannounced to tell the fans: "I just wanted to surprise my husband, and say we've been together about fifteen years, and tonight I just want to announce our divorce. Isn't that the kind of thing that country songs are all about?" This challenge precipitates a variety of smaller crises—and their resolutions. Lily decides that too many people have been hurt by their affair and tells Buck, "It's gotta be wrong." She returns home to apologize to her father, who forgives her. Lily's father follows Buck to Mexico. After a drunken confrontation featuring tequila, a pistol shot, and a brawl, the two old friends make up. We see Lily apologize to Buck's wife, and Buck decide that he still loves his wife and wants to go home. The pair's final reconciliation—like the illicit courtship and the divorce declaration—occurs on stage during a public performance. Buck's wife is singing at another large family picnic when he appears behind her unannounced, steps to the mike, and in a solo apology accompanied only by acoustic guitar, offers "Singing My Song For You." At this, family members signal a communal reconciliation with their smiles, and the assembly of country fans applauds. The film ends with an image of spiritual salvation that amplifies the earthly romantic one, as Buck and Viv join together to lead the crowd in a joyous rendition of the evangelical gospel song "Unclouded Day." The last action is their kiss, and the wild approval of their fans.

Pure Country offers George Strait in a Hollywood movie about the salvation of artistic sincerity and the broken faith of fans (Warner Bros. 1992). Strait plays Dusty Wyatt Chandler, a contemporary hit-maker with an elaborately produced stage show featuring smoke, explosions, a light curtain, sparklers and fireworks. Dusty wears a ponytail, a scruffy beard, a glittering rhinestone jacket and a white hat. He travels with two buses and two transfer trucks. He gives publicity interviews and is a regular figure on The Nashville Network. But Dusty is unhappy. He complains to his female manager that he is tired of the sets, the lights, the smoke, and the loud music—the fans "can't see or hear me," he says. Dusty is so unhappy, in fact, that one night after a big show, he walks out, hitches a ride with a truck driver, and becomes a no-show for his next performance.

Dusty uses his disappearance to return to his roots. He visits Grandma Ivy Chandler, who has saved his original acoustic guitar. He asks how she likes "no smoke, no lights, no amplifiers, no big stage production. Just me and my guitar. You think anybody'd buy that?" "I would," says Grandma. That evening, Dusty goes to the Prairie Bar, a nightclub in rural Texas where he played when he was in high school. While drinking beer and reminiscing, he meets the wholesome daughter of a local rancher. Harley Tucker fails to recognize the famous Dusty, perhaps because he has a fresh haircut and is clean-shaven. In a drunken attempt to defend Harley from the advances of an aggressive boyfriend, Dusty is knocked to the ground. Harley takes him home, where he hangs out, learning rodeo roping and assisting in ranch chores. Soon, Harley and Dusty are in love and Dusty composes a new song with his acoustic guitar, "The King of Broken Hearts."

While Dusty is rediscovering his roots and talent and discovering his love for a woman, his famous stage show goes on without him. His manager arranges a performance so laden with smoke and lights that a member of Dusty's road crew can stand in while lip syncing an entire Dusty concert tape—and the event gets a positive review in the press! Then Dusty's manager finds him, breaks Harley's trust by telling her (falsely) that Dusty is married, and brings Dusty back to his show. Dusty has changed, however. In a recommitment to personal sincerity, he declares: "While I was gone I remembered I could still play the guitar, and I can sing, and I remembered I used to enjoy it. And I'm good at it, so that's what I'm gonna do. I'm gonna play the guitar and sing. No more smoke, no more volcano blasts, no more light shows." But now a TNN reporter has discovered the fake concert and is asking questions on national television. Dusty's new resolution is in crisis—he must restore not only the trust of Harley Tucker, but also the trust of his fans.

It seems that in country music movies, such character dilemmas are resolved by a public performance. Dusty's Las Vegas appearance at the Mirage Hotel allows him the chance to assemble not only his fans but also Harley's entire family and his own personal entourage. To illustrate his renewed authenticity, Dusty brings Grandma Ivy to see the show. And, this time, Dusty appears on stage in simple jeans, a black cowboy hat, and a western shirt with no rhinestones and with his acoustic guitar. Under a single spotlight he invites his fans to indulge him while he does "something different." He then walks to the edge of the stage and pledges his sincere devotion in a new song directed to Harley, "I Cross My Heart." Grandma smiles, Harley's family smiles, Dusty's manager smiles; Dusty's fans erupt in a standing ovation, and Harley cries. Finally, when the song is over, the lovers embrace. With the help of his grandma and his new love, this troubadour has been saved from the compounded tragedies of domestic turmoil and personal insincerity.

Recent novels about male tragic troubadours in country music culture may be read as variations on the salvation theme. The *Lost Get-Back Boogie*, by James Lee Burke, gives us the life and times of Iry Paret, paroled in 1963 from Louisiana's Angola prison farm after serving more than two years for killing a man in a nightclub brawl. Iry worships both country music and the blues. Shortly after his parole, he's again playing in nightclubs and conceptualizing his act as a tragic troubadour:

> My first night I played and sang six Hank Williams songs in a row, then went into "Poison Love" by Johnny and Jack and "Detour" and "I'll Sail My Ship Along [sic]," and the place went wild. . . . Oil-field roughnecks with tin hats and beery faces and drilling mud on their clothes looked up at me with moist, serious eyes when I sang "The Lost Highway." I was good at imitating Hank Williams, and I can make the dobro sound just like the steel that he had used behind him. (Burke 1986, 38)

Despite the reception of his act, Iry is not happy in Louisiana. Haunted by alcohol, pills, and memories of war in Vietnam, Iry manages to transfer his parole to Montana, where he can live with Buddy Riordan, a friend from prison days, who is also a jazz pianist with an elaborate drug habit. In Montana, Iry and Riordan fall into an endless round of drugs, bar fights, and country music. Caught in a battle between Buddy's conservationist father and loggers who fear for their jobs, Iry's truck is burned and his Dobro destroyed. Furious, he retaliates by shooting up the local pulp mill with a rifle. And in the midst of this political violence, Iry precipitates domestic turmoil by making love with Buddy's estranged wife Beth.

Violence escalates when Buddy's father and an environmental action group get a court injunction shutting down every pulp mill in western Montana. Loggers attack the Riordan ranch and Buddy's father suffers a stroke. Lost in a drunken rage, Buddy is killed in a flaming truck accident. By the time Riordan leaves the hospital (with permanent partial paralysis), the injunction has been lifted and the pulp mills are working again. Yet, despite these cycles of political violence and personal destruction, Burke's novel resolves positively for Iry Paret, country musician. Iry marries Beth, settles down on twenty acres of land in a canyon near the mountains where there are apple trees and a small stream, builds a log house with a stone fireplace, and enjoys the view. More important, he writes a song for the first time in years and drives to Vancouver with Beth, where he records the song for West Coast release. Within two months, Nashville calls, asking for more songs. At its close, *The Lost Get-Back Boogie* dissolves in images of domestic harmony, visions of the changing seasons in the mountain west, and Iry's memories of Buddy at home in his cabin.

Burke's story is an attempt to melt the tumultuous experience of working-class violence into a mythic vision of country music as part of an American agrarian dream. Buddy had wanted Iry to play jazz, yet, for almost spiritual reasons, Iry refuses. Speaking of Buddy, Iry explains:

> But what he didn't understand, and what most northerners don't, is that rural southern music is an attitude, a withdrawal into myths and an early agrarian dream about the promise of the new republic. And regardless of its vague quality, its false sense of romance, its restructuring of the reality of our history, it is nevertheless as true to a young boy in southern Louisiana listening to the Grand Ole Opry or the Louisiana Hayride on Saturday night as his grandfather's story, which the grandfather had heard from *his* father, about the Federals burning the courthouse in New Iberia and pulling the bonnets off white women and carrying them on their bayonets. It was true because the boy had been told it was, and he would have no more questioned the veracity of the story than he would have the fact of his birth. (Burke 1986, 166)

In *The Lost Get-Back Boogie*, the imagination of country music through its barn dance traditions becomes a form of agrarian repose that can save tragic troubadours. And after all their hard times, Iry Paret and his new woman are living in it.

Thomas Cobb's novel, *Crazy Heart* (1987), is a detailed account of several months in the life of Bad Blake, a Texas honky-tonk singer who is fifty-six, the veteran of four wives, a heavy smoker with a heart condition, and a serious alcoholic whose decline from previous good fortune leaves his Nudie stage shirt with rotting threads and dripping beads. Bad Blake has learned only two things as a musician—"keep your wrist steady, and don't ever marry nobody" (Cobb 1987, 10). The cover photograph for *Crazy Heart*, an apt visual representation of this message, makes an appropriate contrast to the cover for *The Lost Get-Back Boogie*. For Cobb's novel, a single troubadour stands alone before a blank white background. He is dressed in cowboy boots, western stage shirt, and white cowboy hat and is holding an electric guitar in playing position. His head is bowed so that his face is entirely obscured by the hat—playing hands are the only visible parts of his body. Slightly to the musician's left, and behind him, stands the single prop—a half-filled whiskey bottle. In contrast to this lonesome image of existential individualism, the cover for James Lee Burke's novel offers a rich Montana landscape with a domesticated ranch blending into rising mountains. Beyond the mountains, and merging with them, is a vast sky with billowing white clouds. In the foreground, in rustic rural work clothes with his back to the camera, is a relaxed figure on horseback who is observing this pastoral scene. And, blended into the gentle rise of the mountains, in a middle ground between their distant peaks and the wooden farmhouse in front, is an acoustic guitar—on its side, half visible, an integrated feature of the landscape, its contours extending the gentle visual wave of the mountain range. This contrasting symbolism of agrarian harmony for *The Lost Get-Back Boogie* and existential individualism for *Crazy Heart* is consistent with Cobb's use of the salvation theme. *Crazy Heart* is a story of numerous salvation attempts aimed at creating domestic harmony out of domestic turmoil. They all fail.

We first see Bad Blake in his honky-tonk environment, a bowling alley in Pueblo, Colorado, where he is on tour essentially for room and meals—his agent allows no cash advance and no bar tab. Bad is a veteran of ten albums and a number-one hit, "Slow Boat," that topped country charts for nine weeks. Now deep into middle age, suffering from hemorrhoids, high blood pressure, heart arrhythmia, and chest congestion, he has also lost his recording contract to a younger player who, years earlier, he brought into the business. Bad Blake can still play his music, and his aging fans still love him; but he is miserable. In Pueblo, Bad plays such Hank Williams hits as "Cold, Cold Heart" and "Crazy Arms," and he can still pick up an aging waitress for a one-night stand. But he drinks too much of the whiskey given to him by a fan, and, sweating profusely, interrupts his stage performance to throw up in an alley behind the bar. Later, he cannot sleep. Stumbling around on stage this evening, Bad falls on his amplifier. Looking up, "all he can see is a red amplifier light, pulsing in the dark like the neon red heart of Jesus" (Cobb 1987, 15).

In Las Vegas, New Mexico, Bad discovers that a former member of his road band, Bad's Boys, has retired there to run a construction business, and is raising a family. He brings his grandson to see Bad play. At this encounter with family life, Bad seems wistful about his own stubborn commitment to the road. Then he encounters Jean Craddock, a divorced newspaper reporter in her midthirties. Jean wants to interview him. Attracted to Jean for something more than a one-night stand, Bad spills his life story.

A self-taught player who learned to read music and make guitar chords with the help of an old woman at a church in Judah, Indiana, Bad grew up a Southern Baptist in a family where the father worked in a limestone quarry. He left home at seventeen to play with the Kentucky Bluebirds on WHM radio in Louisville, a radio band that sold auto batteries and once opened for Hank Williams—who gave Bad a drink of bourbon from his own bottle. Jean is captivated by this story and fascinated by Bad's personality; they make love.

Bad taught himself to play by imitating the Carter Family's gospel song, "Can the Circle Be Unbroken," and he has had nightmares about once going to church drunk. Instead of stepping forward at the altar call, Bad ran out the church door and vomited in the bushes. Vaguely troubled about his spirituality, Bad is also troubled about the loss of authenticity in country music. He tells Jean that many real country singers, like Hank Williams, Lefty Frizzell, and Hank Thompson, are dead. On his way to Phoenix, where he is to open for his former side man who is now a star, Bad stops for a drink at a bar outside Tucson, where he tells a bar girl to leave him alone, because "I'm a dead man" (Cobb 1987, 58, 73, 87).

In Tucson, the show at Veteran's Memorial Coliseum goes well, but Bad refuses friendly overtures from his former band member. As Bad leaves town in his aging van, the effects of relentless travel, his heart condition, two packs of cigarettes a day, thirty pounds of obesity, and his alcoholism catch up with him. He falls asleep while driving, hits a tree, and breaks his leg. Bad's recuperation is an opportunity to seek a better life. He takes the initiative in finding his grown son from an earlier wife, now dead, whom Bad thinks he truly loved. Encouraged by Jean, he makes a trip to California to visit this son; but there is no reconciliation. Back home in Houston, Bad invites Jean to visit and bring along her young son, who has made a quick friendship with Bad. Bad is excited and moved to domesticity. He cleans his apartment and cooks; when Jean and her son arrive, he gives them a tour of the city. Bad and Jean make love exhaustingly. She considers moving to Houston, and Bad finds a new level of promise: "Bad cannot remember the last time he woke like this—completely happy" (Cobb 1987, 219).

Bad's most energetic efforts to make a family and be saved from the debilitating troubadour's life are destined to fail. While Jean is interviewing for a newspaper job, Bad takes her son to an underground mall. Bad stops for a drink in a bar, and the energetic boy runs away. Lost for hours, when finally found, the boy is hysterical. Bad apologizes profusely to Jean, proclaims his love for her son, and calls the incident an "accident." Jean's response is a profane evaluation of her own attempt to rescue this honky-tonk singer:

> Oh I believe you feel bad. I believe that. I might even believe you love him, but I know you love your damned bottle more. You had to stop for a drink. Don't you see? You had to stop. You didn't think about him. You had to have that damned drink, or three drinks or four drinks, however many it was. It's not your fault. I know that. It's my fault. You can't help it. I'm a goddamned idiot. (Cobb 1987, 229)

Bad seems to realize that he is now in trouble and tries to make amends by joining Alcoholics Anonymous and enrolling in a detoxification program. Initial results are good. He is able to do an entire show sober, and he signs a new record deal.

At this point, Thomas Cobb's novel exploring the existential quandaries of a tragic troubadour could move in either of two directions and still remain a faithful depiction of country music culture—toward salvation, as in the lives of Johnny Cash and other similar figures for whom Blake is a partial representation, or toward destruction, the heritage of Hank Williams. Cobb elects the latter. Believing that he is well on the mend, Bad Blake ventures a phone call to Jean, asking if she can ever forgive him. She does, but refuses the piety of a nurturing, supportive woman by adding, "but that's not really the point, is it?" Bad is puzzled. "I mean it was all a mistake, my coming there," Jean says. "I knew it before I came. I'm sorry about all of it." Then she hangs up (Cobb 1987, 241). This flat rejection by the woman he loves is followed immediately by a confrontation with Bad's AA counselor. "You have to turn to God," the counselor tells him. "He didn't make you an alcoholic, you did that yourself. But He can get you free. You have to ask Him for help, and He will" (Cobb 1987, 242). Bad refuses.

In the novel's final scene, Bad is back on the road, this time with a woman of indeterminate age who wears heavy makeup and smokes provocatively. When Bad tells her who he is, she responds: "The hell. He's dead." The novel ends in a fog of alcohol and reminiscence about better years in the music business. Driving north on Highway 59, somewhere in north Texas or Arkansas, the van breaks down, the woman falls asleep, and Bad, staggering drunk, stumbles and slides to the bottom of a deep muddy ditch, managing still to keep a grip on his bottle of whiskey. The last word of *Crazy Heart* is appropriately profane. Taking a long pull on his bottle, Bad Blake calls himself by his real name: "'Otis,' he says, 'goddamn'" (Cobb 1987, 248).

If *Honeysuckle Rose, Pure Country,* and *The Lost Get-Back Boogie* endorse the possibility of redeeming male tragic troubadours through romantic love, and *Crazy Heart* opts for the denial of salvation on similar terms, the movies *Honkytonk Man* and *Tender Mercies* also take on the theme of saving tragic troubadours; and both affirm the possibility of it. *Honkytonk Man* (Warner Bros. 1982) suggests that the inspired performance of country music is itself a saving force. *Tender Mercies* (Universal Pictures 1983), by combining the love of music, the love of a devoted woman and her son, and the tradition of gospel evangelism to save an aging and alcoholic country singer, provides the most elaborate country music salvation story in the movies.

Honkytonk Man reaches further back into country music's past by drawing on the legend of Jimmie Rodgers. The setting is the Oklahoma Dust Bowl during the Great Depression. Red Stovall, itinerant singer and songwriter, has finally received an invitation to try out for the Grand Ole Opry. We first meet Red when he crashes (literally) into the front yard of his sister's farm home, "dead drunk" and passed out at the wheel of his fancy automobile. Red invites his sister's boy, Whit, to help him drive to Nashville. While most of the movie is about their travel adventures, family devotion is its central theme. For example, against her inclination, Whit's mother lets her thirteen-year-old son head for Nashville with her alcoholic brother because she knows that Red has an illness and she thinks Whit can take care of him. Whit's grandfather, who wants to die back home in Tennessee after coming to Oklahoma in a nineteenth-century land rush, accompanies them. As the three generations head east to Nashville, we see Red sing in local cafes where he passes the hat, play barrel-house piano in a whorehouse where he introduces Whit to ladies of the evening, enlist Whit's aid in stealing chickens to make pocket money, fake an armed robbery to collect an old debt from a bar owner of questionable reputation, and at one point even stage a local jail break. Whit, played by Kyle Eastwood, is devoted to his uncle Red, who is played by Kyle's father, Clint Eastwood. Along the road, they collaborate in writing a country song featuring the nurturing refrain, "Put your arms 'round this honkytonk man."

By the time this entourage makes it to Beale Street in Memphis, we know that Red has tuberculosis. Red and Whit have begun to talk about the larger meanings of life, Red telling Whit that he once loved a woman in California who was a migrant worker and married with two kids. For two years they were together, then they split up. "What the hell did I have to offer her?" Red explains. "Just honky-tonks and flophouses. That's the life of a country singer. Sound good to you?" Whit answers out of his own experience. "Don't sound so good when you put it like that, but it sure beats picking cotton and living in a sharecropper's shack." Red's response endorses the music business as a route to economic salvation: "Maybe you're right, boy. Maybe you're right. Maybe if I get this break on the Opry we won't have to stay in any flophouses or sharecropper shacks." The stage is set for Stovall's moment at the Grand Ole Opry.

Red sings "Honkytonk Man" at his audition and sings it well; but, before he can finish, he begins coughing uncontrollably. The Opry doctor prescribes hospitalization, but instead Red accepts a recording deal offered by a New York promoter. It will pay him $100 in advance plus $20 a side for his songs, with no royalties. Whit is worried, but the recording scout explains, "He's gonna die anyway and he knows this is his last chance to be somebody. If he makes these recordings, who knows?" Now the movie's quest for economic security has been replaced by a quest for musical immortality.

The last scenes of *Honkytonk Man* are a direct allusion to Jimmie Rodgers's last recording sessions in New York City. Red records for three days; and, like Rodgers, he has to rest between takes. Each night he grows worse, finally requiring oxygen to sleep. But each day he records with heroic determination and, with the help of a side man (played by country star Marty Robbins), finally records all his songs, including "Honkytonk Man," which in this setting reverberates with characteristic Jimmie Rodgers pathos. Then he dies. As early as Red's funeral, we already hear his songs being played on the radio—a musical triumph over physical frailty. One thing more. Despite his tragic-troubadour existence on the margins of the law, Red produces music that comes from a sound heart. His dying words go out to the woman he left behind for her own good: "Mary, my rawboned Okie girl, I love you."

Hollywood creations of domestic romance, country music salvation movies are also in debt to evangelical traditions. This is plainest in *Tender Mercies*. The significant action of the movie occurs at or near the Mariposa Motel, a cheap lodging and service station set in a stark, almost treeless landscape of commercial agriculture, truck-stops, impersonal superhighways, roadside joints, and small towns that is rural post-Vietnam Texas. As the story unfolds in this un-welcoming environment, the broad connotations of rootlessness, alienation from family and home, and a continuing search for endur-ing values are suggested.

Mac Sledge comes to this place broke and hung over from an alcoholic binge. He has been a regional star of honky-tonk music, well known as both a singer and songwriter. He has been twice married and divorced. His second wife, a country star who has be-come wealthy singing his songs, divorced Mac for domestic cruelty. He admits having once tried to kill her but remembers that event only as a drunken haze. Mac has lost his entire family—his former wife will not let him see his teenage daughter.

Out of luck and out of money, Mac offers to work off his bill at the Mariposa Motel, and the owner, Rosa Lee, readily agrees. Rosa Lee has her own story of hard times and a broken heart. She was married at sixteen, a mother at seventeen, and a widow at eighteen when her twenty-eight-year-old husband died in Vietnam. No one, not even the U.S. Army, knew how he died; but Rosa Lee has faith that he was a "good boy." Now she is devoutly religious, thanks God daily for His "tender mercies," raises Sonny, and sings in the local Baptist choir. Rosa Lee seems attracted to Mac's personal sincerity, his open-ness, and, perhaps most important, his effort to give up alcohol. After a time, Mac stops drinking, does chores around the motel, even works in Rosa Lee's garden. Making the most of the circum-stances that brought them together, Rosa Lee and Mac marry.

Tender Mercies proceeds, however, through a series of events that test Mac's recovery and marriage. On the surface, Mac has given up his life as a musician; few in the area know that he was a well-known country star. But, when a newspaper reporter finds Mac and tells him that his former wife is singing at a nearby music palace, we learn that Mac is still committed to his music. He has been writing songs and now makes the trip to the show, partly in the hope of seeing his daughter and partly to sell a song. Mac fails on both counts, and a sharp exchange erupts with his former wife. This is the first severe challenge to Mac's recovery; but, after a night of driving aimlessly in his pickup truck, buying a bottle and then pouring it out, he decides not to leave his new home and family. We learn what Mac has been writing as he sings to his new wife: "Baby, you're the only dream I've ever had that's come true." Mac admits that the lure of the music business still attracts him, but in his new commitment to domesticity he avoids publicity and stardom. Mac turns down a cash offer to have his songs recorded in Nashville, instead choosing to write and perform for a local band of five young men who need his help in making enough money to support their families.

By pursuing more lasting personal relationships than country music stardom seems to offer, Mac Sledge has begun showing affinities for his wife's religious values. He agrees to be baptized along with his new son. Now, however, a new crisis appears. His lost teenage daughter pays him a surprise visit, then runs away from her mother to marry a vagabond, alcoholic musician. When she's killed in a car wreck at some nameless place in Louisiana, Mac's new faith in the possibility of personal happiness is shaken. He reflects on his own earlier escape from just such an automobile accident and puzzles over the nature of justice. He has never trusted happiness, he says, and never will.

Mac underestimates the power of a woman's dedicated, unquestioning love—combined with a son's devoted acceptance—to provide him what he needs. Early in the movie, Sonny expressed curiosity about how his father died, whether Mac ever knew his father, and what kind of man his father was. As the movie progresses, Sonny and Mac become closer. Mac teaches Sonny guitar chords, and Sonny increasingly takes an interest in Mac's happiness. When Mac joins the local band at the Cedar Creek Plowboys Club to sing, "If You'll Hold the Ladder (I'll Climb to the Top)," Sonny watches Mac's personal triumph with pride and satisfaction. Rewarded with vigorous fan applause, Mac, Rosa Lee, and Sonny smile over their soft drinks in a vision of family and community harmony. Rosa Lee has already told Mac, "I love you, you know. And every night when I say my prayers and I thank the Lord for His blessings and His tender mercies to me, you and Sonny head the list."

Mac prays to know why he lived and his daughter died, why his new wife took pity on him and helped him straighten out, why Sonny's daddy died in the war. He gets no direct answers, yet the movie ends with an image of domesticity transcending such questions. Mac and Sonny are tossing a new football that Mac has bought him, Rosa Lee is watching quietly from the door of the motel, the buildings are in good order, and the soundtrack is playing a new song from the pen of Mac Sledge: "You're the good things I threw away, coming back to me every day." The devotion of a religious woman, the personal discipline to resist alcohol, the love of a child, and the support of a community of fans have saved Mac Sledge, country singer.

The salvation motif in country music culture is not confined to evangelical gospel singing, the personal testimony of individual stars, accounts of musicians' life experiences in novels, or Hollywood movies. It has also been used to construct public images of entire careers. *Living Proof: The Hank Williams, Jr. Story*, a 1982 television movie made from the 1979 biography of Hank's son, is a good example (Telecom Entertainment 1982). In this account, from the time he was eight, Hank Junior's mother, Audrey, had him on stage singing his father's songs. The movie opens with the teenager whose act imitates his father—he even wears his father's stage costume. This time Audrey is domineering: "When I married his daddy, Hank Williams was nobody's nothin'. I made him into the greatest country star ever. And I'm gonna do it for Hank, Jr. too." Young Hank is restive at singing only his father's songs. After several confrontations with his mother, he announces his engagement to a local teenager and moves out, taking his guns with him. Audrey warns, "You just remember what happened to your daddy when we split up! He went straight to the bottle without me and so will you!"

Hank Junior's conflict with his mother initiates a pattern of domestic turmoil. On the road his taste for alcohol, women, fraternizing with fans and even fighting with members of his band destroys his engagement. When his fiancee finds him with another woman and says that he needs "someone to make you a home," he retorts: "My home is on a tour bus. That's where I make my livin'. I got a lotta growin' up to do." His estranged fiancée doubts this. "You're just growing mean, and I don't want to be around it."

Hank Junior does stay on the road, but he also marries his new lover and buys a big house in Nashville. True to family tradition, this turns out to be a trap. His new wife, a redhead like Audrey who also seems to live for the accolades of show business and the indulgence of buying clothes, nags him. She wants him to record his father's music so that he will earn more money. "I don't see what's wrong with doin' what's successful," she says. "You know what works, Hank. I just don't see why you wanna fight it." Hank Junior responds with more drinking, drugs, extensive partying, and domestic violence. After beating his wife and appearing on stage so drunk that fans boo him, he ends up in a hospital having his stomach pumped. His wife divorces him.

At this point, the son of country music's most famous tragic troubadour, rejected by his mother and his wife, meets a new kind of woman—a nurturing, stable one who listens to his inner turmoil. "You don't have to listen to much country music to hear my old man's songs," he tells her. "That sucker casts a long shadow. I'm the living proof of that." Becky's response is direct but supportive: "Stop feeling sorry for yourself. Drop all that cowboy bravado." Now Hank admits that he fears giving up the "gimmick" of his father's music in favor of finding his own voice, but Becky reassures him.

In the afterglow of this newfound support, Hank Junior goes mountain-climbing in Montana where he hopes to recover from the stress of life on the road. But hard luck strikes when he falls from a mountainside. His life is saved only because his face "cushioned the fall." In a long, complicated recuperation—which leaves him wearing sunglasses, a full beard, and a large cowboy hat to hide scars—the singer grows sullen and reclusive, swearing that he wants nothing more to do with women or music. Again, the stalwart Becky has a different idea. "I can stand to look at you," she says, "I can't stand you shutting me out. Please don't be so afraid. What do you think I am?" Her unearned love is redemptive. Saved from his own worst nature, Hank replies, "I think you're beautiful."

At the end of the film there occurs a scene typical of country music movies: the country star on stage, an adoring spouse smiling in the wings, and rejoicing fans delivering a standing ovation. "If Heaven ain't a lot like Dixie," Hank Junior sings, "I don't want to go." When Hank Junior found his own voice, he found a strident regionalism that could compare the South to Heaven. By the late 1980s, he could sing such regionalist anthems as "If the South Woulda Won." Yet, he continued to sing his father's songs, and compositions of his own that elaborate on his father's tragic-troubadour legend.

Hank Williams, Jr. was named Country Music Association Entertainer of the Year in 1987 and again in 1988. By the early 1990s, he followed in his father's footsteps to become an icon of American popular culture. He was singing the theme song for *Monday Night Football* on national television; and, in 1992, he headlined a major national tour, the "Budweiser Rock 'N Country" show. His act appeared at the Irvin J. Nutter Center, of Wright State University, in Dayton, Ohio, on April 12, 1992, and at Ray Stadium in Meridian, Mississippi for the Jimmie Rodgers Memorial Festival, on May 30, 1992. At each show, he performed twenty songs and in each, 25 percent celebrated the consumption of alcohol or drugs. Each show included a song that has become a Budweiser commercial in an era of computerized communication, "Please Fax Me a Beer." Each concert emphasized the loud, growling blues tone that is the current signature of Hank Junior's live performances. With time, his early estrangement from his father's image has apparently healed; he talks about his "daddy" on stage as a pioneer of rock and roll. He proudly explains that Hank Senior's music was descended from black blues taught to him by Rufus "Tee-Tot" Payne. And he repeatedly provokes his audience to rowdy behavior.

Many fans attending the Dayton concert displayed a working-class "country tough" style. There were numerous college and high school students, and lots of "farm kids" on dates. Standard dress was cowboy hats, jeans and T-shirts from previous Hank Junior concerts, along with belts, hatbands, vests, and fringe in black leather. There was a higher percentage of men than is usual for country music concerts—probably 50 percent of the audience. The average age appeared to be youngish, in the eighteen-to-twenty-year-old range. These were exuberant fans. They danced in the aisles to recorded warm-up music before the concert began, and throughout the concert, they danced in arena seats and aisles (that incline toward the arena floor at a steep angle). Fans repeatedly shouted, waved, tossed off rebel yells, talked and sang loudly. Lots of beer was consumed. Both men and women smoked in the audience (against arena rules). The business of selling T-shirts—especially ones that pictured Hank in various menacing poses—was brisk. The sales booth in Meridian, Mississippi, sold a "Maverick" shirt for $25, "Hotel Whiskey" shirts for $20, a rebel flag for $20, a Budweiser tour shirt for $20, a poster for $12, caps for $10, a rebel bandanna for $5, and Hank's picture for $2. Panties for women were available for $7, with a hand-lettered sign offering the service "Fitted Free."

A Hank Junior concert is a memorable cultural event. More than any other contemporary country concert setting, it luxuriates in a tone of relentless aggression. Acknowledging his interest in "hard" rock music, amplification is massive, feedback common, and distortion of both sustained guitar tones and song lyrics is the rule rather than the exception. Williams is an accomplished musician who plays keyboard, fiddle, and harmonica as well as guitar on stage. Yet, in some respects, the music is secondary, as the drift of the event seems to be intensive bonding around a popular culture of defiance. Rebel imagery is one indicator of this. Another is a sign that appeared prominently at all entrances to each concert. It warned: "No cans, bottles, or containers. No cameras or video. No weapons." To underline that point, police with metal detectors frisked everyone at the door in Dayton.

Yet the most important bonding agent remains the famous son and his fans remembering his father—the troubadour who, in popular legend, ignored propriety to do things his own way. The son promotes such defiance in many songs, from the aggressive lyrics of "A Country Boy Can Survive" (where Hank warns a New York City mugger who's killed his friend that he'd like to spit tobacco in his eye and shoot him with his .45), to the softer defiance of "Family Tradition." In this anthem that celebrates being his father's son, Hank Junior answers the question, "Why do you live out the songs that you wrote?" "Put yourself in my position," he says. "If I get stoned and sing all night long, it's a family tradition." On a chilly night in early spring, as fans poured out of a packed arena in Dayton, Ohio at 11:20 P.M., following an evening of screaming, waving, dancing, drinking, and rocking with Hank Williams, Jr., in the parking lot, the entire crowd spontaneously broke into a repeated chant of the refrain to "Family Tradition." It rose louder and louder, then fell off into fragments as ecstatic fans found their cars, still singing "If I get stoned, and sing all night long, it's a family tradition. . . ." According to his biographical movie, it was the saving touch of a woman's love that redeemed this country singer from domestic turmoil to family tradition, allowing him, in turn, to create this celebratory fan community.

In October 1992, *Country America* magazine published a "special collector's issue" showcasing their selection of "the top 100 country songs of all time." This ranking was chosen by an elaborate method. Thirty thousand fans who read *Country America* sent votes to be tabulated; separately, the magazine assembled a panel of thirty-seven prominent country music historians and scholars, music business figures, and established stars to make their own selections and rank them. Then an editorial board reconciled the two lists, selecting only those songs that appeared on each when their positions were averaged. The result was a relatively balanced ranking that included about forty songs taken from the 1960s and 70s and distributed the remainder backward as far as the Carter Family and Jimmie Rodgers in the 1920s and forward to Alan Jackson and Travis Tritt in the 1990s. True to the power of the tragic-troubadour legend, Hank Williams appears more than any other artist with six songs, five of those his own compositions and three of them in the top ten (*Country America* 1992). All but one are songs of broken hearts (the sixth is a song of happy love).

But Hank Williams did not top the list. That honor went to George Jones. Many fans, artists, and observers believe that George Jones is the most powerful singer in the history of country music. Jones believes that Hank Williams was. Jones's life and his own growing legend are testimony to the resilience of the tragic troubadour image in country music culture, and to the attraction of the personal-salvation theme.

Born in a log cabin in eastern Texas in 1931, Jones was the last of eight children in a working-class family that featured a religious mother and a father who liked to drink. When he was nine, according to Jones, a couple in the Saratoga, Texas, Assembly of God church taught him guitar chords and the singing of gospel music, and Jones grew up listening to the Grand Ole Opry. During World War II, his family moved to Beaumont, where George was impressed by his earnings as a street singer. At first, he covered the hits of Opry stars and performed gospel tunes. Then he discovered Hank Williams. "Hank Williams came along and oh, oh my goodness, I couldn't think or eat, nothin', unless it was Hank Williams—and I couldn't wait for his next record to come out. He was, had to be, really, the greatest" (Jones 1989). By May 1949, Jones was performing in nightclubs. That month, he met Hank Williams, who was in Beaumont on a promotional tour. In 1950, Jones married, fathered a child, separated from his wife, and joined the military (because, he says, he couldn't afford to pay child support). He spent his enlistment playing bars in San Jose, California, where he learned of Hank Williams's death. "I lay there the rest of the morning and just bawled," he said. "You know it just broke my heart, you know, cause Lord, he was, he was just *everything* as far as I was concerned." After his military service, Jones got a recording contract, became a regional star, and played the Louisiana Hayride with Johnny Cash and Elvis Presley. Other artists remember these days as marked by alcohol, fights, wild parties, and irrational behavior. Jones was still able to move to the Grand Ole Opry, to appear with Red Foley in Missouri, to tour for five years with Buck Owens and Johnny Cash, and to marry for a second time.

By the 1960s, country music touring had become relentless. Jones was said to be on the road 250 nights a year; like Hank Williams, he developed an affinity for whiskey, pills, and casual sex. In 1968, he again divorced, then made an "intense" relationship with country singer Tammy Wynette. Producer Billy Sherrill, at CBS Records, encouraged Jones's talent for singing emotionally in the lower register and paired Jones with Wynette in a memorable duo act. The two were married in 1969, entered the 1970s with numerous hit songs, and had a daughter they named Tamela Georgette. But, according to Wynette, this highly visible marriage was so infested by George's alcoholism that it was undermined. In *Stand By Your Man*, Wynette tells numerous stories of Jones's drinking binges and destructive behavior, the most vivid of which is her claim that he once fired a rifle at her as she ran screaming from their house; then he systematically destroyed their possessions.

> All the Spanish lanterns that had been hanging in the downstairs rooms were smashed to pieces. He had thrown two dining room chairs into my china cabinet and broken all my china and crystal. One of the chairs was still stuck in the shattered glass door. He had ripped the drapes off the windows, thrown furniture against the walls, leaving huge holes in the plaster, and kicked in three television sets. The wall behind one of the sets was scorched where flames had shot up when

he smashed in the screen. Glass figurines had been thrown against walls and windows, and broken glass was scattered everywhere. (Wynette 1979, 201)

Wynette says this incident resulted in Jones being taken in a straitjacket to a sanitarium, where he dried out; then he slinked home shamefully. By 1974, according to Wynette, less dramatic but repeated incidents of this nature were increasing. In that year she divorced George Jones, moved all his belongings out of the house, and wrote a country song about it. The refrain said, "your memory's finally gone to rest" (Wynette 1979, 235). For his part, George Jones remembered Tammy Wynette as lacking understanding: "I don't think she tried to understand me and help me to understand her and the things going on about us. I think she took the quick way out" (Jones 1989).

George Jones's third divorce sent him into a spiral. He traveled the country restlessly, abusing drugs and alcohol. Conway Twitty described him as "set on self-destruct." He disappeared for days and weeks at a time. By 1981, he was said to be "living in the back seat of his car with a bottle of whiskey and a cutout of Hank as his constant companion." He began having delusions, and in an alter ego spoke in the voice of Donald Duck. During this period his weight dropped to 105 pounds, and he was jailed for drunk driving. Yet, in an irony similar to that of his hero Hank Williams, during this emotional trauma George Jones's record sales rose dramatically as he gave authentic voice to songs of heartbreak and loneliness. Describing an important Jones hit from this period, "Bartender's Blues," a CBS Records official said, "It's sort of a love-hate situation when you go through that, because every time George would get in trouble, all I know is we would sell more product. And we were a million albums before we knew it" (Jones 1989).

In the very center of Jones's deepest anguish, he recorded the song named by *Country America* fans and experts as the number-one country song of all time. He began recording "He Stopped Loving Her Today," a song originally written in 1977 and given to Billy Sherrill after other singers had declined it, in 1979. The work was a struggle. Sherrill claims that it took Jones eighteen months to finish the recording, and at the end Jones bet him $100 that the record would never be a hit. "Nobody," Jones told Sherrill, "will buy that morbid sonofabitch" (Jones 1989). Not so. "He Stopped Loving Her

Today" is the only country song ever to win CMA Song of the Year two consecutive years (1980 and 1981). It made George Jones Male Vocalist of the Year twice, and it won him a Grammy.

Jones's performance of this song in the early 1990s retains the power of the original. In concerts at Dayton's Hara Arena in November 1991, and at Cincinnati Gardens in March 1992, "He Stopped Loving Her Today" evoked an eerie silence from thousands of hushed fans who at other points in these concerts were wild and rowdy. For this song, stage lighting dimmed low, and Hara Arena glowed from the power of thousands of lighters held high by fans in ritual acknowledgment of tragic-troubadour emotion. Most of them would probably have agreed with Billy Sherrill:

> Jones' voice, when he unleashes it, has the power of a great primal scream of sorrow, conjuring up a bottomless pathos that is the essence of honkytonk desperation. In more restrained musical moments, he can emote, with similar ease, all the softer emotional shades of tenderness and devotion with a voice that is as pure and soothing as mother's milk. Then, in the next breath, singing through clenched teeth, he can insinuate into even the most mundane of melodies, a compelling sense of sadness, rage and confusion that is as piercing as a cold wind blowing on a dark night. (Sherrill, 1982)

The *New York Times* agreed. Five days before George Jones's 1992 appearance in Cincinnati, its *Sunday Magazine* carried a detailed story announcing his return from the edge of tragedy. "George Jones taught a generation of country-music stars how to sing" said the *Times*. "Now with years of alcohol, cocaine and missed performances behind him, he's competing with his own legacy" (Hunter 1992).

Jones's rehabilitation from years of trauma is a key story for contemporary country music, for it extends the Hank Williams legend in a new direction. In 1986, friends of Jones in the music business convinced him to enter a hospital in Birmingham, Alabama, for detoxification. Jones described the results.

> The first couple of weeks was roughest. Last couple, in there, got time to think. Had an I.Q. of 72 when I went in there. Having some fine cards and letters coming in from so many, so many, fans—that really gave you that big lift that you needed to get you back on the right track. And I met Nancy right after I got out of the hospital. (Jones 1989)

The country-music-salvation formula had appeared in George Jones's life—the vocal support of adoring fans, the nurturing love of a stable woman, and prayer. "I think he was needing someone he could trust and someone that he felt close to," said his new wife, Nancy Sepulvado Jones, "because of the bad times." Remarried and initially living again in Texas near his extended family, Jones recovered—or, perhaps for the first time, gained—personal poise. He readily associates his new life with heavenly intervention: "If it hadn't been for Nancy, and the prayers, and the cards and letters, and the people, the fans that really care—I think that's really what made me think, and to get to thinking, and make my mind up. I said, 'Well, there's somebody still cares and I believe I can do it again'" (Jones 1989).

In 1990, a transformed George Jones released a gospel album entitled *Hallelujah Weekend*. It features the Hank Williams hard times recitation, "A Picture from Life's Other Side," and such titles as "(It's the Bible Against the Bottle) The Battle for Daddy's Soul" and "Jesus Saves Today." The cover picture for this collection shows a gently smiling George Jones with neatly combed silver hair wearing the Christian cross on a neck chain and tidily framed by an intricate wrought-iron fence. In a rolling pastoral background, one can see just over Jones's left shoulder a full-scale rainbow coming to earth. At the end of the rainbow stands a country church (Jones, Epic 1990).

If George Jones has escaped the domestic turmoil that took Hank Williams, "He Stopped Loving Her Today" is the story of someone who did not. As the narrator of the song, Jones tells us about an unnamed friend who has kept alive a lifelong love for a woman who left him. He kept her pictures and letters—where he underlined "every single 'I Love You'." But now we learn that the narrator has gone to see this friend and, instead of the usual tears, found him smiling and "all dressed-up to go away." But the circumstances aren't so attractive as the story at first suggests. For there's a wreath on his door, "and soon they'll carry him away." Although it's never directly stated, his friend's destination is his own burial (Jones, Epic 1987).

Jones's plaintive rendition of this incident of domestic pathos carries all the emotional power that his legend as a country singer suggests. Tension builds slowly through the song, reinforced by a gradual crescendo from a string accompaniment to a crisp, raw wail of grief at the end. The song is a warning—this is what the tragic troubadour wants to avoid. In the literature of domestic romance, "He Stopped Loving Her Today" is a complaint about the absence of love. To its most persistent subject, the trauma of broken love, it applies the ironic strategy common in country songwriting and places the burden of personal responsibility on a faithless woman. Just ahead of the final chorus, we learn (in a narration delivered almost as an aside to preface the narrator's cry of grief) that the lost wife did come back—but only for the funeral. "We all wondered if she would," Jones says. Yet this woman's effort is too late for salvation, for "this time, he's over her for good." While friends remember this man's devotion in loving detail, there is no good woman to save this good man.

Not so for George Jones. He has Nancy, and in the 1990s, he may have a larger array of artist-fans than any other living artist. Younger singers, in particular, pay him respect. In a video version of Alan Jackson's anthem to country music, "Don't Rock the Jukebox," Jackson carefully links the legend of George Jones to that of Hank Williams. In this video, Jackson wears the characteristic white western suit and white cowboy hat associated with Hank Williams. He composes his lanky body in a variation of Hank's slouch and delivers a commentary on rock music. Describing himself as a "heartbroke hillbilly," Jackson says, "I don't feel like rockin'," adding, "I wanna hear some Jones" (Jackson 1993). As Jackson sings, a figure who has been sitting in shadow, alone at a bar table, rises to lean without comment against the stable jukebox beside him. That figure is George Jones, and he is smiling.

In his study of death in pop-music culture, Jeff Pike asks a question that millions of country fans might take only partly in jest:

> Like Jay Gatsby, the figure of Elvis Presley only looms larger in death. His life and career partook of none of death's untidy obsessions. But somehow, like everything else that came into his orbit, Elvis Presley finally embodied and consumed the dark side of life too, including death itself, leaving behind like some smudge from the ash of a great fire this gnawing conundrum: Did Elvis go to heaven, or did he go to hell? (Pike 1993, 58)

Elvis Presley's spiritual destiny has been considered by others. In their short story, "Touring" (1981), science-fiction writers Gardner Dozois, Jack Dann, and Michael Swanwick place the performing spirit of Elvis on stage as the opening act for a three-part billing with Janis Joplin and Buddy Holly. The setting, eerie and futuristic, is presided over by a figure who sports a thin mustache and a cigar, and wears an enigmatic smile. He can quiet the complaints of these legendary stars simply by touching them. In "Touring," Presley is depicted as a self-centered, pushy, gun-toting rock star with an excessive ego. The occasion of the short story is an extraordinary live performance in which fans respond with "rapturous screams" (Sloan and Pierce 1993, 250). When Elvis figures out that "we're caught in a snare and delusion of Satan," he wants to call for help to his mother who is "in Heaven." But, amid "a rolling avalanche of applause," the singers can't stop singing; and Presley, Holly, and Joplin join in a jam session of classic intensity. As they perform, the audience, stage musicians, and stage—and, finally, the three performers—disappear one by one. In their last moments, "Elvis threw back his head and laughed," then continued to sing. Holly perceives this behavior as an important affirmation in the face of impending extinction.

> But the *music* was right, and the *music* was good, and while all the rest—audience, applause, someplace to go when the show was over—was nice, it wasn't necessary. Holly glanced both ways and saw that he was not the only one to understand this. (Sloan and Pierce 1993, 258)

Presley's music may redeem him in "Touring," or it may have an existence separate from Elvis himself, leaving some ambiguity about whether Elvis is, finally, in Heaven or Hell. For Wayne Newton, an important Las Vegas performer with country music roots who tells his audience that he and Elvis "were very dear friends," there is little ambiguity about Presley's spiritual commitment. In "The (Elvis) Letter," a song about Presley's last days in Las Vegas, which Newton used as a finale for his own live performances in 1992 and released as a music video that was a TNN hit, he depicts Presley as a figure praying for guidance in the midst of his glittering and isolated stardom (Newton 1992). When Newton appeared at the Fraze Pavilion, on June 29, 1992, he concluded a two-and-a-half-hour concert with a rendition of this song, which, he told fans, currently was a hit "in the top five." The song's story, Newton said, originated in an incident during Presley's last visit to Las Vegas. Late at night in his hotel room, Presley wrote a note, then crumpled it up. Someone saved the note, and Newton purchased it at auction in 1991. Newton's description of the note suggests that it is about loneliness and suggests a route to salvation. "Elvis may have been lonely," Newton said; "but I guarantee you he was not alone." In Newton's song, Elvis talks about his broken hopes and dreams. His friends have been calling him in Vegas to talk about their own difficulties, Elvis says, yet they don't realize "that I'm there too." Elvis elaborates. He has to wear a false smile because "my pain won't go away." His nights are lonely, and he wants to go home. In a recitation presumably transcribed from the written note, Elvis talks wistfully in the quiet night after his entourage has left him. "I have no need for all of this," he says prayerfully; "Help me, Lord."

Even a cursory inspection of Elvis Presley's life and music suggests that Wayne Newton had good reason to affiliate Elvis Presley with religious devotion. In his *Lost Highway*, Peter Guralnick provides a summary of Elvis Presley's life that appropriately emphasizes his link to evangelical tradition (Guralnick 1989). Elvis Presley was born in 1935, in Tupelo, Mississippi, of working-class parents who apparently suffered much from hard times. They lost their house at least twice before a teenage Elvis could provide for them in Memphis by his success in the music business. The Presley family affiliated with the Pentecostal First Assembly of God, in Tupelo, and Presley's earliest musical inspirations were evangelical:

> We were a religious family, going around together to sing at camp meetings and revivals. Since I was two years old, all I knew was gospel music, that was music to me. We borrowed the style of our psalm singing from the early Negroes. We used to go to these religious singings all the time. The preachers cut up all over the place, jumping on the piano, moving every which way. The audience liked them. I guess I learned from them. I loved the music. It became such a part of my life it was as natural as dancing, a way to escape from the problems and my way of release. (Guralnick 1989, 120–21)

When Presley began a secular career, he was initially attracted to country and gospel music. In 1945, at the age of ten, he won fifth place in a talent contest at the Mississippi–Alabama Fair and Dairy Show by singing a Red Foley number, "Old Shep." He got his first guitar at the age of eleven. He listened to the Grand Ole Opry, Jimmie Rodgers, Bob Wills, and especially to white gospel quartets. After moving to Memphis in 1948, Presley was also interested in black singers Big Bill Broonzy and Big Boy Crudup. In Memphis, Elvis worked odd jobs, finished high school, and by 1954 was driving a truck for Crown Electric Company. Young Elvis cultivated a visible working-class image: "He majored in shop, grew his hair long, carefully slicked it down, and tried to grow sideburns from the time he started shaving, because, he said, he wanted to look like a truck driver." He liked "the all-night gospel sings at the Memphis Auditorium," and in 1954, "almost joined the Songfellows, a junior division of the renowned Blackwood Brothers quartet, whom he had admired for years" (Guralnick 1989, 122–25).

In late spring 1954, a recording event that was to precipitate rockabilly music as a fusion of gospel, blues, and country traditions occurred at Sam Phillips's Sun Records studio in Memphis. A place where Elvis allegedly first went to make a birthday record for his mother, Phillips's studio became a generator of commercial rock and roll marketed to a white audience. That audience intersected significantly with country music culture.

The 1954 sessions teamed Elvis Presley as soloist with guitar and bass players Scotty Moore and Bill Black. Sam Phillips was searching for what he called a "pop song" that would be a market hit because of its musical novelty. Aficionados of rock and roll regard the results as almost spiritual. Describing Presley's cover of the Big Boy Crudup blues song, "That's All Right," Guralnick says it was "a turning point in the history of American popular music," a moment of "easy, unforced, joyous, spontaneous" sound with "irrepressible enthusiasm." Presley's version showed "emotional transcendence" with "a timeless quality" (Guralnick 1989, 126–27). "That's All Right" was recorded July 5, 1954, and released with a cover of Bill Monroe's "Blue Moon of Kentucky" recorded the following day as its backing side. Heavily played on a Memphis radio station that marketed the blues to a young white audience, Presley's first record sold 30,000 copies. It rose to the top of the Memphis country charts, resulting in Presley's being named eighth most promising new hillbilly artist by *Billboard,* and took Elvis to the Grand Ole Opry in September, "where he was advised to go back to truck driving." Instead, following Hank Williams's precedent, he went to the Louisiana Hayride in Shreveport, then to extensive touring in the South as the "Hillbilly Cat" and "King of Western Bop" (Guralnick 1989, 128–29).

In January 1955, following the footsteps of Patsy Cline and seeking a national television audience, Elvis Presley tried out for Arthur Godfrey's talent scouts. The following summer he met his lifetime manager, Colonel Tom Parker, who booked Elvis into concert appearances with Opry star Hank Snow and negotiated a recording contract with RCA records. By the end of 1955, he had a national country hit with "Baby Let's Play House" and was named most promising new country artist (Guralnick 1989, 129–30). Then, in 1956, Presley made the promotional breakthrough that Patsy Cline coveted—he became a national television star.

Television was the leading entertainment novelty of the 1950s. Just as radio listeners had provided an initial audience for barn dance programs in the 1920s and the Carter Family in the 1930s, television now introduced Elvis Presley—and it allowed him to reach an audience well beyond the traditional market for country music. On television, Presley could appeal directly to teenagers of the white middle class. His media exposure began with six appearances on Tommy and Jimmy Dorsey's Saturday night show, where he promoted "Heartbreak Hotel." It rose to number one on both pop and country charts. In 1956, he performed three times on the Ed Sullivan show, the nation's leading variety hour; by the end of the year, he had signed a Hollywood movie contract (Stambler and Landon 1984, 573–74).

The rockabilly fusion of country, gospel, and blues into a new pop music with broad appeal was centered on the figure of Elvis Presley as seen on television. He was also on radio playlists at a time, in the 1950s, when stations were increasingly segmenting the listener market and beginning to program directly for teenagers of the white middle class. As the post World War II baby-boom generation acquired its initial buying power and began the spending habits that would stimulate the nation's economic prosperity into the early 1990s, the Hollywood movie industry followed television and radio into this teenage market. Eventually, these trends contributed to a massive adolescent-oriented popular culture of rock-and-roll star images, ecstatic music, and concert spectacles.

The most perceptive observers of the Elvis phenomenon have been enigmatic when describing his dramatic rise to popularity in the mid-1950s. Like the science-fiction writers of "Touring," the tendency has been to locate the source of Presley's power in his music. Yet these observers acknowledge that music alone cannot adequately explain Presley's impact; often, that impact is described in language borrowed from cultural psychology or social myth. Consider Peter Guralnick's evaluative assessment:

> I don't know what there is to say about the success. There are, of course, the hits. "Heartbreak Hotel," with its bluesy country feel, metallic guitar and dour bass. "Hound Dog," with its reversed sexual imagery, savage musical ride, and spewed-out lyric ("Well, they said you was high class, well that was just a lie"). "Jailhouse Rock," with its frenetic pace and furiously repeated drum roll. "Love Me Tender," "Love Me," "Loving You." The negligent ease of "Don't Be Cruel," the mnemonic pop of "All Shook Up." The impact of hit after hit after hit, fourteen consecutive million sellers, RCA claimed, simultaneously topping pop, country, and r&b charts. The phenomenal explosion of both the mode and the music over a period of twenty-seven months until his March 1958 induction into the army. The elevation to socio/mytho/psycho-sexual status, as Elvis Presley unwittingly became a test of the nation's moral fiber. (Guralnick 1989, 130–31)

It's possible to endorse this view and add to it. Elvis Presley came to a unique visibility in American popular culture on television with a stage performance style that borrowed from ecstatic forms of evangelical worship. This style had never been so systematically exposed to white middle-class youth. It proved to be surprisingly attractive. Presley's cultivated working-class appearance, which would be widely imitated, was consistent for an act probably deep in debt to ritual behaviors of pentecostalism. In these respects, the appeal of evangelical worship forms—and Elvis Presley as their secular agent—should not be underestimated as a phenomenon of popular culture.

In his study of Southern white gospel music, Don Cusic notes that Presley's stage persona featuring "long hair, flashy clothes and flair for showmanship" was in part borrowed from gospel quartets (Cusic 1990, 117). Charles Wolfe explored Presley's links to Southern gospel in a 1977 essay. J. D. Sumner, James Blackwood, and other gospel figures worked with Presley, and the singing style of Jake Hess and the Statesmen quartet may have been a direct influence on Presley's ballad singing. Wolfe reminds us that, in reaction to criticism of his body movements during his first Ed Sullivan television appearance, for his second appearance Presley chose to sing the Red Foley country hymn, "Peace in the Valley" (Quain 1992, 13–27).

At a famous jam session on Tuesday, December 4, 1956, at the Sun studio in Memphis, Elvis Presley was joined by Sam Phillips's other legendary rockabilly artists, Jerry Lee Lewis, Carl Perkins, and Johnny Cash. Performances tape-recorded during that long session have been released as *The Million Dollar Quartet* (Presley 1989). This impromptu encounter at the genesis of rock and roll clearly indicates that white gospel music, country music, and blues were its inspiring musical sources. Yet the imbalance of these traditions is striking—of the thirty-eight renditions that appear in this session, thirteen are clearly white gospel songs and ten are country (four of those bluegrass), for a total of more than half the common repertory of Presley, Lewis, and Perkins at this time. At least nine songs on the album can be described as rock-and-roll creations, four as blues numbers, and two as covers of pop music. Thomas Poole points out that the "gospel set" on *The Million Dollar Quartet* takes twenty-two of its fifty minutes (Poole 1992, 2). In his liner notes for the album, Colin Escott describes the significance of this imbalance:

> The country roots ran deep but the true common ground for *The Million Dollar Quartet* was gospel music. Between songs there is inside chatter about white gospel groups such as the Statesmen Quartet, and one of Presley's first moves after he got a little recognition was to bring the Jordanaires into his entourage. He would warm up for every session with gospel music just as he does here. However, Presley's gospel recordings never captured the atmosphere of pure church as vividly as these performances. There was no need for rehearsal because the songs were so deeply embedded in all the participants; after one singer took the lead, the others instinctively knew where to follow. (Presley 1989)

When Sam Phillips felt a need to defend rock and roll from charges that it was inspired by Satan, he was able to point to the religious belief of his singers. "I dare say that there were never any 'infidels'—or agnostics even—that came in my studio" he said. "There was a deep-seated feeling for God, very much so, in probably every artist I ever worked with. Whether they knew how to express it in any way, they showed it to me in the way they did what they did" (Quain 1992, 18).

Sam Phillips probably did not intend to include Elvis Presley's stage demeanor in that summary remark; yet, if one compares his body motions in early performances with those depicted in Randall Balmer's video documentary of evangelical religion, *Mine Eyes Have Seen the Glory*, there are interesting parallels (Balmer 1992). As shown in the Balmer study, pentecostal religious ceremonies are characterized by ecstatic singing and spasmodic body movements that include a variety of physical jerking motions. These occur when participants experience what they might describe as the spirit of holiness entering their bodies. And, like rock and roll, this spirit crosses racial boundaries freely to embrace both urban black and rural white working-class adherents.

The documentary film *Elvis '56*, a close look at the year 1956 in the career of Elvis Presley, studies the sharp impact of Presley's body movements as promoted on national television. In this film we can see the "Hillbilly Cat" exhibiting a variety of bumps, grinds, pelvic vibrations, leg and body shakes, and spasmodic jerks of his head punctuated by a sneering lip roll followed immediately by a smile and widened eyes—all in time with the crisp, driving rhythm of guitar accompaniment (Cinemax 1987). It's clear that Presley is acting. While his body movements seem effortless and involuntary in a manner parallel to the ecstatic movements of religious seizure, Presley controls his delivery carefully and always brings it to finale with a winning smile and a bow to the audience. We may think of Elvis-on-stage as a novel persona that Presley created out of his religious heritage, a persona that a detractor might call a "secular holy-roller."

In 1956, Presley was the rage of television. He played the Dorsey Brothers, Milton Berle, Steve Allen, and Ed Sullivan (three times). Videos of these performances are enshrined at the Country Music Hall of Fame and Museum in Nashville, to recognize their revolutionary character in American popular culture. For example, when Presley covered Big Mama Thornton's "Hound Dog" on the Milton Berle show from Los Angeles June 5, 40 million people saw him deliver a powerful series of suggestive sexual postures, as well as what many regarded as phallic innuendoes with the microphone stand. Dubbed by critics "Elvis the Pelvis" for this performance, Presley replied: "It's one of the most childish expressions I've ever heard." He described his stage appearance as a natural thing. "Rock and roll music, if you like it, if you feel it, you can't help but move to it. That's what happens to me. I mean I have to move around. I can't stand still. I've tried it, and I can't do it." Asked if he believed that his stage behavior contributed to juvenile delinquency, the non-drinking, nonsmoking twenty-one-year old replied: "If someone saw me singing and dancing I don't see how they could think that it would contribute to juvenile delinquency. If there's anything I've tried to do, I've tried to live a straight, clean life and not set any kind of a bad example."

The scriptwriters of *Elvis '56*, Martin Torgoff and Alan and Susan Raymond, imply that the underlying threat Elvis represented to white middle-class suburban America in 1956 was the way his physical posturing and his music embodied black culture at a time exactly simultaneous with challenges to official segregation from the emerging civil rights movement. "By performing Little Richard's 'Tutti Frutti' on national television," narrator Levon Helm says, "Elvis crosses the racial barrier in music and kicks down the door for scores of artists to follow."

When that door was down, what walked in on American popular culture was a theatrical evocation of adolescent sexual longing. In her short story, "Presleystroika," Kay Sloan has her narrator describe this situation in detail.

> Elvis was revolution, the Lenin of lust. Everybody knew it, especially the P.T.A. parents and the Baptist preachers. In Mississippi in 1956, he stood for everything good Southern girls weren't supposed to want, swiveling hips and rhythm that only black people were rumored to have. Elvis let the black cat out of the pink bag, and it was a slinky, sexy cat. (Sloan and Pierce 1993, 114)

Sloan's narrator is remembering having met Elvis during her childhood from her present perspective of watching a Presley impersonator in Leningrad just before the 1991 Russian revolution. She also makes an exact connection between the intensity of her sexual response to Elvis and her own religious experience of baptism by full immersion. "Meeting Elvis *had* felt like a baptism," she says, "a drowning in hormones that washed away my childhood" (Sloan and Pierce 1993, 115).

For his part, young Presley tried in *Elvis '56* to maintain detachment from the sexual persona of Elvis-on-stage. In an image prefiguring Wayne Newton's vision of Presley turning to religious belief when he felt alone and under stress, Presley was filmed backstage during a rehearsal break for the Steve Allen show on June 28, 1956. At the heart of a national controversy about his television persona, Elvis seated himself alone at a piano in the corner of a New York City studio and began singing a favorite gospel song.

After 1956, Elvis Presley made thirty-three Hollywood films, became the movie industry's highest-paid star, and sold more than a billion records throughout the world. By 1957, the public response to Elvis was so dramatic that Presley essentially stopped touring and moved into his retreat at Graceland, where he lived until his death on August 16, 1977—with the exception of time he spent in Las Vegas and Hollywood, in public appearances or in Germany with the U.S. Army between 1958 and 1960. Presley had his own version of domestic turmoil. He was devoted to his mother, Gladys, who died while he was in Germany. He married in 1967, but his wife later left him, and he was separated from his daughter Lisa. Before he died he was reportedly overweight and possibly addicted to prescription drugs. The ghost of Hank Williams walked through Elvis Presley's autopsy report, where the official cause of death was given as "cardiac arrhythmia."

Elvis Presley's impact on the baby-boom generation was first demonstrated in 1956. At his death, it was again demonstrated. The reaction of country music culture to the unexpected death of a major star had taken its initial public form in 1953 at the Hank Williams death memorial. It was repeated when Patsy Cline died in 1963. In 1977, country music culture again expressed its grief before assembled media, this time for Elvis Presley. Now, the mourning assembly was augmented by fans and artists drawn from social segments well beyond the traditional boundaries of country music culture. Teenagers who had reacted to Elvis Presley on national television in 1956 with unprecedented record buying and concert and movie attendance were in their middle to late thirties in 1977. Some had turned forty. Presley's death was well timed to remind them of adolescent sexual longings enshrined in popular culture imagery but noticeably behind them personally. Now the King of Rock and Roll, who had symbolized unprecedented freedom from restraint for white middle-class teenagers, was dead prematurely at age forty-two. This generational timing enhanced the immediate public response to Presley's death, which was unexpectedly powerful.

Neal and Janice Gregory have meticulously documented reactions to the death of Elvis Presley. Their *When Elvis Died* focuses on the inability of print and television journalists to anticipate adequately the depth of public grief and the fan behavior associated with it (Gregory 1980). They trace the intensity of emotions shown in hundreds of stories from mourners, beginning at the funeral in Memphis, documenting the creation of Elvis memorials (throughout the world), and concluding in 1992 with the creation of a U.S. postal stamp bearing the 1956 image of Elvis-on-stage. The Elvis stamp was the first to allow public selection of the artwork. Again, the 1,121,000 people who voted suggested their nostalgia for the 1950s, when 851,000 of them chose the "Young Elvis" image over a 1990 Las Vegas Elvis.

The most vivid anecdotes in *When Elvis Died* focus on the origins of the perpetual death memorial that Presley's home, Graceland, has become. Reporters at first reacted skeptically to the emotions expressed by thousands of fans who dropped the routine of their daily lives in 1977 and made the trip to Graceland in order to mourn Presley in person.

> Mrs. Nancy Hunter of Plano, Texas, a thirty-five-year-old mother of four, said she had never done anything like it before, but when she heard that the casket would be open for public viewing, she felt she had to go to Memphis. Interviewed by Marilyn Schwartz of the *Dallas Morning News*, Mrs. Hunter said she made her decision at eleven that morning and got a seat on American Airline's twelve-forty-five flight out of Dallas. "I had to fly first class," she added, "but I didn't care. I knew this would be my last chance to be close to Elvis." (Gregory 1980, 79)

Some anecdotes in the Gregory account reinforce the impression that Presley's death touched nostalgia for teenage years. "Mrs. Frank Gregory of Dallas told Schwartz that she was thirteen, her daughter Jean's age, when she fell in love with Elvis. 'I brought her with me because I hope she will catch some of the mood here. She's got to, because after tomorrow, there is no more Elvis. There is no more King. I want her to love him like I do'" (Gregory 1980, 79). With nationwide media coverage and a level of attention that included a formal statement of sympathy from President Jimmy Carter, Presley's funeral would attract far more fans than any previous death memorial of country music culture.

Presley died on Tuesday and was initially buried in a family plot at Forest Hill Cemetery on Thursday. Fifty thousand people visited the cemetery that day. By Friday, 3,500 floral arrangements had been delivered, making Presley's funeral "the biggest day in history for FTD," the national Floral Telegraph Delivery association reported (Gregory 1980, 84). Presley's father, Vernon, gave the funeral flowers to the fans, who treated them with the same sincerity they had shown at Patsy Cline's funeral. Some were "sobbing and hysterical, but most of them [were] quietly and reverently approaching the tomb to receive a remembrance of their sad pilgrimage to Memphis." By noon on Friday, all the flowers, the ribbons, the styrofoam, and anything else available had been taken as relics of the event (Gregory 1980, 98–99).

By the early 1990s, when the white middle-class teenagers who had loved Elvis on television in 1956 were in their early fifties, Elvis Presley had become a distinctive international icon of American popular culture. The controversy that emerged soon after his death—that it was drug-related—has not diminished his importance as primary stimulant for the rock music that, by the mid-1960s, had evolved into a major subculture, substantially obscuring its country and gospel roots. Yet the behavior of Elvis fans at his death and afterward continued to elaborate on an undiminished tradition of affection for singing stars of country music culture. In his absence, that affection continues to focus on Graceland.

In the year following Elvis Presley's death, Graceland became a shrine as fans gathered to light candles and keep all-night vigils on the Graceland grounds near the grave where Presley's body had been moved. In 1982, Graceland was opened to the public, so fans can tour the Presley compound and complete their pilgrimage to the "Meditation Garden." Here, Elvis is buried beside his mother, father, and grandmother. There is also a marker to honor the memory of his twin, Jesse Garon Presley, who died at birth.

By 1992, the tenth anniversary of Graceland as a public shrine and the fifteenth anniversary of Presley's death, the annual memorial event in Memphis had been expanded by Elvis Presley Enterprises, Inc., in cooperation with various Memphis organizations and more than 280 Presley fan clubs. During "Elvis Week '92," August 8 to 16, Graceland sponsored a Memphis Bandstand '92 sock hop at the Mid-South Coliseum, a memorial gospel concert with J. D. Sumner and the Stamps, a nostalgia concert with Elvis band members and personal friends, and an awards ceremony in which RCA records and the Record Industry Association of America recognized the Presley estate for "the largest number of certified gold and platinum record awards ever given at one time to any recording artist or group." Elvis Week also offered Elvis trivia contests, social events for fan clubs and their officers, public showings of Elvis videos in Graceland Plaza across Elvis Presley Boulevard from the mansion, an Elvis Art Exhibit providing awards in categories for amateur, youth, physically challenged, and professional artists, special opportunities for fans to visit the Meditation Garden, and a Candlelight Vigil. The vigil, which began with a ceremony at 10 P.M. on August 15, allowed 25,000 fans to file silently by Presley's grave in continuous procession until 6:15 A.M. on August 16. At the Presley birthplace in Tupelo, Mississippi, there was a memorial ceremony. A theatrical production of Presley music was available at the Libertyland theme park in Memphis, and an Elvis laser light show and concert at the Pink Palace Planetarium in Memphis to remember Presley's "Aloha From Hawaii"—a 1972 live concert broadcast by satellite from Hawaii that reached 40 countries and over 1 billion people (Hazen and Freeman 1992, 68). There was a charity event at the Peabody Hotel featuring the Jordanaires, a karate tournament to benefit Le Bonheur Children's Medical Center, a Five-K Run for United Cerebral Palsy, a memorial gathering of friends at Memphis State University, a rock concert with Carl Perkins and other rockabillies, a photo and memorabilia exhibit on the rockabilly era at the Memphis Center for Southern Folklore on Beale Street, guided tours of Humes High School (where Presley graduated in 1953), an open house at the Elvis Presley Memorial Trauma Center, events benefiting the Humane Society at a restaurant near Graceland, a reunion of Presley's closest friends at a restaurant on Beale Street, and fan-club breakfasts each day hosted by *Elvis World* magazine in a Shoney's restaurant.

If public beneficiaries of the massive memorial activities during Elvis Week are Memphis charitable organizations, private beneficiaries are the Presley fans who take part in the Candlelight Vigil at Graceland. At 7:30 A.M. on August 15, 1992, fans began forming a line outside the gates of Graceland. They waited all day for a 10 P.M. ceremony hosted by the Elvis Country Fan Club to open the graveside procession. By 10 P.M., Elvis Presley Boulevard had been sealed off by the police and was filled with an estimated 25,000 people, most of them wearing decorative mementos of their affection for Elvis. They stood patiently, in silence, before the gates of Graceland, listening to Presley music playing over loudspeakers. At 10:50 P.M., Todd Morgan, of Graceland, welcomed the crowd on behalf of "290 fan clubs throughout the world." The presidents of ninety-five clubs were present and were to be honored by walking first in the graveside procession, "to represent fans all over the world." This announcement was greeted by applause. "Elvis Presley was the greatest and he had the greatest fans in the world," Morgan said. "The night is yours, and we'll be here all night." He then introduced speakers for the Elvis Country Fan Club.

What followed was a spiritual ceremony in which the crowd lit candles, held them high, cheered, then stood in complete silence "to the memory of Elvis Presley." The four women and two men representing the Elvis Country Fan Club ranged from teenagers to grandmothers. Each provided personal testimony about their feelings for Presley, interspersed by moments for the fans to sing along with Elvis recordings played over loudspeakers. As a young woman read a long, vivid poem of her love for Elvis, couples in the street were holding one another, and some were crying. At the poem's end there was a hush, then polite applause. The crowd appeared to be two-thirds to three quarters women, with a tilt toward late middle age. When the Presley rendition of the gospel song "Stand By Me" was played, there was widespread emotional response. When Presley's "Falling in Love with You" was played, the entire street sang with strength, and candles were held high as figures and groups ranging from middle-class families to Elvis impersonators to elderly working-class women with purple hair to small children were crying, hugging, and softly joining in.

The procession opened with fan-club presidents walking up a long winding pathway to the Meditation Garden carrying torches, dressed in all white, as Presley sang "Amazing Grace." As the procession spread out, blacks and whites, families, people of all ages, professionals, yuppies, hippies, rockers, grandmas, good ole boys, teens, twin dress-alikes, gays, straights, daddies with small children on their shoulders, and observers—journalists, photographers, notetakers and writers—carried their candles and moved forward politely to pay their respects. The demeanor of the crowd was remarkably polite; there was no jostling, no loud voices. If someone gave a slight push, they apologized. Fathers held up children to take pictures and to see the crowd, where they could view numerous figures on crutches or in wheelchairs, and some being helped by friends.

No amount of reading, analytic skepticism, or professional detachment is an adequate shield against the emotional power of fan behavior at this memorial service. By the morning of August 16, the Meditation Garden was completely covered with flowers, memorabilia, and personal memorials left by fans. The striking character of these artifacts was their homemade quality—each seemed to have the personal touch of loving individual care. There were poems, heart cut-outs, sprays of flowers, sheet music, stuffed animals, floral exhibits, flags, and thousands of expressions of personal love written on scraps of paper and in floral displays. Outside the gates, on the long stone wall dividing the grounds from Elvis Presley Boulevard and its sidewalk, were thousands of respectful and loving comments to Elvis, meticulously written by the pilgrims who have come to this shrine.

Fan response to the memory of Elvis Presley has received increasing attention in recent years, just as it has continued to grow. The tenth-anniversary memorial attracted 15,000 people to the Candlelight Vigil, compared to 25,000 for the fifteenth anniversary. One critic has described the fascination with Elvis Presley as "a chronicle of a cultural obsession" (Marcus 1991). Yet the most suggestive account of what Elvis fans may be feeling as they engage in this behavior appears in a small book published in 1992 by two younger fans, Cindy Hazen and Mike Freeman. *The Best of Elvis: Recollections of a Great Humanitarian* tells a story of a private Elvis—one who loved people and without calculation gave generously of his personal wealth for their individual benefit (Hazen and Freeman 1992).

The Best of Elvis is an elaborate collection of anecdotes organized around the concept of Presley's personal character. It emphasizes his loyalty and devotion to friends, family, and associates; his commitment to charitable organizations through benefit concerts and personal giving (frequently not made public and often not counted for income-tax purposes); his generosity to people he met casually and to his fans (who received gifts of money, jewelry, automobiles, homes, and other financial support to meet a special need); his inspiration to fan clubs throughout the world (who have their own charitable projects to honor Presley's memory); and, most important, his significant religious convictions.

Hazen and Freeman remind us that, while Presley won more awards for record sales than any other performer, his three Grammy awards for musical excellence all recognize his gospel recordings. Presley had religious humility. "When a fan presented him with a gold crown and said, 'This is for you; you're the King,' he gently corrected her. 'No honey,' he said. 'Christ is the King. I'm just a singer'" (Hazen and Freeman 1992, xvi). J. D. Sumner, the gospel singer who backed Presley on stage, helped arrange his private funeral, and sang there. Sumner remembered Presley's desire to sing gospel music in his live concerts—even in Las Vegas. In a testimony reminiscent of Barbara Mandrell, Sumner said: "He drew in thousands of people and witnessed to them in a way by having us sing some gospel. . . . When he sang 'How Great Thou Art,' he did it with such power and feeling that I know it affected people tremendously" (Hazen and Freeman 1992, 36). This view is consistent with the report that, when Presley was asked what kind of memorial should be created at his birthplace in Tupelo, Mississippi, to remind fans of his life, he replied: "Why don't you build a chapel so my fans can go and meditate and reflect on their own lives and know that no matter what station they reach in life, if they place their talent in the hands of God, He can bless it and they can make a contribution to the world?" (Gregory 1980, 105).

The Best of Elvis is a significant repository of fan memory. In collective memory, Elvis Presley is a mother's boy, a good boy who served his country without protest, one who made it in the music business "his way," and when he had risen successfully from poverty, kept close to his family and original friends. He spent his mature lifetime giving away money in personal philanthropy to help others not fortunate to have the God-given talent that gave him his own success. And he kept his religious faith. This legend of the humble, spiritual Elvis committed to his own form of social gospel is an image of salvation from both the hard times and the domestic turmoil that Presley, like many fans who felt so close to him, endured.

A short story in *Elvis Rising* captures this mood nicely. In "Starlight Coupe," Laura Kalpakian gives us a working-class mother and daughter abandoned by the father. They live on welfare but supplement their income by buying items cheaply at yard sales and refurbishing them for resale. These women are more than crass exploiters of the welfare system; as devoted Elvis fans, their entrepreneurship bears the mark of his generosity:

> Sometimes we go back to the best garage sales Saturday night, when they're closing things up, and we offer, say, five dollars for the leftover clothes. Mama picks through the stuff, and what can be saved or salvaged she mends, washes, irons and puts it in one of the boxes we keep on our living room floor. One each for men, women, children, babies. When the boxes get filled up, Mama delivers them to shelters, schools, small neighborhood grocery stores, people's homes and halfway houses. She gives it all away in Elvis's name. It's good to know we

can carry on the King's work, just like he did it, not making a big fuss, just helping, quiet like. He did it so quiet that people don't even know he helped, but it's true. People still don't believe it when you tell them. (Sloan and Pierce 1993, 181)

"Starlight Coupe" is a story of optimism in the face of hard times and broken hearts. These enterprising women are committed to the welfare of others, as well as themselves; their spirit is rooted in the same tradition that may have produced Elvis Presley's generosity—Christian salvation. When Mama is able to buy a 1946 Studebaker Starlight Coupe, which reminds her of the car her husband drove in their courting days, her family and friends celebrate the new acquisition by dancing to Elvis Presley records.

> There was thunder in the floor and I felt his presence with us and I knew that music could always roll the stone from his tomb and I knew, right then, no tomb could ever hold Elvis or his music. He would never die, and he would never leave us and we could go on loving Elvis forever, and him living forever and his music living forever. He had passed through time, like a sieve, like water or steam through a sieve. His music fell on us like spring rain, and we were, all of us, ready to grow again. (Sloan and Pierce 1993, 215)

In both *The Best of Elvis* and "Starlight Coupe," Elvis fans have provided perpetual salvation for him through kind memory of his devotion to them.

"I believe I will see Elvis Presley in heaven" said evangelist Billy Graham (Hazen and Freeman, 1992, 173). Dolly Parton, Loretta Lynn, and Tammy Wynette agree. In their vocal-event album released near the end of 1993, *Honky Tonk Angels*, they offer twelve songs newly recorded as a trio, including one with guest Kitty Wells on her trademark "It Wasn't God Who Made Honky Tonk Angels," and one where the trio sings with Patsy Cline's recording of Hank Williams's "Lovesick Blues" (Lynn, Parton, Wynette, Columbia 1993). *Honky Tonk Angels* concludes with yet another remake of Hal Southern and Eddie Dean's 1954 vision, "I Dream of a Hillbilly Heaven." This time, Dolly Parton is the dreamer. When she visits "Hillbilly Heaven," Roy Acuff and Tex Ritter are hosting a grand stage show filled with country music artists, and as of late 1993, fifteen men and three women have arrived. On this visit, Parton's hosts tell her that the women members have special qualities: Patsy Cline is "the best singing angel here"; Dottie West is "probably the prettiest"; and Mother Maybelle Carter is "God's favorite." The "Big Tally Book" indicates that within the next forty to sixty years, seventeen more men and eight more women will enter Hillbilly Heaven. But the last angel Dolly actually meets before waking up is Elvis Presley. Dolly's hosts pause to agree with one of Presley's remarks made while he was on earth: "They still call him 'The King' but we know they're not talking about the real King up here."

During four decades when the image of a grand performance in heaven has provided an exact vision of spiritual destiny for country singers, country music culture has maintained and perhaps deepened awareness of its relationship with evangelical religion. Its visions of salvation from hard times, broken hearts, domestic turmoil, and the traumas of tragic troubadours are expressions growing out of that relationship. And its fans, like an extended congregation, honor both the ministers of this faith and their memory, as a way of keeping it.

There's just one place where there ain't no
laughter, and that's Hell. I done made
arrangements to miss Hell. So I won't never
be no place where there ain't somebody
laughing.
                              —Jerry Clower, 1992

She's a sparrow when she's broken
But she's an eagle when she flies.
                              —Dolly Parton, 1991

CHAPTER 5   Success

.

If country music centers on personal salvation from traumas of domestic turmoil and hard times, an important leavening agent that
provides relief from overbearing seriousness is available from country humorists. Since its origins as a commercial enterprise in traveling medicine shows, comedy has been an important feature of country music culture. Many early artists—including Jimmie Rodgers,
Hank Williams, Roy Acuff, Gene Autry, and Bob Wills—earned their
first money in medicine shows, where they were expected to provide
both comic and serious entertainment. By the 1940s, when Grand
Ole Opry tour groups and "package shows" were playing towns
throughout the South, a comedian star system paralleling the one
emerging among singing artists was in place (Green 1976, 78). Hank
Williams was well known for combining a blend of personal pathos
and wry wit that made phrases like "everything's okay," and "I'll
never get out of this world alive" common usage in vernacular

speech for laughing at troubles. The long-running television program *Hee Haw* capitalized on this tradition, adding skits revived from tent shows, minstrels, and vaudeville to create a sustained comic presence still available in 1994 on The Nashville Network. *Country America* magazine showcases jokes from a contemporary country comic on the last page of every issue. Humor sections of suburban bookstores across America that feature compilations of amusing language from supposedly rustic Southerners recently included a collection of "country music's best (and funniest) lines" titled *I've Got Tears in My Ears from Lying on My Back in My Bed While I Cry Over You* (Schwed 1992).

This tradition of comic relief in country music culture has at least three distinct themes. Some artists and groups specialize in relief from the serious tone of country music itself. David Allen Coe's rendition of the Steve Goodman song "You Never Even Called Me By My Name" includes an example. In a narrative preceding the final verse, Coe tells fans that Goodman believed he had written "the perfect country song," but that wasn't so because the original version left out any reference to Mama, trains, trucks, prison, and getting drunk. Then, Coe says, Goodman wrote another last verse, where the singer was drunk when his mother got out of prison, but before he could get to her in his pickup truck, "she got runned over by a damned ole train" (Coe 1985). A more recent parody of the seriousness of country music that makes fun of its persistent rusticity and affection for thematic albums is the *Into the Twangy-First Century* album by the parody group Run C & W (Run C & W 1993). Riders in the Sky take on the "rambling fever" motif of country music culture in High Sheriff Drywall's rendition of "Livin' in a Mobile Home." Here, Drywall and his Mama proudly point out that living in a mobile home resolves a long-standing tension between rambling and family life for country artists, because "We're always gone but we're always home" (Riders 1990).

A second theme of comic relief focuses directly on domestic turmoil. Opry star Mike Snider, who offers a rustic persona specializing in an extreme Southern drawl combined with charismatic banjo-picking, tells stories contrasting his hometown of Gleason, Tennessee, with more modern places. Snider comments on matters ranging from modern food processing ("chicken fingers?") to the Nashville Airport's inability to relieve a good ole boy of his fear of flying ("the first sign you see says terminal"). Yet, the majority of Snider's stories focus on domestic situations, many of them his own marriage. In "Married Life," Snider says that he's been married five years, the best five years of his life, and that he's learned many things during that time. "I've learnt that the man truly is the head of the house. 'Course, I also learnt that the woman is the neck. And the neck turns the head any way it wants it to go" (Snider, undated).

Archie Campbell—one of the founding writer-actors on *Hee Haw* and the inspiration for *Hee Haw Village* in Pigeon Forge, Tennessee—focused on domestic situations of many kinds for his stage show. Well-grounded in vaudeville and minstrel tradition, Campbell in the 1960s pioneered on the Grand Ole Opry as a successful stand-up comedian who refused to dress in rustic garb. His signature story was a "Spoonerism version" of the fairy tale, "Cinderella." Campbell defined a "Spoonerism" as a form of verbal comedy "based on the transposition of consonant sounds in different words." He wrote his comic version of "Cinderella" both to emphasize its romantic dimensions and to make fun of them in verbal absurdity. "Rindercella" achieves her domestic bliss by means that can be instructive to other would-be brides: "If you go to a bancy fall and you want to have a pransome hince lall in fove with you, don't forget to slop your dripper!" (Campbell 1981, 112).

Sarah Ophelia Colley's character Minnie Pearl joined the Grand Ole Opry in 1940. In forty years of performing, she became one of the most prominent figures in country music culture and made a place for her creator in the Country Music Hall of Fame. Colley created a fictitious small town with intricate social relations that provides domestic stories for a memorable stage act. Minnie Pearl's "cousin" persona allowed her to stand outside the domestic turmoil tradition and comment on it with a feisty wit that reinforced the penchant of country music culture for romance while at the same time making light of it. The complexity of Minnie Pearl has been described by Bufwack and Oermann as "a blend of brash and bashful," a "man-hungry old maid with a coy demeanor and a glint in her eye," a "homely wallflower with just enough pluck and grit to keep her chin up," and a "small-town gossip without malice" (Bufwack and Oermann 1993, 248).

The vision of an entire community in Minnie Pearl's stories allows her to move beyond romantic couples and observe the amusing dimensions of extended family life so integral to country music culture. *Minnie Pearl's Diary* includes this entry:

TUESDAY, APRIL 22.

The big social ee-vent of the week wuz the golden weddin' anniversary of the Whittaker Stobbs. The Stobbs had 9 younguns and they got about 40 grandchillun. Well, the fambly and all the relatives wuz thar at the anniversary—and what a hubbub they made with the younguns yellin and squawkin and playin and their pappys and mammys gabbin and arguin politics and crops and things. Finally old Mr. Whit Stobbs turned to his bride of 50 year and said, "Mirandy, that night I took you home from the huskin bee, I sure warn't aimin to start all this!" (Pearl 1953, 60–61)

A third theme of comic relief in country humor is relief from the emphasis on personal salvation associated with evangelical religion. Many country comedians tell stories that deflate the piety of religious ceremonies. A favorite topic is making light of death and funerals. Another story from *Minnie Pearl's Diary*:

FRIDAY, MAY 2.

We all went to Old Lady Splenny's funeral today—pore old thing—she had the reputation of havin the sharpest tongue and the orneriest temper in Hickman County. Jest as the Parson got through asayin the last words at the funeral, a big black cloud come up all of a sudden and they wuz a blindin flash of lightnin and a awful clash of thunder. Ole Lady Splenny's son-in-law looked up and turned to his wife and said, "Well, it looks like she got thar!" (Pearl 1953, 65)

Humorist Jerry Clower satirizes preachers at funerals. In his story "Last Rites," a minister on his way to preach a funeral has a flat tire and misses it. When he arrives at the church, the body has been taken to a nearby graveyard. Unclear about directions, he rushes to a graveyard where "way up on the hill past the graveyard there was two fellows throwing dirt in a hole." Running to them and thinking he must say something, he utters the blessing "Ashes to ashes, dust to dust. We will remember this beautiful lady the rest of our lives. Amen." Then, as he drives away, the diggers lean back on their shovels and one says, "You know, that's the strangest words I ever heared anybody say over a septic tank" (Clower 1992, 94). Clower's "The Dead Cat" digs a bit deeper. Here a lady takes her dead cat in a little casket to two different churches with a request that the cat be buried. Refused each time, she goes to a Baptist church. At first the preacher objects: "How dare you think we would bury a cat." Her answer: "Well, I'm frustrated, and I am prepared to give two thousand dollars to whoever holds a service for my cat." The preacher responds, "Lady, why didn't you tell me your cat was a Baptist?" (Clower 1992, 125)

Jerry Clower is a humorist from rural Mississippi who, in 1993, celebrated twenty-three years as an MCA recording artist by signing a new eight-year contract. Clower is said to have sold over 8 million albums and become the number-one seller among all recording artists at truck stops. Born into a Depression-era childhood in southern Mississippi, Clower was the offspring of an alcoholic father who left his family and a seventeen-year-old mother who taught Clower the values of hard work, personal responsibility, and Baptist religion. Clower regularly tells the story of his own salvation in a revival meeting at the East Fork Baptist Church, Amite County Mississippi, at the age of thirteen. In that same revival meeting, the girl who would become his wife, and to whom he is still married after more than forty years, also confessed her religious faith. Clower says both were baptized the same day in the Amite River. After serving in the Navy during World War II, Clower attended Mississippi State University on a football scholarship and studied agriculture. He briefly worked as a county agricultural agent, then became a successful fertilizer salesman based in Yazoo City, Mississippi. Clower told humorous stories as a company banquet speaker, and in 1971, he began recording them. His early recordings found a good regional audience and in 1973 he joined the Grand Ole Opry (Clower 1992, 3–49; Bronner 1989, 467).

In the early 1990s, Jerry Clower has become an important representative of country music culture. He tours more than 200 days per year and has seen 124 of his stories collected in a volume published by the university press of his native state. If one theme of Clower's humor is to temper the seriousness of country music culture with amusing stories that deflate religious piety, another is to elevate the naive ingenuity, pride, and gumption of rural and working-class people. Many of Clower's stories are structured by assuming these traits for favorable characters and putting them into conflict with characters who lack them. "Marcel's Talking Chain Saw" is a good example. Here, Marcel Ledbetter who, despite his "fine Christian teaching," liked to dress in nothing but overalls for hot weather, is a hard-working poor man who on a summer day stops at a county line "beer joint" to buy a soda. Marcel politely asks the proprietor to hand the soda through the door, saying he will pay for the drink and its bottle. But Marcel is refused service and called a "redneck." "We don't want the likes of you in here," he's told. Marcel's reaction is deliberate and convincing. He picks up a chain saw from the back of his truck, saws out the screen door, steps inside, and snips two legs off a table. Told in live performance, this story displays Clower's signature ability to imitate the sounds of machinery. As it builds to a climactic confrontation between an innocent working man and those who would deny his dignity, Clower embellishes the tension with the roaring of a chain saw, then ends with a kind of rustic justice: "They gave Marcel the beer joint!!" (Clower 1992, 109–10).

An extended family named Ledbetter supplies many of Clower's stories. In "Railroad Man," "old man Claymore Ledbetter" illustrates the value of knowledge earned through personal experience rather than through formal education or position. One day a train is stalled at Chatawa, Mississippi, because the engine won't crank. As Clower tells it: "They sent to McComb where they have a roundhouse and they know all about engines. The top dog come down there, his assistant dog come down there, and assistant to that dog come down to Chatawa. They went to looking and fumbling and turning knobs and bolts and screws and electrical things, and it wouldn't crank." A crowd gathered. Someone said that Ledbetter, who worked the railroad for fifty years, could crank it. The exasperated superintendent sent for him. Ledbetter's solution was to mark an "X" in a key spot on the side of the engine and have the strongest boy standing around hit it with a sledgehammer. This done, the engine "began running like a sewing machine." While the crowd applauds, the superintendent asks, "Sir, what do I owe you?" The answer is $100. Asked how he got that figure, Ledbetter says "Well, give that boy that slung that sledgehammer a dollar for hitting the engine with the sledgehammer, and give me ninety-nine dollars for knowing where to hit the thing" (Clower 1992, 94–95).

Another variation among Clower's stories of working-class dignity are those in which individuals deftly slither out of embarrassing situations into which their own entrepreneurship has gotten them. In "The Chauffeur and the Professor," "a technical fellow with a Ph.D. from the School of Mines" becomes a brilliant traveling speaker on behalf of the Independent Oil Dealers Association of

Hal Ketchum and Ferlin Husky on stage at the Grand
Ole Opry for Ketchum's induction, January 22, 1994

Fans of the Grand Ole Opry at the Ryman Auditorium in Nashville, 1950s

Jimmie Rodgers as country singer

Jimmie Rodgers as western singer

Publicity photograph of the original Carter Family: Maybelle, A. P., and Sara Carter

Roy Acuff, friends, and fans performing at the Ryman

Bill Monroe, inventor of bluegrass

Dean Mitchell promotional photograph with Jimmie Rodgers

Patsy Cline on stage

Hank Williams on stage

Alan Jackson and fans live at Fan Fair in Nashville, 1992

Above: Jerry Clower, humorist;
Right: Cousin Minnie Pearl

Hubert and Jeanette Cooke sing after reaffirming wedding vows at their
Thirtieth Anniversary Concert in Harrogate, Tennessee, April 25, 1992.

Recollections of a
Great Humanitarian

THE
BEST
OF
ELVIS

Cindy Hazen and Mike Freeman

Elvis Presley: the fans' view, 1992

George Jones smiles, 1990.

Loretta Lynn's tour bus parked at the Double L Ranch,
Hurricane Mills, Tennessee, 1992

Loretta, Loudilla, and Kay Johnson

Right: Dolly in 1993;
below: Tina Jackson and Jeanette
Williams at the Dollywood
Foundation Benefit Concert,
April 25, 1992

photograph by Curtis W. Ellison

Fans meeting Garth Brooks, June 11, 1992

Fans line up to meet Garth Brooks at Fan Fair in Nashville, June 11, 1992.

A fan remembers Conway Twitty on the day of his memorial service in Hendersonville, Tennessee, June 9, 1993.

America. A chauffeur drives him from meeting to meeting in a limousine. After hearing the speech for five months, the chauffeur decides he can improve upon it. "Sir, there ain't no justice in this country," he tells the professor. "I can make that speech better than you. I can! I've heard you make it a hundred times and I memorized it. I'm a better speaker than you. You are making so much money you can't spend it all, and I go hungry, just driving this car. I guarantee you I can make a speech as good as you, and I ought to get a raise." Challenged and irritated, the professor decides to embarrass his chauffeur. At a place where he is unknown, he swaps clothing with the chauffeur, daring him to make a fool of himself. Sure enough, the chauffeur gives a successful oration before 22,000 people. Then he invites questions. Someone in his "egghead" university audience poses a complicated inquiry about the pH of soil on a drill bit that passes through the decayed carcass of a dinosaur buried 8,943 feet beneath the earth's surface. Apparently caught, the chauffeur is, however, not defeated. Clower explains: "That ole boy on that stage stared right at him. He said: 'Long as I've been in this business I ain't never been asked a question that simple. Just to show you how simple that question is, my chauffeur is in the back of the room, and I'm going to ask him to stand up and answer it!'" (Clower 1992, 189–91).

Gumption, pride, and dignity are key themes in Clower's best-known stage presentation, "A Coon Huntin' Story." This tale is one of Clower's earliest recorded hits, and he often uses it as a signature finale to his stage show. One of his longest items and an auto-biographical one, "A Coon Huntin' Story" allows Clower to describe both growing up in rural southern Mississippi before World War II and the hunting rituals important to outdoor life of men there. As the story begins, Clower is hunting raccoons with his friends and his dogs at night on a neighbor's property when the neighbor surprises him. The neighbor has with him John Eubanks, "a great American" who doesn't believe in shooting raccoons out of trees. He taught hunters to "give everything a sporting chance." Eubanks's approach to coon hunting was to take along a cross-cut saw and when a dog treed a raccoon, to "hold the dog and cut the tree down, or either climb the tree and make the coon jump in amongst the dogs." This was "sporting," because "at least he had the option of whipping all them dogs and walking off if he wanted to."

This time, Jerry's dogs tree a raccoon up the biggest sweet gum tree in the entire swamp. The hunting party can't see into the top of this tree nor can they reach around it, and Jerry challenges John Eubanks to climb this tree. John did climb the tree. As the party stands below, he makes his way out of their sight, pulls out his stick to punch the raccoon, and discovers that instead of a raccoon the dogs have treed a lynx. This situation allows Clower to graphically depict sounds of the obscure fight in the top of the tree. They hear John Eubanks calling "WOW! OOOO! This thing's killing me!" and finally, "*Shoot this thing!*" John Eubanks's desire to protect his tree-climbing reputation has gotten him into a situation his hunting principles may not survive. Now the hunters reply that they can't shoot because they might hit Eubanks. But he offers them a solution respecting the mutual dignity of animals and men that is Clower's punch line: "Well, just shoot up in here amongst us. One of us has got to have some relief" (Clower 1992, 141–44).

Beyond tales that deflate piety and explore working-class dignity, Jerry Clower offers stories that celebrate entrepreneurial zeal, as well as those that testify to the personal satisfaction available through the faith of his Baptist upbringing. George Jones is loved by country fans partly because he is confessional—that is, his songs disclose in open emotion the pain of domestic turmoil, thus giving a kind of testimony paralleling that of evangelical tradition. Clower has called George Jones "the greatest country singer God ever allowed to be birthed in the world" (Clower 1992, 20). The affinity is understandable because Jerry Clower also provides testimony for his fans. But Clower celebrates the relief of the saved instead of the guilt of the tormented.

In "Salesman at the Funeral," Clower (who sometimes tells audiences that there are people who think he is still selling fertilizer) provides a story meant to illustrate his admiration of salesmen. In this instance, a traveling salesman comes into a small Southern town at midafternoon, but all businesses are closed because every person in town has gone to the funeral of a prominent local citizen. When the salesman arrives at the funeral, the crowd is packed around the gravesite because there are too many people to go into the church. After the preacher says words, he invites anyone present to say something "about our departed brother." None respond. After a short pause the salesman's natural instinct to fill the void moves him to step forward:

Sir, Mr. Jones must have been a wonderful, respected man, and I'm just in awe of so many turning out for the funeral. But if none of y'all have anything you want to say, I'd like to take this opportunity to say a few words about Red Man chewing tobacco. (Clower 1992, 183–84)

Listening to a Jerry Clower tape, seeing a video or witnessing his stage performance leaves little doubt that Clower has a deep religious faith. Though in many stories he punctures his own ego by making humor from personal mistakes and embarrassment, Clower's underlying faith in his salvation nurtures his advocacy of a success ethic. In his twentieth-anniversary album, *Jerry Clower: The Mouth of the Mighty Mississip' Just Keeps Rolling Along*, Clower concludes with an autobiographical confessional entitled "Twenty Years (A Synopsis)." This long story details Clower's life in show business, which he dates from his decision to join the 4-H club in grammar school. He carries the story through his college life at Mississippi State University playing football, his work with 4-H clubs as a county agent in Oxford, Mississippi, his achievement as a salesman for agricultural chemicals, discovery by MCA records as a storyteller, and his first record label contract in 1970. Clower says his family listened to the Grand Ole Opry on Saturday nights as he was growing up but he never dreamed then that he might be a member today. In 1990, when this album was recorded, he looked back over twenty years of success as a country artist to evaluate himself as a country boy who kept his religious faith, stayed close to his wife and family, worked hard all his life, maintained consistent honesty in his treatment of others, and, in effect, was rewarded by the blessing of a successful entertainment career. In this story, company executives are characterized as sophisticates and Clower as an innocent whose inherent cleverness and natural common sense take him to stardom (Clower 1990).

A year later, Jerry Clower made a recording that elaborates on the values behind his self-regard. In "Celebrate You," he speaks directly to country music fans about a philosophy of life. You need to "celebrate you" because you have immense potential, talents, experience, and gifts. Your age, color, or whether your parents loved you do not matter, Clower says. The mistakes you've made, the people you've hurt, these don't matter—because "that belongs to the past." Now, today, you are accepted, okay and loved, in spite of everything.

Forgiveness is freely available because of "the miracle called God." And spiritual salvation can lead directly to personal success, "So celebrate the miracle, and celebrate you!" (Clower 1991).

Jerry Clower has played a distinctive role as a country humorist by giving voice to a goal of many artists and fans: achieving personal success through ingenuity, pride, gumption, entrepreneurship, and religious faith. In the 1970s, 80s, and 90s, a series of important women artists brought forward their own examples of personal success and became icons of American popular culture. Loretta Lynn, Dolly Parton, and Reba McEntire have presented variations on a personal success ethic that has become an important alternative to the emphasis of male tragic troubadours on hard times and broken hearts.

"It wasn't God who made honky tonk angels," sang Loretta Lynn, Dolly Parton, Tammy Wynette, and Kitty Wells on the opening cut of their 1993 event album *Honky Tonk Angels* (Lynn 1993). This 1952 "answer song" to the tragic-troubadour lament "Wild Side of Life," a number-one hit for Kitty Wells in the early 1950s, became virtually an anthem for aspiring female country artists who elected not to focus on compliant femininity in their careers. It challenged in particular the domestic-turmoil tradition by centering the blame for marital traumas on faithless husbands themselves instead of hard times (Horstman 1986, 224). In Custer, Washington, a migrant Appalachian housewife who loved singing to her children heard Kitty Wells's smash hit, and it left a lasting impression. Loretta Lynn later recalled how Wells had changed her thinking about the audience for country music:

> In the old days, country music was directed at the men—truck-driving songs, easy women, cheating songs. I remember how excited I got back in 1952, the first time I heard Kitty Wells sing "It Wasn't God Who Made Honky-Tonk Angels." That was the women's answer to that Hank Thompson record. . . . See, Kitty was presenting the woman's point of view, which is different from the man's. And I always remembered that when I started writing songs. (Lynn and Vecsey 1977, 155–56)

Women gospel singers had already offered a spiritual alternative to worldly trauma through gospel salvation, and Loretta Lynn now offered a secular alternative—an image of the woman's assertive role in domestic relationships that affirmed traditional marriage yet required of men a new degree of direct personal attention. Lynn combined her message with a visible business career identifying her in popular culture as a spirited, successful woman who could be a model for multitudes of female fans. In effect, she presented an alternative to domestic turmoil and a challenge to the tragic-troubadour tradition.

It's reasonable to think of the star system in country music as exemplary of popular mythology about American commercial success. Most highly productive artists come from economic and social circumstances that are far from privileged. Their devotion to the hard work of their artistry is legendary, and many have had the good fortune to be supported by benefactors at key moments in their careers. Horatio Alger's dictum for success in America might seem to fit—financial rewards and public attention follow pluck, perseverance, and luck. Loretta Lynn's life has been seen this way.

At the age of forty-one, with a million dollars in the bank, an elaborate dude ranch in Tennessee, and a visibility unprecedented for a female artist (including million-selling records, prominence on national television talk shows, and selection as the first female CMA Entertainer of the Year) Loretta Lynn published her autobiography. Written with George Vecsey, *Coal Miner's Daughter* became a best-selling paperback, then in 1980 was made into a biographical movie that won an Oscar for Sissy Spacek's depiction of Loretta's life. The movie *Coal Miner's Daughter* became the official biography of country music's leading female figure of the 1970s. It showed a hillbilly singer who challenged conventions of domestic turmoil and affirmed American success in terms applicable to ordinary women (MCA Home Video 1980).

Two years before Lynn published her autobiography, Hollywood director Robert Altman released a movie that used country music culture in Nashville to meditate on American politics (Altman 1975). In *Nashville,* Altman exaggerates the culture's rhinestone garishness, drawing characters motivated almost solely by materialism, greed, power and sexual lust. He focuses on a female artist and her husband whose lives have an unflattering resemblance to Loretta Lynn and her husband. *Nashville* lacks any sympathy for the warm relationship that distinguishes the bond between country artists and their fans. In a telling scene, Altman's Loretta figure is performing before fans who, in stark contrast to typical fan behavior in live-performance situations, stare sullenly and vacuously toward the stage and show no positive interaction, either with one another or with the artist they supposedly have come to see. This unlikely environment is sustained for more than two and a half hours in a movie that ends when a psychopath assassinates the Loretta figure while she sings at a political rally. In Lynn's autobiography she claims not to have seen Altman's movie and, in any case, expresses a preference for Walt Disney movies. She makes it plain, however, that her autobiography represents a correction of Altman's negative image: "So if you're wondering whether that character in the movie is me, it ain't. This book is me" (Lynn and Vecsey 1977, 15).

The movie version of *Coal Miner's Daughter* is developed with attention to detail suggesting a desire to "answer" *Nashville*. Actress Sissy Spacek studied Lynn with great care and sang Lynn's original songs in the movie, complete with an impressive grasp of Lynn's characteristic mannerisms and voicing patterns. Significant figures in Nashville's country music business gave the movie *Coal Miner's Daughter* their official endorsement by playing themselves in their actual relationship to Lynn in the situations and places where life events occurred.

Loretta Lynn's movie tells her life history in four parts, each designed to reveal a dimension of country music culture. Part one occurs in the Appalachian mountain setting of Butcher Holler, Johnson County, Kentucky. Born in 1935 the second of eight children, when the movie opens, Loretta Webb has just entered her teenage years. Her father at this time is a sturdy, hard-working coal miner and her mother, who is one-fourth Cherokee Indian, provides a disciplined home in a coal mine camp. In this part of the movie, Loretta's life is centered entirely on traditional family values, the community of an isolated mountain coal town that she has never left, and a daily life that lacks any amenities other than the Grand Ole Opry on the radio Saturday night and mail-order clothing from Sears and Roebuck.

Loretta's childhood prematurely comes to an end when a brash young man, Doolittle Lynn, returns from Army service in World War II, vowing not to spend his life in the coal mines and intent on marrying Loretta. Despite the objections of her family to Doolittle's more advanced age and worldly ways, Loretta's first love is a deep one, and this marriage will not be denied. Doolittle does go to work in the mines he hates, in order to support them; and his response to

Loretta's childish ways—especially her sexual naiveté and her inability to cook—adds domestic turmoil to their economic hard times. At age fourteen, Loretta is both pregnant and sent home to her parents, while Doolittle apparently takes an interest in women of the town. But, right here, Loretta takes a first step to assert her rights: she physically chases away a woman who is paying attention to her husband, saying that by their marriage, he's her man and she expects to be respected.

Doolittle and Loretta reconcile; then he decides they must leave the economically depressed coal country. They move to Washington state, where he works on a ranch, then in the timber industry. The final scene of part one draws the curtain on Appalachian hard times and domestic turmoil in a touching good-bye between Loretta and her father. They stand beside a waiting locomotive where the coal miner, now suffering from respiratory disease, tells his daughter he will never see her again.

The second part of *Coal Miner's Daughter* shows us Loretta's domestic life in the state of Washington, where she keeps house and takes care of her children, now numbering four. Memories of Appalachia remain strong and she listens to country music. Doolittle likes the way Loretta sings. He buys a guitar for her birthday, which she learns to chord well enough to accompany the renditions of songs she is writing. Doolittle is impressed. At his instigation, Loretta begins performing in a local honky-tonk. By the time Loretta's father dies a few years later, Doolittle is, in effect, Loretta's manager, and they are in position to promote a demonstration record she has made. Back in Butcher Holler for the funeral, they decide to tour radio stations across Kentucky and Tennessee, calling on disc jockeys and encouraging them to spin her "Honky Tonk Girl."

This part of the movie, however, is not focused mainly on Loretta's singing. The movie omits Loretta's winning a talent contest sponsored by Buck Owens in Tacoma, and the role of a wealthy benefactor, a Vancouver lumberman who was a recent widower. In her written autobiography, Lynn says, "Doo and I were just like a couple of kids, and Norm Burley kind of adopted us. He said he wanted to help us by giving us a contract to make a record. He didn't wear any red suit or black boots, but that man sure looked like Santa Claus to us" (Lynn and Vecsey 1977, 108). This part of the movie continues to emphasize the domestic relationship between Doolittle and Loretta, suggesting that his desire to improve their lot in life by capitalizing on Loretta's talent motivates Doolittle to work night and day for their mutual benefit. The key scene in part two of the movie occurs in the aftermath of Loretta's father's funeral. She has experienced extreme guilt about leaving Kentucky, as well as homesickness for her original family life that she knows will never be recovered. She's unclear about the life of a professional country singer that her husband offers as an alternative to the image of family her father provided in Butcher Holler, and now she must make an entrepreneurial decision. While riding away from her father's grave seated on a bulldozer her husband has used to make a new road, she decides to invest everything in pursuit of country music success. "I want it real bad," she tells him.

Part three of *Coal Miner's Daughter* outlines Lynn's steps to stardom in country music culture. In the late 1950s and early 60s, country music was a dynamic business with stage shows, radio plays, recording contracts and television appearances; yet it remained fluid enough to provide openings for new hits from independent record labels (Zwisohn 1993, 9–11). The path Loretta Lynn followed to stardom included an initial period of performing regionally followed by a demonstration record that was promoted nationwide on radio, leading to a nationwide hit recognized on the country music charts. All these events occur in the movie. They result in an appearance on the Grand Ole Opry and entry into the inner circle of artists and business people. Supported by Opry stars Ernest Tubb and Patsy Cline, Loretta begins her ascent.

At the time Loretta Lynn and George Vecsey wrote *Coal Miner's Daughter*, Lynn was entangled in professional separation proceedings with the Wilburn Brothers and details of the Wilburns' influence on Lynn were omitted. Laurence Zwisohn suggests that Teddy and Doyle Wilburn were "unsung heroes" in Lynn's emergence. Soon after arriving in Nashville, Loretta made contact with the Wilburn Brothers, whom Zwisohn describes as "among the most foresighted businessmen in country music at the time, with a touring show, a successful publishing company, Sure-Fire Music, and an important booking agency, Wil-Helm, which handled many of the decade's biggest country stars" (Zwisohn 1993, 10). Zwisohn states that Doyle Wilburn arranged Loretta's initial Opry appearance on October 15, 1960, and may have played a role in the considerable attention given her by the Opry until she was made a permanent member in 1962. Doyle Wilburn also arranged Loretta's first recording contract with Owen Bradley, at Decca Records, producer of the Wilburn Brothers and Patsy Cline. In 1963, Loretta became a regular on the Wilburn Brothers syndicated television show, a move that gave her important visibility in an era when television exposure was a crucial route into national popular culture.

Instead of showing these business connections with men that assisted Loretta Lynn at a crucial point in her career, the movie version of her autobiography emphasizes Lynn's relationship to Patsy Cline. Cline is shown to be a mentor for what became Loretta's signature image, a woman singer who challenges compliant femininity. In the movie, Loretta is influenced by Patsy Cline's combative yet loving attitude toward her stormy marital relationship with Charlie Dick, and she learns to apply Cline's attitude to her own marriage. Under Patsy's tutelage she begins to write and sing convincing songs about women who object to their husband's "cheating" behavior with other women. In her actual career between 1964 and 1969, Lynn was at first recording conventional duets with male star Ernest Tubb. Those carried such titles as "Wine, Women and Song." Yet, in this same period, Lynn's songwriting and solo recording took an important turn toward self-conscious gender statement. In 1966, she wrote her famous challenge to domestic turmoil, a wife's ultimatum to an alcoholic husband, "Don't Come Home A Drinkin' (with Lovin' on Your Mind)." The year before, she wrote "You Ain't Woman Enough (To Take My Man)" as a challenge to a female competitor. Other feisty woman titles included "Your Squaw Is on the Warpath," "Fist City," and the 1972 endorsement of a form of sexual independence for women through contraception, "The Pill." This particular song crystallized Lynn's challenge to domestic turmoil. It argues that women's control of procreation gives them the power to explore extramarital sex just as men had previously done in the traditional scenario of domestic turmoil. For Lynn, this means women have a new bargaining power that can be used to keep errant men at home.

In part three of the movie, these forceful songs are written in response to Doolittle Lynn's affection for alcohol and his occasional attention to other women. Their effect is a signature image for Lynn as a noncompliant female who is sexually assertive while simultaneously defending traditional family values. Loretta's stage persona in the film magnifies this effect. It emphasizes her petite stature, her mystique of youthful innocence (garbed in the ladylike attire of long white formal dresses) and her soulful delivery featuring a sincere "catch" or "tearful" articulation combined with a rustic regional accent. This image became a badge of working-class sincerity.

In part four of the movie, Loretta's challenge to conventions of domestic turmoil pays off. When Patsy Cline dies in a plane crash, Loretta's career soars. She tours incessantly while Doolittle becomes a more attentive husband, living on their ranch in middle Tennessee and caring for their twin daughters. The movie depicts road life as exhausting. With a woman in the role of the circuit-riding country music star who weaves across the nation by bus to perform for fans in their hometowns, we see less romance of nomadic travel and more pressure from constant attention by adoring fans. There is reliance on prescription drugs for sleeping, for waking, and for physical relief from fatigue. There is strain on family relationships created by prolonged absence from spouse and children. In the classic tradition of troubadour musicians, Loretta suffers a near breakdown. But Doolittle leaves the ranch temporarily to join her on the road, and finally, he takes her off the road for a period of recovery at home. Although this part of the movie tells a prototypical success story of country music stardom, it never loses its focus on the domestic relationship between the star and her husband. In the concluding scene, Doolittle proposes building a new home on their ranch, and Loretta objects—not to the idea of a new home, but to her husband's presumption that he can make the decisions to design and build it without her participation. In the end, he relents without, the movie seems to say, losing his personality. For Loretta, achieving full partnership in domestic decisions appears to be the final step to mature stardom.

Coal Miner's Daughter is a kind of resistance to the tragic domestic turmoil popularized in country music culture by Hank Williams and Patsy Cline. Both in her songwriting and in her personal life, Loretta Lynn is shown to be a fully independent woman who favors traditional family values in a larger environment where personal behavior is opportunistic, social experience is migratory, and emotions are often fragmented. Much of Lynn's music speaks to broken promises, displacement from home, and a strong determination to establish satisfactory love relationships where women hold the keys to independent behavior that can open doors previously open to men. Lynn's autobiographical song, "Coal Miner's Daughter," looks at marriage reflectively in a nostalgic daughter's tribute to the conventional values of her father and mother during times of economic hardship. Born into hard times, a daughter looking back from success can remember her parents' strength as a heritage of pride: "I'm proud to be a coal miner's daughter," she sings. At the same time, her movie life celebrates commercial success and stardom, despite the pressures of celebrity status and life on the road.

The country music culture of Loretta Lynn offers compelling rewards that a vernacular singer with charisma and rustic sincerity might not find elsewhere—financial gain and public notice combined with a supporting home life through domestic accommodation. Unlike the image of country music stardom presented in Hank Williams's biographical movie, the coal miner's daughter is not saved in retrospect. She has success now, achieved by a tough-minded woman who will not allow destruction of her personal life in domestic turmoil.

Loretta Lynn's image was attractive in American popular culture of the early 1970s. "Coal Miner's Daughter" rose to number 83 on the pop charts in 1970 and in 1971, 1972, and 1973, Lynn was named CMA Female Vocalist of the Year. In 1972, she became the first woman named CMA Entertainer of the Year and in 1973 earned honorable mention in a Gallup Poll of the world's ten most admired women. Between 1971 and 1976, she recorded five number-one hits in a duet partnership with Conway Twitty. She was also the first female to be named Entertainer of the Year by the Academy of Country Music, who awarded her "Artist of the Decade" for the 1970s. For her songwriting Lynn was elected to the Nashville Songwriters Association Hall of Fame. By June 1977, her written autobiography had sold over a million copies. Nine years later, *Music City News*, a leading fan magazine, gave her its Living Legend Award.

In 1966, Loretta Lynn and her husband purchased a 1,200-acre plantation at Hurricane Mills, west of Nashville in central Tennessee. By 1975, the Lynns had considerably expanded its acreage, bought the town of Hurricane Mills, and opened a dude ranch named the "Double L." Loretta wrote in her autobiography that the ranch had pastureland for 300 head of cattle and accommodations for 180 trailers, that it featured "square dances, fishing, games, a recreation room, tennis court, laundry, and bathrooms and more than 150 miles of horseback trails" (Lynn and Vecsey 1977, 166). The ranch has expanded; in the 1990s, it provides Loretta's fans a walking tour of her home and a visit to a simulated coal mine from Van Lear, Kentucky, where Loretta's father worked. Hurricane Mills includes a re-creation of Loretta Lynn's childhood home built on a landscape that evokes its original site in Butcher Holler (complete with outhouse, dug well, iron bed, oil lamps, Warm Morning heater, spittoon, washboard, lye soap, slop jar, wood stove, wallpaper made from newspapers and Sears catalogs, and wasp nests on the back porch). The only clue to Lynn's future career in her replica house may be the battery-operated radio.

The town of Hurricane Mills was founded in 1896 as a site for carding wool and processing grain, corn and flour. In 1974, the Lynns restored the town with its mill and dam. Today it is a "working ranch" with 500 head of cattle and its own post office. In the center of Hurricane Mills is a museum showing Loretta's music awards, gold records, pictures, and extensive memento collection. This museum bears Loretta's distinctly personal touch—many items on display are identified by her handwritten notes. Lynn regards her fans as a kind of extended family with whom she maintains personal friendship. There is a prominent picture of Max and Mary MacMullen, fans of Loretta who over more than twenty years have attended 500-plus live performances in forty-eight states, five Canadian provinces, and five foreign countries. You can learn about and talk with Loretta's actual family members in this museum. Early personal letters from Doolittle are on display here, in addition to a postcard sent to her family about Loretta's first airplane ride. The special chair of her "favorite uncle, John Webb," who died in May 1990, sits beside the door. Uncle John's widow, Loretta Webb, who works in the museum, identifies herself as "Loretta's Aunt Loretta." Both of us, she says, were named after the movie star, Loretta Young.

The cozy atmosphere of fans as extended family is pervasive at the Double L Ranch. On June 6, 1992, Loretta Lynn staged her annual concert for fans, which occurs the weekend preceding Nashville's Fan Fair. A sold-out crowd of more than 2,000 ticketholders gathered in a new open-air shelter designed with a stage at one end, floor seating for approximately 800 people, and bleachers for at least 1,200 more. The concert began at 8 P.M. and ended at 10:10, with attentive fans lingering afterward to socialize—encouraged by the pouring rain of a true thunderstorm that began near the concert's conclusion. A living legend in her late fifties, a member of the Country Music Hall of Fame, owner of a ranch valued well above a million dollars, and western clothing stores, restaurants, the nation's largest rodeo, and three publishing companies, Loretta Lynn arguably is a revolutionary model for successful women in country music. Even so, this concert in 1993 was more like a family reunion and back-porch singing in a small Southern town than a showcase for one of country music's most successful businesswomen.

Before the concert began, fans bought beer and souvenirs at tents outside the shelter, mingled and strolled, conversed briefly with Doolittle through a chain-link fence that separated the backstage area, took pictures, and chatted with one another. Just before 8:00 P.M., an announcer stated that he was planning to fix the audio so everybody could hear well. He told fans they could take all the pictures they wished, but they would need to stay behind yellow ropes in front of the low stage so that seated members of the audience could see the stage show at all times. Loretta walked on promptly at 8:00 P.M. and opened with "They Don't Make 'em Like My Daddy Any More," a tribute to the strong character of her father. She followed with "I Wanna Be Free," a 1970 single that introduced her feisty woman persona. After a third number in this same vein, Loretta offered her fans a series of personal remarks that seemed to resume a conversation already in progress. She acknowledged the discomfort of fans about the heat of the day and commented on the newly constructed sound system: "It's hotterin' the dickens, ain't it? It's bouncin' off the wall here. Keep that bass drum down. In fact it's too loud, ain't it? Give me a Holiday Inn towel. Had so many of 'em on the line I's ashamed. I want to thank you-all for comin' to see us. Turn some lights down. We don't need 'em."

Lynn returned to performing with three more numbers in the motif of the assertive woman: "You Ain't Woman Enough," "Wouldn't That Be Great," and "Don't Come Home A Drinkin' (with Lovin' on Your Mind)," the last two a wife's challenge to a husband's attraction to alcohol. On stage, Loretta Lynn stands front and center of her band, walks back and forth, comes to the edge of the stage, cocks her head, smiles, and makes friendly hand gestures to fans. After the second set of three renditions, Loretta resumed her conversation with the audience. This time she puzzled aloud over the effectiveness of the new concert shelter, particularly its sound system. "This is the first time I've worked the new building. It's bouncin' off the ceiling. At least we got y'all out of the rain. We're out of the sun too. We've had concerts out here where it was so hot people fainted." She closed this patter with the first of many direct references from the stage to particular people in the audience—this one to her long-time friends and fan-club organizers Loretta, Loudilla, and Kay Johnson. "We'll do this one for the Johnson sisters," she said, moving into "I'll Lose My Mind Before I'm Over You." This was the seventh song of the concert and by this time Loretta was well involved, both with the audience and with her band, the Coal Miners, spread on stage behind her. For the eighth song she called her son Ernest Ray from the band for a duet of "Sweet Thing." By its end, fans in the audience were actively calling out requests, with Loretta responding, "We'll do a little bit of that. . . ." Two songs about childbearing and contraception followed, "One's on the Way" and "The Pill." Then Loretta backed into a more conventional mode with "Here I Am Again," a cover of Bill Monroe's "Blue Moon of Kentucky," and her own "Somebody, Somewhere," and "Out of My Head, Back in My Bed."

The first fourteen songs of this concert were delivered in loosely thematic groups of two to four songs each. Groups alternated thematically. One group presented nostalgia, romantic longing, and loving; the next focused on Loretta's trademark, a woman's assertiveness with her husband. There were twenty-eight songs in this concert, and at the end of the first fourteen, halfway through, Loretta switched tone decisively. The next eight songs—at the heart of the concert—were designed to involve members of Loretta's family with her fans. First, Loretta brought on her daughter, "Sissy," and her son-in-law, John, to sing a duet of the old minstrel song, "Yellow Rose of Texas." Sissy then addressed fans with a testimony about a solo she wanted to sing: "This is a special song to me. This is a song that was written for Mama. I took it up to the house. Mama left the room. Daddy listened but had fear in his eyes. Whenever Mama left I wanted to be on that bus." Sissy followed this with her "Letter to Loretta," which explains her desire to be a country singer, and added, "I'm the daughter of the Coal Miner's Daughter." This rendition moved the audience to the most vocal response so far. Sissy closed her stage appearance by telling the fans, "I hadn't got to see Mama since April 2nd. I want to wish her happy birthday and happy Mother's Day and I love her." Lynn came back on stage at this point to introduce her twins, whom she called "Ding and Dong," and she introduced as many grandchildren as would come forward. The twins, Patsy and Peggy, have a singing act under the name "The Lynns." They offered a rendition of the Everly Brothers' "Bye, Bye Love." That moment was followed by Anthony, Patsy's young son, donning a pair of sunglasses and doing a very credible rendition of "Achy Breaky Heart." This brought great pleasure to both fans and the assembled family on stage. Loretta called forward more grandchildren, saying, "We got a hundred." When she had her entire family on stage she looked off to ask, "Where's Papaw at? Here he is." Doolittle Lynn then ambled on stage wearing casual clothing and a baseball cap. He told the crowd a joke, at which they laughed politely, and then he became visibly serious. "Hey," he said. "I appreciate all the years you've supported Mama. Thank you and God bless you."

Without skipping a beat, Lynn introduced her fan-club presidents, the Johnson sisters. "We've been together all these years and had a good time, haven't we girls?" she said, then moved easily into two Patsy Cline songs, "She's Got You" and "Back in Baby's Arms." Loretta thanked her son-in-law for building the concert shelter and for running the dude ranch, then took requests from the audience. This led to a rendition of "When the Tingle Becomes the Chill." Next, she introduced a group of twenty-four people from Dublin, Ireland, who were attending this special concert for a third consecutive year. They had with them a man Lynn called "Ernie from Ireland." She said Ernie had the number one song on the charts there and added, "I went back to Ireland to find out where my roots were." "I kissed the Blarney stone twice." Then she brought Ernie to the stage to sing his "Nobody's Child," a song about an orphan. Ernie concluded this impromptu appearance by saying to Loretta, "I want you to know that your music is up there at the top. It's number one."

The appearance of Ernie from Ireland ended the eight-song central segment of this concert—where four of the songs were sung not by Loretta but by her children and grandchildren, one was sung by a fan from Ireland, one was sung in response to a request from a member of the audience, and two were sung for Loretta's longtime friends and fan-club presidents, the Johnson sisters. This thorough mingling of Loretta's own professional persona with that of her immediate family *and* representatives of her fans—who are singled out, brought on stage, and invited to perform—exemplifies the informality and casual down-home rusticity pervasive in country music culture. To this, it adds the infectious domesticity of Loretta Lynn's personal touch. A concluding set of five songs gave thanks for the blessings of this moment: the gospel number "Put Your Hand In The Hand," the evangelical standards "Amazing Grace" and "Peace in the Valley," Hank Williams's signature "I Saw the Light," then "God Bless America Again." Now, Loretta Lynn received a prolonged, intense standing ovation. "Thank you," she said, "we love you too." Then she did her last song, "Coal Miner's Daughter."

Described by Lynn as a "true story of my early life," "Coal Miner's Daughter" is a thirty-line narrative that pays homage to the memory of domestic life in Butcher Holler, Kentucky (Horstman 1975, 9). "We were born poor, but we had love," says Loretta in the song's first evaluation of her home life, because, "that's the one thing that Daddy made sure of." The story has her father working all night in the coal mine and all day in the field to raise eight children "on a miner's pay." Loretta's mother rocked babies, "read the Bible by the coal oil light," and scrubbed clothes on a washboard until her fingers bled; but she always presented a smile. The song is spoken in the present as a memory of the past. As for modern Butcher Holler, "nothing lives here anymore"; but Lynn is "proud to be a coal miner's daughter." The song's undercurrent is the reconciliation of an assertive woman with her working-class origins. Lynn intends to keep a positive image of her family of origin in a mature life where economic circumstances are utterly different; she also intends to suggest pride in both her family and her extended fan family, those who made possible her success. The annual concert at Hurricane Mills celebrates these connections through everyday rituals of familiarity—chatting with the audience while on stage; taking the immediate comfort of the fans into account; introducing her spouse, children, and grandchildren; inviting fans on stage to sing; and celebrating the good fortune of the group instead of agonizing about hard times, broken hearts, and domestic turmoil. There is a broader suggestion in all of this. In discussing Lynn's movie, Allen Batteau points out one of its key cultural messages:

> This story of upward mobility from hardship, aided by nothing more than talent, effort, and pride, is a story that is repeated time and again in the world of country music: many singers and groups, when introducing themselves and their biography on stage, will tell what a difficult time they had breaking into "the business" and how grateful they

are that they have made it, if not to the stars, at least to stardom. To the local audience, which has a close identification with the singers, there is nothing sentimental about this: it is a message that one of ours has succeeded. (Batteau 1990, 195)

One of the most significant annual events of country music culture is directly descended from Loretta Lynn's relationship with her fans, particularly her women fans.

> I've got so many fans that I recognize all around the country. If I go to the West Coast, there're the same faces from last year. If I'm up North somewhere, there're my same fans. I'd list all of 'em but I know I can't. Most of my fan club is women, which is how I want it. The men have enough things going for 'em in this life. We women have got to stick together. (Lynn and Vecsey 1977, 115)

The sisterhood Loretta Lynn refers to has been an important force in organizing fans in country music culture. As a device for promoting a living artist, fan clubs have been active at least since the late 1940s; 3,000 people belonged to the Ernest Tubb Fan Club in 1947. Tubb reached out to his fans in a variety of ways. In addition to promoting an active fan club, he toured "some 75,000 miles per year, by train, plane and car," and in 1947 opened the Ernest Tubb Record Shop in Nashville—"first and foremost so that the country music fan could buy country records more easily, Tubb's and everyone else's." At times, as much as 70 percent of Tubb's record business has been mail order (Pugh 1993, 10–11).

Ernest Tubb was a patron of Loretta Lynn when she was learning the music business in Nashville. In 1960, Lynn became a pen pal of Loretta Johnson, a fan then a high school senior in Wild Horse, Colorado. In 1963, two years after she had joined the Grand Ole Opry and the same year she became a star of the Wilburn Brothers television show, Lynn asked Loretta Johnson to take over her fan club. With the help of sisters Loudilla and Kay, and advice from Norma Barthel, president of the Ernest Tubb Fan Club, Loretta Johnson began what has become more than thirty years of organizing fans for the promotion of country music. In 1965, the Johnson sisters founded the International Fan Club Organization (IFCO), "dedicated to the promotion of country music artists and the furtherance of fan clubs affiliated with us—individually and collectively—on a worldwide basis" (IFCO 1993, 1). For an annual membership fee of $5, IFCO membership provides access to a registry of fan clubs that have "monitored ratings." This means that—in addition to listing the fan club president, the address, telephone, dues schedule, and information about fan club services (newsletters, photographs, autographed photographs, yearbooks, buttons, biographies; discographies, V.I.P. concert seating and backstage passes)—every club in the registry is rated on the quality of its services.

The *IFCO Clubhouse*, the registry for October–December 1993, rates a total of 345 country music fan clubs in the following categories: a Gold Star for 100 percent or more of promised materials delivered; a smile logo for clubs delivering 50–75 percent of promised materials; a frown logo for those delivering less than 50 percent; a blank circle for known clubs who have not provided information to IFCO; a "compliance program" where clubs are placed for a six-month grace period to demonstrate that they will meet commitments they have made to members; and a "new" category for new clubs. Of the clubs listed in this registry, 62.6 percent (216) achieved Gold Star ratings. Only 4.9 percent (17) met fewer than 50 percent of their commitments, and 15 percent (52) of the fan clubs were new, in keeping with the current growth rate of country music culture. Only three fan-club presidents had first names that were not gender specific, and 80 percent (276) of fan club presidents were women. Another 5.8 percent (20) of fan club presidents are male-female couples. Loretta Lynn's wish for female fan leadership has been amply fulfilled—over 85 percent of those fans who are publicly committed to organizing others are women (IFCO 1993, 6–20). And, in Loretta Lynn's spirit, their activity is consciously meant as an antidote to the hard times mood of much country music. In their introductory letter to each issue of the *IFCO Clubhouse*, Loudilla, Loretta, and Kay Johnson close their remarks to fans with the phrase, "If you GOTTA be blue, be a real BRIGHT BLUE!" (IFCO 1993, 2).

In 1967, the Johnson sisters organized their first concert in Nashville to showcase country music stars for devoted fans. The show, held in the Hermitage Hotel, featured such established artists as Charlie Pride and then-newcomer Barbara Mandrell and attracted 200 fans. By 1970, the event had become annual and had moved to larger quarters in Nashville's Sheraton Ballroom. In 1972—co-sponsored for the first time by the Grand Ole Opry and the Country Music Association and held in the Municipal Auditorium—it attracted 5,000 fans. The very next year, this event, now called Fan Fair, doubled its attendance to 10,000 fans and featured 130 entertainers. In 1982, it moved to the Tennessee State Fairgrounds, sold

18,000 tickets, and filled five fairgrounds buildings with 220 exhibits showcasing country music stars and music-business institutions. In 1991, Fan Fair sold out the fairgrounds by late May for a June event that attracted 24,000 people. Since then Fan Fair has sold out annually and earlier each year. The 1992 twentieth anniversary Fan Fair (which closed with the twenty-fifth anniversary IFCO Show) sold its 24,000 tickets in April. In 1993, it sold out by February 5 (*Country Fever* 1993, 74–77).

Despite its scale and growing popularity as the most visible annual event of country music culture, Fan Fair maintains the friendly down-home manner modeled by Loretta Lynn and the Johnson sisters as a trademark of country music culture. Because the 1992 Fan Fair coincided with a sharp rise in the popularity of country music among middle-class listeners, it received considerable media attention. A *New York Times* article of June 14, 1992, describes Fan Fair as a "seven-day country music festival, love feast and fan club extravaganza that brings fans and country music stars together in what may be the world's largest autograph session." Fan Fair, reported the *Times*, is worth $7.9 million to the city of Nashville and "has become a madcap fiesta filled with industry wheeling and dealing, autograph booths lavishly decorated by fan clubs and zany events." Much fan attention is given to autograph booths where stars—including multi-millionaires like Garth Brooks—sign autographs, pose for pictures and chat with fans all day, every day and sometimes into the evening for a week, when they are not appearing in three showcase concerts per day featured in the grandstand. Fans of individual artists organize club events during Fan Fair; in 1992, these included a "floating country luau aboard a riverboat that Doug Stone sponsored to thank his fans for their support during his recent quadruple bypass operation," and others.

> At a Randy Travis "early bird" get together at the Maxwell House Hotel Tuesday morning (not to be confused with the Ricky Skaggs picnic, the Alan Jackson ice cream festival or Mark Collie's "Mark in the Park" party, where Mr. Collie greeted fans with his dog Amos, a collie), Mr. Travis welcomed some 300 fans, many wearing "Randy Travis: Always And Forever" buttons and carrying "The Randy Travis Cookbook," which includes "favorite anytime country ham." (Brown 1992, 39)

Fan Fair 1992 opened Monday, June 8, and closed Saturday, June 13. It featured bluegrass and cajun shows Monday evening; three showcase programs on Tuesday from Curb, Polygram, and MCA records; showcases on Wednesday and Thursday from Liberty, Warner Brothers, RCA, Atlantic, Arista, and Columbia/Epic Records; a "multi-label" show on Friday and a "Grand Masters Fiddling Championship" at Opryland on Saturday. On Sunday morning, at the end of Fan Fair, the Music City Christian Fellowship hosted Sunday Mornin' Country at the Grand Ole Opryhouse. Ninety performing acts appeared on stage before 24,000 fans during Fan Fair. Additionally, the Silver Anniversary IFCO Show featured twenty-two artists in the traditional IFCO mix, ranging from established stars such as Charlie Pride, Gary Morris, and Mark Chestnutt to a "new country showcase" of hopefuls seeking recording contracts.

Aside from listening to the latest releases of country music's top acts all week and mingling with other fans and with artists, participants in Fan Fair had other options in Nashville. Country music shrines and such sites as the Ryman Auditorium, the Country Music Hall of Fame and Museum, and Opryland offered free admission with the Fan Fair package registration—which costs $75 for the entire week. Hotels and nightclubs throughout the city sponsored live performances; tours of star home districts were available, and charitable events were common. The Y.W.C.A. All Star Celebrity Auction, on Thursday afternoon, hosted by TNN celebrities Lorianne Crook and Charlie Chase, was held in a large tent outside the state fairgrounds. It featured memorabilia and items donated by eighty-five stars of country music. Bidding was friendly but excited, with auctioned items including a handwritten copy of the lyrics for Collin Raye's "Love, Me" for $120, Holly Dunn's boots for $350, Alan Jackson's autographed blue jeans for $900, an autographed jacket from Reba McEntire for $900, and Garth Brooks's autographed Stetson for $3,800. In a specially contested moment, a handful of items given by Wynonna Judd (backstage passes to her first solo concert in Milwaukee, an autographed copy of her first solo album, a tape recording of a personal interview just before her first solo performance) brought the tidy sum of $6,600.

Meanwhile, in seven fairgrounds exhibit buildings, 336 booths featured artists fraternizing with fans, plus representatives of record companies, magazines, country music theme parks, television shows, festivals, production companies, cable television, museums, and western wear manufacturers. The scene in the Tennessee State Fairgrounds was crowded, bustling, and excitable when a star moved through. Yet the atmosphere remained astonishingly personable and mannerly. This tone was evident at the daily barbecue luncheon served by the Odessa Chuck Wagon Gang, a 250-member charitable organization of the Odessa, Texas, Chamber of Commerce. They arrive in a forty-three-foot van with 250-gallon bean pots and organize serving lines that can accommodate 1,000 people per hour. The Chuck Wagon Gang works throughout the United States, Canada, and Europe, dresses in brown and gold western uniforms with cowboy boots and hats, and reports serving 30,000 people for Klondike days in Edmonton, Canada, 10,000 people at the Smithsonian Institution in Washington, D.C., and, in its largest endeavor, 41,100 for Fan Fair in Nashville. Yet, massive as the luncheon is, when fans, artists, and music business people eat Chuck Wagon Gang barbecue under large fairground shelters, the overwhelming sense returns of country music culture as an extended family at an endless church supper in a rural American small town. Ample food and friendly talk is everywhere. The first day, I sat next to a middle-aged couple from Virginia who told stories of Ricky Van Shelton's parents. After lunch, at a refreshment counter in the Grandstand, this atmosphere continued as fans talked freely about Roger Miller's health and the dispute between Travis Tritt and Billy Ray Cyrus, which they seemed to take calmly but seriously.

The week of Fan Fair in Nashville opens with the TNN/*Music City News* Awards Show, the only country music awards devoted exclusively to fan-voted nominations and selections. This event, elaborately staged in the Grand Ole Opryhouse and carried nationwide by The Nashville Network, is an important formal validation of personal connections among fans and artists. Fan Fair extends and amplifies those connections for an entire week in diverse ceremonies of affection that have evolved from efforts of the organizing women associated with Loretta Lynn. While Fan Fair certainly celebrates the financial success of country music and promotes adulation of its stars, it retains a commitment to homey rusticity and informality. In her autobiography, Loretta Lynn notes an event she had co-sponsored at Fan Fair almost twenty years earlier. She described it in a manner that ably sums up the attraction of this elaborate fan-artist ceremony:

> I get a chance to say "Thank you" just before the Fan Fair—a convention for over 10,000 fans—every year in June. My fan club presidents

and Conway Twitty's are invited to a banquet at one of the big hotels in Nashville. Jimmy Jay from my booking agency cooks a pig for two days, getting that thick barbecue sauce all over it. Everybody helps themselves to potato salad and cole slaw and all the soda they can drink, and I just sit there and get barbecue sauce all over my face from kissing everybody for all the help they've been. By the time we go home, we're all full of sauce, just a bunch of country bumpkins. And that's the way we like it. (Lynn and Vecsey 1977, 119)

Loretta Lynn's public persona suggests some relief from the conventions of domestic turmoil in country music. Dolly Parton's public personas play with conventional gender stereotypes and suggest relief from hard times in Appalachia. Jimmie N. Rogers has analyzed 137 songs by Loretta Lynn, "describing love relationships between men and women," and "found 99 that did not support the stereotypical women's role" (Rogers 1989, 65). A parallel view has not always prevailed when Dolly Parton is observed. A letterwriter to *T.V. Guide* in December 1993 expresses her dismay:

I have never been so thoroughly sickened by a magazine cover that has come into the house as I was with your Dolly Parton issue. What type of "family-oriented" message were your corrupt photographers attempting to convey? What kind of woman is Dolly Parton to actually *agree* to be photographed in such a manner?

I am 16 years old and just hope that this incident does not help send the women's movement hurtling so far backward into the Stone Age that a recovery would be highly improbable—if not useless. And while I realize that things *are* improving, our struggles are far from over—something the picture on your cover makes perfectly clear. (Hancock 1993, 45, 84)

The image that roused this young woman's ire appeared in *T.V. Guide* under the headline "Good Golly Miss Dolly!" The magazine trumpets Dolly Parton's latest venture into television—"those amazing get-rich infomercials"—and offers as its principal visual impact a dramatically posed Dolly in a gold-rhinestoned gown displaying an ample bosom, a wasp waist, slender legs, tousled long blonde wig, and a make-up job that renders her skin in a porcelain doll-like quality with highly defined eyes, red lips, and "dragon" red fingernails. In every respect, this Dolly is a vivid depiction of working-class sexuality. Whether or not her image sets back the women's movement is open to debate. In 1987, Gloria Steinem honored Dolly Parton in *Ms.* magazine for becoming a highly visible female who "has turned all the devalued symbols of womanliness to her own ends" (Steinem, 1987, 66).

The conscious manipulation of stereotypes has been a steady note in Dolly Parton's career. Mary Bufwack and Robert Oermann credit Loretta Lynn with becoming the most important symbol of working-class pride among country music women and a role model to fans and women artists (Bufwack and Oermann 1993, 304–25). They quote Dolly Parton speaking in a different, and characteristically more humorous, tone: "I was always impressed with Cinderella and Mother Goose and all those things when I was a kid, because we didn't have television or movies then. I kinda patterned my look after Cinderella and Mother Goose—and the local hooker" (Bufwack and Oermann 1993, 363). The *T.V. Guide* interview occasioned by Parton's infomercial entrepreneurship, a $2 million deal with Revlon to market cosmetics, is a study in Parton's ability to manipulate pop media successfully, with exaggerated images drawn from her regional and working class origins, leavened by a generous dose of self-deprecating country humor. Here, this star of Nashville, Las Vegas, and Hollywood, described by *People* magazine as worth $70 million in 1993, emphasized her origins in Appalachian poverty. Asked where she gets her ambition, Parton replied,

> I just didn't want to stay back there, get married, have a house full of kids, let my teeth rot out, and have no clothes and nothin'. But it wasn't about what I *didn't* want—it was about what I *did* want. And what I *needed*. I needed the attention. Mama and Daddy loved us, but they didn't have time for us unless we were sick or in trouble. The only time we really got picked up was when we were being nursed or when we were gonna get our butts popped. (Murphy 1993, 15–16)

Parton was the fourth of twelve children, born to a working-class family near Sevierville, Tennessee, in 1946. Her 1993 interview is filled with references to her childhood when she wore bright make-up and bleached her hair " 'cause it made me feel prettier." That stretched the constraints of an evangelical family. "Grandpa would have a fit. He would say, 'the devil has got into that young'un'" (Murphy 1993, 11). A good part of Parton's public image has been one of rustic coziness rendered in picturesque regional idioms. She left for Nashville and a music career the day after graduating from high school, and was immediately homesick. Here's how she remembered home in 1994:

> We had runnin' water when we'd run and git it. We basically all slept in the same bed—three, four in the same bed, most like army cots. It wasn't so bad 'cept everybody peed in the bed. You know, when I went to Nashville to become a star, I was so homesick I said, its amazin', how you miss stuff. Like pee! (Murphy 1993, 16)

At a time when ethnic pride is a prominent feature of American popular culture—and, for most ethnic groups not something to be amused by—white Appalachians may be the last social group who can be made fun of in public without repercussions and the last to frequently display their own self-deprecating humor as a route to popular fame. "I'm not tryin' to preach that people should look like me, 'cause everybody don't want the dragon nails and town-tramp look," Parton told the world as she entered her infomercial venture to sell cosmetics. In the same year that Hollywood promoted humorous Appalachian stereotypes in a feature film that reproduced the popular television series *The Beverly Hillbillies*, Dolly Parton showed an analogous grasp of the marketability of witty self-parody:

> TVG: A friend said you're one of the smartest and most perceptive women he knows, but that you camouflage it—I presume by the way you look, with your wig and four-inch heels and makeup.
> DP: It's a nice compliment. But I ain't all that smart, to be honest. I'm just smart about what I know. I'm a very professional Dolly Parton. (Murphy 1993, 17)

In live performances, Dolly Parton has developed a sophisticated use of her Appalachian autobiography to construct a stage persona that organizes concerts theatrically. At Fraze Pavilion, in Kettering, Ohio, August 1, 1993, she provided a standup comic as a thirty-minute warm-up act. The comic's jokes were focused almost entirely on domestic-relations relief from the country music conventions of heartbreak and romantic trauma. Want to know the secret to a good marriage? he asked. "Yard work. Every old couple you know has a nice yard." On women: "My wife needs mall air. She comes into a mall, takes a deep breath, says 'this is a good mall.'" On men: "The only species that will shower and put their underwear back on." The last joke was for young parents—a rap version of the Dr. Seuss number, "Green Eggs and Ham."

At 8:50 P.M., Dolly Parton's stage show began in darkness, with the sound of crickets at night and a distant lonesome fiddler. Then, in a burst of dramatic flair, Parton entered center stage down a flight of stairs wearing a blue sequined dress. She opened with three "party" numbers: "Baby I'm Burnin'," "Two Doors Down," and a declaration that said, "I wanna be your lover, friend, full-time woman." Parton's stage chatter between songs, which began immediately after the first number, emphasized the friendliness of the audience, what a nice man her comedian is ("he cracks us up"), a comment on the full moon visible tonight in this outdoor pavilion, and a characteristically witty expression of gratitude to the fans: "Thank you for coming to this show. I know it costs a lot of money. I need the money. It costs a lot to look this cheap."

The stage arrangement for Parton's show was more elaborate than that for most country singers (who tend to display their five- or six-piece band in a straight line or semicircle across the back of the stage with the star slightly ahead and in front, drum-set near the middle, keyboard and steel guitar on the outside ends, rhythm, bass, and lead guitars toward the center). In Parton's strategy, she occupies all of center stage, with open depth behind her, and instrumentalists group in clusters on either side. To her left was a string band consisting of fiddle, two guitars, banjo, and drums; to her right were keyboard and steel guitar, with four backup singers positioned in front of them. This arrangement facilitates theatrical variation between elaborate production numbers and more modestly produced acoustic renditions.

The first three party songs, for example, were done with full musical backings and vocal accompaniments. Songs 4 through 7 were a cluster of autobiographical ballads comprising 20 percent of the total concert and positioned for dramatic effect as a calm, intimate sharing with the audience, in contrast to the vigorous opening. Here, Parton performed "My Tennessee Mountain Home," "Coat of Many Colors," "Appalachian Memories," and "Applejack." Each song was introduced by a story from Parton's personal life; she referred to her autobiographical songs as "little pictures." To magnify the tone of cozy intimacy, Parton performed the set with the acoustic string band under spotlights that left the remainder of the stage in darkness. "Pretend like this is our front porch," she told the fans. "The boys will gather 'round."

"Tennessee Mountain Home" is a number Parton said "kinda sets up the picture." It's an idyllic vision of sitting on a front porch in Appalachia on a Sunday afternoon, kids playing with June bugs on strings and chasing fireflies at dusk. Honeysuckle grows "along the lane," songbirds, and even the national symbol of stability and power, eagles, are in the background. Dolly's Tennessee mountain home is a place where "life is as peaceful as a baby's sigh" (Parton 1975). The only purposeful human action in this picture is a pair of lovers walking home from church to sit on the porch, where they laugh, talk, and make plans. Not one note of personal or social turmoil is present.

The tone shifted with the second song of Parton's autobiographical set, "Coat of Many Colors," which Parton took great care to explain before singing. It's a true story, she said, that people who "grew up poor" like herself can relate to. "I've written thousands of songs about those days, and this is my personal favorite of all the thousands of songs I've written." In "Coat of Many Colors," the idyllic environment of "Tennessee Mountain Home" yields to a human drama that sets family love, especially Mother's love, against the world's cruelty and indifference. The story is a ballad about an incident when Parton was very young, the family was poor, fall was coming, and she had no coat to wear. Someone gave Dolly's mother a box of rags and she sewed Dolly a coat from them. This is a lesson about attitude: Dolly's mother not only made the best of what she had, she gave the situation depth by linking it to the biblical account of Joseph's coat of many colors. She told Dolly that story while sewing the coat, then she "blessed it with a kiss." Young Dolly wore her new garment "proudly" as a symbol of spiritual wealth. Yet, at school, because she was different, other children laughed at her colorful garb. Parton's memory of her response from the perspective of a mature songwriter emphasizes the pathos of this incident, enhanced by her ability to depict the voice of an incredulous little girl. "I couldn't understand it," she says, because "I felt I was rich." Nevertheless, in an important sense, there is no self-pity. The moral of Dolly Parton's favorite song is its emotional high point. On stage it is delivered with a flair that links Dolly Parton to the personal grit of Loretta Lynn. The moral also suggests the determination that has helped make Lynn and Parton models for successful women in the country music business, as well as distinct voices speaking dreams of American prosperity. With her coat of many colors warming her in the love of her mother, and the resonance of biblical tradition, young Dolly defies the other children and tells the world, "one is only poor only if they choose to be" (Parton 1987).

The third, and most dramatic, song of the autobiographical set was Parton's "Appalachian Memories." Another true story, this song is an account of her father's attempt to move to Detroit to find better employment and his desire to return home. Unlike the tragic troubadours of country music culture, he did come home again. Parton uses this story to create a full-scale account of the failure of Appalachian migration to achieve the American dream: "there was no land of promise," just reliance on "sweet Jesus" (Parton 1987). The final song of the autobiographical set returned to an upbeat hillbilly motif to idealize "Applejack," a man named Jackson Taylor who lived near Dolly when she was growing up and taught her music, smoking tobacco, and sipping moonshine whiskey. For this number, Parton played banjo in a frolicking manner, and in a stage aside made fun of her own playing while passing on a bonding reference to other women artists when she said, "Eat your heart out, Barbara Mandrell!"

The "autobiographical" persona of Dolly Parton is a rags-to-riches story in which riches are good and rags have love and spiritual commitment. The "professional" Dolly Parton, a Cinderella/hooker witty persona who sings about romantic love and domestic trauma, is the second focus of Dolly Parton's public image. The eighth song of the Fraze Pavilion concert served as a transition to this image when the "boys on the porch" joined Dolly front and center stage to do two versions of her Nashville hit, "Do I Ever Cross Your Mind"— first an *a capella* gospel evocative of a church service, then an attention-getting fast version done as if playing a 33 rpm record at 78 rpm speed. A third version of the same number was done by a black singer Parton introduced as "my distant relative, Howard." He sang, "Do I Ever Cross Your Mind" in "Smokey Robinson style." The effect of this theatrical interlude immediately after Parton's autobiographical set was to make it perfectly clear that Dolly Parton thinks of herself as a professional entertainer to whom many personas are available in the quest for stardom.

The next four songs showcased hits from the early, middle, and recent stages of Parton's career. "Jolene," the title song of a 1974 album, was a major hit in which Parton projects the Cinderella/hooker image on a competing female who has the power to "take my man." Unlike the combative response of Loretta Lynn's

"Fist City," here, the singer pleads, "please don't take him just because you can" (Parton 1974). Then came three songs in which Parton teamed with male singers in a duet. "Here You Come Again" and "Islands in the Stream" (originally done with Kenny Rogers), and the 1993 release, "Romeo."

"Romeo" is a production number with several targets. One is the country dance club market; another is the country video market. The video is set in a dance club where Dolly and her friends Mary Chapin Carpenter, Tanya Tucker, and Kathy Mattea are hanging out when Romeo enters in the person of Billy Ray Cyrus. A larger target of this song is parody of the romantic love tradition by exaggerating sexuality. In the video, the attraction between Billy Ray Cyrus and the four women is flauntingly sexual, featuring Billy Ray's exposed bicep and tight blue jeans flashed in opposition to Parton's hyper-voluptuous figure in a tight dress. This is used to reverse conventional male innuendo about female sexuality. Here, the women are sexual aggressors and the male has to endure their taunting as they chatter: "He is *hot*," "Check it *out*," "*Don't* look," "What kind of jeans *are* those, anyway?", "Wish I had a swing like *that* in my back yard." Both the record and the video come directly to the point: "I may not be in love/but let me tell you/I'm in heat" (Parton 1993). This line created some public controversy and Parton omitted it from her Fraze Pavilion rendition. After she performed the song, Parton carefully explained, "All the money from that particular video went to the Red Cross," and "Actually, I wrote that song about my little sixteen-year-old nephew." Another level of her philanthropy might have been to boost the career of Billy Ray Cyrus in the face of Travis Tritt's critique of him or to employ their controversy to her own benefit.

The concluding six songs of Parton's concert were addressed to women. This set began with Parton's 1991 anthem, "Eagle When She Flies." It speaks directly to the generic experience of being a woman while making a statement for the women's movement as translated into country music culture. "You'll never keep her down," the song says; she's a lover, mother, friend and wife, "a sparrow when she's broken, but she's an eagle when she flies" (Parton 1991). This commentary on women carries a mood of gospel spirituality. It was greeted by fans with absolute silence—a response near to awe—and a solid ovation at the end. Parton followed this by commenting on the gifts and flowers brought backstage by fans. She keeps the gifts, she said, but donates the flowers to a local hospital or children's home. The second song in her "women" set was a story song sung in a little girl's voice, evoking pathos about a domestic trauma. In "Me and Little Andy," mommy's gone and daddy's drunk again in town, and at the end, even little dog Andy dies. Considered apart from its performance, this song is a stereotype of the impact of domestic turmoil on young children. Yet, in live performance, Parton's comments about the song make it a figure in a larger tapestry of women's success stories. Introducing the song, Parton said, "It's absolutely plum pitiful." After she sang it, she told the rest of the story:

> I told ya it's sad. Sometimes when I'm in a sad mood that sucker makes me cry, and I wrote it! It's based on a true story, but the girl did not die. She married a doctor in Louisville, Kentucky. Now she's rich and has a big house and a big car. I thought it would make you feel better. It does me. Some people ask me why'd you have to knock off the dog? That dog grew up to be Spuds MacKenzie.

Parton performed "Slow Dancing with the Moon," the title song from a 1993 album; it comments ambiguously on romantic dreams of suburban housewives. "Put a Little Love in Your Heart" was a Las Vegas-style production number that appeals for personal philanthropy. She did "Nine to Five," a movie theme that protests troubles of working girls stuck in a corporate world controlled by men, and concluded the concert with her three-time number one hit, "I Will Always Love You."

Apparently written as she was ending her mentoring relationship with Porter Wagoner, "I Will Always Love You" speaks about the breakup of a relationship between a man and a woman that does not descend into unremitting domestic turmoil, but instead envisions parting with respect—because of the initiative of the woman.

> You get in these love-hate relationships with people that you work with. Porter and I were very competitive and passionate. Then you'd get all jealous, too. And I am not ashamed of feeling this way. But finally, it was just breaking my heart because I thought, well, I'm going. He won't listen. There's nothing I can say that will make it easier. So I just sat down and wrote this song. [She leans forward, and tears come into her eyes.] "If I should stay/I would only be in your way/and so I'll go/but I know I'll think of you each step of the way/and I will always love you." And now I'm in tears! (Murphy 1993, 17)

This song first appeared on Parton's 1974 album *Jolene* and went to number one on the *Billboard* country charts, June 8, 1974 (Roland 1991, 113–14). On October 16, 1982, Dolly Parton entered country music history as "the first artist ever to earn a number one record twice with the same song" when "I Will Always Love You" went to number one again with the popularity of the movie soundtrack from *The Best Little Whorehouse in Texas* (Roland 1991, 333). In the early 1990s, when ambiguity in romantic relationships accompanies changing expectations for both men and women, this song demonstrates Dolly Parton's appeal as a songwriter in the pop music market. For its third trip to number one as a cover by pop singer Whitney Houston, Parton's song helped Houston win an unprecedented eleven *Billboard* awards, including No. 1 world artist, No. 1 world single, no. 1 Hot 100 Single, No. 1 R & B single and "special honor for single with the most weeks at No. 1 for its 14-week reign, which made it the longest-running No. 1 Single of the rock era" (Rosen 1993, 140). At Fraze Pavilion, Parton showcased the Whitney Houston soul version of this song by bringing forward a background singer to do it "Whitney Houston style." Parton then performed her original styling of "I Will Always Love You" to close the concert and, in this position, to make her signature statement to fans. At the end, amid an unrestrained standing ovation, Parton shouted, "Thank you and God bless you!" and walked off stage over the central steps.

She returned to do one more number. Her encore was a major production of a 1977 gospel number that concluded Parton's 1989 album produced by Ricky Skaggs, *White Limozeen* (Parton 1989). As the only encore for her live concert, "He's Alive" specifically brings forward the third focus of Dolly Parton's public image—her "spiritual" persona. In this persona, the autobiographical Parton and the professional Dolly testify that Dolly Parton is rooted in an evangelical faith that arms her for encountering the world. "He's Alive" begins with a lengthy narration of the resurrection of Jesus, told in a detailed, intimate manner that covers the biblical account of crucifixion, death, burial, and denial by believers, followed by the return of Jesus from the tomb. The chorus of this number is an elaborate gospel rendition that can, quite visibly, move an audience with evangelical leanings, whether performed by the Singing Cookes or by Dolly Parton. "He's alive, yes He's alive/Oh He's alive and I'm forgiven" exults the chorus. In Parton's version, this finale of gospel ecstasy is accompanied by an instrumental and choral backing reminiscent of Las Vegas stage shows; and smoke rises from the stage. By 10:13 P.M., when Parton left the Fraze Pavilion stage, her fans in Kettering, Ohio, had seen her professional, autobiographical, and spiritual personas come together in a charismatic presentation preaching faith and personal action as a means to both spiritual and material reward.

In 1977, in comments to interviewer Alanna Nash, Dolly Parton made her theology of success quite explicit:

> I think you can do anything you want to do. And if I believe I can, I can. And I believe I can. I certainly don't mean it as a vain statement. I am one of those people from the old faith—the old church—that believes that all things are possible, only believe. The Bible doesn't say, "Some things are possible." It says, "*All* things are possible," and I believe that. I grew up with all the faith and belief in the world. It was faith and belief that led us through all kinds of problems when we were growin' up. No doctors—with illness, and believin' that we'd make it, that we'd get well. Believin' in prayer, believin' that there was somethin' bigger than us that would take care of us. I think that's the healthiest attitude in the world. And I believe in my heart that if I've got enough faith, and enough grit and determination, that if there is anything in this business or in this world that I truly want to do, I can give it as good a shot as anybody can. I just believe I can do it, because I work hard enough to do it, if nothin' else. I'll get it done. Let's just put it that way. (Nash 1988, 386–87)

A prominent focus of Dolly Parton's entrepreneurship has been the creation of an entertainment park near her home in Sevier County, Tennessee. "I love the Smoky Mountains, and I wanted to create a prestigious place and jobs for the people in the area where I grew up. I just felt it was a great thing—a Smoky Mountain fantasy to preserve the mountain heritage" (Nash 1988, 376).

The entertainment park that is now Dollywood opened near Pigeon Forge, Tennessee, in 1961. It featured a steam train, general store, blacksmith shop, and saloon and was called "Rebel Railroad." When the Cleveland Browns purchased it in 1970, they added a sawmill, log cabins, camping facilities, and church. In 1976, Herschend Enterprises, owners of Silver Dollar City, in Branson, Missouri, acquired the park. They added a working grist mill and crafts area that today feature candle-dipping, woodcarving, broom and basketmaking, wagon making, wood-turning, sand casting, pottery, leatherworking, and a demonstration of making lye soap. In 1980, carnival rides were added. Dolly Parton invested in Silver Dollar City in 1986, opening the park renamed for her on May 3 of that year. Since that time, more than 12 million people have visited this 90-plus acre park. Parton's personal association with the park created a dramatic improvement in business. The first year it operated under her name, attendance increased 75 percent, to more than 1.3 million. Between 1985 and 1992, attendance increased some 160 percent, to more than 2 million annually. By 1992, it was the twenty-fifth largest theme park in the United States. In addition to Parton's visibility, a factor in Dollywood's success is its location just outside the Great Smoky Mountains National Park, the country's most popular national park. The Smokies drew almost 9 million people in 1992 (compared to the runner-up Grand Canyon, at 4 million).

Dollywood incorporates references to all facets of Dolly Parton's public image. The autobiographical Parton is present in the strong emphasis on Appalachian heritage and crafts, in a voluminous "rags to riches museum" that tells her life story in a large building at the center of Dollywood, and in a replica of Parton's childhood home. Dolly's actual coat, for which her autobiographical "Coat of Many Colors" is named, can be seen in the museum. Directly behind the replica of her "Tennessee Mountain Home" is a covered Back Porch Theatre where actual members of her extended family present a show featuring the musical traditions that have influenced Parton's life and music.

The professional Dolly is evoked in a variety of live-performance venues throughout the park, the most important of which is the Dollywood Celebrity Theatre, a 1,739-seat auditorium that hosts major artists. This theater, which provides excellent acoustics, as well as intimacy between fans and artists, was honored as Theater of the Year by the Country Music Association in 1990. In 1992, the Celebrity Theatre featured thirty major acts between May 23 and November 1, ten of them women. A "Starwalk," in nearby Friendship Gardens, honors more than a hundred figures of country music culture including recording artists and entertainment business figures. During the summer of 1993, Dollywood inaugurated the "Sunset Musicfest" between July 10 and August 1. Sixteen young stars appeared in an outdoor environment that featured a total of 3,300 performers on twenty-two stages throughout the park, while a "Songwriters Showcase" ran three times nightly, showing off more than thirty songwriters.

The spiritual Dolly Parton, though less visible at Dollywood, is definitely here. The 400-seat Valley Theatre is a venue that hosts Dollywood's Southern gospel singing group, the Kingdom Heirs. There is also an active church in the park named for Dr. Robert F. Thomas, a country doctor in Sevier County from 1926 to 1980, who presided at Dolly's birth. Services are held each Sunday morning when the park is open.

Dollywood loves special events. In 1993, these included the Fourth Annual American Quilt Showcase (billed as a "living history lesson"), a championship clogging competition with five hundred clogging groups in the spring, a fall National Crafts Festival, and during November and December, "Smoky Mountain Christmas." For this event, the park is decorated with more than 1.5 million twinkling lights and the theater behind Dolly's replica home hosts a living nativity scene (Long 1993; *Country America* 1994).

The professed mission of Dollywood is to "create memories worth repeating." Parton has also created the Dollywood Foundation with the mission "to protect and perpetuate the legacy of Dolly Parton as an inspiration for future generations." As a nonprofit public foundation committed to education in Sevier County, its board includes a variety of local figures, Dollywood officials, and Parton as president and chairman of the board. The Foundation raises funds through benefit concerts at Dollywood; between 1988 and 1993, these earned more than $1.5 million. By May 1993, the Foundation had provided $1 million to college scholarships (for academic merit and to study music and environmental studies), to elementary and high school programs, and to the Dr. Robert F. Thomas Foundation in support of a nearby medical center. In 1990, Parton was awarded an honorary doctor of letters by Carson-Newman College, in Jefferson City, Tennessee, recognizing her contributions to education in Appalachia.

The philanthropic emphasis of the Dollywood Foundation is the organizing rationale for Dolly Parton's fan club. In 1992, there were approximately 3,000 active members of the Dollywood Ambassadors, and 900 of them appeared at Dollywood April 26, 1992, for Ambassador Day V. About 500 of these gathered at 10 A.M., in the Showstreet Palace Theatre, to talk with officials of the Foundation, win door prizes, and meet Dolly Parton. This inner circle of Dolly

Parton fans is a clean-cut lot. Many wore collegiate middle-class clothing. There were families with children, retired people, and a scattering of good ole boys and girls as well as middle-aged couples. The crowd was reserved in manner and extremely orderly. The motif was "country" rather than "western"—in a crowd of five hundred or more, you could see only four cowboy hats but sixteen baseball caps. Many fans wore memorabilia of earlier Ambassador Day events, pictures of Dolly, or fan club jackets. The stage for Dolly's appearance was simply arranged, with three metal folding chairs and two life-size cutouts of Parton (created to promote her most recent movie, *Straight Talk*).

The opening of this event was conversational, almost casual. Her fans wanted to know: Would Dolly be at *Ameriflora* (an exhibition in Columbus, Ohio, to recognize the five-hundredth-year anniversary of the arrival of Christopher Columbus); would Dolly open a theme park in Japan; would Dolly be at the opening of a new Dixie Stampede restaurant at Myrtle Beach, South Carolina; would Dolly play the part of Mary Kay in a movie about the life of this cosmetics entrepreneur. Answers to these inquiries were interspersed with giving away door prizes—stand-up cut-outs and posters for *Straight Talk*, a book of Kenny Rogers's photographs, a T-shirt made in Massachusetts by two female fans, autographed caps, cassettes, fan magazines, a signed copy of the movie script for *Straight Talk*, a shirt promoting Dolly's radio station WDLY. Every ambassador received a packet that included glossy photos, a Dolly auto tag, a clip-on photograph, and other items, including a small stuffed catfish. This was explained. Dolly kept the drapes from her dressing room on the set of *Straight Talk* and had them made into a large catfish and many small ones as a memento of a song done for the movie, "Fish Out of Water." Even though the song was cut from the film, the catfish were presents for her fans. The mama catfish, given away as a door prize, was won by a little girl.

The response to a fan's question, "Where's Dolly?" was, "She's getting dressed up for you all—a little bit different than normal." When Parton appeared on stage, she was wearing a flamboyant antebellum costume. She posed elaborately in silence to strong applause, then told her fans that this "Miss Scarlett dress" had been made especially for today, and "it's yaller!" She then thanked three women—Eunice, Jan and Jo—who had organized the event. Using a line from her movie, she said: "They keep me busier than a one-legged man in a butt-kickin' contest." Then Dolly took fan questions. Fans from England and Scotland wanted to know when she was coming to their countries. Four men introduced by Parton as the "Dolly Brothers" were asked to stand in their seats and show off their custom-made Dolly shirts. A young girl asked if she could bring up a gift. Parton thanked her profusely but said she needed to bring it down afterward. Then a precocious thirteen-year-old said, "You hugged me when I was ten. I'm thirteen now, and would you hug me again?" To this, Parton replied: "I'm gonna make an exception." The girl was invited on stage where a large hug was exchanged to a blizzard of flashbulbs from surging fans. In response to a request, Parton did an *a capella* version of the song "Straight Talk," then gave away special door prizes. These included butterfly earrings ("They look like they're made out of real good stuff!"), a framed poster, and "some fun summer earrings" ("I wore these. I wouldn't just go out and get something that hadn't been mine to give to you. They've even got some make-up on 'em"). In the last moments, Parton gave away two front-row tickets to each of her benefit concerts that would occur later that day. At 11:53 A.M., Dolly Parton left the stage and the ambassadors' luncheon was announced—a picnic served buffet-style under an outdoor covered area near the rides. Door prizes had been numerous for the ambassadors who met Dolly—86 women and 56 men brought away 142 souvenirs.

Throughout the day, Dollywood Ambassadors patronized features of the park and talked with figures on the grounds, such as "Howard A. Hogwaller, Mayor of Dollywood." The mayor, a portly figure with a full black beard, sported black pants, a top hat, walking cane, pink shirt, and vest displaying numerous badges given him by law-enforcement officials. He introduced himself with the line, "If you can't remember the name, remember the question." Food for Ambassador Day was evocative of Southern church suppers. The luncheon served salad, melon, beans, black-eyed peas, carrots, corn, ham, fried chicken, catfish, and iced tea. Similar fare was available in the park's most popular restaurant, Aunt Granny's, named for a term of affection used by Parton's nieces and nephews to describe her. The Backporch Theatre show featured Dorothy Jo Owens, Bill Owens, and other Parton relatives portraying her career in song— seventeen numbers organized in thematic similarity to the Fraze Pavilion show, opening with "Tennessee Mountain Home" and closing with "I Will Always Love You."

For donations ranging from $35 to $500 to the Dollywood Foundation Benefit Concert, fans could attend one of four performances held during the weekend. At 2:00 and 7:00 P.M., on Saturday, April 25, 1992, Dolly Parton appeared with Burt Reynolds (her co-star in *The Best Little Whorehouse in Texas*). At the same hours on Sunday, Dolly appeared with Reba McEntire as her opening act. For the 7:00 P.M. concert that day, a bloc of seats was reserved for special guests from the nearby Church of God Children's Home.

When fans got to their assigned seats for this concert, they found a printed replica of the Dollywood Foundation Buddy Contract, the main document of a five-year pilot project meant to increase high school graduation rates in Sevier County. That project began with seventh and eighth graders in 1988. Approximately 100 students participated from three high schools, and their dropout rate was reduced from 35 to 14.6 percent for 1992 graduation. The Foundation followed this program with other initiatives aimed at increasing literacy and graduation rates. The Dollywood Assistant program funded a teaching assistant for every first-grade classroom in Sevier County during 1992–93. The PALS (Principles of Alphabet Literacy) project partnered with IBM to create high-school computer laboratories for individualized instruction of "at risk" students, and for science workstations. In 1994, an educational field-trip project utilized Dollywood rides for teaching laws of physics to seventy high-school students.

The Buddy Contract document distributed at the 1992 benefit concert "certifies to all the world that we are buddies with each other and with Dolly Parton." By signing, two high-school students pledged not to drop out of school, to give and seek help for "all problems that might keep one of us from graduating," to help others, and to "write Dolly Parton at Dollywood if we have a problem we cannot solve." Each buddy who signed this contract earned $500 from the Foundation upon graduation. In 1992, they received their checks at a Dollywood ceremony the day after the Sunday concert.

By investing the $250,000 needed in 1992–93 to operate the buddy contract program, the Dollywood Foundation achieved direct links for Parton with emerging Appalachian adults, as well as pledged commitments to self-help, personal responsibility, and individual action. These values are entirely consistent with Parton's success philosophy and her themes as a songwriter. Additionally, the strategy promotes philanthropy among Dolly Parton's fans, who donate Foundation funds.

In the tradition of the Johnson sisters and Loretta Lynn, most country stars have active fan clubs that communicate through newsletters. Parton's *Dollywood Foundation Newsletter* serves that function. This quarterly publication offers news about her activities and tour schedule, as well as photos of Dolly and of Dolly with buddies, public officials, other stars, and fans. It includes a "Pen Pal Corner," to facilitate communication among fan club members, and an "Ambassador's Corner," where members can seek help in finding Dolly items they desire. ("Wants old albums, postcards, and a 1978 Dolly doll." "Wants old records and a Dolly metal trash can.") Parton sometimes prints poems she has written in the *Newsletter*, along with the occasional homey recipe. Yet there is always an emphasis on philanthropic assistance to others, moving ahead successfully in the world, the growth of Dolly's enterprises, and encouragement of fans toward self-help and personal success. Foundation executive director Jerry R. Herman captured this tone in the September 1993 issue: "There is something about Dolly that motivates us to become all we can be, to strive for the best, to reach for the stars, and to help others to reach out too" (Herman 1993, 2).

At the benefit concert on Sunday evening, fans did report inspiration by Parton's philanthropy and positive attitude. Those seated near me had traveled from Australia (for the fourth consecutive year), Norway, and England (second year), Scotland (a mother and son), and from points throughout the United States. Many volunteered their appreciation for Parton's philanthropic commitments. Two fans who spoke freely about their affection for her were Tina Jackson and Jeanette Williams, from Santa Rosa and Los Angeles, California. Tina was twenty-seven, and Jeanette twenty-one. They were dressed as look-alikes in faded jeans and denim jackets heavily laid on with Dolly items. Many homemade Dolly items were applied to their clothing—butterflies, movie marquees, references to song titles, flowers and album cover representations, pictures, buttons, and appliqué hearts and lettering. Tina and Jeanette explained that they had met at a concert in Las Vegas, where they learned that each had a "Dolly room" in their home. Subsequently they started dressing alike. Their phone bills, they said, were "outrageous." They had each attended more than thirty-five live performances and in the past six years had collected a complete set of fifty-three albums, read all available books, and filled twelve hundred-page scrapbooks with clippings about Dolly Parton's life. "We won't take a job unless we can get time off to go to concerts," Tina said. "Jeanette was working at a grocery store and had to quit to come to this concert. She's done that before." Asked what they liked most about Dolly, Tina responded: her clothes, the way she dresses, and the way she captivates little kids.

> I got captivated six years ago when she was promoting the old *Dolly!* show. People call us obsessed, people actually think we're nuts. But Jeanette lost 60 pounds because Dolly went on a diet and lost weight. We see her as a role model. We have her view of life—always open-minded, with a sense of humor. She teaches you to be open-minded.

Seated next to me at the Dollywood Foundation Benefit Concert was a working man from eastern Pennsylvania, attending this concert for the fifth consecutive year. His wife, he said, was at home. He had apparently driven to Tennessee that day and was still wearing work clothes. In a tone of camaraderie and awe he volunteered, "I saw Reba in Erie last year." The object of this attention appeared on stage promptly at 7:00 P.M., without introduction, and after renditions of three of her hit songs, paused to talk with fans. Reba McEntire's first words were: "I'm a fan of Dolly Parton. She's done a lot for women in country music and a lot for people everywhere. On behalf of me and my organization I want to thank her for letting us be here." The part of McEntire's organization that appeared on stage with her was a sophisticated band that included a variety of guitars, drums, keyboards, and a saxophone player. One of the guitarists, who also doubled on vocals, was female. The ninth song of McEntire's sixteen-song set was a cover of Aretha Franklin's "Respect." Earning respect for one's achievements as a woman has been an evolving theme for Reba McEntire, who has emerged as perhaps country music culture's most determined female artist of the early 1990s.

Reba McEntire has shown an extremely competitive desire to succeed in the music business. She has used live performance, television, and music video to speak to an audience of women who, in the 1980s and early 90s, welcomed commentaries on social issues. In

Reba McEntire: Country Music's Queen, Don Cusic describes her emergence into country music superstardom.

McEntire's father and grandfather were champion rodeo stars and her mother was a strong woman who loved country music. Born in rural Oklahoma in 1955, McEntire and her siblings grew up traveling the rodeo circuit, working their family ranch, and playing music. Reba was a precocious singer who as early as second grade was singing solos for high school functions (Cusic 1991, 33). Reba, her sister Susie, and brother Pake formed the Singing McEntires, which enabled them to compete successfully in area talent contests. By 1974, when she was in her late teens, Reba was a rodeo barrel racer who had her eyes on a professional singing career. Her first major opportunity was singing the National Anthem at the National Rodeo finals in Oklahoma City in 1974, an event that appeared on *ABC Wide World of Sports.* Country singer Red Steagall heard this performance and, at the request of Reba's mother, agreed to let Reba appear with him at a rodeo event for Justin Boots. A student of voice at Southeast Oklahoma State University, who had been singing for years in public, McEntire was well prepared to make a positive impression on Steagall. That occurred when she did her rendition of Dolly Parton's "Joshua" (Cusic 1991, 52–54).

Steagall was so impressed that he arranged for McEntire to make a demonstration record in Nashville, and he convinced Mercury Records to sign her to a recording contract. Her first album was issued in 1977. She toured with Steagall's band that year and on September 17, made a guest appearance on the Grand Ole Opry, where she performed Patsy Cline's "Sweet Dreams." Charlie Dick telephoned her after the event to express his appreciation. By 1979, McEntire's recording of "Sweet Dreams" had risen to number 19 on the country charts, and in the opening year of the 1980s "(You Lift Me) Up to Heaven" broke her into the top ten at number eight, and stayed on the charts fifteen weeks (Cusic 1991, 67, 70–73).

In 1983, Reba McEntire made a series of moves intended to advance her career significantly. She moved to MCA Records, the label that had recorded Kitty Wells, Patsy Cline, and Loretta Lynn. She hired a lighting designer, choreographers, and dance instructors to give professional advice about her stage persona. She took steps to magnify the impact of her fan club by locating its headquarters at her ranch in Oklahoma and publishing a monthly newsletter. She formed an association with record producer Jimmy Bowen, who had an important influence in Nashville during the 1980s and 90s by emphasizing musical professionalism and artist discretion. "I think my contribution to country music has been that I put trust in and control of the music back with the artist where it belongs," Bowen said (Cusic 1991, 103–21).

In a crucial step to broaden her audience and long-term visibility, McEntire began appearing on the new cable television channel, The Nashville Network. TNN was inaugurated March 7, 1983, at the Stage Door Lounge, in the Opryland Hotel. Eleven days later Reba McEntire appeared on the program that would become the cable channel's most famous live show, *Nashville Now*. This was a night-time variety and talk show showcasing country artists, hosted by WSM radio and television personality Ralph Emery. Three more appearances on TNN in 1983 increased her visibility, and her first album with Jimmy Bowen, *My Kind of Country* (1984), used fiddles and steel guitars to create a western swing motif. It features McEntire covering older Grand Ole Opry stars such as Connie Smith, Faron Young, and Carl Smith and positions her as a leader in the country "traditional" movement. This trend had part of its origins in the work of Emmylou Harris in the 1970s and 80s, and descended to McEntire through Ricky Skaggs, George Strait, and Randy Travis. "We're trying to go back," McEntire said, to the sound of artists like Ray Price (Cusic 1991, 123). In her earliest bid for stardom, Reba McEntire had invoked the heritage of Patsy Cline and Dolly Parton; now she invoked the heritage of Loretta Lynn:

> Loretta's been laughed at for talking hokey and being hokey and country. Her footsteps are the ones I want to walk in—not to do *exactly* what she's done, because she's Loretta and you can't *be* her, but I want to be country, and Loretta's definitely country. I don't want to go crossover, I don't want to be rock'n'roll, I just want to stay country. (Cusic 1991, 132)

The year 1984 was the last time that Reba McEntire sang *The Star Spangled Banner* for the National Rodeo Finals in Oklahoma City. Within a few years, she began to cultivate an audience of women by appealing to their consciousness of gender and social relations. Her stated goal was to "bond" with her female fans:

> I don't want their husbands. I can just barely handle my own. I want to be those women's friend. You know, they've got problems. Like if I was

a woman whose husband was cheatin' on me, or who worked nine to five, sick to death of my job, sick to death of the kids, sick to death of my husband, sick to death of what I'm havin' to go through—that's the kind of songs I pick. There's a lot of women out there who just want to have that three minutes of rebellion. (Cusic 1991, 154)

Reba McEntire cultivated her "three minutes of rebellion" strategy in albums and especially in music videos. She continued to populate television programs—as the first artist to join the Grand Ole Opry during a televised broadcast, on *Nashville Now* with her entire family, and on heavily watched country music awards shows. She won four consecutive CMA Female Vocalist of the Year awards and in 1988 became the fourth female singer (after Loretta Lynn, Dolly Parton, and Barbara Mandrell) to win CMA Entertainer of the Year (Cusic 1991, 163, 179).

McEntire's first music video, a tearful depiction of the impact of infidelity on a faithful woman for "Whoever's in New England," was filmed in Boston and premiered on the network television show *Entertainment Tonight.* Soon her music videos were running between movies on the Home Box Office premium cable movie channel (Cusic 1991, 166, 185). Cusic reports that McEntire toured 275 days in each of the years 1986 and 1987 and that her rodeo-star husband Charlie Battles reported her "into a religious thing" where "she was talking in tongues and things I didn't understand" (Cusic 1991, 192).

In 1987, McEntire divorced her husband and named her steel guitar player and road manager, Narvel Blackstock, as her new business manager; she married Blackstock in 1989. McEntire's domestic turmoil was, however, entirely unlike the public traumas of Hank Williams, George Jones, and other representatives of the tragic-troubadour tradition. "I thought when I got divorced, some songs would come out of it, but none did, so I guess it wasn't meant to be talked about," McEntire said. Her second marriage bore one resemblance to Hank Williams. She performed in public twice on the day of her second wedding, with one show between the marriage ceremony and the wedding reception, and another after it (Cusic 1991, 209, 211). In 1977, Dolly Parton told Alanna Nash that she liked having her marriage separate from her life as a music business professional. "Although I do mention the fact that I'm married," Parton had said, "It's certainly not a business arrangement. If it is, it's smart business" (Nash 1988, 391). In 1993, McEntire told a *McCall's* interviewer that she was pleased to be married to her business manager and that Narvel Blackstock played a significant role in her professional life, both as a critic of her public image and of her stage shows. Then with a flash of wit, McEntire presented her domestic arrangement as fully harmonious with her life as a professional businesswoman and left little doubt about who was in charge of her career:

> I know he has my best interests at heart, and that he's the best at what he does. And that his percentage goes into my checking account! His management fee goes into our checking account. We always talk about business, but I don't think that's a bad thing. . . . I can't think of what's bad about working with him. (Frankel 1993, 92)

Entering the 1990s, Reba McEntire's music videos became short dramatic presentations about women's pride and the salvation of dignity through hard work and determination. McEntire went beyond the usual conventions of domestic trauma and heartbreak to take on such issues as wife-beating, prostitution, working women recovering from divorce, and adult homemakers returning to college. Occasionally, McEntire's videos gave her songs a perspective not predicted by the music alone, as in the 1993 video of her duet with Vince Gill, "The Heart Won't Lie." The original song (written by Kim Carnes and Donna Terry Weiss) is a wistful exchange between estranged lovers; the video version features McEntire as a cadet at the U.S. Naval Academy, striving mightily to meet exacting standards of a superior officer played by Gill (Bufwack and Oermann 1993b, 19). Like this one, several of McEntire's music videos in the early 1990s presented visual images of women intent on controlling their own destiny:

> I choose songs with a little different attitude toward women. Loretta Lynn and I both sing songs for women, and we sing things that they can't always say to men but would like to. The difference, though, is that back in the Sixties or Seventies Loretta would sing a song like "Don't Come Home A' Drinkin' With Lovin' on Your Mind" but nowadays I'll sing a song with a message like, "Don't even consider coming home, because we're not gonna put up with it any longer." That's the difference with the Eighties and Nineties women. (Cusic 1991, 187)

On April 1, 1991, Reba McEntire appeared on the cover of *People* magazine. The occasion was another premature-death disaster in country music culture, the death of seven members of McEntire's band and her tour manager in the crash of a chartered plane leaving San Diego, California, after McEntire had performed at an IBM convention. Evocative of the tragic-troubadour tradition, McEntire had performed Patsy Cline's "Sweet Dreams" as one of her final numbers with this band before it died. McEntire was unwilling, however, to slacken her pace. She told *People* interviewer Steve Dougherty that it was an act of divine will that she stayed behind in San Diego recovering from bronchitis: "Evidently, I was meant not to go on that plane, and God has other things for me to do." The decision to form a new band immediately and continue her performance schedule was made, she said, with the encouragement of her road manager's widow, who reportedly told her: "Jim Hammond worked all this time to help get you where you are today. He'd kick your butt if you thought about quitting" (Dougherty 1991, 30–33). McEntire never considered quitting:

> She organized a memorial service, auditioned a new band, and got a standing ovation for singing "I'm Checking Out" on the Oscar telecast nine days later. She resumed touring two weeks after the tragedy. "I'm not going to quit, because there are too many opportunities that I have open to me," she said. "Staying busy is the best thing for all of us." (Bufwack and Oermann 1993b, 19)

McEntire's ability to focus personal pain through professional performance is revealed in her music video collection *For My Broken Heart* (McEntire 1992). It presents dramatizations of five songs from the album of the same title, which McEntire regarded as a memorial to her band. "It was a healing album for me," she told the *Dayton Daily News* in November 1993. "It'll always be a very special album. That'll be my favorite album until I die" (Larsen 1993e, 17).

The music video of "For My Broken Heart" is a clear example of McEntire's concern with the dignity and determination of women. This "three minutes of rebellion" pays homage to the strength of women who go on with their lives despite broken romantic relationships. The song's story is a first-person account of carrying packed boxes down to a car as the singer, a woman, says good-bye for the last time to a partner who is leaving her. While the exact circumstances are not revealed, the parting is not an angry one, and it's plain that life will go on. That evening the woman says her prayers, then cries herself to sleep. The next morning, awakened by the sunshine, the song's message is revealed: "I guess the world ain't gonna stop for my broken heart."

The music video format allows McEntire to make a visual statement to augment the verbal one. McEntire sings the song, but a sisterhood of three women is shown lip-syncing the words along with her. These women include a distinguished white-haired white woman past middle age who is finely dressed and surrounded by icons of upper-middle-class culture; a young white working girl, probably in her late teens or early twenties, with long hair; and a slightly older, apparently middle-class black woman. At the beginning of the video, each woman wears an expression of pain as she and Reba tell their common story of parting and loss. At the end, each of them takes an action that illustrates recovery. The older white woman walks downtown, buys a newspaper, and smiles as she enters a busy revolving door. Coming out of the door is the black woman wearing a blue business suit and walking with professional deliberation. Just then, the working girl crosses the street with a preoccupied but deliberate air. In the last scene, Reba McEntire herself smiles at the sun and walks away from camera down the busy major street where these women have just been, dressed in a finely tailored business suit and briskly swinging a briefcase. Her demeanor is one of unmistakable self-determination and personal poise. The musical and visual images of "For My Broken Heart" suggest a common bond among women crossing race, age and occupation, a bond that may conquer domestic turmoil through both individual strength and collective example. And now the image of female strength is that of a professional working woman whose worldly achievements can submerge a broken heart. In this direct challenge to country music culture's domestic turmoil tradition, these women, even without their men, are successful and visibly happy.

In 1993, Mary Bufwack and Robert Oermann published *Finding Her Voice*, a major study of women in country music culture. While most of this detailed 594-page work is devoted to the history of women performers, the book also considers another kind of woman—successful businesswomen whose achievements have been important for establishing the position of country music in American popular culture.

Jo Walker-Meador is one of these. The Country Music Association was formed in 1958. Jo Walker-Meador, the Country Music Association's initial executive director, served in that position thirty-three years. The lead professional support organization for secular country music, Bufwack and Oermann cite an important indicator of the CMA's business impact: "Country was a backwater style being programmed by fewer than one hundred radio stations" in 1958; but, "when Jo retired, one-fourth of America's 8,000 stations were country, and the $735 in the CMA bank account had swollen to $2 million. From a one-woman office with borrowed equipment, the organization grew to a staff of eighteen in its own Music Row palace." Throughout the 1980s and 90s, women rose to important music industry positions in "tourism businesses, video companies, booking agencies, song publishers, management offices, and public relations firms" (Bufwack and Oermann 1993a, 384).

Finding Her Voice highlights the striking story of Frances Preston. In 1950, Preston was "working as a receptionist at WSM, opening fan mail for Hank Williams and other Opry stars." New York executives of Broadcast Music Incorporated, a performance rights organization that "distributes five hundred million dollars annually" as the world leader in this field, met Preston during WSM's celebration of the Grand Ole Opry birthday at Country Music Week in 1953. She "was offered a job coordinating a BMI branch" in Nashville; at first, she "worked out of her home." Preston's rise to prominence as a professional woman paralleled the growth of the country music business. She opened an office in 1958, and in 1965 was appointed a BMI vice president, "the first female corporate executive in Tennessee." In the 1970s, "BMI-affiliated songwriters increased by 233 percent," and Preston promoted legislation on songwriter rights, tape piracy, and cable TV licensing. In 1982, *Esquire* called her "the most influential and powerful person in the country music business," and in 1986, she was named president of BMI. In 1990, *Ladies Home Journal* cited her as "one of the fifty most powerful women in America" (Bufwack and Oermann 1993a, 385–87).

As the post-World War II country music business expanded in the national popular music market, room was opened for determined women. They followed the standards of grit and dedication implicit in the ambition of country music's legendary singers, not the standards of compliant femininity implicit in conventions of the songs themselves. Walker-Meador made this explicit. "Just forget you're a woman and go to work," she said. "Think of yourself as a businessperson, not as a woman. Think of yourself as an equal" (Bufwack and Oermann 1993a, 387). The authors leave little doubt that successful women in country music culture have done this. Despite a "conventional wisdom" that country female singers cannot compete effectively with men in record sales, there was an indicator in 1992 that this is not true:

> Arista Records publicist Merissa Ide had a gut feeling that even though they were in the vast minority, country's women were selling proportionally as well as the men were. So she tallied all the gold and platinum sellers then active. At the time, only 36 women were recording artists on major labels, but 15 of them had won these sales awards (42 percent). Men and male groups, on the other hand, represented 117 album-making acts, of whom 44 had sold in the millions (38 percent). (Bufwack and Oermann 1993a, 551)

Trisha Yearwood is a good example of a rising young female star who thinks of herself as a businesswoman. The first female singer in country music to have her debut single rise to number 1 and her initial album reach a million in sales during its first year, Yearwood is the daughter of college-educated parents from a small town in Georgia. She is also a fan who has Reba McEntire's autograph hanging on a wall in her parent's home, and the holder of a degree in music business from Belmont College in Nashville (Gubernick 1993, 313). In commenting on her first marriage, which occurred her junior year in college, she was more direct about its relationship to her ambition than either Reba McEntire or Dolly Parton. "If I had been madly, passionately in love with somebody, I might have been really distracted," she said. "That probably doesn't sound very nice, but the support was there, and I was able to put all my passion into my career" (Gubernick 1993, 36).

As told by Lisa Gubernick in *Get Hot or Go Home,* Yearwood's career is a study in calculated determination. She was determined to go to Nashville after finishing high school, and Belmont College offered the opportunity to make contacts in the music business. While a student there, she gained a considerable reputation as a singer of "demos," recordings made to showcase songwriters' efforts to artists, and she sang in local nightclubs. This brought her to the attention of record producer Garth Fundis, who showcased her talent successfully to MCA Records executive Tony Brown. It was Yearwood's good fortune to meet Garth Brooks while he too was singing demos—and to impress him. Brooks promised to take her on the road as his opening act, and in 1990 he made good on the pledge.

> A brand-new act usually spends the first year or two touring small-time county fairs and midsize honky-tonks, lucky to get a crowd of a thousand or two. But June 1990 found Trisha Yearwood, who had sung a dozen times at Douglas Corner and the Bluebird Cafe—not to mention those memorable months at the Eleventh Frame—standing before a crowd of six thousand at the Universal Amphitheater in Burbank, California, the opening act for the biggest thing to hit country music since Hank Williams. Her first album would still not be released for a month. (Gubernick 1993, 62)

By 1991, Yearwood told Gubernick "I'm the head of a corporation, and my name is the bottom line." The following year, "Trisha Yearwood, Inc. stood to gross nearly two million dollars, ten times what Hank Williams was making in his heyday" (Gubernick 1993, 22, 51–52, 62–64).

A significant part of Lisa Gubernick's study, which focuses on seven months in 1991 for the purpose of documenting the process of emergent stardom in country music culture, is an inside account of professional decisions made by Yearwood to advance her career. In the midst of her first flush of success, Yearwood fired her manager and hired Ken Kragen, a graduate of the University of California at Berkeley and Harvard Business School. Kragen had managed the Limeliters and the Smothers Brothers in the 1960s, the solo career of Kenny Rogers in Nashville in 1975, the career of rising star Travis Tritt in the 1990s, and had organized the popular events "USA for Africa" and "Hands Across America." Kragen had already appeared in *Doonesbury* and in *Lifestyles of the Rich and Famous* (Gubernick 1993, 18, 67–69).

Kragen wanted to market both Yearwood's voice and her beauty. Throughout 1991, Yearwood hired additional advisors—a stylist for "supervising her look on album covers, videos, and television appearances, as well as outfitting her for performances on the road," a trainer for keeping her physical condition and stamina responsive to her demanding schedule, and professional photographers, choreographers, and hairdressers, as well as a full-time publicist. In 1991, these supporting players for Trisha Yearwood required more than $200,000 (Gubernick 1993, 71–75, 80–81). There was a clear sense of direction to this activity; the plan was to create a high-impact image for Yearwood as a woman country singer who was "sensual and sexy without being slutty" (Gubernick 1993, 83). Throughout 1991, Yearwood and her people were negotiating with Revlon for a cosmetics endorsement contract, which they achieved. Gubernick specified Yearwood's marketing strategy in that effort.

> As for Revlon, she was convinced that as long as the image conveyed by the perfume jibed with her aesthetic image, it could do no damage. "They told me that a hundred million people buy Revlon," she said. "That's a potential audience for country music, a potential audience for me—people I can't get to another way. No matter what I do, I'm being marketed. Why shouldn't I try for more exposure?" (Gubernick, 341)

In addition to revealing the marketing strategies of a rising star, Gubernick's study also documents artist-fan interactions in the process of star-making. Yearwood and her managers took advantage of every opportunity offered by country music culture to broaden her impact. For her first appearance at Fan Fair, she bought ten billboards in Nashville to advertise her presence and spent $20,000 on her Fan Fair booth—a working sound studio where fans could sing along with Trisha on the chorus of her initial hit, "She's in Love with the Boy." Fans could keep the cassette (Gubernick 1993, 222). For the high-impact CMA awards show, where she performed with rock star Don Henley, Yearwood was nominated for the Horizon Award. This was a target of her promotional campaign because it would recognize her as "the performer whose career has seen the most growth in the past year" (Gubernick 1993, 80). Gubernick's account of Yearwood's appearance on the CMA Awards in 1991 is the concluding event of this story. Yearwood needed to do more than win the award; to advance her record sales and career significantly, she needed to perform well, look good, and win. This episode did not end on an entirely happy note for Yearwood. Another rising female star, Suzy Bogguss, won the Horizon Award. Yearwood responded to this disappointment like the businesswoman she has trained herself to be: "Basically I was okay," she said. "But I felt like I let down the team" (Gubernick 1993, 332, 336).

On May 6, 1993, CBS television hosted a two-hour special entitled *The Women of Country*. Based on *Finding Her Voice*, this program showcased the history of women in country music culture and presented an elaborate group of contemporary female stars. As opening credits roll, the announcing voice proclaims the significance of this moment: "Tonight the largest gathering of women performers in the history of country music come together to celebrate a century of sisterhood" (CBS 1993). Thirty-three women performed live on this program, and more than forty others were mentioned or shown. *Women of Country* opens with Mary Chapin Carpenter singing her satirical commentary on conventional marriage and nuclear families, "He Thinks He'll Keep Her"; it ends two hours later with Carpenter leading the assembled singers in a song that here served as an anthem to women, "The Hard Way." At the finale, the assembled group vigorously repeats the refrain "Everything we got, we got the hard way" (Carpenter 1993).

Born in 1958, in Princeton, New Jersey, the daughter of a *Life* magazine executive who lived in Japan before her teenage years, at age sixteen, Carpenter moved to Washington, D.C., and became involved in acoustic music and songwriting in the District's club scene. Albums appeared in 1987 and 1989, and in 1990 she was named top new female vocalist by the Academy of Country Music. In 1992, a Cajun-style number done with a Cajun band, "Down at the Twist and Shout," won a Grammy.

Carpenter has consistently been attracted to issues of social concern and is self-conscious about the status of women. *Women of Country* was not her first involvement in a project of this kind; in *'Til Their Eyes Shine: The Lullaby Album*, she collected children's songs and featured Dionne Warwick, Emmylou Harris, Gloria Estefan, Rosanne Cash, Laura Nyro, Carole King, Deniece Williams, and Maura O'Connell. Mary Chapin Carpenter earned a B.A. in American Civilization from Brown University in 1981. Eleven years later, after two gold record albums, she was named CMA Female Vocalist of the Year. Her rapid rise in country music paralleled a seeming rise in self-consciousness among women singers—one that extended the success ethic modeled by Loretta Lynn and Dolly Parton, and the show-business savvy of Reba McEntire and Trisha Yearwood.

In the early 1990s, images of sisterhood were achieving high visibility in country music culture. On *Women of Country*, Grand Ole

Opry star Jeannie Seely said, "You know, when you share the same dreams and goals, and you face the same problems, there has to be a sisterhood." In November 1993, *Country Music City News* featured two pictures on the cover of its issue carrying fan nomination ballots for the 1993 TNN/*Music City News* Country Awards. The reigning CMA Entertainer of the Year, Vince Gill, was pictured in the upper right-hand corner, in a head shot the size of a large U.S. postal stamp. Three quarters of the front cover was occupied by three women. Loretta Lynn, Dolly Parton and Tammy Wynette stood in regal smiling poses, shown from the waist up, well coiffured, highly dressed, and looking straight at the fans. The picture's title referred to a new album by these living legends memorializing country music's historic sisterhood: "Country's Honky Tonk Angels" (*Country Music City News* 1993c). When fans watched the successful sisterhood of female country singers extending from Patsy Montana and Patsy Cline to the youngest stars in the business on CBS television, they heard from Alison Krauss, a new 1993 member of the Grand Ole Opry and the most nominated act for that year's International Bluegrass Music Association Awards, as well as winner of Female Vocalist of the Year and Album of the Year. Krauss spoke of her awe in the presence of Dolly Parton and described Parton's singing in an image that transcends worldly success and suggests a larger aspiration:

> I was lucky enough to get to sing on her new record. I was probably two feet away from her. She started singing and my eyes just filled up with tears and I turned into this basket case because, you know, that's what Heaven sounds like. Dolly Parton singing is what Heaven sounds like.

Hello darlin'.
—Conway Twitty, 1969

That road isn't going to beat me.
—Mel Tillis, 1984

I believe in the Wal-Mart school of business.
—Garth Brooks, 1992

CHAPTER 6   **The Marketplace**
of Emotions

In the 1990s, entrepreneurs of the country music business created an unprecedented market niche in the national economy. Social factors supplementing the availability of charismatic talent were important to their achievement. Among those factors were a changing demographic profile of American popular culture consumers and shifts in cultural attitudes that accommodated the music's interest in salvation from hard times and broken hearts. In this milieu, the zeal of savvy music business professionals was strikingly effective.

A good example is the marketing of Billy Ray Cyrus. According to Paul Kingsbury, the Cyrus recording of "Achy Breaky Heart" was a "nearly identical" cover of an earlier recording of the same song by the Marcy Brothers. The earlier version made no dent in the market, while the Cyrus version "rode in on a massive promotional blitz and had a great-looking poster boy." Recorded between February and July of 1991, the Cyrus album *Some Gave All* and its lead single "Achy Breaky Heart" were given a carefully orchestrated marketing treatment after six months of deliberation by Mercury Records.

> What Mercury eventually hit upon was to have a line dance choreographed by Lee Greenwood's ex-wife Melanie, which they shipped (via video) to dance clubs across the country, along with instructions. Then they gave TNN and CMT a video . . . that made Cyrus look like the second coming of Elvis. And then—only when folks were clamoring for more—did they finally give radio the "Achy Breaky" single. After that, the deluge: Within a month, "Achy Breaky Heart" was Top Ten on country radio. In mid-May the album shipped gold (500,000 units). In the first week of June, the album crashed into *Billboard*'s Hot 200 at #4. It was the fastest-selling debut in the history of pop music. (Kingsbury 1993, 10)

The entertainment niche Mercury Records sought to exploit linked the popularity of suburban country dance clubs with music video promoted on cable television. Such specialized strategies for magnifying star visibility and record sales became common in Nashville in the early 1990s.

By 1992, Robert Oermann could identify the marketing approaches of emerging artists Travis Tritt, Vince Gill, Wynonna Judd, Marty Stuart, Sammy Kershaw, and Marty Brown. He described them as variations on the promotional strategy of country music's most lucrative act in the 1990s, Garth Brooks. In "How Garth Conquered America" for the *Journal of Country Music*, Oermann notes that between 1989 and 1991, thirty country stars achieved gold (500,000) and platinum (1,000,000) sales status and "doubled country's share of the music marketplace from roughly 10 percent to nearly 20 percent" (Oermann 1992, 17).

Coordinated by managers Bob Doyle and Pam Lewis, as well as Liberty Record operatives and Liberty president Jimmy Bowen, the Brooks strategy was to isolate his image as a distinctive voice, promote him on cable television through music video, emphasize the experiential impact of his live performances, and sell key songs as a focal point of controversy in country music culture. To keep his identity separate from that of Clint Black, Brooks's managers turned down an offer to appear with Black on the cover of *People* magazine. "The Dance," a music video from Brooks's initial album, associated Brooks's theme of commitment to intense experience whatever the cost with the lives of slain civil rights leader Martin Luther King, Jr., assassinated President John F. Kennedy, ill-fated astronauts of the *Challenger* disaster, actor John Wayne's losing battle with cancer, and the premature deaths of rodeo star Lane Frost and country artist Keith Whitley. Brooks gave elaborate attention to convention performances for business "gatekeepers" of country radio and "live-performance industries," and his concerts magnified the concept of intense personal experience by borrowing theatrical effects from rock music.

An important catalyst in propelling Brooks was the public image of controversy. His second album was played on a country radio station in Oklahoma City prior to its official release; Brooks's managers exploited that with "a whole media push about the fact that he's so hot people stole the record." Building on opportunity, a decision was made to pursue a target of 6 million sales. This required planning, as explained by Pam Lewis:

> Basically we put together a marketing campaign which included television advertisements, print ads, radio buys, and Garth really working really, really hard doing in-store appearances, retailers and buyers conventions. The live shows were catching on, the reviews were great, he was coming into his own, and everything was working to our advantage. He was like the butterfly emerging from the cocoon. The timing was right. (Oermann 1992, 17)

More good fortune followed. "Friends in Low Places" "became a fraternity pop anthem at the time of the year when kids were going back to college." "The Thunder Rolls," a domestic-turmoil song about spouse abuse by a philandering husband, was released in a music video that has the faithful wife kill the faithless husband. It was rewarded by being banned on cable television. "We had no idea CMT or TNN was going to ban it," Lewis said. "We're not that smart. You can't manufacture controversy that way."

Brooks's third album, *Ropin' the Wind*, was marketed with even more attention—discounted albums, "store displays, posters, TV ads, print ads, radio." Joe Mansfield, marketing executive of Liberty Records, "bought up all these ads in blocks, cornered the market so no one else could buy them and basically got all the retail accounts to push the *Ropin' the Wind* album." By 1991, Brooks had sold 17 million albums. Ken Kragen, manager of Trisha Yearwood and Travis Tritt, commented that the Brooks team "set the standard for the industry, to take it to another level" (Oermann 1992, 17).

According to Oermann, each new singer breaking through in the early 1990s represents the work of a team of managers with what Kragen calls an "overall game plan." For Travis Tritt, the strategy emphasized public exposure in live performances, backed by professional booking and public relations agencies. Vince Gill was positioned to sing "When I Call Your Name" on the Country Music Association Awards show before a national audience. Bruce Hinton, of Arista Records, explained the effect of Gill's exposure: "At that instant on that show, the career built. Sales took off. And we've been building ever since." Wynonna Judd was marketed as a solo act by building on the publicity generated by her mother's retirement from their mother-daughter act because of illness. The release of her first solo album was coordinated with a concert tour so heavily advertised that Ken Kragen described it admiringly as "a burst of attention." Judd's single, "She Is His Only Need," "was timed to go #1 nationally during the same week her album appeared." The first album did go to number 1 on the *Billboard* country chart and entered the *Billboard* Hot 100 Chart at number 4, and "was declared platinum within days of its release" (Oermann 1992, 19).

Marty Stuart and Travis Tritt toured in 1992 under the "attention-getting concept" of "no hats," to differentiate these two performers with rockabilly leanings from cowboy imagery. Sammy Kershaw's song "Cadillac Style" was marketed in Texas, Oklahoma, Louisiana, and Arkansas in coordination with a sales campaign for Cadillac automobiles. It had Kershaw autographing at car dealers and giving away both records and chances on a trip to Nashville in return for test driving a car. Perhaps the most historically conscious creation of a market niche described by Oermann is the one that sold between 120,000 and 150,000 albums for rustic newcomer Marty Brown. Borrowing from the behavior of Loretta Lynn, Hank Williams, and Jimmie Rodgers and updating strategies for earning popularity by using cable television, Brown's managers used a novel approach. "Brown was sent on a forty-stop tour of small towns in the Southeast visiting Wal-Mart stores for eight weeks" as a way of getting his music "to the people."

> Someone talked about Loretta Lynn and Mooney driving from station to station with her record. . . . The Wal-Mart tour wasn't our first idea, but that's what it evolved into. "How do we do this backroads barnstorming tour?" we asked. "In a Cadillac convertible!" someone said. And that led to the idea of a giveaway and tying the whole thing

in with the TNN cable TV shows "Nashville Now" and "Video Morning." (Oermann 1992, 19)

The role of cable television is an important theme running through Oermann's account of contemporary country music marketing. Patsy Cline, Elvis Presley, and Dolly Parton came to national prominence on network television, and country music award shows broadcast by networks were important early in the careers of Reba McEntire and Vince Gill. For recent acts as diverse as Garth Brooks, Billy Ray Cyrus, and Marty Brown, cable television has been crucial. Lloyd Werner of The Nashville Network and Country Music Television has suggested this: "The fact is that we connect the voices to the faces for country music fans in more than 60 million homes in North America every day. . . . Before TNN and CMT, it used to take six years to establish a country act; now it takes six months" (Oermann 1992, 21).

As the view of a professional journalist and writer based in Nashville specializing in country music, Robert Oermann's account of marketing strategy provides an important perspective on the national growth of country music culture in the early 1990s. Another perspective was available from national and regional journalists, as the phenomenon of country music culture's financial success became an important news story after 1992. A review of key items in both national print media and regional newspapers for the Miami Valley of Ohio between February 1992 and February 1994 indicates how well the story played.

On February 18, 1992, the *Dayton Daily News* media page headlined the metropolitan area radio Arbitron ratings for three fall months of 1991 in a market population of 823,100. Four of the top twenty radio stations (20 percent) featured secular country formats, and all but one of these showed an upward ratings trend. These four stations occupied positions 20, 12, 11, and 1. The top-ranked station, WHKO-FM, was the only Dayton metro-area station to achieve a double-digit percentage rating—10.7 percent of the reported listening audience. A fifth station in the top twenty also featured programming affiliated with country music culture; a "Christian" music station tied for position 15. Stations with the most rapid declining trends in this survey had top-forty and urban rhythm-and-blues formats (Batz February 18, 1992, 6B).

On March 2, 1992, *Forbes* magazine took note of the growing country music market by featuring Garth Brooks in a cover story by Lisa Gubernick and Peter Newcomb, entitled "The Wal-Mart School of Music." This article showed off a blizzard of trend impressions. Denim & Diamonds in Santa Monica, California, had converted from disco dancing to country dancing. The rock concert business was hurting financially while three of the top ten tours were country acts. A Judds cable TV pay-per-view event outdrew both the Rolling Stones and New Kids on the Block. In the first month of 1992, 20 percent of all record albums sold were country music. In three months, country music revenues had exceeded $3 billion. In the previous year, thirty-three country albums went gold and thirty-five platinum. In one week of January, Garth Brooks sold 340,000 records and netted $500,000. In the last decade, country radio stations had increased from 1,800 to 2,500. A Simmons Market Research study indicated that households with incomes of over $40,000 were partial to country radio over other formats. An MCA executive said that fifteen- to twenty-five-year-olds are "the driving demographics" for the new country audience. A small town in the Ozarks (Branson, Missouri) was attracting 4 million tourists per year, who were spending $750 million in a setting of mountain rusticity and live country music theaters. Venerable stars of country music Waylon Jennings, Willie Nelson, Kris Kristofferson, and Johnny Cash were touring Europe and drawing large audiences as The Highwaymen. In January 1992, Tokyo, Japan, inaugurated full-time country radio station KTYO. Garth Brooks concerts were selling out in record time at an average 1991 price of $15—substantially less than the price for leading rock acts—and Brooks was averaging $8.50 in merchandise sales for each fan who saw him live. *Forbes* concluded from all this that the market was healthy: "Good quality at a reasonable price. What more can you ask from the entertainment industry—or any other business?" (Gubernick and Newcomb 1992, 72–76).

The rising popularity of country music was not lost on musical entrepreneurs in Dayton, Ohio. On Sunday, April 5, 1992, the *Daily News* carried a review of a pop concert by the Dayton Philharmonic Orchestra. Here, critic Betty Dietz Krebs objected to the orchestra's "drift from its original purpose." "The pair of pops concerts this weekend at the Convention Center are an example—for this listener, at least—of what not to do to sell tickets. In this case, it had to do with bringing in Emmylou Harris to belt out her songs in strident fashion" (Krebs April 5, 1992, 3C). After praising the first half of the program (a rendition of the "George Gershwin Songbook"), Krebs noted dourly: "The second half of the program was given over to Harris and her guitar. She clearly has a lively following for her songs." That same day, the *New York Times* reported record guitar sales nationwide, with fretted instruments returning $400 million in 1990, led by acoustic guitars. The head of Umanov Guitars, in New York City, told the *Times*: "I have a lot of 40-year-olds who now can afford to buy the guitar they wanted when they were 15. So, they do" (*Times* April 5, 1992, 9).

In *Forbes'* annual report of entertainer earnings for fall 1992, a group including actors, film producers, directors, singers of all varieties, cartoonists, magicians, producers, writers, novelists and TV hosts, Garth Brooks was the only figure of country music culture to make "The Top 40." He did enter impressively at number 13, positioned between number 12, Prince, and number 14, Arnold Schwarzenegger. *Forbes* reported that Brooks had earned $20 million in 1991 and $24 million in 1992 for a total in the survey period of $44 million. "It's been a good year for cowboys . . ." the story began (Newcomb and Chatzky 1992, 87–91).

In its December 1992 retrospective issue, "1992: The Year in Music," *Billboard* attempted to provide perspective on the country music boom. This double issue featured a color cover with a centered picture of Garth Brooks on stage. A front-page article by Edward Morris, "Country's Fan Base Is Wider Than Ever," reported perceptions of the growing country music market from industry demographic studies. Without losing "rural dwellers in the 25-to-54 age range," Morris reports, these studies show that "country also appeals now to listeners/viewers/buyers who are younger, more musically eclectic, and more geographically diverse than ever before." Singers like Garth Brooks, Clint Black, Hal Ketchum and Billy Dean appeal to mid-teens and to twenty-year-olds. Women remain numerically dominant in the market.

> According to data compiled for the County Music Assn., more women who are 18 and older listen to country than to adult contemporary and rock; 56.9% of all country album purchases are by women; just over 48% of TNN viewers are women; and 54.1% of the viewing audience for the 1992 CMA awards show were women. (Morris 1992, 5, 98)

Morris quotes researcher Paul Keckley who identified "distinct country markets" in three areas: "traditionalists," "transition-30s," and "country converts." "Traditionalists" are midteen to late-fifties fans with "a fairly narrow band of artist preferences"—those who sound "traditional." This group is probably influenced by Appalachian migrants; it is "concentrated in the area from Canada through the Midwest into Tennessee and the Ohio Valley," comprises 25 percent of the market, and purchases 15 percent of albums in a ratio preferring cassettes to CDs by five-to-one. "Transition-30s" are in their early twenties to early forties, "generally grew up not liking nor listening to country music" but now prefer it over other types "because it has understandable beats and lyrics and because they feel that it's more in sync with their values [and] their passage through life." They are 45 percent of the market buying 55 percent of albums in a ratio of three-to-one CDs to cassettes. They listen to both new artists and traditionalists, and may watch TNN and CMT. "Transition-30s" will "divide their radio listening among three stations, two of which are country," and televised award shows are important to them. They "watch religiously." "Country converts" are 30 percent of the market and buy 30 percent of its product. Their musical tastes are eclectic. "They'll buy 'Ropin' the Wind' and turn around and buy Rick Astley or Phil Collins or 'The Bodyguard' soundtrack." Converts are "typically in the mid-20s up to the late-40s and predominantly in the 30s," and are the "fastest growing portion of the market," particularly expanding in the Northeast and the West. In addition to spreading geographically and to a broader age segment, by 1991, country music was moving decidedly into the middle class. That year, Simmons Market Research reported to the Country Music Association "that country music listeners are neck and neck in income with those who listen to adult contemporary radio and earn more, on average, than those who listen to rock. A greater percentage of college graduates, the study said, listen to country music than to AC and rock" (Morris 1992, 98).

If 1992 closed with news about a new demographic profile for country music fans, 1993 opened with commentary on fragmentation across the pop music market. In a front-page article for the Arts & Leisure section of the *New York Times*, Sunday, January 3, 1993, Jon Pareles praised new forms of rock music that defy the "esthetics of the baby boomers who have dominated rock for a generation." With instrumentation augmented by computers, a tendency to "play distortion instead of harmony" and a preference for "rootless" sounds over "clarity," rock bands such as Arrested Development, Pearl Jam, Nine Inch Nails, and My Bloody Valentine had become leading rock acts. This happened as part of a larger cultural phenomenon Pareles called "narrowcasting," where "recording companies pitch to specific markets, whether that means collegiate rock or techno dance music or gangster rap. But just as nobody watches just one cable channel, very few people are actually stuck in a single subgenre."

> Music from the margins has grown more important as the popular music audience has fragmented by age, geography, class and inclination. (Radio stations trying to carve out tiny individual niches have also moved the process along.) Entertainment moguls can still score blockbusters with heavily marketed movie tie-ins and, away from the coasts, with good-hearted Garth Brooks. But they bemoan the absence of across-the-board hit-makers like the Beatles in the 1960's or Michael Jackson in the 1980's. Let them. As sure things disappear and cultism rules the charts—Def Leppard one week, Ice Cube another—the business has to offer more choices; corporate disarray leads to diversity. (Pareles 1993a, II, 1, 27)

For country music, Pareles says, market fragmentation means "boomers' last chance to enjoy melodies and straightforward storytelling."

If the national pop music market was sizzling in early 1993—with grunge, rap, heavy metal, and other traditions diverging from the rock music that baby boomers (born generally between the mid-forties and mid-fifties) knew in their youth—in Ohio's Miami River Valley, the *Dayton Daily News* reported twice in 1992 on an important new trend in night life: country dancing. In February, Lolita M. Rhodes wrote that Dayton featured fourteen clubs for dancing, three of them specializing in country dance action and instruction. Other February dance options included traditional ballroom dancing, top-forty, pop, classic rock, big band and rhythm and blues. Yet the lead trend was downtown with the Yellow Rose Saloon and Dance Hall, where couples dressed in western outfits and Garth Brooks hats had adapted the cha-cha, the two step, and other maneuvers to music of the new country entertainers (Rhodes February 15, 1992, C1). By April 24, the newspaper's weekend entertainment section could showcase several country dance clubs that were eclipsing other dance forms. In a story detailing night life at the Yellow Rose, Billy Bob's Saloon, and Breakers, Bob Batz interviewed patrons in their thirties who described their participation in group dancing to the Texas Two-Step, Cowboy Motion, Roundup, Berlin Boogie, Denver, Flying 8, Reggae Cowboy, Slo Cadillac and Cherokee Kick. Thirty-three-year-old Frank Rose, of Kettering, told Batz that he liked country music dancing because "you don't have to get blitzed on booze to have a good time" and that in this era of increased caution about sexual advances, "What I like best is that when you ask a woman to dance at a country music nightclub, she doesn't look at you like you're trying to pick her up." Perhaps the closest evocation of dance club euphoria in Batz's account was this random moment:

> The tall, thick-armed doorman collects a cover charge from a husband and wife, then sends them into The Yellow Rose Saloon and Dance Hall with a smile.
> Inside the door, a woman employee of the downtown Dayton dance emporium greets them with a cheerful, "How about a couple of cold beers?"
> When they nod she plunks a pair of frosty Bud Lights from an ice-filled tub, saying, "That'll be $4."
> The dance floor—with its western mural backdrop—is a sea of Stetsons.
> Recorded music blares. Candles flicker on the bartop.
> A woman, wearing sequined designer bluejeans, is standing near the center of the room, swaying to the beat of the music.
> "Is this heaven?" she asks dreamily.
> "No," replies her companion, taking another swig of his beer. "It's Dayton." (Batz April 24, 1992, 16–17)

If Dayton nightlife was dancing increasingly to country, it was also buying concert tickets. On February 26, 1993, the *Daily News* told readers that the Ervin J. Nutter Center, at Wright State University, had been "ranked as one of the world's ten top-grossing concert facilities of its size for 1992 by *Amusement Business*, an entertainment industry trade publication." Between December 9, 1991, and November 30, 1992, Nutter Center reported attendance of 161,776 at concert events and a gross income of $3,228,412, ranking it seventh "among buildings with a seating capacity of 10,001 to 15,000." Opened in 1991, in its second year Nutter Center featured twenty-three shows, nine of them sell-outs. It had seated more than 10,000 for Hank Williams, Jr. and sold out for Garth Brooks. Nutter was a particularly lucrative venue for Brooks:

> Sales of concert merchandise, such as T-shirts and programs, at Nutter have exceeded national averages, [director Tom] Oddy said. For example, concert-goers at the Dec. 10 Garth Brooks concert spent an average of almost $14 per person on merchandise. It was one of the highest per capita spending figures on Brooks' tour. (Larsen 1993a, 1B)

Located on a freeway loop just west of downtown Dayton, in southwestern Ohio—easily accessible from Cincinnati, Columbus, and Indianapolis and strategically positioned in a region heavily populated with Appalachian migrants and their descendants near the Kentucky border—the Nutter Center is well positioned to attract top country acts. Just over 300 miles from Nashville by freeway, Dayton is also convenient for supplemental show dates on tours playing Indianapolis, Detroit, Cleveland and Pittsburgh.

Nutter Center wasn't the only Dayton metro-area concert venue flourishing in the early 1990s. In other 1992 concerts, Alan Jackson packed the University of Dayton arena with 7,632 fans, and Travis Tritt sold out Memorial Hall's 2,501 seats (Batz 1992, 16). In its second season during the summer of 1993, the Fraze Pavilion for the Performing Arts in Kettering (a community of south Dayton heavily populated by white upper-middle-class suburbanites) offered a calendar of forty-seven events in an outdoor setting between May 20 and September 8. Bookings ranged in style from the community college wind symphony and the Dayton Philharmonic to comedian Gallagher and pop musician Yanni. Four country music concerts were included: Hal Ketchum, with Riders in the Sky; the Lone Star Country Dancers and Eldorado Band; Dolly Parton; and Lyle Lovett.

On June 29, 1993, Lyle Lovett played a concert at Fraze Pavilion that lasted more than two hours and presented twenty-six songs. Lovett opened with the Tammy Wynette hit, "Stand By Your Man," and closed with his own "She Makes Me Feel Good." This event was on a Tuesday evening; the preceding Sunday afternoon, Lovett had married Hollywood starlet Julia Roberts in neighboring Indiana, precipitating a deluge of publicity in newspapers, magazines, and electronic media. On the day of his marriage, Lovett had played an evening concert where Roberts appeared to introduce him. The morning after Lovett's Dayton appearance, the *Daily News* headlined a front-page story detailing fan reactions to this marriage. Entitled "Fans at Fraze wait for Lovett's love," it focused on fan expectation that Julia Roberts might come to Kettering. She didn't, but she might have understood the zeal. Originally from Georgia and a fan of Lovett's who owned all his records before meeting him, Roberts had told *Time* magazine: "It's like a dream. I'm scared it's going to be over, and I don't want to wake up" (Corliss *1993*, 6; Debrosse June 30, 1993, 1).

If country music culture was leading in radio Arbitron charts, broadening into upper-middle class venues like the Fraze Pavilion, helping the Nutter Center gain prominence, opening dance clubs and being played by the Dayton Philharmonic, it was also expanding in Miami Valley youth culture. In July 1993, amid much local publicity, "Country Concert '93" was held just north of Dayton for the thirteenth year at Hickory Hill Lakes Campground, Ft. Loramie. An event that originated as a weekend of local entertainment for campers, in 1992, more than 120,000 fans showed up. In 1993, for the $52 price of a three-day ticket (and an additional $35 to camp out) you could spend July 9, 10, and 11 outdoors listening to sixteen country stars headlined by Vince Gill, Kathy Mattea, and Mark Chestnutt. Known in the business as a good venue for rising acts, the 160-acre RV park was saturated with a middle-class youth culture reminiscent of Woodstock that mingled with traditional working-class fans in a crowd that exceeded 80,000 people per day. In the early 1990s, Ohio was host to another massive July outdoor festival as well—the WWVA Jamboree in the Hills, just across the state line from Wheeling, West Virginia (Larsen 1993b, 14–15; Larsen 1993d, 1).

By August 1993, the inroads of country music into new listening and live-participation audiences in southern Ohio were so notable that the Sunday *Cincinnati Enquirer* could devote the cover page of its Arts & Leisure section to interviewing new country fans. Its emphasis was on professional people in the Cincinnati area who had favorite country stars: the superintendent of Cincinnati Public Schools liked Reba McEntire; the judge of Hamilton County Municipal Court, Charlie Daniels; the assistant director of the Cincinnati Downtown Council, Willie Nelson; the president of a celebrity hairdressing salon, Hank Williams, Sr.; the president of the Greater Cincinnati Flower and Garden Show Society, Kenny Rogers; the owner of a prominent Ford dealership, Garth Brooks and Wynonna Judd; and a senior vice president and portfolio manager at a major securities company, Dolly Parton (Radel August 1, 1993, G1, G3). In September, on the eve of the CMA awards show, the *Dayton Daily News* devoted half its front page to country music. Under the banner headline BIG COUNTRY, Gary Graff, of the Knight-Ridder News Service, reported that, in 1992, country music had 67 million radio listeners nationwide, eclipsing adult contemporary music at 56.8 million and rock at 46.9 million; that 25 percent of albums on the *Billboard* Top 200 were currently by country artists; and that country music sales had almost doubled since 1990, from 9 percent to 17 percent, while the leading share of pop music—still held by rock—had declined from 37 percent to 33 percent in the same period (Graff September 29, 1993, 1).

By late 1993, Nashville insiders were reflecting on the need to maintain their new market. In *Billboard* for December 25, Liberty Records' Jimmy Bowen expressed reservations about the industry "getting very tunneled and very traditional and safe." Even with new construction on Music Row, the expansion of record labels, and the emergence of new superstars like Vince Gill (winner of five CMA awards, including Best Male Vocalist and Entertainer of the Year), there was desire for new marketing techniques. Tony Brown, of MCA Records, saw this as a matter of public education. "Our job is, yes, to deliver what the public wants to hear, but our real job is to introduce the public to things that they *ought* to hear" (Morris and Cronin 1993, 48).

If the country album marketing business in Nashville was beginning to stretch its entrepreneurs by early 1994, according to the *Wall Street Journal*, country cable television was just coming into its own. A front-page story January 19—about the financial success of Gaylord Entertainment Company (parent company of the Grand Ole Opry, Opryland, The Nashville Network and Country Music Television)—reported that Gaylord's net income rose dramatically from $2 million in 1991 to $21 million in 1992. Its revenue increased by $42 million that year and was expected to go to $700 million for 1993 with a profit of $38 million. The main focus of this sharp growth was cable television. Country Music Television (CMT) tripled its subscribers in two years to 25 million homes, and the prime-time ratings of TNN beat MTV. Gaylord offered public stock in 1991; its value more than doubled, and split, by 1994.

Majority owner Edward L. Gaylord, a wealthy newspaperman who is "an unabashed devotee of *Hee Haw*," entered the country music business in the 1980s. The initial vision for TNN was a "country lifestyle" network centering on music, and its dramatic success in middle-America attracted important advertising revenues. Ralph Emery, host of *Nashville Now*, became "the Johnny Carson of the pickup-truck circuit" and the author of an autobiography that went to number two on the *New York Times* bestseller list. CMT features an MTV-style format of continuous music videos that especially appeals to younger fans. "By 1993, the 18 to 34 age group and people earning more than $60,000 a year had become the fastest-growing segments of the country music audience." CMT has also helped move country music into new geographic regions. In 1993, country fans increased 48 percent in the Northeast and 19 percent in the West. CMT has expanded into Europe, signing 8 million subscribers "in such unlikely places as Israel, Russia, and Scandinavia." Back at home base, Gaylord is adding a thousand rooms to the Opryland Hotel, building a water taxi route to downtown Nashville, making arrangements for hosting franchises of the National Basketball Association and National Hockey League, and considering a venture into TV home shopping (Sharpe January 19, 1994, 1, 8).

By 1994, two young male stars who frequently grace TNN and CMT entered the *Forbes* Top 40 earning entertainers for 1992–1993; Garth Brooks moved up to ninth rank at $47 million and Billy Ray Cyrus entered at twenty-second place with $29 million (*Country America* 1994, 91). On February 4, 1994, the *Daily News* told readers that the final survey for 1993 top album sales showed continued growth for country music. For the second year, Garth Brooks was the number one seller among albums. Billy Ray Cyrus was number five, Reba McEntire number ten, Brooks and Dunn number eleven, and George Strait number twelve. This gave country music one-third of the entire album market (Holden 1994, 3C).

Coverage in the national and regional press of country music culture's 1990s expansion emphasized rising sales figures, broadening market demographics, the role of new technologies, the human interest of fans new to the culture, and the effectiveness of business entrepreneurs. The charismatic talent of new stars—especially male ones—was taken for granted. Less direct attention was given to shifting cultural attitudes that opened public taste to the themes of hard times, broken hearts, domestic turmoil, and salvation that had been evolving specialties of country music culture since the 1920s.

In its seventy-fifth anniversary issue of September 14, 1992, *Forbes* assembled an array of cultural critics speaking to the theme, "Why we feel so bad when we have it so good." Peggy Noonan, former CBS News writer and presidential speechwriter, explored the psychology of the aging middle-class baby-boomer generation, a group she described as feeling "obscurely oppressed." In their late forties, burdened with the responsibilities of young children and aging parents, enmeshed in high-income jobs that yet fail to equal their parents' actual wealth at this age, facing large mortgages, underfunded pensions, anxiety about social security, and savings bank failures, this generation is seen by Noonan as plagued by anxiety about the future. She also sees it moving toward a recovery of religious belief. Noonan connects the phenomena of New Age religiosity and cynicism about political and cultural deterioration with declining faith in the country's future. For her, the ultimate characterization of boomer psychology is its reticence to act, to take leadership in changing its way of life. A generation that matured in an era which romanticized the destruction of oppressive institutions and traditions has difficulty, Noonan suggests, exerting mature responsibility. We "white-collar boomers have recused ourselves from a world we never made," she says, to focus attention instead on arts and entertainment. We watch, support, and contribute to them, "because they are the only places we can imagine progress" (Noonan 1992, 58–69).

Noonan's view of baby-boomer psychology makes no reference to the appeal of country music culture, yet it may be that the public values of entertainers who trade in domestic stories of salvation from hard times play well to the emotions she describes. A catalog of popular culture enthusiasms in the early 1990s complements this notion. The persistent rusticity of country music culture harmonizes with 1990s trends in environmentalism, the popularity of casual "outdoor" clothing bought from mailorder houses like L.L. Bean and Land's End, the growth in sales of "rugged" four-wheel-drive vehicles as routine means of suburban transportation, the witty localism of popular television dramas such as *Northern Exposure* and *Picket Fences*, and the marketing success of "natural" foods, from their reasonably authentic expressions in bran cereal, heavy-grain bread and multi-bean soup to perhaps their more suspect expression in "dirty" potato chips. The pervasiveness of rusticity in popular culture of the early 1990s lends perspective to the reception of such items as *Country America,* a magazine of "country life and entertainment." In the June 1992 issue, editor Danita Allen reported that, since its debut in October 1989, this magazine had grown to 900,000 readers—at a rate of two to three hundred thousand readers per year. By 1992, *Country America* was among the nation's seventy-five largest-circulation magazines and one of its fastest growing, adding 550 new readers each day (Allen 1992, 10). In addition to glossy stories on country music entertainers from the aging to the neophyte, *Country America* includes regular features on country crafts, travel, cooking, and entertainment. It features a country comedian each month and carries the TNN viewing guide.

The popularity of rusticity and country lifestyle lent special interest to the presidential campaign of 1992. Every president since Richard Nixon had openly endorsed country music, and George Bush was no exception. Lee Greenwood's rendition of "God Bless the U.S.A." was a campaign song in both the Reagan and Bush campaigns. Bush himself was reported to be a subscriber to *Country Music* magazine. He appeared on *Nashville Now* during his campaign and attended the 1992 CMA Awards show at the Grand Ole Opryhouse. Naomi Judd and Tanya Tucker performed at the Republican convention where Bush was nominated. On the platform with the President, November 2, for his last campaign rally were singers Ricky Skaggs, Lee Greenwood, and Naomi Judd. Bush's speeches late in the campaign were peppered with phrases from country song lyrics that, Bush felt, presented his opponent in a bad light.

Despite his appropriation of it for campaign strategy, George Bush showed an affection for country music, its values and its artists, that,very likely, is genuine. For his part, Bill Clinton shied away from embracing country music outright. During the campaign, Hillary Rodham Clinton made a strategic error by publicly criticizing what she understood to be negative values of compliant femininity in Tammy Wynette's "Stand By Your Man." Yet, Clinton's campaign strategy was more carefully synchronized with the rhythms of the country music business in the 1990s than was the approach of George Bush. As Jon Pareles pointed out in the *New York Times,* Clinton's campaign paralleled the commitments of country music entrepreneurs by acknowledging (but not emphasizing) Southern roots, using modern showmanship, and making a direct pitch to suburban baby boomers (Pareles 1993b, 27). Like contemporary country music stars, Clinton used television to make personal contact with the public. In a pitch aimed at baby-boomer nostalgia, Clinton revealed his affection for Elvis Presley and earlier forms of rock and roll, including Fleetwood Mac, who provided him the campaign song, "Don't Stop Thinking About Tomorrow." An important icon of country music culture was prominent in Clinton's public imagery—he was shown on his campaign plane sleeping beside an Elvis picture. In fact, the Secret Service code name for Clinton was reported to be "Elvis."

Moreover, Clinton's key strategic move to impress American voters with his sincerity and personal touch was taken directly from the playbook of country music stars—a six-day bus tour of 1,000 miles through seven states from New York City to St. Louis immediately after his nomination. This bus tour was a glad-handing quick-stop touch-the-people affair that at least outwardly paralleled artist-fan interaction in country music culture. Coupled with his campaign pitch for restoring "family values" and lifting tax burdens from the "middle class," Clinton was moving effectively in the same terrain as Nashville entrepreneurs. When Travis Tritt released a music video of "Lord Have Mercy on the Working Man" that confronted a litany of personal oppressions attributed to government policy with a large sign saying "Vote," the insurgent spirit of Clinton's popular campaign—and a touch of Ross Perot's—seemed to have reached its target (Specter 1992, E3; Ifill 1992, A13; Kelly 1992, A7).

If, in the 1990s, presidential politics worked its own niche in the marketplace of emotions alongside new Nashville entrepreneurs, older country music stars were also active. The Ryman Auditorium was being renovated, and a continuing show depicting the career of Patsy Cline was planned for it. Cline appeared (via recording) on the *Honky Tonk Angels* album. Willie Nelson—elected to the Country Music Hall of Fame in 1993, after recovering from a bankruptcy debt of $9 million owed the Internal Revenue Service—released *Across the Border Line*, an album that showcases his flair for penetrating popular music markets. Songwriters Bob Dylan, Peter Gabriel, and Paul Simon had songs on the album, and Nelson sang duets with Dylan, Simon, Bonnie Raitt, and Sinead O'Connor (Nelson 1993). Nelson continued his involvement in an annual charity festival he calls "Farm Aid." At "Farm Aid V," the 1992 version, 55,000 fans heard twelve hours of country, rock, and pop music. Half of the show was broadcast live on TNN (*Daily News* March 15, 1992, 8A).

One of the more attractive market niches for aging country music stars has proved to be that of tourism. The demographic growth in senior citizens and retirees as the nation's population ages is underwriting a general expansion of tourist options. One option is Caribbean cruises. On November 14, 1992, country music fans boarded the *M.S. Westerdam* for a seven-night cruise hosted by the Bill Anderson Fan Club. In addition to Anderson, Tanya Tucker, and rising star Collin Raye, this event featured eminent stars of the Grand Ole Opry Jan Howard, Del Reeves, and Little Jimmie Dickens. In January 1993, *Music City News* offered a Celebrity Cruise hosted by George Jones and Ralph Emery, which stopped in St. Maarten, St. John, and St. Thomas.

Cruising with venerated stars was not the only tourist option heavily promoted in the early 1990s. In Nashville, plans were underway to make the city more attractive to aging country artists by establishing a retirement home for them, to be funded partly by proceeds from a West Coast version of Fan Fair inaugurated in 1994. Nashville also made a commitment to provide more live entertainment for tourists, to supplement the Grand Ole Opry and such songwriter showcases as the Bluebird Cafe. Opryland announced an expanded offering of live performances, including George Jones and Tammy Wynette for 1994; and the city of Nashville, where the overall 1990s growth rate is predicted to be 22 percent, is witnessing renovation of a warehouse district near the Cumberland River that features shops, restaurants, and "a huge country dance emporium" (Applebome 1993, A8).

In Pigeon Forge, Tennessee, Dolly Parton announced plans to invest $20 million in a series of music theaters to be called "Music Road." Her plan was to have the city of Pigeon Forge provide land leases and improvements that would attract music theater entrepreneurs to "an industrial park for tourism attractions in a show business zone" (Chance 1993), adding momentum to a tourist town where revenues in the period 1982–1992 increased from $72.6 million to $416.7 million (*Dollywood Foundation Newsletter* 1993, 1). Country music tourism even came to the seventeenth-century reconstruction site at Colonial Williamsburg in the form of the "Old Dominion Opry," whose tourism brochures promoted family entertainment, live country music, country comedy, and special rates for groups and children.

This ferment in country music tourism was very likely precipitated by the rise of Branson, Missouri, as a country music theme town. Located in the Ozark Mountains not far from Arkansas, Branson in the 1880s was a logging center. In 1903, the Missouri Pacific Railroad arrived, and in 1912 the town was incorporated. The following year, the White River was dammed for electric power generation, creating Lake Taneycomo, and it promptly became an Ozark tourist attraction. The population of Branson in 1912 was 1,200. More tourism was stimulated by a theme park depicting sites in Harold Bell Wright's novel, *The Shepherd of the Hills* (1907). Next, in 1950, Hugo Herschend, an Illinois businessman, took a ninety-nine-year lease on Marvel Cave just west of Branson. Herschend died in 1955, but his sons, Jack and Pete, developed Marvel Cave as a theme park and changed its name to "Silver Dollar City." The Herschends purchased the theme park in Pigeon Forge that was to become Dollywood when Dolly Parton bought a minority interest. In 1992, Silver Dollar City, Inc., had revenues exceeding $110 million. The Herschends also own Branson's largest country music theater, The Grand Palace, a $12.5 million investment opened in 1992, which seats 4,000. By 1993, Branson had a permanent population of 3,700 and thirty-five music theaters offering 50,172 theater seats to more than 5 million visitors annually (Gubernick 1992, 418–19; Buckstaff, 1993, 9–116).

In casual conversation some permanent residents of Branson, Missouri, will describe the long music history of their community as an unbroken line of progress. In the early days of party telephone lines, one story has it, extended families would pick up the phone and sing to one another. Early music shows with an Ozark hillbilly theme, the Presleys and the Baldknobbers, operated on the Branson waterfront for many years and are still active on the Branson theater strip. Branson has attracted pop stars Andy Williams and Christy Lane, and Japanese country fiddler Shoji Tabuchi with a show evocative of Las Vegas. Country comedians Ray Stevens and Jim Stafford have popular theaters here.

The principal attraction of Branson is well-known mature country singers who are tired of road life although they still wish to perform frequently. Guitarist and entertainer Roy Clark was the first national country music figure to invest in Branson. In 1983, he opened *Roy*

Clark's Celebrity Theater, which quickly gained a level of success attractive to other stars of his generation. In the early 1990s, stars such as Boxcar Willie, Wayne Newton, Mickey Gilley, and Loretta Lynn have active theaters in Branson and the town has become a national tourist mecca. In early February 1994, AAA Miami Valley, in Dayton, Ohio, offered seven week-long bus tours to Branson for 1994—two in October, two in June, and others in May, July, and August. (At the same time, this agency was offering only one three-day bus trip to Nashville, for Country Christmas at the Opryland Hotel in November.)

Entrepreneurial tourism activity in Nashville, Pigeon Forge, and other sites of country music is recognition of Branson's success in reversing traditional migratory patterns of country music culture. Instead of traveling constantly for more than two hundred days annually to meet and entertain their fans throughout the nation, in Branson, artists can work in their own comfortable venue where they may perform daily for fans who come to them—and at night go home to an artist community living in a rustic setting on a mountain lake. If Branson is a prototype, successful efforts to create country music tourist towns will need to feature several elements. A tradition of tourism that precedes the investment in country music will be useful, as will geographic location on accessible travel routes that tourists, vacationers and tour buses are likely to take. Attractions that appeal to men, women, and children need to be located in close proximity. In Branson's case, there is fishing, camping, and other outdoor recreation traditionally appealing to men; combined with discount and other shopping in five malls, plus the village of Branson, traditionally appealing to women. For children there are rides and other amusements at Silver Dollar City theme park. Then, every afternoon and evening—and, in a few instances, during the morning, as well—there are country music shows in comfortable theaters designed to showcase live country music performance for the entire family.

Mel Tillis is a leading example of an established country music star and business entrepreneur who has high visibility in Branson. Tillis's 1984 autobiography, *Stutterin' Boy*, written with Walter Wager, is a revealing account of a mature star's view of the long-term costs of country music road life. Born in 1932, in Pahokee, Florida, Tillis was fifty-two when his autobiography was published. Although Branson, Missouri, is not mentioned in it, the hazards of road life are.

In 1984, Tillis traveled with his band approximately 250 days. A self-taught musician who won talent shows in the 1950s and sang with country bands while stationed in the Pacific as an Air Force cook, Tillis met Wesley Rose, of Acuff-Rose publishing in Nashville, in 1956. Influenced by the western swing style and the professional advice of Bob Wills, Tillis hired a large show band, rehearsed heavily, disciplined his performers, and provided an orchestrated stage show that featured fiddle players, big-band instrumentation, and Tillis vocals and comedy routines—many of them playing off his natural tendency to stutter. Tillis was a regular with the Porter Wagoner television show when Dolly Parton made her first splash there, became a successful Nashville songwriter, appeared in nine movies, was named Entertainer of the Year in 1976, then bought his own music publishing company (Tillis and Wager 1984).

Stutterin' Boy tells Mel Tillis's success story in a chronology of incidents, many of them amusing; yet, approximately the last half of the book can be read as extended comment on negative aspects of road life. Tillis tells road stories of excessive drinking, bad food, and the deepest enemies—boredom, monotony, and idleness. The "lonesome highways" keep country artists "cooped up in the bus like sardines with the same bunch of guys, who've already told you their family problems and jokes eighty-nine times." On the road, says Tillis, the routine opportunities of domestic life—movies, ball games, fishing—are rare (Tillis and Wager 1984, 149). The story of Tillis's divorce and remarriage is told in this context and attributed partly to road life. By 1984 Tillis and his new wife had a farm outside Nashville, a place, he said, that "gives me the renewed strength to go on with the touring" (Tillis and Wager 1984, 241).

At one point in the book, lamenting his discourteous treatment by a newcomer to country music culture, Tillis complains about prospects for mature stars: "Don't put the old road warriors out to pasture. Don't slap them in their road-weary faces, 'cause that ain't country" (Tillis and Wager 1984, 185). Mel Tillis found a highly productive way to avoid that fate when he opened the Mel Tillis Theater, an elaborate venue in Branson, Missouri, in 1991. This theater seats 2,100 people in a luxurious descendant of the Grand Ole Opryhouse complete with fine acoustics, outstanding visual sight lines, and a "rain curtain" of actual glycerin-treated water that falls during his stage show across a 40-foot stage (Buckstaff 1993, 29–30). From April through December, Tillis offers matinee and evening performances daily. On May 23, 1992, the 8:00 P.M. show featured a sixteen-member band with four fiddles, two guitars, a steel guitar, two keyboards, drums, three wind instruments (including clarinet and trumpet), and two female backup singers. The band provided a polished musical presentation in an intense, highly professional stage show. Tillis's band is named the Statesiders (perhaps in contrast to his military experience), and he introduced his singers as "the Stutterettes." Tillis opened with a set of nine songs, including the Bob Wills favorite "San Antonio Rose," comic-recitation songs such as "Smoke, Smoke, Smoke that Cigarette," songs Tillis had written for movies, and instrumental specialties like "Steel Guitar Rag," which featured a player Tillis said had been with the Statesiders for twenty-five years. Tillis performed "Digging Up Bones," a song that sold 4 million copies for Randy Travis and was published by Tillis's publishing company. "So, every record ol' Randy sold," said Tillis, "they had to pay me, too."

Tillis divided his first set by introducing Levi Garrett, a thirteen-year-old singer who had appeared on the TV program *Star Search* and who now performed "Little Liza Jane." Tillis returned for five more numbers before intermission, one of which brought six dancers on stage for a well-choreographed performance. Another featured a strobe light; and another—where Tillis played guitar with his band—showcased dancers wearing trench coats and Navy uniforms in a production version of the pop favorite "Sentimental Journey." The finale produced impressive thunder effects and a rainstorm from the water curtain. At the break, an announcer welcomed tourist groups, including the Fellowship Baptist Church of Joplin, Missouri. After the break, Barbara Fairchild, a country singer who has moved into contemporary Christian music, did four songs, among them her 1973 number-one secular hit "Teddy Bear Song," and a gospel hit "Could You Walk A Mile?" from her 1991 album, *The Light*.

During Tillis's second set he introduced each member of his band, emphasizing their home states—initially Missouri, Texas, Arkansas, and Louisiana. The Mel Tillis Theater has an intense green color scheme, and Tillis was dressed in a suit to match it for the first half of his show. For the second half he wore a fitted sport coat to accent his tall, trim figure. Tillis did more relaxed story songs in this set, featured comedians from the band in a saxophone and harmonica duet of "Danny Boy," and told a variety of jokes. He introduced band members from more distant states—Florida, Montana, and Vermont. Tillis talked about his children (five girls and a boy), his daughter Pam, and his son-in-law and grandchildren. He told his fans that Mel Junior was in Nashville and that he had a daughter who was a sophomore at Samford University. In a show-stopping moment, he introduced his four-year-old daughter, Hannah Elizabeth, who told some riddles with her father, sang "You Are My Sunshine," and took three bows to a tremendous ovation. At the end of the show, Tillis told his fans that he had started his career at the nearby Springfield, Missouri, Ozark Jubilee "with Red Foley." In honor of that past, he ended with an inspired, up-tempo rendition of "I Believe."

In 1993, admission to the Mel Tillis Theatre was $15.50 for adults and $5 for children under twelve. For eight and a half months out of the year Tillis appears to be filling most of 4,000 seats five days a week. His show markets country music history, showcases his own hit songs, provides a tight professional performance in an intimate venue that is a pleasant accommodation for fans, and offers comedy, humor, and gospel music, as well as performers of all ages. In the spirit of extended family perhaps modeled in country music culture by Loretta Lynn, Tillis shares members of his own family with his fans. After the show, Tillis descended to the theater floor and moved to a specially designed area at the side of the stage, where hundreds of country fans, with their typical patience, formed a long slow line to meet Mel Tillis, shake his hand, obtain his autograph, buy his autobiography and a cassette tape, have their picture made, and just talk to Mel. While Barbara Fairchild also autographed and talked with fans behind a table in the lobby, Tillis stayed late to attend to every fan who sought him out. In country music culture's marketplace of emotions, the Mel Tillis Theater in Branson, Missouri, is a rising stock.

If the Mel Tillis Theater represents a new dimension of country music as a favored destination for vacationing families and fans who have retirement time to spend as well as the means for bus travel, in the early 1990s, the marketplace of emotions still requires a vigorous road life for its artists, especially the young ones.

The tradition of touring is descended from medicine shows and repertory theaters. It entered and was firmly established in country music culture with Jimmie Rodgers and the Grand Ole Opry, and it remains lively in the 1990s. Southern gospel singers have combined touring with the heritage of evangelical circuit riding to keep a withering pace of performing to save souls. The *Singing Cookes Newsletter* told their followers of seventy-five "bus stops" between February and November of 1993 in nine Southern and four Border states, plus the fertile Appalachian-migrant state of Michigan. *Singing News* magazine, a leading comprehensive information source for devotees of Southern gospel music, provided in its November 1993 issue detailed itineraries of seventy-six acts during November and early December. That information required eleven pages in the magazine to document plans for well over a thousand personal appearances scheduled for a period of less than two months (*Singing News* 1993, 82–93). Four additional pages were devoted to listings for gospel concerts featuring multiple groups in eighteen states.

The circuit riders of the gospel were traveling the nation's highways alongside circuit riders of the heart. Tour itineraries for secular country musicians are printed for fans in *Country Music City News*. In October 1993, it detailed plans for sixty major artists. Inspection of the list suggests that older artists tour less, yet maintain time in their lives for this important commitment. Between mid-October and early December, Kitty Wells planned seven personal appearances in six states, and Chet Atkins listed five performances in as many states. Younger stars still building their fan base were much more active. Michelle Wright offered thirteen concerts in this period; Collin Raye, fourteen; Doug Supernaw, nineteen; and Radney Foster, twenty-two appearances criss-crossing the country from Chicago to Arizona to California to Florida, Tennessee, Wisconsin, Texas, and Oklahoma. Established hitmakers were on the road as well. In slightly less than two months during the fall of 1993, Garth Brooks appeared in thirteen live concerts and Vince Gill in seventeen. In a separate advertisement, "Star Quest Concert Info" advertised a 900-number where fans could learn dates, places, and ticket phone numbers for 127 concert listings in 28 distinct areas of the United States (*Country Music City News* 1993b, 12–13).

In their autobiographies, Loretta Lynn and Mel Tillis complain of incessant boredom in the road life of country music culture. By the early 1990s, bus company entrepreneurs had taken steps to address that. Eagle Coach and Prevost offered elaborate custom-designed buses with interiors tailored to individual personalities. The Hemphill Brothers Coach Company of Nashville was in its second decade of custom bus design based on the personal experience of a gospel-singing family. Lisa Gubernick reports in her biography of Trisha Yearwood that Hemphill adds eight inches to the top of a bus so that cowboy hats can be worn inside. They rented a 1982 Silver Eagle to Yearwood for approximately $10,000 a month, plus $135 to $150 a day for a trained driver. When Gubernick traveled with Yearwood, her bus was a 1982 Silver Eagle with a first-class cabin, ten bunks with individual air conditioning, and a bathroom, kitchen, and "stateroom" with television and stereo equipment (Gubernick 1993, 101–102).

In November 1993, *Country America* magazine gave its readers a special feature on star bus life, with eight pages of color photography and detailed descriptions of the "bus sweet bus" that hosts Aaron Tippin, George and Nancy Jones, Patty Loveless, T. Graham Brown, Billy Dean, and Doug Stone. Tippin's bus was of special interest to the magazine. They reported that he spent a year with a computer designing it to be "a spectacular work of art" featuring western decor—"horseshoe bar, gaslight fixtures, brass spittoons and a nearly full-sized wooden Indian," all rendered in "mahogany, brass and burgundy velvet" (*Country America* November, 1993, 41–48). Tippin has a saloon motif in his stateroom and a brass bed in his private quarters.

Deficiencies of "road food" are a prominent theme in bus life. The Jones bus has a full-size kitchen for Nancy and a satellite dish for George's TV. Doug Stone responded to his quadruple bypass surgery by customizing a kitchen for low-fat eating requirements. "We've got a full size refrigerator, an oven, a microwave and a stove," Stone told *Country America*, "and I do a lot of stir frying in my electric wok." The Patty Loveless bus, purchased from Reba McEntire, features an elaborate vanity for make-up application. T. Graham Brown loves the Andy Griffith show. His bus features a video archive that has allowed him to watch Andy Griffith every day that he's been on his bus since April 1986. Billy Dean's design showcases his commitment to family life. A queen-size feather bed and a baby crib are in his bedroom. His goals, he said, are "being able to sleep comfortably and having room for my wife, Kathy, and our new baby to travel with me when they want to."

A sidebar for the *Country America* report notes that Music Concepts, Inc., of Nashville, and the Country Music Collectors Club, of Smyrna, Georgia, offer scale-model replica buses. Music Concepts, Inc. features models for thirteen artists, including Billy Ray Cyrus, Travis Tritt, George Jones, and Lorrie Morgan. Their versions sell "for about $7.00 in such stores as Wal-Mart, Target and Toys-R-Us," while the Country Music Collectors Club offers more elaborate versions. In December 1993, this company was running full-page color advertisements for their latest creation, the Conway Twitty "Twittybird" 1/64th scale model of Twitty's Prevost touring bus (*Country Music City News* 1993d). Only 5,000 would be available at $59.95 each, plus the cost of club membership. The previous spring, Twitty had collapsed on this bus while traveling from Branson, Missouri.

When Lorrie Morgan appeared with Conway Twitty and George Jones at the Cincinnati Gardens on March 21, 1992, she performed a ten-song set that concluded with a dramatic rendition of "Faithfully." This is a song of the road in country music culture—a dramatic pledge of fidelity by a woman married to "a music man." It evokes the sense of physical separation caused by constant touring, where "wheels go round and round in my mind." The road, says the song, "is no place to start a family," yet the pledge is exact: "I'm forever yours, faithfully" (Morgan 1991).

For Lorrie Morgan's debut on the Grand Ole Opry in 1975, she was introduced by her father, Opry star George Morgan. After eighteen years as a country singer, Morgan, in the early 1990s, had recorded songs challenging the domestic turmoil tradition of country music. One of those challenges came as the second in her set at the Cincinnati Gardens. In Beth Nielsen Chapman's "Five Minutes," Morgan had a substantial hit in the tradition of Loretta Lynn's feisty woman. Here, the female in a domestic partnership addresses her mate, telling him he looks "disbelievin'" that she's packed her bag and called a taxi to leave. "Lately you've forgotten what lovin' me's about," she sings; "now you've got five minutes to figure it out." The domestic problems in "Five Minutes" seem to be boredom and lack of communication. The singer implores her partner to talk to her, to tell her what she needs to hear, to ask her to stay, to be passionate, to kiss her. The demand, in short, is for commitment: "to show me that you're really sincere" (Morgan 1989).

The popularity of Lorrie Morgan's demand for male commitment in the early 1990s is consistent with the emergence of younger female singers who give voice to higher expectations for men than have been conventional in the domestic turmoil tradition of country music culture. Take, for instance, Michelle Wright. In "Take It Like a Man," showcased on the 1993 CBS television special, *The Women of Country*, Wright's challenge to nineties men is unequivocal. She introduces "Take It Like a Man" as not a "man-bashing song." "It's just a guideline," she says with an assertive smile, "for all you fellows out there." Written by Tony Haselden and recorded as the lead cut on Wright's 1991 album, "Take It Like a Man" is a story song about a woman who wants both a lover and a friend in a romantic relationship. But the men she has encountered have consistently failed; they actually want a maid or a mother, too much or too little space. This song is not a lament, however. In an upbeat tone, Wright issues a challenge. She seeks someone who will "take it like a man, steady and strong," someone true to their promises, someone sincerely committed to her (Wright 1992).

The challenge by female country singers of the 1990s to male sincerity has generated responses from male singers. Some are parodies of women's expectations. A popular debut album of 1992, by the group Confederate Railroad, opens and closes with this type of song. In the finale, the male response is "I like my women a little on the trashy side." When Confederate Railroad appeared in concert with George Jones for the 1994 "High-Tech Redneck" tour at Dayton's Nutter Center, they performed "Trashy Women" as their climactic number. To the front of the stage, they brought three female singers dressed in black silk shirts and tight pants (with glitter and studs), where they did a sexually suggestive chorus line. This act achieved a raucous standing ovation from three quarters of the crowd, especially male fans. The opening song on Confederate Railroad's debut album is one that might be taken as an "answer" to Michelle Wright: "She Took It Like a Man." The singer "had a tender moment planned" for the instant when he would tell his partner they "were through." He expected her heart to break, that she would "beg me not to go," or "be devastated." But, in an account rendered in rustic inflection with a jaunty swing, the singer describes the woman's unexpected response: "She cussed me like a sailor," kicked a hole in the wall, threw a telephone down the hallway, and stormed out of the house slamming the front door, saying "I'll be down at the bar." The moral is "she took it like a man" (Confederate Railroad 1992).

Other rising male stars of the 1990s are trading with traditional currency in the marketplace of emotions. Doug Stone's lead cut from his self-titled 1990 album was "I'd Be Better Off (In a Pine Box)," an exotic broken-heart lament in which the singer protests that he would rather die, "go to hell and face the devil" than think of his partner, who wanted to "spread her wings and fly," with another man (Stone 1990). Mark Chestnutt, in a 1990 album endorsed by George Jones, extends the link between domestic turmoil and spiritual imagery with "Broken Promise Land," where a wife takes revenge for a husband's infidelity by trying infidelity herself. True to the tragic-troubadour tradition, this revenge leaves both partners in an anti-heaven where "streets are paved with misery" and "lives are built on lies" (Chestnutt 1990). Joe Diffie could resurrect and update Jimmie Rodgers's blue yodel in the broken-heart lament "Startin' Over Blues," the lead cut to his *Regular Joe* album of 1992. Here, the singer is disoriented because a woman has left him. The last time this happened, he says, he started over "down at my local Wal-Mart" (Diffie 1992). In early 1994, Billy Ray Cyrus and his Sly Dog Band toured for Budweiser under the aggressive masculine title of "Ain't Your Dog No More," a song from his second album.

Despite the persistence of conventional domestic visions among young male singers of the 1990s, the most popular singers took a different tone. In 1994, John Michael Montgomery went to number one on *Billboard's Top Country* and *Billboard 200* charts with an album that featured an earnest pledge of devotion, "I Swear." "You can be sure I know my part," he sings. "I'll make mistakes," but "I'll never break your heart" (Montgomery 1994). Montgomery's "I Swear" represents a trend of sensitive males devoted to women that emerged in the early 1990s as country music culture's leading masculine image. This trend was precipitated by the success of Garth Brooks and Vince Gill, but it had an earlier voice.

On Sunday, June 6, 1993, the *New York Times* carried an important obituary for country music culture. The headline read "Conway Twitty, 59, Dies on Tour; Country Star Had 50 No. 1 Songs." In a lengthy account of Twitty's life and recording career, Dennis Hevesi reported the key strategy that he pioneered: "Mr. Twitty once said, 'I like a song that says things a man wants to say and doesn't know how to say it'" (Hevesi 1993, 19). Then, in a vivid circuit-riding image, Hevesi reports that "Mr. Twitty collapsed Friday night on his tour bus after a performance in nearby Branson, Mo." Four days later, at the First Baptist Church of Hendersonville, Tennessee, near Nashville, a public memorial service was held for Conway Twitty. It was in the exact center of Fan Fair week.

The *Tennesseean* reported a capacity crowd of 2,000 for Twitty's memorial and told fans that he died of "heart failure related to an abdominal aortic aneurysm" (Rogers and Bluitt 1993, 1–2). Mourners lined up at the church at 5:30 A.M. to assure entry for the 2:00 P.M. service. When they entered, they could see fifty-four bouquets of flowers spread symmetrically across the front of this modern tabernacle built in 1991. Its interior design is reminiscent of the Ryman Auditorium, with a sweeping balcony around two-thirds of the building facing on an open stage with a central pulpit and a choir area behind. Conway Twitty had already been buried in a private ceremony at an undisclosed location. To remember him vividly, a picture posing Twitty in a casual sitting position, wearing an aqua green golf shirt and white shorts, smiled at assembled mourners from the center front of the church just below the pulpit.

At 1:30 P.M., a tape recording of Twitty's songs began playing, while family, figures in the music business, stars, and fans entered the church. George Jones, with whom Twitty had toured for the last two years, came in early, wearing a gray suit, black shirt, and sunglasses. He was followed by the Statler Brothers, Porter Wagoner, and other major performers. At 2:04 P.M., Ralph Emery, who hosted the memorial service, took a seat beside the minister at the front of the church, and the service began. The minister opened with a gospel commentary focused on celebrating Twitty's life, and noted that Twitty once considered entering the ministry. Twitty's daughter, Kathy, spoke for the family about the quality of her father's life. Then a series of musical performances was headlined by Vince Gill. Accompanying himself on acoustic guitar with a piano background, Gill sang his lonely lament, "When I Call Your Name." Gill introduced this song with a soft-spoken commentary about his personal debt to Conway Twitty. "This is a tough gig," he said. Gill remembered that his first job after moving to Nashville was playing at Twitty City, and serving as a backup singer on Twitty's recordings. Gill closed by paying Conway Twitty a compliment: "Some of the old singers say we're from a new school, and in some ways that's true. That old school is the best school to go to, and I'm glad I got to go."

Gill was followed by nine country music entertainers and songwriters, each introduced by Ralph Emery. Eight of them paid brief verbal tribute to Conway Twitty, and four sang for him. George Jones remembered their touring life: "I feel sorry for thousands and thousands of fans who loved him so much. I loved him too, and I'm speechless," he said. Porter Wagoner also referred to Twitty's unique bond with fans. "He didn't move in political circles to promote his music," Wagoner said. "He left it up to his fans. I'm *sure* that's why he had the most hits in the history of country music." Five prominent women were introduced: Barbara Mandrell, songwriter Mae Axton, Tammy Wynette, Connie Smith, and Reba McEntire. Wynette and Smith sang the evangelical hymns "Precious Memories" and "How Great Thou Art." McEntire was the final speaker. Early in her career, she had been an opening act for Conway Twitty, and now she expressed her admiration for him as a role model of hard work and steady, sound business practice. McEntire also confessed that she had never told Conway Twitty what a fan of his she was. "I loved opening for Conway," she said, because when he closed the show she "loved the roar of the crowd." Conway Twitty then closed his own memorial service with a recorded version of Kris Kristofferson's "Why Me," a reflective commentary on the unearned blessings of Jesus.

The Conway Twitty memorial service was a quietly impressive affair; many fans were visibly moved. Twitty's life was held up as exemplary of his personal salvation and as a model for other entertainers. Appropriately, in this memorial gathering of country music culture to honor a star regularly introduced as "the best friend a song ever had," the emphasis was on songs themselves—texts of both heavenly and romantic love.

Early in Conway Twitty's authorized biography, *The Conway Twitty Story*, by Wilbur Cross and Michael Kosser, Twitty describes his motivation for abandoning a successful career as a rock music performer in 1965. His managers, producers and agents couldn't understand why a singer who had a series of hits, including a number-one song on the pop music charts in 1958, wished to give up his commitment to rock and roll in order to sing country music. "They kept bringing up the subject of money," Twitty said, "and I kept trying to tell them singing country meant a lot more to me than making money" (Cross and Kosser 1987, x).

Conway Twitty came from a background affectionate about country music. Twitty was born Harold Jenkins, of working-class parents in Friars Point, Mississippi, September 1, 1933. His father worked for the WPA during the Depression, eventually becoming a riverboat pilot. As a teenager, Jenkins worked at odd jobs and played baseball. He was a favorite of a female high school principal who loved country music and allowed him to sing over the school intercom. Harold played country music in high school and formed a close friendship with John Hughey, a steel guitar player who later had a major professional career with Conway's Twittybirds before becoming a steel guitarist for Vince Gill in 1992 (Cross and Kosser 1987, 29–35; Gill 1992). Harold listened to the Grand Ole Opry as a child; as a teenager, he sang with the Arkansas Cotton Choppers on the Helena, Arkansas, radio station KFFA. Before he was twenty, he was leading Baptist youth revivals at a church in Smith's Station, Alabama. Yet, from an early age he was active in both spiritual and worldly dimensions of love. A romantic relationship in high school led to an unwanted pregnancy, brief marriage to provide his son Mike with legitimacy, and early divorce. By 1953, Jenkins was working in Chicago at International Harvester and considering a professional baseball career (he had a spring-training offer from the Philadelphia Phillies). Inducted into the army in 1954, he was eventually stationed as a clerk in Japan where he formed a band and won an army talent show (Cross and Kosser 1987, 30–51).

Immediately after his discharge in 1956, Jenkins underwent a life-changing experience: He heard an Elvis Presley record on the radio. "I heard Elvis singing 'Mystery Train' and I said to myself that *I* could do that too. It was like the feelings I was having about getting out of the Army—a new sense of freedom and purpose." Presley's impact on fans was particularly impressive to Jenkins. The origins of rock and roll, he said, have been attributed to Bill Haley, Bo Diddley, or others. "But it was Elvis and no one else. He was the one. Nothing like it. Period. He bowled people over. He changed the whole damn world" (Cross and Kosser 1987, 55–57).

Jenkins soon put a band together and met a woman country singer who introduced him to "The Ozark Jubilee," a television show in Springfield, Missouri, where he sang Elvis Presley songs successfully. In the proliferating market for rock and roll in 1956,

Jenkins went to Memphis to record for Sam Phillips at Sun Records, but no songs were issued. Later that year, with help from an army friend, he acquired a manager based in New York City, Don Seat. By 1957, he had a Mercury recording contract, an initial record that failed to rise on the charts, a plan instigated by his manager to spend two years in Canada building his fan base, and a new name chosen by selecting town names from an atlas—Conway, Arkansas, and Twitty, Texas (Cross and Kosser 1987, 57–69). After a year in Hamilton and London, Ontario, playing jazz and other clubs, Twitty developed a reputation as the first rock-and-roll singer in Canada, and by 1958, he had an MGM recording session at Owen Bradley's studio in Nashville. "It's Only Make Believe," a Twitty composition that went to number one in Canada before becoming a hit in the United States (initially in Columbus, Ohio), eventually sold 8 million copies, became number one in twenty-two countries and created a mystique around Conway Twitty as a rockabilly singer with a distinctive signature "growl" (Cross and Kosser 1987, 75–83). Rock and roll touring shows now showcased Conway Twitty as a pop culture hit; but, by 1965, he was disillusioned by the behavior of rock and roll fans: "They weren't afraid to do almost anything right out in the open—things we never dreamed about doing in our day. We were brought up under the old idea that kids should be seen and not heard" (Cross and Kosser 1987, 91).

Twitty had to sue his manager for release from his contract. He paid off his bills and started over, moving to Oklahoma City, where he found work playing in country music nightclubs for $200 a night and sang for fewer than a hundred people each evening. From then on, Conway Twitty was his own manager. He carefully cultivated a public image and developed a distinctive performance influenced by the emotional pop singer, Johnnie Ray. Twitty elected to distinguish himself further from other country singers by relinquishing stage chatter in order to communicate with his fans entirely through music and stage production (Cross and Kosser 1987, 103–106). These decisions magnified the Conway Twitty mystique. Twitty could easily slip into his original persona of Harold Jenkins to comment on his stage persona:

> I made up my mind years ago that I never would try to be that image. Understand me, I'd never destroy the image, because it belongs to the people who created it. I protect the image at all times, but I don't ever kid myself into thinking that's really me. I always treat Conway Twit-

ty as something separate from myself. And I'm the one who has to breathe the life into it, while other people make it grow. So I go to great lengths to keep from being consumed by the make-believe world. (Cross and Kosser 1987, 97–98)

The creation of country music star Conway Twitty had another intricate strategy—nurturing a strong appeal to women fans as a sensitive man. Twitty commented on this intention at length for his biographers:

> I've understood that the way to develop an appeal was to aim at women as the primary audience. I knew it way back then, and almost every song I've ever written was created first of all with women in mind and anticipating how they were going to react. Second, and very close to that, most men want to say these things to women, but they just don't know how. They may end up expressing themselves all wrong, and not even knowing why or how they've hurt a woman's feelings. A lot of us men have made this mistake. (Cross and Kosser 1987, 135)

One of Twitty's compositions, "Hello Darlin'," became the signature of his intentional appeal to women through songs that spoke to them casually and in detail about everyday experience from the point of view of a sensitive man. Twitty used the song as a dramatic show opener, beginning offstage with the lights darkened and walking slowly on stage as fan approval crescendos. He stayed with his successful formula of sensitive-man love songs as a way to build long-term fan trust:

> Women understand why and how I select the songs I do. They reach a point where they trust me to deal with their feelings and emotions. That confidence takes a long time to develop, for one reason because women need time to reach the point where they can trust you to be able to deal with the emotions they go through. It may take *years*. (Cross and Kosser 1987, 134)

By 1975, ten years after taking up his mission as a country singer, Twitty's "Hello Darlin'" achieved international acclaim when it was played in both its English-language version and a Russian-language version that Twitty recorded for the initial rendezvous between American and Russian spacecraft (Cross and Kosser 1987, 138–40).

Beginning in 1970, Conway Twitty and Loretta Lynn recorded a series of duets that displaced Porter Wagoner and Dolly Parton as CMA Vocal Duo of the Year (1972, 1973, 1974, 1975). The joint venture with Loretta Lynn, perhaps country music's most effective star with women fans, enshrined Conway Twitty as a fan favorite. He had less success with individual recognition by the Country Music Association however. Nominated for Entertainer of the Year in 1971 and 1975 and for Male Vocalist of the Year five times between 1970 and 1976, he received none of these awards (Cross and Kosser 1987, 157). Yet he became the undisputed leader in fan popularity, with thirty-two consecutive number one hits before 1977 and a reported total of fifty-five by the time of his death (Cross and Kosser 1987, 157–59).

One reason Conway Twitty may have lacked appeal to business insiders was his independence. He produced and marketed his own show, developing elaborate variations on the "sensitive man on stage" who for more than twenty years in "a world of tight-lipped macho American males" presented himself as "powerful, communicative, and daring to reveal his vulnerable side to a woman." This production was achieved almost entirely in hit recordings and live concerts; Twitty said he avoided both television productions and appearances on awards shows, fearing that television would blunt the effect of his cultivated product. In 1981, he formed an alliance with producer Jimmy Bowen that refined his sound, marketed him more carefully as a recording artist, and increased the pace of his number-one hits, with four in 1981 alone. Ever wary of overexposure, Twitty claimed he occasionally released a song he felt could not achieve number one status, "just to cool things down a little bit." To carry off that daring strategy, he had to convince the entrepreneurial Bowen "that the company is looking for the home run but I'm looking for the long run" (Cross and Kosser 1987, 173–82). Bowen was convinced.

A lifelong workaholic, Conway Twitty diversified his financial interests by establishing a "Twittyburger" restaurant chain that failed (whereupon he assumed the total loss and paid back all his investors), and he bought a majority interest in Nashville's minor league baseball team, the Nashville Sounds. But a lifetime of hard work and touring took its toll. He was married in 1956, divorced after fourteen years, remarried to the same woman for another fourteen years, divorced again, and married for a fourth time (to a different woman) not long before his death (Cross and Kosser 1987, 17, 111, 187).

Twitty Enterprises eventually expanded to include "a travel agency, health clubs, other minor league baseball teams, restaurants, a novelty company, landholdings, and several music publishing companies" (Cross and Kosser 1987, 188). In 1992, Twitty formed a partnership with Wal-Mart to distribute Twitty Bird Seed, with a strategy that "Twitty Bird Seed can dominate bird food for the same reason Jimmy Dean dominates sausage—there is no nationally recognized brand in the field" (*Country Song Roundup* 1992, 7). The year 1992 was also the tenth anniversary of Twitty's most elaborate investment, a tourist complex and family compound in Hendersonville, Tennessee, which featured Twitty's private home, office, homes for his children and mother, an entertainment center, an elaborate museum telling his life story and displaying his recording awards, gardens, a pavilion, and a gift shop. "I built Twitty City for my fans," he said, but he did it with a marketing strategy. A feasibility study was done to determine what tourists visiting Nashville were seeking. The study showed that fans wanted to see places where they might "catch a glimpse of the stars themselves as they went about their work"—a star's home, office, "or even parking spaces with their names on them." "I can understand those kind of hopes," Twitty said, "because I'm a fan myself." By 1984, Twitty City was receiving 700,000 visitors per year and by 1985 more than 1 million per year (Cross and Kosser 1987, 188–90).

In 1992, Chris Praetor, manager of Twitty City, attributed part of Twitty City's initial popularity to the visibility of the World's Fair held in Knoxville in 1982. By its tenth anniversary, paid attendance to Twitty City was running at 100,000 visitors per year, with 30 to 40 thousand concentrated during the heavily-advertised "Christmas at Twitty City." Twitty City was originally intended as part of a country music complex called "Music Valley," that would include venues for other major stars and attract fans to live concerts in Nashville. But financial and management problems, the perception of Nashville suburbanites that the intent was to create a "Las Vegas" atmosphere, and the inability to obtain alcohol licenses that could attract major hotels were cited by Praetor as shortcomings of the more elaborate project. Even though Twitty's family compound and tourist attraction sustained its appeal for his own fans, with the right support, Praetor felt, it could have been the center of something larger. "We should have been Branson," he said.

Conway Twitty appeared in concert at the Cincinnati Gardens March 21, 1992. For this event, opened by George Jones and Lorrie Morgan, the audience was predominantly female. In the two sections nearest my seat, 122 of 181 fans were female, with an average age I estimated at over forty-five. In my own section, 127 of 173 fans were female. The youngest fans visible appeared to be of high school age; but there were far more who may well have been retired couples and grandmothers. Unlike the dress for concerts by younger country stars, this audience sported very little cowboy clothing. There were many T-shirts and blue jeans. Men in this audience had "haircuts," not "stylecuts," and many women had "home perms." The crowd was quiet and orderly, indulged in modest drinking and smoking, and respected the sign for no alcohol inside the arena. There was very little "dating" behavior.

After the second intermission, the house lights went dark and a spotlight hit a sparkling ball that had begun revolving just in front of the stage. For this concert, Conway Twitty began singing offstage the opening words of "It's Only Make Believe"—then stopped for an announcer to say dramatically: "One of the best friends a song ever had, please make welcome Conway Twitty!" As the announcer drew out the pronunciation of the name a long drum roll began, the sparkle-ball threw confetti-like light throughout the crowd, smoke emerged from stage, and Twitty walked from stage left into a blue light that shifted to a white spotlight as he began the opening words of "Hello Darlin'." The cheering crowd rose to its feet in unison.

Twitty was dressed in a dark blue suit, black patent shoes, and a pink high-necked satin shirt decorated with a single jewel at the throat. Spotlighted against a dark background, this presentation of Conway Twitty was an impressive evocation of another slogan applied to him, "the high priest of country music." Twitty stood alone holding a hand mike during "Hello Darlin'," while a mob of fan-photographers streamed forward in orderly fashion to capture the moment on film as others stood, or sat on the edge of their seats.

Immediately after his first song, Twitty nodded politely with a soft "Thank you." The band hit a fast beat, with Twitty picking up a small electric guitar to open a medley of hits beginning with "Boogie Grass Band." Twitty's third through seventh songs were "sensitive man" love songs. These began with "I'd Love to Lay You Down"—a proposition song sung by a man to his wife on how to love correctly—then "Tight Fittin' Jeans," a commentary on the dalliance of an upper-class woman in a working-man's world. This sequence ended with "Desperado Love," a pledge of total commitment. Songs in this set were done in rapid-fire fashion, spotlighting key lines from hit songs. Twitty played guitar and introduced modest body language, and at the end the stage went totally black.

When the lights came up again, Conway Twitty was standing center stage without his guitar, holding a hand microphone and bending his right knee in a slight kneeling gesture, an image of intense concentration to prepare for the eighth (and centerpiece) song of his concert. A slow production number that builds to intense emotion, "Good-bye Time" sets a tone of resignation at the dissolution of love in a long-time marriage. The song begins with gentle questions: "How can you walk away?" and "Don't I matter anymore?" Then an emotional shrug: "Well, it's been fun. What else can I say?" The central refrain of the song is a plaintive play on the marketplace of emotions. "If being free's worth what you leave behind," the singer says, "then it's good-bye time." This song includes a range of moods, from gentle talking to wailing pain. All the while, the involvement of fans builds. Twitty delivered it intently and at the conclusion made a gesture of finger-pointing at more than a forty-five-degree angle, with the right hand moving rhythmically up and down in a manner resembling a blessing of the multitudes. When he was finished, Twitty uttered a polite "Thank you" (Twitty 1990).

The next six songs elaborated the slow-tempo-production-number motif of sincere commentary on romantic relationships. "Crazy in Love" is a reminiscence about a time when the intensity of romance was more lively in a couple's relationship. "Who Did They Think He Was?" is a memorial song with a gospel tint that honors Elvis Presley, John Kennedy, and Jesus. This song questions the enigma of hero worship but doesn't dismiss its significance (Twitty 1991). At the end of the song, Twitty addressed his fans briefly for the only time during this concert. "Isn't that a pretty song?" he said. "If you like it, when you get back to wherever it is that you came from, call your local radio station and tell 'em you like it, and sock it to 'em one time for ol' Conway." "Slow Hand," the eleventh song, was delivered as one verse and one chorus. This slightly up-tempo song is a good example of the potential double meanings often provided by Twitty's songs. The refrain, "when it comes to love you want a slow hand," is both sexually suggestive and connotative of attentiveness

(Twitty 1990). At the end of "Slow Hand," Twitty again provided the blessing gesture. Finally, the auditorium blacked out entirely.

When the lights came up again, there was a soft red spotlight shining directly down on Conway Twitty sitting Jimmie Rodgers-style on a stool in center stage, in preparation for the theological statement of the Conway Twitty show, his cover of "The Rose." Like "Slow Hand," "The Rose" was a pop hit. Bette Midler performed this song for the sound-track recording of the film memorializing the rock singer Janis Joplin. For Conway Twitty, "The Rose" offered an extended commentary on the power of love, depicted here as a gentle force of nature that will overcome loneliness, and moments when "the road has been too long" (Twitty 1990). It also provided Twitty a piece for theatrical display. With the entire Cincinnati Gardens in eerie silence at the beginning of his delivery, he talked the first two verses in a slowly building, rumbling growl featuring long hesitations and pauses. As the intensity rose, members of the audience engaged the mood with spontaneous yells and screams. When Twitty returned abruptly to a softer manner for a second verse, the audience responded by going to total silence. Then, as he built vocal power again, his rising growls brought more screams. By the end of this song, couples in the audience were hugging and crying, many hands were raised in the manner of evangelical responses at a gospel religious service, and clapping, shouting, and screaming urged Twitty on to more emotional demonstration. Although the gesture was prohibited in the Gardens, when Twitty reached this point in concerts at Hara Arena thousands of butane lighters were held aloft to symbolize the quasi-religious candle-lighting of emotional communion.

After "The Rose," fans were fully engaged; and Twitty provided three more songs. "That's My Job" focuses on warm nurture in a loving father-son relationship. "You've Never Been This Far Before" is another double-meaning song that connotes either potential adultery, or as Twitty explained it elsewhere, tenderness:

> The lyrics are really about a woman who's married, and you in the song have admired her for years. It's an off-limits situation. She doesn't love her husband and she's outside the boundaries of her marriage for the first time. And that's what the line means, "You've never been this far before." Now she's with you, this woman you've admired, and simply holding her hand has been a forbidden thing. And that's what the words really mean—not something dirty or risqué.

The implication is just like putting your arm around her. Women are sensitive like that and they understood that line. (Cross and Kosser 1987, 134)

For his final number, Twitty returned to his opening to complete a rendition of "It's Only Make Believe." Here, he was bringing the image of Conway Twitty to full presentation, framing his concert with a direct commentary on its character as produced entertainment. In addition, he was revealing himself to his fans as a conscious showman, within the show itself. As they had at the beginning, Twitty's fans loved it. Spotlights panned the crowd and Twitty again made the finger-blessing gesture. He waved to the floor, to the bleachers on each side and in the back, nodded his head in a gesture of appreciation, and slowly left the stage. The show had been carefully constructed theatre communicating through a sequence of song statements. No encore was planned or expected. As the public-address announcer asked for one more round of applause for Conway's Twittybirds, the lights came up, and the crowd—now that the service was over, amazingly subdued by comparison with their recent ecstatic demonstration—filed out of the hall in an orderly way.

On the first album he released after Conway Twitty's death, George Jones, country music's most highly respected living honky-tonk singer, recorded a tribute to postwar country music culture's most enduring showman when he ended the *High-Tech Redneck* album with a vivid rendition of "Hello Darlin'." In keeping with Conway Twitty's style, there was no written commentary in the album notes—just the song.

Vince Gill has acknowledged the importance of Conway Twitty to male singers of the 1990s who specialize in sensitive masculinity. That sensitivity comes in several varieties. Billy Dean's self-titled debut album of 1991 features tender ballads about his childhood and family as a contrast to an ambiguous maturity. His autobiographical "Billy the Kid" presents his childhood as an era of macho high-life, in contrast to his adulthood when, he says, he does the best he can because "there's only so much you can do as a man." "Only the Wind" remembers a mother comforting a child, telling it not to fear the sounds of a storm, and wishes for this reassurance in adulthood as a romantic relationship ends, but knows that cannot come. Dean's inaugural album concludes with homage to his father's love ("Daddy's Will"). When read, his father's will says that "family fortune lies within our hearts" (Dean 1991).

In 1994, Collin Raye was a thirty-three-year-old singer from Texas, with three album releases. He told *Country Music City News,*

> I go for the songs that sound like the writer cut a hole in his heart and just let it pour out. I don't like the songs that have the cool little hooks and clever lines. I've had three songs that have been played at massive amounts of weddings and funerals. That's the greatest compliment in the world and that's because those songs touch people. (Harden 1994, 22)

Raye's signature song from his 1991 album, "Love, Me," is a balladeer's tribute to the lifelong devotion of grandparents remembered nostalgically as an object lesson in romantic love and masculine fidelity (Raye 1991).

Vince Gill has gone beyond his own songs of sensitive masculinity to fashion a public persona of the road musician as caring husband, friend, and benefactor of the country-music business. An important instrumentalist often honored for his virtuosity, on February 7, 1994, Gill appeared on television with Gladys Knight at the American Music Awards to inaugurate promotion of an ambitious project teaming "legends of R & B" with "legends of country" in an MCA album that offered an innovating blend of these entertainment subcultures (*Billboard* 1994, 2–3).

Born in Norman, Oklahoma, in 1957, Gill played bluegrass music with various groups before obtaining a solo recording contract with MCA Records in 1984. By 1985, he had two singles in the top ten, and in 1990, "When I Call Your Name" hit number one. The following year Gill joined the Grand Ole Opry. His national visibility was substantially advanced by attractive appearances on televised music award programs, where his self-effacing manner and all-American boyish looks combine with gestures of personal sincerity that have lingering appeal.

At the June 1993 fan-voted TNN/*Music City News* Country Awards (targeted to country music fans on the TNN cable network), Gill was given his third Instrumentalist of the Year award. In an unrehearsed moment of generosity and gratitude, Gill called forward John Hughey, now steel guitar player with Gill's band, and gave him the award in honor of his long years of musical commitment to Conway Twitty. That same year, Gill received the Minnie Pearl

Award, recognizing his humanitarian efforts on behalf of charitable causes aided by the country music community. In receiving the award, Gill cried openly. As the camera panned assembled stars and music business figures, it appeared that many had joined him. Gill's most important awards-show moment for indelibly forging an image of a caring husband occurred in March 1993 at the *Music City News* Country Songwriters Awards. Readers of *Music City News* that year chose "I Still Believe in You," written by Vince Gill and John Barlow Jarvis, as Song of the Year. In the course of the evening, Gill— dressed in a conservative dark suit, white shirt, and tie—appeared on stage several times. Each time he commented on his marriage: "Sometimes what I'm doing takes me away from Janis and our daughter Jenny. It's really tough." At another point, he described how the song was written; he went directly to a songwriting session after "probably the worst fight of our thirteen-year marriage." In his acceptance speech for the highest honor, Song of the Year, Gill again cried. This time he invited his wife Janis—also crying—to join him on stage, where, before the entire viewing audience of country music culture, he gave his wife the award. Noting that she too was an entertainer, and that women were, in his opinion, notably absent from music award shows, he said: "There is no better inspiration than my wife. She's done this for a long time. She's a good songwriter, too. So, honey, I'm giving this to you" (*Country Music City News* 1993a, 38–40). By this gesture, Gill, in effect, endorsed the posture of assertive young women country singers who expect men to show self-conscious attention to the emotional needs of women. By commenting publicly on the resistance of the music business to the achievement of women artists, Gill positioned himself alongside such outspoken female performers as Mary Chapin Carpenter and in sympathy with a long line of successful women.

On March 20, 1993, Mary Chapin Carpenter and Vince Gill appeared in concert at Hara Arena, in Dayton, Ohio. Carpenter, the opening act, played a one-hour set that, in this traditional working-class venue, did not emphasize her political views. For her encore of "Party Doll," she leaped from the stage to mug with fans on the floor. Surrounded by the arena's security team, she picked out a large young guard, sang to him, and to the delight of fans, concluded her act by kissing him forcefully on the mouth. Gill's set picked up on the "party" mood set by Carpenter. Most of his songs were upbeat fast numbers emphasizing instrumental virtuosity and frequently showcasing John Hughey on steel guitar. Gill stood front and center on stage with seven players in a crescent arc behind him. His stage manner was animated yet he did not rely on such theatrical effects as dramatic movement across stage, smoke machines, and elaborate lighting—or extended banter with fans. In an uninterrupted two-hour set, Gill played twenty songs in a snappy back-to-back style reminiscent of Conway Twitty's strategy of speaking to the fans through the music.

His concluding number was the signature song, "I Still Believe in You." For this moment, the house, which had been raucous during previous numbers featuring Gill's ecstatic guitar-playing, fell silent, and a sea of lighters came out. Gill chose a single white rose from the array of flowers brought to the stage and inserted it in his guitar strings. On the repeat of the chorus Gill said gently to the fans, "y'all sing it for us now, come on, one more time, everybody come on." The song itself is a confessional account by a musician who recognizes his failure to give proper attention to his spouse and asks for a chance to make amends. He's been thinking only of himself, but now says, "for all the times I've hurt you, I apologize," and "I'm sorry it took so long." As fans at Hara Arena sang softly with Gill on the refrain of "I Still Believe in You," he performed a gesture reminiscent of Conway Twitty's hand-blessing. But Gill's was verbal: "This is for Margaret and Vesy," he said, "may it heal all your pain. God Bless you." After four repetitions of "I Still Believe in You" with the sold-out crowd, Vince Gill received a standing ovation throughout the hall, waved gently, said "Good night, thank you," and left the stage.

At the end of the first third of his show at Hara Arena, Vince Gill told his fans, "I got something real special now." He then brought his father on stage with the introduction, "It's always special for me to come to Ohio because that's where my Dad lives. I've not forgotten where I learned these three chords. I want him to come out and do the one he first taught me." Then Vince Gill's father, dressed in a black sport coat and gray slacks with a white shirt and tie, sang the pop hit, "When My Blue Moon Turns to Gold Again," while Gill stood slightly behind him, playing guitar. At the end of this ritual of family feeling, Gill gave flowers to his father in the midst of a wild ovation from the fans.

At the very same minute that Vince Gill was performing with his father to the warm praise of fans at Hara Arena in west Dayton, across town, at the Ervin J. Nutter Center, the "pop metal" band Def Leppard was rocking its 9,123 fans with "a menacing rendition" of "Gods of War" from its album *Hysteria* at $20 a ticket (Weaver 1993, 4B). In a heavy-metal concert at Nutter Center three months later, the lead singer of Megadeath, Dave Mustaine, left the stage in fury after forty minutes of confrontation with fans that included "challenging one fan to a fight for flipping him the finger," goading "a girl down front into exposing her breasts to the crowd, belittling her when she refused," and berating fans "for shouting out requests." This four-hour event, also featuring the bands Pantera and White Zombie, offered Megadeath numbers such as "Angry Again," "My Darkest Hour," and "Symphony of Destruction" (Larsen 1993c, 6B).

As the pop music market of the early 1990s continued to fragment into emotional displays of diverse tone, Garth Brooks took up the challenge to offer sincere masculinity by positioning himself in popular culture as a devoted family man with deep sensitivity to white middle-class social concerns. In his commitment to a music of "message," Brooks did not shrink from cultural politics. In six record albums between 1989 and early 1994, and in numerous appearances on cable and network television as well as in print media, he embraced the causes of hungry children, exploited fans, homosexuality, war, environmental concern, domestic violence, foreclosures, civil rights, and date rape. In early September 1992, when Brooks had sold 21 million records and was offering two new albums, he told a reporter for the *New York Times* that "We Shall Be Free," the lead single from one of those albums, was a song about "family values." Then he explained.

> I think the Republicans' big problem is that they believe family values are June and Walt and 2.3 children. To me it means laughing, being able to dream. It means that if a set of parents are black and white, or two people of the same sex, or if one man or one woman acts as the parent, that the children grow up happy and healthy: that's what family values are. (Watrous 1992, B5)

Brooks also pointed out that one dollar from the sale of each CD of his Christmas album would be donated to Feed the Children, a group that "specializes in helping to fight poverty and starvation in the United States." The *Times* reported that "at some of Mr. Brooks' shows he has the charity collect canned goods to distribute locally."

The Marketplace of Emotions   259

Said Brooks, "it's an effective way to have people think of what's going on: to get involved."

A massive wave of publicity supported Brooks's breakthrough to popular culture icon. It penetrated all segments of American electronic and print media, yet Brooks was especially popular with media targeted to white working- and middle-class families. One of the ways he was promoted was as a sensitive man. A biography of Brooks, written in 1993 by Rick Mitchell, established this tone in its early pages by quoting Brooks's memories of his father:

> If I could wrap my dad up in two words, it would be thundering tenderness. He's a man with the shortest temper I ever saw, and at the same time he's got the biggest heart. Some of the greatest conflicts are not between two people but between one person and himself. He knows what's right and he doesn't have any tolerance for what isn't right but at the same time he is so forgiving. I learned from him that you gotta be thankful for what you got and treat people like you want to be treated. My Dad drilled that into my head all my life. We're a lot alike in that way. (Mitchell 1993, 17)

"Thundering tenderness" might be a description of the impression Brooks himself hopes to leave on American popular culture. In Edward Morris's 1993 biography, a chronology of Brooks's achievements is presented which centers on family experiences. In this version of his life, family provides a foundation for success in the music business. Among the events cited for Brooks's first thirty-three years are: his birth February 7, 1962, in Tulsa, Oklahoma; getting a banjo for his sixteenth birthday; graduating from high school; listening to George Strait in 1981 and deciding to be a country singer; winning a talent show in college at Oklahoma State University; making a one-day trip to Nashville in 1985; and marrying Sandy Mahl on May 24, 1986. At this point in the chronology the significant events selected by Morris shift to music business activities: his second effort to win a recording contract in Nashville; his agreement (on a handshake) to record for Capital Records after a performance at the Bluebird Cafe in 1988; video promotion of "The Dance" in 1990; winning the CMA Horizon Award that year; the breakthrough popularity of "Friends in Low Places"; publicity surrounding TNN's ban of "The Thunder Rolls" video; triumphs in 1991 and 1992 at the CMA awards; a 1992 Grammy for *Ropin' the Wind*; and selection by *Entertainment Weekly* as America's favorite male singer (Morris 1993).

Interspersed with this personal progress in Morris's account is a story about Brooks's handling of domestic turmoil. In 1989, while Brooks was touring, Sandy Brooks learned "that Garth was cheating on her." She telephoned her husband and issued an ultimatum demanding faithfulness. Her bags were packed, she supposedly told him, and it was "my way or the highway" (Morris 1993, 77,188). The next day, while performing in Cape Girardeau, Missouri, Brooks allegedly broke down on stage while performing "If Tomorrow Never Comes"—a song he wrote to express love for his wife. Brooks has said that at the end of that concert an unidentified fan called out to him distinctly, "Go home to her, Garth." He did.

Soon stories that Sandy was expecting were everywhere in the news. So detailed were they that Garth's baby-boomer fans who had delayed their own child-bearing years could follow every detail of the pregnancy, including Brooks's failure to appear for the January 27, 1992, American Music Awards (where he won Best Country Male Performer, Best Country Album, and Best Country Single) because Sandy Brooks was hospitalized in fear of a miscarriage (Morris 1993, 194–95). Vince Gill's public affirmation of sensitive masculinity and commitment to his marriage occurred on national television at a songwriter awards show on TNN. For Garth Brooks, the sensitive-masculinity commitment was escalated by media attention to suggest the full-blown creation of his nuclear family under the watchful eyes of television, radio, newspapers, and magazines.

In 1992, Garth Brooks appeared in fan magazines, financial magazines, music business magazines, tabloids, and on the covers of *Time*, *Life*, and the *Saturday Evening Post*. The latter three in particular were aimed at the "family" market. Here, Brooks emphasized his sensitive masculinity. He told Marjie McGraw of the *Saturday Evening Post* that his music was more important to him than his showmanship. "It has to *mean* something to me," he said.

> I would rather have one song that was from the heart than 80 songs that were clever and went to No. 1 on the charts. If I get a song that I feel is on a parallel from my heart to yours, instead of coming from my mouth to your ears . . . then I think I've got something. (McGraw 1992, 102)

For *Post* readers, Brooks emphasized the richness of his own family life. He stayed off the road during latter months of the pregnancy to "be a husband" to Sandy. "I introduced myself to her and she introduced me to one of the neatest people I've ever met—I've been living with her for six years and didn't know her" (McGraw 1992, 103). All of his music awards, he said, were hidden under the stairs in the basement, because he didn't want the music business to intrude on family life:

> Our house is a house for loving, for fighting and making up, for learning, for screaming at each other, for laughing—it's not a house for music. Music has given us the house, music has given us the food to eat, but that house is for Sandy and me as a family. (McGraw 1992, 103)

So pervasive was the Garth Brooks media image of sincere masculinity in 1992 that readers of *Country America* magazine—polled that year, along with a panel of music business figures, to vote for "the Top 100 country songs of all time"—chose "The Dance," written by Tony Arata and performed by Garth Brooks, as number three (*Country America* 1992, 28–29). When the eighth annual People's Choice Awards (said to be the only awards voted by the public for performers in television, film, and music) were given on March 17, Garth Brooks and Reba McEntire won best male and female performers in both country and overall musical categories (*Daily News* 1992, 8A).

In 1993, a coffee-table book of photographs illustrating the lyrics of "The Dance" was published (Hyperion 1993). True to the connotations of Brooks's image, every photograph depicted an intense moment of family experience or a life-marking event—birthdays of the elderly, the birth of a child, a high-school football game, a christening, a college graduation, a little leaguer at bat, children hearing Halloween stories from elders, teenagers victorious in small-town sporting events, a young couple introducing their infant child to an elderly gentleman, groups of children eating watermelon at a local festival, veterans at a reunion, a young girl on a swing, an ecstatic bride preparing for marriage, a young boy's early haircut, a couple at a country dance. Only four of twenty-two images omit family situations, and all these show pastoral scenes. One is of a peaceful graveyard.

In the summer of 1992, Brooks himself was nearing a life-marking event with the anticipated birth of his daughter. She would be named Taylor Mayne Pearl Brooks, after James Taylor, Minnie Pearl, and the vacation spot where Brooks said the child was conceived

(Mitchell 1993, 110). At Fan Fair in June of 1992, Brooks and Sandy received an impromptu public baby shower. Brooks had made a public commitment to spend at least five minutes with each of his fans, and they lined up across the entire Fairgrounds parking lot from early morning hours every day to meet him. Media reported Brooks autographing for more than nine hours a day. At the Liberty Records show on the third morning, Brooks performed his cover of Billy Joel's "Shameless" by going to his knees near the edge of the stage, then lying down to bestow a symbolic kiss on an adoring fan. Throughout his showcase performance, which included renditions of "Rodeo," "The Thunder Rolls," "Friends in Low Places" and "The Dance," fans streamed forward in urgent but orderly fashion to offer flowers, notes, and gifts for Taylor Mayne Pearl Brooks. This scene was repeated at the Grand Ole Opry Superstar Spectacular that evening. On every public occasion during Fan Fair week, Brooks accepted each gift individually and bestowed thanks for the giver's generosity. Before his final number, Brooks brought a visibly pregnant Sandy on stage to the excited applause of fans and introduced her with the phrase, "I know a lot of you might be wondering how Sandy's doing. Well, I brought her here with me today." At the end of his show, Brooks gave what Edward Morris described as "a long, benign wave, strongly reminiscent of a papal benediction" (Morris 1993, 135–38). Then, carefully loading up every single gift, the Garth Brooks nuclear family left the stage.

Taylor Mayne Pearl Brooks was born July 8, 1992. Two months later, Garth Brooks was talking about retiring from country music. This public gesture received another burst of extended coverage in print and electronic media. On November 17, in an interview with Jane Pauley on NBC television, Brooks expressed deep concern about his personal future. As he talked, he wiped away tears. In September, *Billboard* had reported as front page news the focus of Brooks's concern. "I feel God put me down here to play music," he told *Billboard*, "but it's very evident to see because of the baby, God put me down here to be a father also." The problem seemed to be achieving the proper mix of money, time, ambition, and family life.

> Sandy and I have 50,000 times more money than we could spend in the rest of our lives. . . . The parents, the whole crew is set up on pension plans, so I can walk away from it. I must decide what I want to do. I think parents work to provide for their children because they

have to, and if I don't have to, is it my duty to stay home? And that's a war that's going on right now. (Newman and Morris 1992, 1)

The authenticity of Brooks's dilemma was undeniably rooted in his actual situation. Yet, at the very end of their coverage of it, *Billboard* made passing reference to an additional dimension of Brooks's concern in the marketplace of emotions. At that moment, Brooks was renegotiating his contract with Liberty Records.

I've been amazed at all the other labels who have given me numbers and said, "Look, if you're ever unhappy, give me a call." I'm not in this thing to be the highest-paid ball player on the field. I did, however, want to negotiate a deal that stated if I did sell product, I got rewarded and that's what we've worked out. (Newman and Morris 1992, 85)

Garth Brooks's promotion of sincere masculinity and the cultivation of his image as a devoted family man are essential ingredients of his unprecedented appeal in American popular culture. But there is more to him. Brooks seems personally responsible for a performing style that has brought country music culture its most flamboyant live-concert experience in almost seventy years. That production may be viewed on video tape; *This Is Garth Brooks* amply depicts his on-stage maneuvers and strategies for fan engagement as he performs fifteen songs (Liberty 1992). Compiled from films of two sold-out concerts in Dallas, September 20 and 21, 1991, and presented on NBC television, January 17, 1992, the live-performance style documented there is a preoccupation of Brooks's critics. Influenced by his fondness for the rock and roll groups Boston, Journey, REO Speedwagon, and Fleetwood Mac, Brooks blends frenetic personal extravagance on stage (including swinging over his fans on lighting cables, bashing guitars, and commandeering a spotlight to connect with individuals throughout the hall) with tender ballads evocative of compliant masculinity and ritualized moments of emotion that focus on Brooks as a popular theologian.

Daniel Cooper describes Garth Brooks's appeal as "a musical überculture that's very middle American, very 1970s, and unfortunately very white." According to Cooper, 1970s rock and roll was an emotional expression by white teenagers living in safe suburbs where white flight had placed them; and, consequently, Brooks's merging of country music with this tradition is undesirable. Says Cooper, "Garth serves one master: the spectacle" (Cooper 1993, 55–57). While Cooper's critique may be pertinent to the social origins of rock and roll culture in the 1970s, the "spectacle" aspects of fan behavior displayed at a Brooks concert have roots in earlier secular country performance and in evangelical religious practices going back at least to the nineteenth century. There is no doubt that Garth Brooks loves spectacle. Possibly his largest audience ever watched him sing the national anthem at professional football's Superbowl on January 30, 1993. And during September 1993, he filled Texas Stadium three consecutive days for a concert event of unprecedented fan volume for a single performer in country music culture, one with overtones of evangelical revival meetings from the days of Billy Sunday and Captain Ryman's auditorium in Nashville to the continuing appeal of Billy Graham. It's probably not entirely accidental that Brooks's fan club magazine is titled *The Believer*.

Trend lines in American religious practice may suggest a context for the phenomena of Garth Brooks concerts. Church membership has increased approximately 30 percent since 1960, although church membership as a percentage of the total national population declined 4 percent. These changes mask internal shifts in the nature of American churchgoing. Since 1965, Methodist, Presbyterian, Congregationalist, and Episcopal churches have declined in membership 20–33 percent, while evangelical and conservative denominations and movements have grown rapidly—especially in metropolitan areas (Bennett 1994, 115–16). Robert Oermann reports results of a study suggesting that the retail audience for "Christian" music may grow "by an estimated 50.5 million" people in the 1990s (Oermann 1993, 1E). The cumulative significance of these fragmentary indicators—revival-style concerts in Texas, dramatic growth in evangelical religious practice, suggestions of sharply increasing volume for "Christian" music—is not entirely plain. Yet, when one visits Fan Fair and watches Garth Brooks greet his fans beneath a larger banner spelling out *"The Believer"* and sees those fans wearing shirts with a philosophic lesson printed across the back saying the "true lesson" of life is not its outcome but the "struggle" "between the dream and reality," links between "Garthmania" and a secularized version of religious feelings seem possible.

On December 10, 1992, Garth Brooks appeared at the Nutter Center in Dayton, Ohio, which sold out in record time for Brooks and his opening act, Martina McBride. Early in his career, Brooks had opened for Reba McEntire and for the Judds; now as a headliner, he chooses women to promote as opening acts. McBride's thirty-minute set featured seven songs, including a cover of Hank Williams's "Your Cheatin' Heart," a song for working women, and a then-current single on the country charts.

The crowd had clearly come to see Garth Brooks. The audience included more teenagers than is usual for a country music event. Many were dressed in highly styled "Garth shirts" with bold stripes or striking color patterns, crisply clean bluejeans, and black Garth-style Stetson hats. The audience was well-manicured. There were many women costumed in country garb, the majority of them appearing to be in their mid- to late-twenties. The crowd was extremely well-behaved, orderly and polite; virtually no drinking or smoking was visible. The black Garth-hat with its silver band and rhinestones could be found on six-year-old girls, teenage boys, and grandfathers. The age range of this crowd included babies, toddlers, teenagers, young adults, middle-aged people, and couples who appeared to be in their sixties. Compared to a Conway Twitty crowd, late-middle-age working-class couples did not visibly dominate. The broadening demographic of country music culture was entirely the norm.

At 9:10 P.M., the announcer told the sell-out crowd that, while no video or audio recording was allowed, flash photographs were encouraged. At this point, the crowd began to clap in anticipation. At 9:17, the house lights went down and the crowd rose uniformly to its feet—not to sit again the entire evening. Smoke rose from the stage, a loud explosion was heard over the public address system, and a countdown of rim-shots and a drum roll filled the hall as a mechanical platform from the rear of the stage lifted Garth Brooks into view, emerging in his characteristic bow-leg cowboy stance, with guitar and head bowed. To ecstatic cheers in the packed arena bright lights came on, Garth's band of six players fanned out onto the stage (displaying red and blue guitars), and Brooks came forward wearing his black hat, red, white and black shirt, bluejeans, and guitar.

Without comment, Brooks launched into the initial framing song for the concert, "Rodeo." As an opening statement, "Rodeo" serves as a song about entertainment culture and introduces anticipation of a high level of action, as it sums up through a catalog of specific images "the joy and the pain" of rodeo entertainment (Brooks 1991). From the moment Brooks appeared on stage, couples in the audience were hugging in excited pleasure and women formed an orderly but urgent procession toward the stage, where they held up babies for him to touch. As Brooks sang each song, individuals in the crowd watched closely, intent on studying the words as if following an important text, many of them singing along with his inflections. Yet, at the end of each song, they erupted in ecstatic applause. After his first number, Brooks spoke directly to his fans with this question: "Is everybody ok?" Through the next few numbers, fans responded by taking up loads of flowers and more children to be touched.

Song three began a trio of songs focused on domestic commitment. Brooks introduced the first song by speaking earnestly to his fans. "Something very sweet has happened to me," he said, and in honor of that tonight he dedicated "Two of a Kind, Workin' on a Full House" to himself. The choice of this song suggested that the event of importance was his recommitment to passion in his marriage and the recent birth of his daughter. If "Two of a Kind" represented testimony about Brooks's conversion to devoted family man, the crowd liked the idea. They sang along ardently. His fourth song, "Somewhere Other Than the Night," came from his then-current album, *The Chase*. It told the story of an older married woman's need for passion and her husband's discovery of that fact. The fifth song, "Papa Loved Mama," concluded the initial three-song set of commentaries on domestic commitment with domestic relief—a humorous account of misplaced passion and revenge for infidelity.

Brooks had opened with a framing song about entertainment in a manner analogous to the strategy of Conway Twitty, then offered a sequence of story songs meant to be instructive about passion in romantic relationships, including his own personal testimony. Now the tone of the concert shifted. Songs six and seven spoke to the role of God's will in everyday affairs, offering the philosophic position that life is not under the control of individual desire but instead flows "like a river." Song six, "Unanswered Prayers," proved to be one of two emotional high points for fans and the most directly theological utterance of the evening. A ballad that tells a story of meeting an "old flame," this song is a testimonial by a man to a third person about his realization that an unanswered adolescent prayer was, in fact, answered. As a mature man, when he looks at his actual wife, he realizes that divine intent and immediate human desire don't always coincide (Brooks 1990). The strategy of this song is reminiscent of Conway Twitty's claim that his songs spoke the words men would like to say but often cannot. Garth Brooks fans received "Unanswered Prayers" in impressive silence until Brooks played a solo guitar accompaniment and invited everyone to sing along. They knew all the words. Brooks's seventh song, "The River," generated more armloads of flowers, a vast array of ceremonial lighters held aloft, and embracing by many couples as Brooks sang that we should dare to "chance the rapids" and "dance the tide" even though rough waters are doubtless in store (Brooks 1991).

The next three songs—numbers eight through ten—were statements about justice. "We Shall Be Free" was introduced as a "righteous song," a "gospel song" that takes up matters of public justice. "The Thunder Rolls," a story of domestic violence and retribution, is an account of private justice. "Much Too Young (To Feel This Damn Old)," Brooks's first hit, tells the story of a rodeo rider who admits that he got his appropriate reward when his partner left him—another variation on domestic justice.

Again, Brooks changed tone, reverting to the theme of domestic commitment to give a sermon and make a point. The sermon exists within "If Tomorrow Never Comes," advice to his followers that they should tell their lovers how much they care in case their "time on earth" ends before they have another opportunity to do so. In song twelve, a cover of Billy Joel's "Shameless," Brooks demonstrated *how* one should make that testimony—passionately, directly, with open emotion. During these two songs, which serve as exemplary testimony to Brooks's theology of passion and commitment in personal relationships, the audience took action. First, they filed to the stage where, during "If Tomorrow Never Comes," Brooks paced back and forth, shaking hands with them in a ritual reminiscent of communion. Then they hugged and kissed as Garth stood alone, acting out his rendition of "Shameless" while holding a single flower, which at the song's conclusion he presented gently to a woman singled out in the front row. A tremendous ovation rolled through the hall as Brooks made personal contact.

This moment of high feeling was followed with another song of domestic justice—this time, one providing humor and comic relief from the seriousness of Brooks's sermonizing—a bawdy rendition of "Friends in Low Places." Another witty commentary on domestic justice, as it is sung in live concert, this ballad tells the story of a rejected lover who brashly tells off his former lover on the day she is about to marry into high society (Brooks 1990). Just before beginning this song Brooks threw a towel into the audience; throughout the song, he enjoyed ecstatic overhand clapping from fans and more singing along.

After this moment of comic relief, Brooks turned serious again. In a departure speech to his fans, Brooks returned to family matters. "This tour ends in two days," he said. "I'm gettin' ready to take a few months off and go home and be a dad." By now, however, Brooks had resolved his retirement dilemma: "After that I'm gonna pack up Sandy and Taylor and come back out" on the road, to be with the fans. This comment introduced his finale, Brooks's signature song "The Dance." A hymn to the role of chance in ordinary lives, "The Dance" is meant as an incentive to take chances and make passionate commitments. It brought lighters throughout the hall, and solid singing with Brooks, who stood isolated under a single spotlight. At 10:35 P.M., Brooks waved good-bye and said humbly to his fans, "In our eight months off, please don't forget us."

As Garth Brooks left the stage, the hall erupted in a deafening roar more intense in its appreciation than any other moment I had witnessed in two years and five thousand miles of travel across country music culture. Perhaps this response was the more impressive because it came from an audience blended of both traditional and new country fans. There was no doubting the genuine desire for an encore. When Brooks returned, accompanied by a long drum roll, the fifteenth song of the evening provided a platform for his only significant dalliance with rock-and-roll stage effects. Up to this time—with the exception of moments when he was kissing babies, taking flowers, or shaking hands with fans—Brooks had remained essentially at center stage, with his band spread out on risers behind him in a half-semicircle not significantly different from the placement of other country bands. But, for this single encore, that changed. During a fervent cover of the rock-and-roll number, "Keep Your Hands to Yourself," Brooks acted out the theatrics that so preoccupy his critics. He threw a water bottle into the crowd, climbed a rope ladder, rode a dangling cable out over the audience in a dramatic swinging arc, picked up a spotlight and focused it around the hall to make direct contact with small groups, took off his hat, let his shirttail hang out—building enthusiastic audience involvement with every trick. This action was intense but brief; after seven minutes, and without further comment, Garth Brooks and his band left the stage.

The Marketplace of Emotions   269

The lights came up then, and the crowd filed politely out of the hall. Crowded exit sidewalks outside the arena revealed no jostling, or even loud talk. Many fans had to enter shuttle buses for distant parking lots that accommodated the sell-out crowd; even here, demeanor was mannerly and respectful—no pushing. At that moment, it seemed that Garth Brooks's fans had been inspired to be good to one another.

Garth Brooks's 1992 concert in Dayton, Ohio, possessed a crowd-rousing strategy that evoked aspects of evangelical church services. Framed by two songs that clearly referred to its status as entertainment, the interior structure of the concert was serious. It introduced a personal testimony of domestic commitment with examples, shifted to a commentary on God's will and the role of chance in ordinary lives, raised issues of public and private justice in the domestic realm, returned to sermonizing to instruct fans about openly declaring their deepest feelings, then demonstrated how to do that. A moment of comic relief followed, then a statement of summary theology: personal commitment to passionate involvement is worth it, whatever the outcome. The structure and content of this concert linked it to Garth Brooks's popular image of sincere masculinity and devotion to family values and to the ministerial role that major country artists can play in popular culture.

There is little doubt that—like his predecessors, Jimmie Rodgers, the Carter Family, Hank Williams, Patsy Cline, Loretta Lynn, Dolly Parton, Reba McEntire, Mel Tillis, and Conway Twitty—Garth Brooks means to sell himself as a commercial star. Like them, he trades in the currency of both romantic love and spiritual commitment. Song titles printed on the *Ropin' the Wind* album jacket highlight a single letter in each title. Garth Brooks has confirmed that this was intentional and that the highlighted letters can be arranged to read "God Bless Us." *Ropin' the Wind* had unprecedented sales for a country music artist, one who came to prominence in the early 1990s demonstrating his affection for a theme sustained in country music culture during seventy years of growth and evolution: this music can lead us from hard times to heaven.

APPENDIX A   **Log of Concerts, Events,**

Places, and Artists

1991

Nov 16 *Conway Twitty, Mark Chestnutt, George Jones,* Hara Arena, Dayton, Ohio

1992

Feb 15 *Alan Jackson, Diamond Rio,* University of Dayton Arena, Dayton, Ohio

Feb 23 *Mark O'Connor,* Canal Street Tavern, Dayton, Ohio

Mar 20 *Conway Twitty, George Jones, Lorrie Morgan,* Cincinnati Gardens, Cincinnati, Ohio

Mar 27 *Norm's Gospel Sing,* Memorial Hall, Dayton, Ohio, *Singing Cookes, Spencers, McKameys*

Mar 28 *WWVA Jamboree,* Capitol Music Hall, Wheeling, West Virginia, *Tom T. Hall*

Apr 3,4 *Emmylou Harris* with Dayton Philharmonic Orchestra, Convention Center, Dayton, Ohio

Apr 12	*Hank Williams, Jr., Patty Loveless, Doug Stone,* Nutter Center, Dayton, Ohio
Apr 24	*Renfro Valley Jamboree,* Renfro Village, John Lair Museum, Renfro Valley, Kentucky
Apr 24–26	Grand Opening Benefit Concert, *Dollywood,* Pigeon Forge, Tennessee
	Dolly Parton, Reba McEntire, Dolly Parton Museum, "Dollywood Ambassadors" Fan Club
Apr 25	*The Singing Cookes* 30th Anniversary Concert, Harrogate, Tennessee
May 22–25	*Jerry Clower, Mel Tillis, Loretta Lynn, Merle Haggard, Charlie Pride,* Branson, Missouri
May 26–31	Jimmie Rodgers Memorial Festival, Meridian, Mississippi
	Travis Tritt, Tanya Tucker, Collin Raye, Joe Diffie, T. G. Sheppard, Rich McWilliams, Charlie McCoy, Paulette Carlson, Hank Williams, Jr., Jason D. Williams
	Peavey Museum, Peavey Amplifier Co., Meridian
May 29–30	9th Annual International Country Music Conference, Mississippi State University, Meridian, Mississippi
June 5	*Loretta Lynn Ranch & Western Town,* Hurricane Mills, Tennessee, Annual Fan Club Concert
June 6–14	Fan Fair, Opryland, Grand Ole Opry, Ryman Auditorium, Twitty City, Nashville, Tennessee
	Wayne Newton, Garth Brooks, Brooks and Dunn, Hal Ketchum, Ronna Reeves, Ricky Skaggs, Alan Jackson, Sawyer Brown, Tanya Tucker, Diamond Rio, Joe Diffie, Roy Acuff, Dan Seals, Billy Dean, Marty Brown, Clive Francis, Jack Greene, Country Music Hall of Fame
June 13	*Alabama June Jam,* Ft. Payne, Alabama
June 15–16	Archie Campbell Memorial Theater, Pigeon Forge, Tennessee, *Hee-Haw Show, Phil Campbell*
June 16	*Museum of Appalachia,* Norris, Tennessee
June 29	*Wayne Newton,* Fraze Pavilion, Kettering, Ohio
July 10–12	12th Annual *Country Concert '92* at Hickory Hill Lakes, Ft. Loramie, Ohio
	Nitty Gritty Dirt Band
July 26	*Sumiton Church of God Choir,* Princeton Pike Church of God, Hamilton, Ohio
Aug 1	*Lorrie Morgan, Ricky Van Shelton,* Preble County Fair, Eaton, Ohio
Aug 14	*Dean Mitchell,* "Jimmie Rodgers at the Ft. Payne Opera House, July 1932," Gadsden, Alabama
Aug 15	*Alabama Music Hall of Fame,* Florence, Alabama

Aug 15–16 *Elvis Week*, 15th Anniversary Candlelight Vigil, *Graceland*, August 15, Memphis, Tennessee

Sep 8 *Lyle Lovett, Bonnie Raitt*, Nutter Center, Dayton, Ohio

Sep 12 *Billy Ray Cyrus*, Hara Arena, Dayton, Ohio

Oct 4 *Willie Nelson*, Nutter Center, Dayton, Ohio

Oct 25 *Kenny Rogers, Pirates of the Mississippi, Michelle Wright*, Nutter Center, Dayton, Ohio

Nov 7 *Conway Twitty, George Jones, Vern Gosdin*, Hara Arena, Dayton, Ohio

Dec 10 *Garth Brooks, Martina McBride*, Nutter Center, Dayton, Ohio

1993

Feb 13 *Alabama, Diamond Rio*, University of Dayton Arena, Dayton, Ohio

Mar 20 *Vince Gill, Mary Chapin Carpenter*, Hara Arena, Dayton, Ohio

Apr 15 *Alan Jackson, Billy Dean, John Michael Montgomery*, University of Dayton Arena, Dayton, Ohio

May 27–31 Jimmie Rodgers Memorial Festival and 10th Annual Country Music Conference, Meridian, Mississippi
Billy Joe Royal, Collin Raye, Marie Osmond, Ricky Skaggs, Patsy Montana, Tanya Tucker, Justin Tubb, Charlie McCoy, Willie Nelson

June 7–11 *Fan Fair, TNN/Music City News Awards; Conway Twitty Memorial Service*, Nashville, Tennessee

June 29 *Lyle Lovett, Roseanne Cash*, Fraze Pavilion, Kettering, Ohio

Aug 1 *Dolly Parton*, Fraze Pavilion, Kettering, Ohio

Hank Williams: Song Assignments by Category

TOTAL THEMES

Domestic Situations (54)
See list on page 276.

Broken Hearts (37)

All the Love I Ever Had
Alone And Forsaken
Are You Lonely Too [Hank
  Williams, Jr.]*
The Blues Come Around
Cold, Cold Heart
Cowboys Don't Cry
Heaven Holds All My Treasures

I Can't Escape from You
I Can't Get You Off of My Mind
I Can't Help It (If I'm Still in Love
  With You)
I Don't Care (If Tomorrow Never
  Comes)
(Last Night) I Heard You Crying in
  Your Sleep

---

*[co-writers]

I Lost the Only Love I Knew [Don
  Helms]
I Told a Lie to My Heart
I Watched My Dream World
  Crumble Like Clay
I'd Still Want You
I'm Just Crying 'Cause I Care
  [Hank Williams, Jr.]
I'm So Lonesome I Could Cry
In My Dreams You Still Belong to
  Me
Just Me and My Broken Heart
  [Hank Williams, Jr.]
Kaw-Liga [Fred Rose]
Long Gone Lonesome Blues
Lost on the River
May You Never Be Alone

Me and My Broken Heart
Men with Broken Hearts
My Love for You (Has Turned to
  Hate)
My Sweet Love Ain't Around
A Stranger in the Night [Bill
  Morgan]
A Teardrop on a Rose
There'll Be No Teardrops Tonight
There's a Tear in My Beer
Weary Blues from Waitin'
When You're Tired of Breaking
  Other Hearts [Curley Williams]
Why Should I Cry
Won't You Sometimes Think of Me
You Can't Take My Memories of
  You [Hank Williams, Jr.]

Gospel (21)

The Angel Of Death
Are You Walking and A-Talking for
  the Lord
Calling You
Countryfied
The Funeral
A Home in Heaven
A House of Gold
How Can You Refuse Him Now
I Saw the Light
I'm Going Home
I'm Going Home

I'm Gonna Sing
Jesus Died for Me
Jesus Is Calling [Charlie Monroe]
Jesus Remembered Me
Last Night I Dreamed of Heaven
Ready to Go Home
Wealth Won't Save Your Soul
We're Getting Closer to the Grave
  Each Day
When God Comes and Gathers His
  Jewels
When the Book of Life Is Read

Happy Love (13)

The Alabama Walk
Baby, We're Really in Love
Bayou Pon Pon [Jimmie Davis]
Cajun Baby [Hank Williams, Jr.]
Hey, Good Lookin'
Honey, Do You Love Me, Huh?
  [Curley Williams]
Honky Tonkin'

Howlin' at the Moon
I Ain't Got Nothing But Time
I Could Never Be Ashamed of You
If You'll Be a Baby (to Me)
Jambalaya (on the Bayou)
There's Nothing as Sweet as My
  Baby

Hard Times (5)

Everything's Okay
I'll Never Get Out of This World
    Alive [Fred Rose]
A Picture from Life's Other Side

Rockin' Chair Daddy [Braxton
    Shooford]
W.P.A. Blues

Death Lament (3)

On the Evening Train [Audrey
    Williams]

Singing Waterfall
Six More Miles

Trains (2)

California Zephyr

Pan American

Other (3)

Warning About Fighting Men: I've
    Been Down That Road Before
Prison Lament: On the Banks of
    the Old Pontchartrain [Ramona
    Vincent]

Against War: (I'm Praying for the
    Day that) Peace Will Come [Pee
    Wee King]

DOMESTIC SITUATIONS

Complaint (31)

See list on page 277.

Loneliness (10)

Homesick
Honky Tonk Blues
I'm So Tired of It All [Hank
    Williams, Jr.]
If I Didn't Love You [Fred Rose]
Low Down Blues

A Mansion on the Hill [Fred Rose]
Moanin' the Blues
'Neath a Cold Gray Tomb of Stone
    [Mel Foree]
Never Been So Lonesome
Nobody's Lonesome for Me

Defiance (8)

Satisfaction: I Won't Be Home No More
              You Broke Your Own Heart [Hank Williams, Jr.]
              You Broke Your Own Heart
              Your Turn to Cry [Hank Williams, Jr.]
   Warning: You're Barkin' up the Wrong Tree Now [Fred Rose]
              You're Gonna Change (or I'm Gonna Leave)
              Your Cheatin' Heart
   Kissoff: I'm a Long Gone Daddy

Family (5)

Mother: Dear Brother
             Message to My Mother
             Mother is Gone
Dad: The Log Train
Son: Little Bocephus

DOMESTIC COMPLAINT

Women's Changing Mood (5)

I Wish You Didn't Love Me So Much
Is This Good-bye [Hank Williams, Jr.]
Please Make Up Your Mind
Wearin' out Your Walkin' Shoes
Why Don't You Love Me

Loveless Marriage (4)

A House without Love
I Just Don't Like This Kind of Livin'
Where Do I Go From Here
Why Should We Try Anymore

Remorse (4)

Let's Turn Back the Years
My Cold, Cold Heart Is Melted Now [Johnnie Master]
My Heart Would Know
Somebody's Lonesome [Hank Williams, Jr.]

Shame (4)

The Little House We Built (Just O'er the Hill) [Don Helms]
(I Heard That) Lonesome Whistle [Jimmie Davis]
Move It on Over
My Son Calls Another Man Daddy [Jewell House]

Infidelity (3)

I'm Not Coming Home Anymore
Never Again (Will I Knock on Your Door)
You Win Again

Warning About Women (2)

Mind Your Own Business
You Better Keep It on Your Mind [Vic McAlpin]

Other (9)

Ambitious Wife:	For Me There Is No Place
Unresponsive Wife:	No, Not Now [Curley Williams, Mel Foree]
Doubt of Love:	Forever's a Long, Long Time
Waiting for Love:	Just Waitin' [Bob Gazzaway]
Unreturned Love:	My Heart Won't Let Me Go [Hank Williams, Jr.]
Fear of Marriage Constraints:	I'll Be a Bachelor Till I Die
Divorce Trauma:	Help Me Understand
Sympathy for Broken Hearts:	I'm Sorry for You, My Friend
Rambling Man:	Ramblin' Man

WIT

Laughing at Treatment by Woman (21)

Homesick
Howlin' at the Moon
I Won't Be Home No More
I Wish You Didn't Love Me So Much
I'm a Long Gone Daddy
If You'll Be a Baby (to Me)
Is This Good-bye
Just Waitin' [Bob Gazzaway]
Long Gone Lonesome Blues
Mind Your Own Business
No, Not Now [Curley Williams, Mel Foree]
Nobody's Lonesome for Me

Please Make Up Your Mind
There's a Tear in My Beer
Wearin' Out Your Walkin' Shoes
When You're Tired of Breaking Other Hearts [Curley Williams]
Why Don't You Love Me
You Better Keep It on Your Mind [Vic McAlpin]
You're Barkin' up the Wrong Tree Now [Fred Rose]
You're Gonna Change (or I'm Gonna Leave)
Move It on Over

Laughing at Hard Times (5)

Everything's Okay
I'll Never Get Out of This World Alive [Fred Rose]
I've Been Down That Road Before

Low Down Blues
Rockin' Chair Daddy [Braxton Shooford]

Other (2)

Put Down of City Folks: Countryfied

Laughing at Shy Man: Kaw-Liga [Fred Rose]

Source of Titles: Don Cusic, Ed. 1993. *Hank Williams: The Complete Lyrics.* New York: St. Martin's Press.

Alan Jackson: Song Assignments by Category

TOTAL THEMES

Domestic Situations (9)
See list on page 280.

Broken Hearts (11)
Dog River Blues
Don't Rock the Jukebox [Roger Murrah, Keith Stegall]*
From A Distance [Randy Travis]
Here in the Real World [Mark Irwin]
Just Playin' Possum [Jim McBride, Gary Overton]
Merry Christmas to Me
She Don't Get The Blues [Jim McBride]
Short Sweet Ride [Jim McBride]
Up To My Ears in Tears [Don Sampson]

———

*[co-writers]

Walkin' The Floor Over Me [Don Sampson]
(Who Says) You Can't Have It All [Jim McBride]

Happy Love (3)

Blue Blooded Woman [Keith Stegall, Roger Murrah]
I'd Love You All Over Again
Tonight I Climbed the Wall

Home Nostalgia (1)

Chattahoochee [Jim McBride]

Becoming a Star (1)

Chasin' That Neon Rainbow [Jim McBride]

Honoring Country Music Legend (1)

Midnight in Montgomery [Don Sampson]

DOMESTIC SITUATIONS

Complaint (6)

See list below.

Family (2)

Home
Working Class Hero [Don Sampson]

Loneliness (1)

Tropical Depression [Jim McBride, Charlie Craig]

DOMESTIC COMPLAINT

Remorse (3)

If It Ain't One Thing (It's You) [Jim McBride]
She's Got The Rhythm (And I Got The Blues) [Randy Travis]
Wanted [Charlie Craig]

Abandoned (2)

Dallas [Keith Stegall]
Someday [Jim McBride]

Waiting for Love (1)

That's All I Need To Know [Jim McBride]

REFERENCES

BOOKS, ARTICLES, PERIODICALS

Allen, Danita. 1992. "Country Respect." *Country America* (June): 10.

Balmer, Randall. [1989] 1993. *Mine Eyes Have Seen the Glory: A Journey into the Evangelical Subculture in America.* New York, Oxford: Oxford University Press.

Batteau, Allen W. 1990. *The Invention of Appalachia.* Tucson: University of Arizona Press.

Bennett, William J. 1994. *The Index of Leading Cultural Indicators: Facts and Figures on the State of American Society.* New York: Simon & Schuster.

Billboard. 1994. "Rhythm, Country & Blues" (February 26): 2–3.

Bronner, Simon J. 1989. "Jerry Clower." In *Encyclopedia of Southern Culture.* Charles Reagan Wilson and William Ferris, eds. Chapel Hill: University of North Carolina Press.

Buckstaff, Katheryn. 1993. *Branson and Beyond.* New York: St. Martin's Press.

Bufwack, Mary A., and Robert K. Oermann. 1993a. *Finding Her Voice: The Saga of Women in Country Music.* New York: Crown.

———. 1993b. "Reba McEntire Walks On." *Journal of Country Music.* Vol. 16, no. 1, pp. 16–19.

Burke, James Lee. [1978] [1986] 1987. *The Lost Get-Back Boogie.* New York: Owl Book, Henry Holt.

Campbell, Archie, with Ben Byrd. 1981. *Archie Campbell: An Autobiography.* Memphis, Tenn.: Memphis State University Press.

Cantwell, Robert. 1972. "Believing in Bluegrass." *Atlantic* (March): 52–60.

Cash, June Carter. [1979] 1981. *Among My Klediments*. Grand Rapids, Mich.: Zondervan Publishing House.

Clower, Jerry. 1992. *Stories from Home*. Jackson and London: University Press of Mississippi.

Cobb, Thomas. 1987. *Crazy Heart*. New York: Harper & Row.

Cohen, Norm. 1981. *Long Steel Rail: The Railroad in American Folksong*. Urbana: University of Illinois Press.

Collins, Andrew "Ace." 1993. *I Saw Him in Your Eyes*. Cheyenne, Wyo.: Vision Press.

Coontz, Stephanie. 1992. *The Way We Never Were: American Families and the Nostalgia Trap*. New York: Basicbooks, Harper Collins.

Cooper, Daniel. 1993. "No Fences." *Journal of Country Music*. Vol.16, no. 1, pp. 55–57.

Corliss, Richard, and Georgia Harbison. 1993. "The Barefoot Bride: Julia's Got a Lovett." *Time* (July 12): 6.

Country: The Music and the Musicians. 1988. Edited by Paul Kingsbury and Alan Axelrod. Country Music Foundation. New York: Abbeville Press. Included in this work are: Bill Ivey, "The Bottom Line: Business Practices That Shaped Country Music"; Alanna Nash, "Home Is Where the Gig Is: Life On and Off the Road"; Nolan Porterfield, "Hey, Hey Tell 'Em 'Bout Us: Jimmie Rodgers Visits the Carter Family"; Nick Tosches, "Honky-Tonkin': Ernest Tubb, Hank Williams, and the Bartender's Muse"; Charles Wolfe, "The Triumph of the Hills: Country Radio, 1920–50."

Country America. 1994. "Christmas at Dollywood" (January): 64–67, 91.

———. 1993 (November): 41–48.

———. 1992. "The Top 100 Country Songs of All Time." Vol. 4, no. 1 (October): 8, 91, 26–52.

Country Fever. 1993. "The 'Godmothers' of Fan Fair" (June): 74–77.

Country Music City News. 1993a (April).

———. 1993b (October).

———. 1993c (November).

———. 1993d (December).

Country Song Roundup. 1992 (May): 7.

Cross, Wilbur, and Michael Kosser. 1987. *The Conway Twitty Story: An Authorized Biography*. Toronto and New York: PaperJacks.

Cusic, Don, Ed. 1993. *Hank Williams: The Complete Lyrics*. New York: St. Martin's Press.

———. 1991. *Reba McEntire: Country Music's Queen*. New York: St. Martin's Press.

———. 1990. *The Sound of Light: A History of Gospel Music*. Bowling Green, Ohio: Bowling Green State University Popular Press.

Delmore, Alton. 1977. *Truth Is Stranger than Publicity*. Edited with introduction, commentary, and discography by Charles K. Wolfe. Nashville, Tenn.: Country Music Foundation Press.

Dorgan, Howard. 1987. *Giving Glory To God in Appalachia: Worship Practices of Six Baptist Subdenominations*. Knoxville: University of Tennessee Press.

Dougherty, Steve. 1991. "Sweet Dreams No More." *People Weekly* (April 1): 30–33.

Eiland, William U. 1992. *Nashville's Mother Church: The History of the Ryman Auditorium*. Old Hickory, Tenn.: Opryland USA.

Eller, Ronald D. 1982. *Miners, Millhands, and Mountaineers: Industrialization of the Appalachian South, 1880–1930*. Knoxville: University of Tennessee Press.

Faragher, Scott. 1992. *Music City Babylon*. New York: Birch Lane Press.

Flippo, Chet. 1981. *Your Cheatin' Heart: A Biography of Hank Williams*. New York: St. Martin's Press.

Fowler, Gene, and Bill Crawford. [1987] 1990. *Border Radio*. New York: Proscenium Inc.

Frankel, Martha. 1993. "Heaven on Earth, Reba's Charmed Life." *McCall's* (December): 90–95, 148.

Green, Archie. 1972. *Only a Miner: Studies in Recorded Coal-Mining Songs*. Urbana: University of Illinois Press.

Green, Douglas B. 1976. *Country Roots: The Origins of Country Music*. New York: Hawthorne Books.

Gregory, Neal, and Janice Gregory. 1980. *When Elvis Died: Media Overload & the Origins of the Elvis Cult*. New York: Pharos Books.

Gubernick, Lisa Rebecca. 1993. *Get Hot or Go Home: Trisha Yearwood, The Making of a Nashville Star*. New York: William Morrow.

———. 1992. "A Curb on the Ego." *Forbes* (September 14): 418–19.

Gubernick, Lisa, and Peter Newcomb. 1992. "The Wal-Mart School of Music." *Forbes* (March 2): 72–76.

Guralnick, Peter. [1979] 1989. *Lost Highway*. New York: Perennial Library, Harper & Row.

Hancock, Rebecca. 1993. "Letters." *TV Guide* (December 18–24): 45, 84.

Harden, Lydia Dixon. 1994. "Collin Raye Gives a Tip of His Hat to Musical Heroes." *Country Music City News* (February): 22.

Hazen, Cindy, and Mike Freeman. 1992. *The Best of Elvis: Recollections of a Great Humanitarian*. Memphis: Memphis Explorations.

Hemphill, Paul. 1975. "Merle Haggard." In *Stars of Country Music: Uncle Dave Macon to Johnny Rodriguez*. Bill C. Malone and Judith McCulloh, eds. Urbana: University of Illinois Press.

Horstman, Dorothy. [1975] 1986. *Sing Your Heart Out, Country Boy.* Revised edition. Nashville: Country Music Foundation.

Hyperion. 1993. *The Dance.* Lyrics by Tony Arata. New York: Round Stone Press.

Jensen, Joli. 1982. "Patsy Cline's Recording Career: The Search for a Sound." *Journal of Country Music.* Vol. 9, no. 2, pp. 34–36.

Kingsbury, Paul. 1993. "Journey to the Center of Billy Ray Cyrus." *Journal of Country Music.* Vol. 15, no. 2, pp. 9–17.

Kirby, Jack Temple. 1987. *Rural Worlds Lost: The American South, 1920–1960.* Baton Rouge and London: Louisiana State University Press.

Koon, George William. 1983. *Hank Williams: A Bio-Bibliography.* Westport, Conn.: Greenwood Press.

Lee, Judith Yaross. 1991. *Garrison Keillor: A Voice of America.* Jackson and London: University Press of Mississippi.

Levine, Lawrence W. 1988. *Highbrow/Lowbrow: The Emergence of Cultural Hierarchy in America.* Cambridge, Mass.: Harvard University Press.

Lomax III, John. 1985. *Nashville: Music City USA.* New York: Abrams.

Lyle, Katie Letcher. 1991. *Scalded to Death by the Steam: Authentic Stories of Railroad Disasters and the Ballads That Were Written About Them.* Chapel Hill, N.C.: Algonquin Books.

Lynn, Loretta with George Vecsey. 1977. *Coal Miner's Daughter.* New York: Warner Books.

Malone, Bill C. 1993. *Singing Cowboys and Musical Mountaineers: Southern Culture and the Roots of Country Music.* Athens and London: University of Georgia Press.

———. 1992. "Hank Williams." *Journal of the American Academy for the Preservation of Old Time Country Music.* Vol. 2, no.1, pp. 9–11.

———. [1968] 1985. *Country Music U.S.A.* Rev. ed. Austin: University of Texas Press.

Marcus, Greil. 1991. *Dead Elvis: A Chronicle of a Cultural Obsession.* New York: Doubleday.

McCall, Michael. 1991. *Garth Brooks: A Biography.* New York: Bantam.

McGraw, Marjie. 1992. "Garth Brooks: Hitting 'em in the Heart." *Saturday Evening Post* (July/August): 38, 102–103.

Millard, Bob. 1993. *Country Music.* New York: HarperCollins.

Mitchell, Rick. 1993. *Garth Brooks, One of A Kind, Workin' On a Full House.* New York: Fireside, Simon and Schuster.

Morris, Ed, and Peter Cronin. 1993. "Nashville's Still Booming But Industry's Leaders Warn of Creeping Complacency." *Billboard* (December 25): 48, 50.

Morris, Edward. 1993. *Garth Brooks: Platinum Cowboy*. New York: St. Martin's Press.

———. 1992. "Country's Fan Base Is Wider Than Ever." *Billboard* (December 26): 5, 98.

Murphy, Mary. 1993. "Dolly Parton." *TV Guide* (November 27–December 3): 10–17.

Nash, Alanna. 1988. *Behind Closed Doors: Talking With The Legends of Country Music*. New York: Knopf.

Nassour, Ellis. 1993. *Honky Tonk Angel: The Intimate Story of Patsy Cline*. New York: St. Martin's Press.

Newcomb, Peter, and Jean Sherman Chatzky. 1992. "The Top 40." *Forbes* (September 28): 87–91.

Newman, Melinda, and Edward Morris. 1992. "Garth Bows Latest (Last?) Sets." *Billboard* (September 5): 1, 85.

Noonan, Peggy. 1992. "You'd Cry Too If It'd Happened to You." *Forbes* (September 14): 58–69.

Oermann, Robert K. 1992. "How Garth Conquered America." *Journal of Country Music* Vol. 14, no. 3, pp. 16–21.

Pearl, Minnie. 1953. *Minnie Pearl's Diary*. Nashville, Tenn.: Minnie Pearl Museum.

Peterson, Richard A. 1992. "Class Unconsciousness in Country Music." In *You Wrote My Life: Lyrical Themes in Country Music*. Edited by Melton A. McLaurin and Richard A. Peterson. Montreux, Switzerland: Gordon and Breech.

Pike, Jeff. 1993. *The Death of Rock 'n' Roll: Untimely Demises, Morbid Preoccupations and Premature Forecasts of Doom in Pop Music*. Boston, London: Faber and Faber.

Porterfield, Nolan. 1979. *Jimmie Rodgers: The Life and Times of America's Blue Yodeler*. Urbana: University of Illinois Press.

Pugh, Ronnie. 1993. "Ernest Tubb." *The Journal of the American Academy for the Preservation of Old Time Country Music*. No. 14 (April): 9–11.

Quain, Kevin. 1992. *The Elvis Reader: Texts and Sources on the King of Rock 'n' Roll*. New York: St. Martin's Press. Includes: Charles Wolfe, "Presley and the Gospel Tradition."

Randall, Lee. 1992. *The Garth Brooks Scrapbook*. New York: Citadel Press.

Rhodes, Joe. 1993. "The Voices of Billy Ray Cyrus." *TV Guide*. (February 13): 20–23.

Richards, Tad and Melvin B. Shestack. 1993. *The New Country Music Encyclopedia*. New York: Fireside, Simon & Schuster.

Ritchie, Jean. [1955] 1988. *Singing Family of the Cumberlands*. Lexington: University Press of Kentucky.

Rogers, Jimmie N. 1989. *The Country Music Message: Revisited.* Fayetteville: University of Arkansas Press.

Roland, Tom. 1991. *The Billboard Book of Number One Country Hits.* New York: Billboard Books, Watson-Guptill Publications.

Rosen, Craig. 1993. "Whitney Houston Takes Record 11 Billboard Awards." *Billboard* (December 18): 1, 140.

Rosenberg, Neal V. 1985. *Bluegrass: A History.* Urbana and Chicago: University of Illinois Press.

Schlappi, Elizabeth. [1978] 1980. *Roy Acuff: The Smokey Mountain Boy.* Gretna, La.: Pelican Publishing.

Singing News. 1993. (November): 82–93.

Sloan, Kay, and Constance Pierce. 1993. *Elvis Rising: Stories on the King.* New York: Avon. Includes: Gardner Dozois, Jack Dann and Michael Swanwick, "Touring"; Laura Kalpakian, "Starlight Coupe"; Kay Sloan, "Presleystroika."

Smith, Lee. 1992. *The Devil's Dream.* New York: Ballantine.

Stambler, Irwin, and Grelun Landon. [1969] [1982] 1984. *The Encyclopedia of Folk, Country & Western Music.* 2nd ed. New York: St. Martin's Press.

Stark, Phyllis. 1992. " 'Achy Breaky' Embraced by Pop Stations Across Nation." *Billboard.* (June 20): 1, 89.

Tillis, Mel and Walter Wager. 1984. *Stutterin' Boy.* New York: Rawson Associates.

White, Howard, with Ruth White. 1990. *Every Highway Out of Nashville.* Nashville, Tenn.: JM Productions.

Williams, Peter W. 1990. *America's Religions: Traditions and Cultures.* New York: MacMillan.

Williams, Roger M. 1973. *Sing a Sad Song: The Life of Hank Williams.* New York: Ballantine.

Wilson, Charles Reagan. 1992. "Digging Up Bones: Death in Country Music." In *You Wrote My Life: Lyrical Themes in Country Music.* Edited by Melton A. McLaurin and Richard A. Peterson. Montreux, Switzerland: Gordon and Breech.

Wolfe, Charles K. 1982. *Kentucky Country: Folk and Country Music of Kentucky.* Lexington: University Press of Kentucky.

———. 1977. *Tennessee Strings: The Story of Country Music in Tennessee.* Knoxville: University of Tennessee Press.

———. 1973. *The Grand Ole Opry: The Early Years, 1925–35.* London: Old Time Music.

Wynette, Tammy, and Joan Dew. 1979. *Stand By Your Man: An Autobiography.* New York: Pocketbooks.

Zwisohn, Laurence J. 1993. "Loretta Lynn." *Journal of the American*

Academy for the Preservation of Old Time Country Music. No. 17, pp. 9–11.

MOVIES, VIDEOS, RECORDINGS, TELEVISION

Altman, Robert. 1975. *Nashville.* Hollywood: Paramount Pictures. VHS.

Anderson, Bill. 1993. "Country Music Heaven." Revision of Hal Southern and Eddie Dean. *Country Music Heaven.* Curb CD.

Balmer, Randall. 1992. *Mine Eyes Have Seen The Glory: Exploring the Amazing Vitality and Diversity of Evangelicalism and Its Role in American Life.* PBS television documentary. 3 vols. Chicago: WTTW and Isis Productions. VHS.

Brooks, Garth. 1991. "The River." "Rodeo." *Ropin' the Wind.* Capitol Nashville CD.

———. 1990. "Friends In Low Places." "Unanswered Prayers." *No Fences.* Capitol Nashville CD.

Cash, Johnny. 1971. "Man In Black." *Man In Black.* Columbia LP.

CBS Television. 1993. *The Women of Country* (May 6).

Chestnutt, Mark. 1990. "Broken Promise Land." Written by Bill Rice and Mary Sharon Rice. *Too Cold at Home.* MCA CD.

Cinemax. 1987. *Elvis '56.* Television documentary.

Clower, Jerry. 1992. *The Mouth of the Mighty Mississip' Just Keeps Rolling Along.* MCA Cassette.

———. 1991. "Celebrate You." *Racoonteur.* MCA Cassette.

Coe, David Allen. 1985. "You Never Even Called Me By My Name." Written by Steve Goodman. *Seventeen Greatist Hits.* Columbia CD.

Confederate Railroad. 1992. "Trashy Women." Written by Chris Wall. *Confederate Railroad.* Atlantic CD.

Cyrus, Billy Ray. 1993. "Ain't Your Dog No More." Written by Don Von Tress. *It Won't Be the Last.* Mercury CD.

———. 1992. "Achy Breaky Heart." Written by Don Von Tress. *Some Gave All.* Mercury CD.

Dean, Billy. 1991. "Billy the Kid." Written by Billy Dean and Paul Nelson. *Billy Dean.* Liberty Records CD.

DeMent, Iris. 1992. "Mama's Opry." *Infamous Angel.* Warner Brothers CD.

Diffie, Joe. 1992. "Startin' Over Blues." Written by Lonnie Williams and Sanger D. Shafer. *Regular Joe.* Epic CD.

Escott, Colin. 1993. *Hank Williams' Health & Happiness Shows.* The Country Music Foundation. New York: Polygram Records. Mercury CD.

Gill, Vince. 1992. *I Still Believe in You*. MCA CD.

Greene, Jack. 1991. "He Is My Everything." Written by Dallas Frazier. *He Is My Everything*. Nashville, Tenn.: Step One Records. Cassette.

HBO Pictures. 1985. *Sweet Dreams*. Bernard Schwartz, Producer. Starring Jessica Lange and Ed Harris. HBO Video. VHS.

Jackson, Alan. 1993. "Don't Rock the Jukebox." *Livin', Lovin', and Rockin' that Jukebox*. Produced by Keith Stegall and Scott Hendricks. The Home Video Collection. VHS.

———. 1992. "Chattahoochee." *A Lot About Livin' (and a Little 'Bout Love)*. Arista CD.

———. 1991. "Midnight in Montgomery." *Don't Rock the Jukebox*. Arista CD.

JEMF. 1977. *The Carter Family on Border Radio*. Liner notes by Norm Cohen, Archie Green, and William H. Koon. Los Angeles: The John Edwards Memorial Foundation.

Jones, George. 1990. *Hallelujah Weekend*. Epic CD.

———. 1989. *George Jones: Same Ole Me, The Authorized Video Biography*. Nashville, Tenn.: Hallway Productions. VHS.

———. 1987. "He Stopped Loving Her Today." Written by Bobby Braddock and Curly Putnam. *George Jones Super Hits*. Produced by Billy Sherrill. Epic CD.

Liberty. 1992. *This Is Garth Brooks*. Liberty Home Video. VHS.

Lynn, Loretta, Dolly Parton and Tammy Wynette. 1993. *Honky Tonk Angels*. Columbia CD.

MCA Home Video. 1980. *Coal Miner's Daughter*. Produced by Bernard Schwartz. Hollywood: Universal City Studios. VHS.

McEntire, Reba. 1992. *For My Broken Heart*. MCA Video. VHS.

M.G.M. Metro-Goldwyn-Mayer. 1964. *Your Cheatin' Heart (The Hank Williams Story)*. Produced by Sam Katzman; directed by Gene Nelson. Hollywood.

Montgomery, John Michael. 1994. "I Swear." *Kickin' It Up*. Atlantic CD.

Morgan, Lorrie. 1991. "Faithfully." Written by Jonathan Cain. *Something in Red*. RCA CD.

———. 1989. "Five Minutes." Written by Beth Neilsen Chapman. *Leave the Light On*. RCA CD.

MCCF. Music City Christian Fellowship. 1990. *Live Sunday Mornin' Country from the Grand Ole Opryhouse*. Vol. 2. Nashville, Tenn. Video VHS.

———. 1986. *Sunday Mornin' Country Live From the Grand Ole Opryhouse*. Nashville, Tenn.: Mastervision, Inc. Video. VHS.

Nashville Bluegrass Band. 1987. "The Train Carryin' Jimmie Rodgers

Home." Written by Greg Brown. *The Nashville Bluegrass Band*. Cambridge, Mass. Rounder CD.

NBC Television. 1992. "The World According to Garth," *Dateline NBC*. Elizabeth Revetas, Producer. November 17, 1992.

Nelson, Willie. 1993. *Across the Borderline*. Columbia CD.

Newton, Wayne. 1992. "The (Elvis) Letter." Written by Rick Goodman, Johnny Minick and Wayne Newton. *Moods & Moments*. Curb Records CD.

Parton, Dolly. 1993. "Romeo." *Slow Dancing With The Moon*. Columbia CD.

———. 1991. "Eagle When She Flies." *Eagle When She Flies*. Columbia CD.

———. 1989. "He's Alive." Written by Don Francisco. *White Limozeen*. CBS CD.

———. 1987. "Appalachian Memories." "Coat of Many Colors." *Dolly: The Best There Is*. RCA CD.

———. 1975. "My Tennessee Mountain Home." *The Best of Dolly Parton*. RCA CD.

———. 1974. "Jolene." *Jolene*. RCA LP.

Presley, Elvis. 1989. *Elvis Presley: The Million Dollar Quartet*. Liner notes by Colin Escott. RCA CD.

Raye, Collin. 1991. "Love, Me." Written by Skip Ewing and Max T. Barnes. *All I Can Be*. Epic CD.

Riders in the Sky. 1990. "Livin' in a Mobile Home." Written by Ronnie Scalf and Rory Michael Bourke. *Horse Opera*. MCA CD.

Ritter, Tex. 1981. Revision of Hal Southern and Eddie Dean. 1954. "I Dreamed of a Hillbilly Heaven." King: Gusto Records.

———. 1961. Revision of Hal Southern and Eddie Dean. 1954. "I Dreamed of a Hillbilly Heaven." Country Music Foundation Collection.

Run C&W. 1993. *Into the Twangy-First Century*. MCA CD.

Singing Cookes. 1991. *One Live Family*. Prime Video Productions. VHS.

Smithsonian Institution. 1986. *Jimmie Rodgers On Record: America's Blue Yodeler*. Selected and annotated by Nolan Porterfield. RCA. Cassettes.

Snider, Mike. Undated. *Live on the Boat*. Gleason, Tennessee. Cassette.

Southern, Hal, and Eddie Dean. 1954. "I Dreamed of a Hillbilly Heaven." Country Music Foundation Collection.

Spencers. 1990. "Let's Meet By The River." *It'll Be Worth It After All*. Peaceful Stream Music CD.

Stone, Doug. 1990. "I'd Be Better Off (in a Pine Box)." Written by Johnny MacRae and Steve Clark. *Doug Stone*. CBS Cassette.

Stuart, Marty. 1992. "Me and Hank & Jumpin' Jack Flash." *This One's Gonna Hurt You.* MCA CD.

Telecom Entertainment. 1982. *Living Proof: The Hank Williams, Jr. Story.*

TNN. The Nashville Network. 1994. *Opry Backstage. Grand Old Opry Live.* January 22.

———. 1993. "Mark Collie." *Path To Stardom.* June 24.

Twitty, Conway. 1991. "Who Did They Think He Was?" Written by Richard Leigh and Pat McManus. *Even Now.* MCA. Cassette.

———. 1990. "Good-bye Time." Written by Roger Murrah and James Dean Hicks. "The Rose." Written by Amanda McBroom. *Conway Twitty Silver Anniversary Collection.* MCA CD.

Universal Pictures. 1983. *Tender Mercies.* Horton Foote and Robert Duvall, Co-Producers. Hollywood. VHS.

Warner Brothers. 1992. *Pure Country.* Hollywood. VHS.

———. 1982. *Honkytonk Man.* Executive Producer Fritz Manes. Produced and Directed by Clint Eastwood. Hollywood. VHS.

———. 1980. *Honeysuckle Rose a.k.a. On the Road Again.* Produced by Sidney S. Pollack and Gene Taft. Directed by Jerry Schatzberg. Hollywood. VHS.

Wright, Michelle. 1992. "Take It Like a Man." Written by Tony Hasalden. *Now & Then.* Arista CD.

NEWSPAPERS, OTHER SOURCES

Adkinson, Tom. 1992. "Opryland USA Fact Sheet." Photocopy, 5 pp. Nashville, Tenn.: Opryland USA.

Akenson, James. 1993. Correspondence. December 1.

Applebome, Peter. 1993. "Country Music Boom Highlights New Allure of Cities Like Nashville." *New York Times* (September 29): A8.

Batz, Bob. 1992. "WHKO-FM Tops Arbitron List Again." *Dayton Daily News* (February 18): 6B.

Bazyari, Habib. 1992. Interview. May 27. Meridian: Mississippi State University, Meridian.

Brown, Patricia Leigh. 1992. "Reaching for the Stars: A Nashville Fair Celebrates the Fans of Country Music." *New York Times* (June 14): 39.

Carpenter, Mary Chapin. 1993. Biographical Fact Sheet. Columbia Records.

Cash, Johnny. 1980. *The Original Carter Family Songbook.* New York: Peer International Corporation.

Castagno, Paul. 1991. "A Survey of Theaters and Theatrical Practices in

Meridian and Lauderdale County, Mississippi from 1870–1927 Including the Cultural, Economic and Social Effects of Traveling Theater and Silent Movies in Lauderdale County." Meridian: The Grand Opera House of Mississippi.

Chance, Ralph. 1993. News release. *Pigeon Forge Carrier News.* July 10.

Daily News. 1992. "Rockin' on for Rural America." *Dayton Daily News* (March 15): 8A.

Debrosse, Jim. 1993. "Fans at Fraze Wait for Lovett's Love." *Dayton Daily News* (June 30): 1.

Dollywood Foundation Newsletter. 1993. Vol. 4, no. 3 (September): 1.

Fryd, Vivien G. 1993. "'The Sad Twang of Mountain Voices': Thomas Hart Benton's *Sources of Country Music.*" Nashville, Tenn.: manuscript.

Graff, Gary. 1993. "BIG COUNTRY!" *Dayton Daily News* (September 29): 1.

Herman, Jerry. *Dollywood Foundation Newsletter.* 1993. Vol. 4, no. 3 (September): 1.

Hevesi, Dennis. "Conway Twitty, 59, Dies on Tour; Country Star Had 50 No. 1 Songs." *New York Times* (June 6): Y19.

Holden, Stephen. 1994. "Adult Contemporary Music Remains Strong." *Dayton Daily News* (February 4): 3C.

Hunter, James. 1992. "The Ballad of No-Show Jones." *New York Times Magazine* (March 15): 51, 60, 64.

IFCO Club House. 1993. October-December. Nashville, Tenn.: International Fan Club Organization.

Ifill, Gwen. 1992. "Clinton-Gore Caravan Refuels With Spirit From Adoring Crowd." *New York Times* (July 19): A13.

JRMF. 1953–1993. *Jimmie Rodgers' Memorial Festival Scrapbooks.* Compiled by Eddie Bishop. 5 Vols. Meridian, Miss.: Jimmie Rodgers Museum.

Kelly, Michael. 1992. "Road Show Of Togetherness Is New Kind Of Political Act." *New York Times* (July 22): A7.

Krebs, Betty. 1992. "Symphony's Pops Concert Too Extreme." *Dayton Daily News* (April 5): 3C.

Larsen, Dave. 1993a. "Nutter Center Has the Ticket, Sales Report Says." *Dayton Daily News* (February 26): 1B.

———. 1993b. "Country Concert in the Hills." *Dayton Daily News GO!* (July 2): 14–15.

———. 1993c. "Tantrum Highlights Megadeath Debacle." *Dayton Daily News* (July 5): 6B.

———. 1993d. "Wild About Country." *Dayton Daily News.* (July 12): 1.

———. 1993e. "Reba McEntire." *Dayton Daily News GO!* (November 5): 17.

Long, Ellen A. 1993. Dollywood Public Relations Packet. Pigeon Forge, Tenn.: Dollywood.

Meridian Historic Preservation Commission. 1992. *Historic Neighborhoods of Meridian, Mississippi.* Meridian: pamphlet.

Oermann, Robert K. 1993. "Christian Music May Be Booming." *Tennesseean* (May 27): 1E.

Pareles, Jon. 1993a. "It's Noisy! It's New! It's 90's!" *New York Times* (January 3): sec. 2, pp. 1, 27.

———. 1993b. "Pop Can Survive Almost Anything. But Respect?" *New York Times* (January 10): 27.

Poole, Thomas. 1992. "Rock and Roll: A Country and Gospel Connection?" Mississippi State University, Meridian: 9th Annual Country Music Conference. May 29.

Radel, Cliff. 1993. "Their Hearts Belong to Country." *Cincinnati Enquirer* (August 1): G1, G3.

Rhodes, Lolita M. 1992. "Flight of Fancy Footwork." *Dayton Daily News* (February 15): C1.

Riders in the Sky (Too Slim, Ranger Doug, Woody Paul with Texas Bix Bender). 1992. Layton, Utah: Gibbs Smith.

Rogers, Joe and Jocelyn Bluitt. 1993. "Twitty 'a man of his fans'." *Tennesseean* (June 10): 1–2.

Schwed, Paula. 1992. *I've Got Tears In My Ears From Lying on My Back In My Bed While I Cry Over You.* Kansas City: Andrews and McMeel.

Sharpe, Anita. 1994. "Right In Tune: Country Music Finds New Fans And a Firm in Nashville Prospers." *Wall Street Journal* (January 19): 1, 8.

Sherrill, Billy. 1982. *George Jones' Anniversary: Ten Years of Hits.* Liner notes. CBS/Epic LP.

Specter, Michael. 1992. "Crazy for Country Music." *New York Times* (August 23): E3.

Steinem, Gloria. 1987. "Dolly Parton." *Ms.* (January): 66, 94.

Strobel, Jerry, ed. 1992. *Official Grand Ole Opry Picture-History Book.* Nashville, Tenn.: Opryland USA.

Times. 1992. "Vintage Guitar for Grown-ups." *New York Times* (April 5): 9.

Watrous, Peter. 1992. "Brooks Seizes a Chance to Make Changes." *New York Times* (September 2): B5.

Weaver, Gary. 1993. "Def Leppard Rocks Crowd at Nutter." *Dayton Daily News* (March 21): 4B.

Wolfe, Charles. 1987. "The Bristol Sessions." Liner notes. *The Bristol Sessions.* 2 vols. Nashville, Tenn.: Country Music Foundation. Cassettes.

INDEX